PLATINUM EDITION

4

Series Director: Diane Larsen-Freeman

GRAMMAR DIMENSIONS

FORM, MEANING, and USE

D0573118

Jan Frodesen
University of California
Santa Barbara

Janet Eyring
California State University
Fullerton

HH Heinle & Heinle
Thomson Learning

Australia • Canada • Denmark • Japan • Mexico • New Zealand
Philippines • Puerto Rico • Singapore • Spain • United Kingdom • United States

Acquisitions Editor: Eric Bredenberg
Senior Developmental Editor: Amy Lawler
Production Editor: Michael Burggren
Senior Marketing Manager: Charlotte Sturdy
Manufacturing Coordinator: Mary Beth Hennebury
Composition/Project Management: The PRD Group, Inc.
Text Design: Sue Gerould, Perspectives
Cover Design: Hannus Design Associates
Printer: Quebecor World/Taunton

For permission to use material from this text, contact us:
web www.thomsonrights.com
fax 1-800-730-2215
phone 1-800-730-2214

Heinle & Heinle Publishers
20 Park Plaza
Boston, MA 02116

AUSTRALIA/NEW ZEALAND:
Nelson/Thomson Learning
102 Dodds Street
South Melbourne
Victoria 3205 Australia

CANADA:
Nelson/Thomson Learning
1120 Birchmount Road
Scarborough, Ontario
Canada M1K 5G4

UK/EUROPE/MIDDLE EAST:
Thomson Learning
Berkshire House
168-173 High Holborn
London, WC1V 7AA, United Kingdom

LATIN AMERICA:
Thomson Learning
Seneca, 53
Colonia Polanco
11560 México D.F. México

SPAIN:
Thomson Learning
Calle Magallanes, 25
28015-Madrid
Espana

ASIA (excluding Japan):
Thomson Learning
60 Albert Street #15-01
Albert Complex
Singapore 189969

JAPAN:
Thomson Learning
Palaceside Building, 5F
1-1-1 Hitotsubashi, Chiyoda-ku
Tokyo 100 0003, Japan

ISBN: 0-8384-0286-0

 This book is printed on acid-free recycled paper.

Printed in the United States of America
1 2 3 4 5 6 7 8 9 04 03 02 01 00

TOEFL® is a registered trademark of Educational Testing Service (ETS). This product is not
endorsed or approved by ETS.

A Special Thanks

The series director, authors, and publisher would like to thank the following individuals who offered many helpful insights and suggestions for change throughout the development of *Grammar Dimensions*.

Jane Berger
*Solano Community College,
   California*
Mary Bottega
San Jose State University
Mary Brooks
Eastern Washington University
Christina Broucqsault
*California State Polytechnic
   University*
José Carmona
Hudson Community College
Susan Carnell
*University of Texas at
   Arlington*
Susana Christie
San Diego State University
Diana Christopher
Georgetown University
Gwendolyn Cooper
Rutgers University
Sue Cozzarelli
EF International, San Diego
Catherine Crystal
Laney College, California
Kevin Cross
University of San Francisco
Julie Damron
*Interlink at Valparaiso
   University, Indiana*
Glen Deckert
Eastern Michigan University
Eric Dwyer
*University of Texas at
   Austin*
Ann Eubank
Jefferson Community College
Alice Fine
UCLA Extension
Alicia Going
*The English Language Study
   Center, Oregon*
Molly Gould
University of Delaware
Maren M. Hargis
San Diego Mesa College
Mary Herbert
*University of California, Davis
   Extension*

Jane Hilbert
*ELS Language Center, Florida
   International University*
Eli Hinkel
Xavier University
Kathy Hitchcox
*International English Institute,
   Fresno*
Joyce Hutchings
Georgetown University
Heather Jeddy
*Northern Virginia Community
   College*
Judi Keen
*University of California, Davis,
   and Sacramento City College*
Karli Kelber
*American Language Institute,
   New York University*
Anne Kornfeld
LaGuardia Community College
Kay Longmire
*Interlink at Valparaiso
   University, Indiana*
Robin Longshaw
Rhode Island School of Design
Bernadette McGlynn
*ELS Language Center,
St. Joseph's University*
Billy McGowan
Aspect International, Boston
Margaret Mehran
Queens College
Richard Moore
University of Washington
Karen Moreno
*Teikyo Post University,
   Connecticut*
Gino Muzzetti
*Santa Rosa Junior College,
   California*
Mary Nance-Tager
*LaGuardia Community College,
   City University of New York*
Karen O'Neill
San Jose State University
Mary O'Neal
*Northern Virginia Community
   College*

Nancy Pagliara
*Northern Virginia Community
   College*
Keith Pharis
Southern Illinois University
Amy Parker
*ELS Language Center, San
   Francisco*
Margene Petersen
*ELS Language Center,
   Philadelphia*
Nancy Pfingstag
*University of North Carolina,
   Charlotte*
Sally Prieto
*Grand Rapids Community
   College*
India Plough
Michigan State University
Mostafa Rahbar
*University of Tennessee at
   Knoxville*
Dudley Reynolds
Indiana University
Ann Salzman
*University of Illinois at Urbana-
   Champaign*
Jennifer Schmidt
San Francisco State University
Cynthia Schuemann
Miami-Dade Community College
Jennifer Schultz
*Golden Gate University,
   California*
Mary Beth Selbo
*Wright College, City Colleges of
   Chicago*
Stephen Sheeran
*Bishop's University, Lenoxville,
   Quebec*
Kathy Sherak
San Francisco State University
Keith Smith
*ELS Language Center, San
   Francisco*
Helen Solorzano
Northeastern University

Contents

Unit 25 Focusing and Emphasizing Structures
It-Clefts and *Wh*-Clefts 432

APPENDICES   A-1

A Word from Diane Larsen-Freeman, Series Director

Before ***Grammar Dimensions*** was published, teachers would always ask me, "What is the role of grammar in a communicative approach?" These teachers recognized the importance of teaching grammar, but they associated grammar with form and communication with meaning, and thus could not see how the two easily fit together. ***Grammar Dimensions*** was created to help teachers and students appreciate the fact that grammar is not just about form. While grammar does indeed involve form, in order to communicate, language users also need to know the meaning of the forms and when to use them appropriately. In fact, it is sometimes not the form, but the *meaning* or *appropriate use* of a grammatical structure that represents the greatest long-term learning challenge for students. For instance, learning when it is appropriate to use the present perfect tense instead of the past tense, or being able to use two-word or phrasal verbs meaningfully, represent formidable challenges for ESL students.

The three dimensions of form, meaning, and use can be depicted in a pie chart with their interrelationship illustrated by the three arrows:

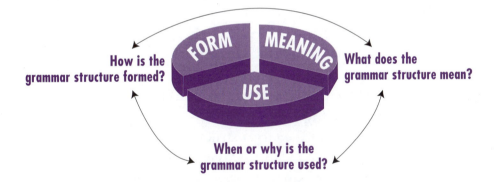

Helping students learn to use grammatical structures accurately, meaningfully, and appropriately is the fundamental goal of ***Grammar Dimensions.*** It is consistent with the goal of helping students to communicate meaningfully in English, and one that recognizes the undeniable interdependence of grammar and communication.

Enjoy the Platinum Edition!

To learn more about form, meaning, and use, read ***The Grammar Book: An ESL/EFL Teacher's Course,*** Second Edition, by Marianne Celce-Murcia and Diane Larsen-Freeman, also from Heinle & Heinle. It helps both prospective and practicing teachers of ESL/EFL enhance their understanding of English grammar, expand their skills in linguistic analysis, and develop a pedagogical approach to teaching English grammar that builds on the three dimensions. ISBN: 0-8384-4725-2.

Welcome to Grammar Dimensions, Platinum Edition!
The most comprehensive communicative grammar series available.

Updated and revised, *Grammar Dimensions, Platinum Edition,* makes teaching grammar easy and more effective than ever. Clear grammar explanations, a wealth of exercises, lively communicative activities, technology resources, and fully annotated Teacher's Editions help both beginning and experienced teachers give their students the practice and skills they need to communicate accurately, meaningfully, and appropriately.

Grammar Dimensions, Platinum Edition, is:

Communicative	• Students practice the **form, meaning,** and **use** of each grammar structure.
	• **Improved! A variety of communicative activities** helps students practice grammar and communication in tandem, eliciting self-expression and personalized practice.
	• Students learn to communicate accurately, meaningfully, and appropriately.
Comprehensive	• **Improved!** Grammar is presented in **clear charts.**
	• **A wealth of exercises** helps students practice and master their new language.
	• **The Workbook** provides extra practice and helps students prepare for the TOEFL® Test.
	• **Engaging listening activities** on audiocassette further reinforce the target structure.
	• **New! Enclosed CD-ROM** includes over 500 activities and gives students even more practice in mastering grammar and its use in language. **FREE!**
Clear	• **Improved! Simplified grammar explanations** help both students and teachers easily understand and comprehend each language structure.
	• **Improved! A fresh new design** makes each activity engaging.
	• **New! Communicative activities** ("the Purple Pages") are now labeled with the skill being practiced.
	• **New!** The Teacher's Edition has **page references** for the Student Book and Workbook, minimizing extra preparation time.

User-Friendly for Students	• **Contextualized grammar explanations and examples** help students understand the target language.
	• **New! Goals** at the beginning of each unit focus students' attention on the learning they will do.
	• **Sample phrases and sentences** model the appropriate use of the structure.
User-Friendly for Teachers	• **New!** Teacher's Edition now contains answers, tests, tape scripts, and complete, **step-by-step teaching suggestions** for every activity.
	• **New!** "Purple Page" activities are now labeled with the skill.
	• **Improved! A tight integration** among the Student Book, the Workbook and the Teacher's Edition make extension activities easy to do.
Flexible	• Instructors can use the units in order or as set by their curriculum.
	• Exercises can be used in order or as needed by the students.
	• "Purple Page" activities can be used at the end of the unit or interspersed throughout the unit.
Effective	Students who learn the form, meaning, and use of each grammar structure will be able to communicate more accurately, meaningfully, and appropriately.

Grammar Dimensions, Platinum Edition

Within *Grammar Dimensions, Platinum Edition,* students progress from the sentence level to the discourse level, and learn to communicate appropriately at all levels.

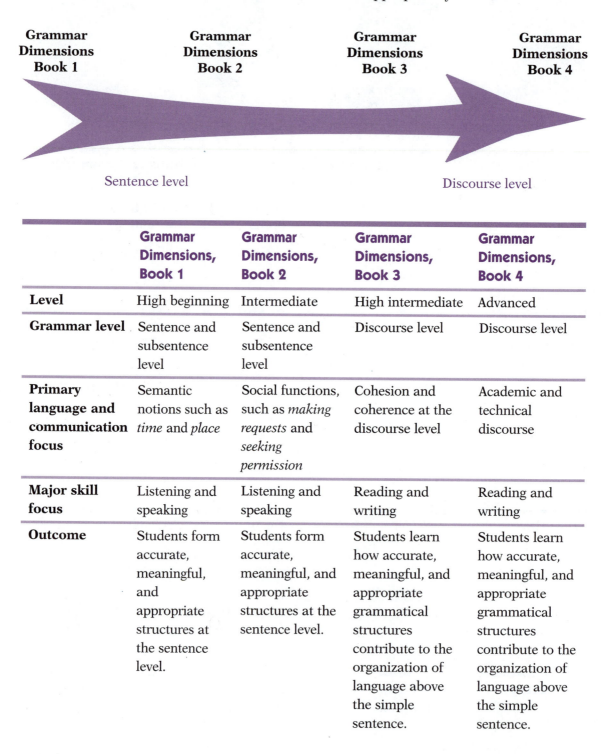

	Grammar Dimensions, Book 1	Grammar Dimensions, Book 2	Grammar Dimensions, Book 3	Grammar Dimensions, Book 4
Level	High beginning	Intermediate	High intermediate	Advanced
Grammar level	Sentence and subsentence level	Sentence and subsentence level	Discourse level	Discourse level
Primary language and communication focus	Semantic notions such as *time* and *place*	Social functions, such as *making requests* and *seeking permission*	Cohesion and coherence at the discourse level	Academic and technical discourse
Major skill focus	Listening and speaking	Listening and speaking	Reading and writing	Reading and writing
Outcome	Students form accurate, meaningful, and appropriate structures at the sentence level.	Students form accurate, meaningful, and appropriate structures at the sentence level.	Students learn how accurate, meaningful, and appropriate grammatical structures contribute to the organization of language above the simple sentence.	Students learn how accurate, meaningful, and appropriate grammatical structures contribute to the organization of language above the simple sentence.

Unit Organization

Used with or without the Workbook and the *Grammar 3D* CD-ROM, ***Grammar Dimensions*** Student Book units are designed to be clear, comprehensive, flexible, and communicative.

Goals	• **Focus students' attention** on the learning they will do in each chapter.
Opening Task	• **Contextualizes** the target grammatical structure. • **Enables teachers to diagnose** their students' performance and identify the aspect of the structure with which their students have the most difficulty. • **Provides a roadmap** for the grammar points students need to work on in that chapter.
Focus Boxes	• **Present the form, meaning,** or **use** of a particular grammatical structure. • **Focus students' attention** to a particular feature of the target structure. Each rule or explanation is preceded by examples, so teachers can have students work inductively to try to discover the rule on their own.
Exercises	• Provide a wealth of opportunity to **practice** the form and meaning of the grammar structures. • Help students develop the skill of **"grammaring"**—the ability to use structures accurately, meaningfully, and appropriately. • Are varied, thematically coherent, but purposeful. • Give students many opportunities to personalize and own the language.
Communicative Activities ("The Purple Pages")	• Help students practice **grammar and communication in tandem.** • **Are engaging!** • Encourage students to **use their new language** both inside and outside the classroom. • Provide an opportunity to **practice reading, writing, listening, and speaking skills,** helping students realize the communicative value of the grammar they are learning.

Student Book Supplements

Audiocassettes	• **Provide listening activities for** each unit so students can practice listening to **grammar structures in context.**
Workbooks	• **Provide additional exercises** for each grammar point presented in the student text.
	• Offer question types found on the TOEFL® Test.
CD-ROM	• *Grammar 3D* **provides additional practice** for 34 of the key grammar structures found in the text series.
	• Offers over **500 activities** for beginning to advanced students.
	• **Provides an instructional "help page"** that allows students to access grammar explanations at any point.
	• **Provides feedback** that helps students understand their errors and guides them toward correct answers.
	• **Free** with each Student Book!
Teacher's Editions	• **Facilitate teaching** by providing in one place notes and examples, answer keys to the Student Book and Workbook, page references to all of the components, the tapescript for the audiocassette activities, and tests with answer keys for each unit.
	• **Minimize teacher preparation time** by providing step-by-step teaching suggestions for every focus box and activity in the Student Book.

The ***Grammar Dimensions, Platinum Edition*** Student Books and the additional components help teachers teach and students learn to use English grammar structures in communication accurately, meaningfully, and appropriately.

Dedication

To Jeanne and George Frodesen
and
In memory of Lavon and Joseph Eyring

Acknowledgments

Series Director Acknowledgments

This edition would not have come about if it had not been for the enthusiastic response of teachers and students using the previous editions. I am very grateful for the reception *Grammar Dimensions* has been given.

I am also grateful for all the authors' efforts. To be a teacher, and at the same time a writer, is a difficult balance to achieve . . . so is being an innovative creator of materials, and yet, a team player. They have met these challenges exceedingly well in my opinion. Then, too, the Heinle & Heinle team has been impressive. I am grateful for the leadership exercised by Erik Gundersen, formerly of Heinle & Heinle. I also appreciate all the support from Charlotte Sturdy, Eric Bredenberg, Mike Burggren, Mary Beth Hennebury, and Marianne Bartow. Deserving special mention are Amy Lawler and Nancy Jordan, who never lost the vision while they attended to the detail with good humor and professionalism.

I have also benefited from the counsel of Marianne Celce-Murcia, consultant for the first edition this project, and my friend. Finally, I wish to thank my family members, Elliott, Brent, and Gavin, for not once asking the (negative yes–no) question that must have occurred to them countless times: "Haven't you finished yet?"

Author Acknowledgments

With this edition of *Grammar Dimensions,* as with the previous one, we are grateful for the thoughtful comments and suggestions from ESL teachers and students who have used Book 4. We especially hope that teachers will find the annotated Teacher's Edition useful and that the teaching suggestions will inspire creative ways to help their students meet learning challenges.

As always, we appreciate the guidance, expertise and ongoing support of Diane Larsen-Freeman, our series director. We thank the Heinle and Heinle team for their constant support of the *Grammar Dimensions* series. Many thanks to our editor, Amy Lawler, for her patience and flexibility, as well as her valuable assistance with annotations for the Teacher's Edition. The PRD Group, Inc. deserves thanks for so smoothly managing the final stages of this project.

To the *Grammar Dimensions* authors of Books 1, 2 and 3—Carolyn, Victoria, Heidi, Gin, and Steve—we extend special thanks. The friendship and understanding of the author team resulting from shared efforts have meant a great deal to us over the last decade.

Once again we end with thanks to our family members, friends and colleagues for their continuous support and good will.

UNIT 1

VERB TENSES IN WRITTEN AND SPOKEN COMMUNICATION

UNIT GOALS:

- To use verb tenses correctly to describe events and situations
- To use verb tenses consistently
- To understand why tense and time frames may change

▶ OPENING TASK
Describing In-Groups

STEP 1 Read the following information about *in-groups* and find the definition of this term.

Gordon Allport, a Harvard psychologist, used the term *in-groups* to describe the groups that individuals are part of at one time or another. We are born into some in-groups, such as our ethnic groups, our hometowns, and our nationalities. We join other in-groups through our activities, such as going to school, making friends, entering a profession, or getting married. Some in-groups, such as ethnic groups, are permanent, but others change as our activities, beliefs, and loyalties change.

The following some of the in-group memberships, both past and present, of Kay, a Thai-American woman in her mid-thirties.

the family she grew up in
her own family (husband Phil and
    child Andrea)
Thai (ethnic group)
native speakers of Thai
Bangkok (the city she was born in)
Chicago (where she lived from ages eight
    to eighteen)
Palo Alto, California (the city she lives
    in now)
her girlhood circle of friends

the Girl Scouts
her elementary and secondary school
Princeton University
Stanford Medical School
physicians (her profession)
the Buddhist religion
the National Organization for Women
her neighborhood volleyball team
the Sierra Club
the Democratic party
the United States

STEP 2 Make a list of some in-groups to which you belonged as a child (pick an age between five and twelve years old). Some of these groups might be the same as present ones. Next, make a list of in-groups that you belong to now. Finally, create a third list which includes your present in-groups that you believe will remain significant groups for you ten years from now.

STEP 3 Compare your lists with those of two or three other class members. Discuss which groups on your childhood lists have changed and which have remained important groups to you at the present time.

STEP 4 As an out-of-class assignment, write three paragraphs. For the first paragraph, describe a childhood in-group that was especially important to you. For the second paragraph, write about your current involvement in an in-group. In the third paragraph, speculate about what might be some new in-groups for you in the future—for example, a new school, a profession, your own family (as contrasted to your family of origin)—and when you think some of them might become a part of your life. Save your paragraphs for Exercise 2.

▶ The English Verb System: Overview

Verbs in English express how events take place in time. The verb tenses give two main kinds of information:

Time Frame   When the event takes place: now, at some time in the past, or at some time in the future

Aspect   The way we look at an action or state: whether it occurs at a certain point in time (for example, *study*) or lasts for period of time (for example, *speak*). (See Unit 2 for more detail.)

Time frame and **aspect** combine in twelve different ways in English.

	TIME FRAME		
ASPECT	**Present**	**Past**	**Future***
Simple Ø-aspect (at that point in time)	*study/studies* *speak/speaks* (simple present)	*studied* *spoke* (simple past)	*will study* *will speak* (simple future)
Progressive (in progress at that point in time)	*am/is/are studying* *am/is/are speaking* (present progressive)	*was/were studying* *was/were speaking* (past progressive)	*will be studying* *will be speaking* (future progressive)
Perfect (before that time)	*has/have studied* *has/have spoken* (present perfect)	*had studied* *had spoken* (past perfect)	*will have studied* *will have spoken* (future perfect)
Perfect Progressive (in progress during and before that time)	*has/have been studying* *has/have been speaking* (present perfect progressive)	*had been studying* *had been speaking* (past perfect progressive)	*will have been studying* *will have been speaking* (future perfect progressive)

*Please note that there are many ways to express the future time frame in English. The chart above gives examples of the future using *will* only. See Focus 7 in Unit 2 for other ways.

EXERCISE 1

In his autobiography, *The Hunger of Memory*, Richard Rodriguez describes his struggles growing up in two different worlds: Mexican culture and the American educational system. The following passages are from his book. Underline the verbs of main clauses in each sentence. Then identify the time frame for each passage: present, past, or future. Circle words and phrases that help to signal the time frame. The first one has been done as an example.

▶ **EXAMPLE:** 1. (a) From an early age I knew that my mother and father could read and write both Spanish and English. (b) I had observed my father making his way through what, I now suppose, must have been income tax forms. (c) On other occasions I waited apprehensively while my mother read onion-paper letters air-mailed from Mexico with news of a relative's illness or death. (d) For both my parents, however, reading was something done out of necessity and as quickly as possible.
Time frame: *past*

2. (a) Lately, I have begun to wonder how the family will gather even three times a year when [my mother] is not there with her phone to unite us. (b) For the time being, however, she presides at the table. (c) She—not my father, who sits opposite her—says the grace before meals. (d) She busies herself throughout the meal.

3. (a) Someday . . . you will all grow up and all be very rich. (b) You'll have lots of money to buy me presents. (c) But I'll be a little old lady. (d) I won't have any teeth or hair. (e) So you'll have to buy me soft food and put a blue wig on my head. (f) And you'll buy me a big fur coat. (g) But you'll only be able to see my eyes.

4. (a) The third of four children, I had been preceded to a neighborhood Roman Catholic school by an older brother and sister. (b) But neither of them had revealed very much about their classroom experiences. (c) Each afternoon they returned, as they left in the morning, always together, speaking in Spanish, as they climbed the five steps of the porch.

5. (a) Visiting the East Coast or the gray capitals of Europe during the long months of winter, I often meet people at deluxe hotels who comment on my complexion. (b) (In such hotels it appears nowadays a mark of leisure and wealth to have a complexion like mine.) (c) Have I been skiing? In the Swiss Alps? (d) Have I just returned from a Caribbean vacation? (e) No. I say no softly but in a firm voice that intends to explain: My complexion is dark.

6. (a) [My nephew] smiles. (b) I wonder: Am I watching myself in this boy? (c) In this face where I can scarcely trace a family resemblance? (d) Have I

foreseen his past? (e) He lives in a world of Little League and Pop Warner.
(f) He has spoken English all his life. (g) His father is of German descent, a
fourth-generation American.

7. (a) I had known a writer's loneliness before, working on my dissertation in
the British Museum. (b) But that experience did not prepare me for the task
of writing these pages where my own life is the subject. (c) Many days I
feared I had stopped living by committing myself to remember the past.
(d) I feared that my absorption with events in my past amounted to an immature refusal to live in the present.

EXERCISE 2

Exchange the paragraphs you wrote for the Opening Task with a classmate. After reading the paragraphs, write one or two questions that you have about your classmate's
in-groups and ask him or her to respond to them. Then decide whether there is a consistent time frame used for each paragraph. If so, identify the time frames and underline any time indicators. Check with your classmate to see if he or she agrees with
your analysis. Discuss any changes you think should be made.

FOCUS **2**

▶ Moment of Focus

Verbs can describe events that happen at a point in time (for example, *last night, three
weeks ago*) or an event that lasts a period of time (for example, *all night long, three
weeks*). We can call this the **moment of focus**.

Here are examples of **moment of focus** for each of the three time frames: present,
past, and future.

Moment of Focus

	POINT OF TIME	PERIOD OF TIME
Present	(a) Her son is four years old **today**.	(b) Her son listens to music **for hours at a time**.
Past	(c) The tornado touched down **just before dawn**.	(d) **During the early nineteenth century**, millions of Italians immigrated to the United States.
Future	(e) **On Saturday morning**, they will leave for their trip.	(f) **In the decades to come**, com-puter technology will continue to change our lives.

The time focus may be stated explicitly or it may be implied in the context.

	POINT OF TIME	PERIOD OF TIME
Present	(g) I can't talk **now**; I'm trying to study.	(h) Her son goes to a private school. (Implied: now)
Past	(i) **Until the end of the Cretaceous period**, dinosaurs roamed the earth.	(j) Dinosaurs evolved into two distinct groups. (Implied: During a period of time in the past)
Future	(k) **After you finish that chapter**, I'll give you a ride to school.	(l) The weather will continue to be warm and sunny. (Implied: for a future period of time)

In written and spoken communication, the moment of focus may be the same for a number of sentences or it may change from sentence to sentence:

SAME POINT OF FOCUS	CHANGING POINT/PERIOD OF FOCUS
(m) **When Kay first moved to Chicago** from Bangkok, she had a hard time adjusting to her new life. She didn't like the food at school. Other children seldom talked to her and she had no one to play with.	(n) Kay met Phil **the summer after she graduated from college**. They dated **for two years. When they got married**, it was on the same date, July 15th, that they had first met. **This year** they celebrated their fifteenth anniversary.

EXERCISE 3

The following oral interview passages are from Studs Terkel's book *The Great Divide*, in which Americans talk about their lives and thoughts on changes in America. In small groups, take turns identifying the moment or moments of focus for each passage. (1) Determine whether each moment of focus is (a) a point of time or (b) a period of time. (2) State whether moment of focus is (a) past or (b) present. (3) State whether the moment of focus is (a) explicitly stated or (b) implied.

1. (a) Right now, he's working the night shift at a twenty-four hour service station, with ten or twelve pumps. (b) He pumps the cash register. (c) His goals are very short-term, to get through the day

2. (a) Back in the early eighties when the draft-resistance movement began, many of us who were resisters first appeared in public. (b) We debated representatives of the Selective Service. (c) Frankly, we'd usually make them look pretty silly.

3. (a) In the last five years, there's been much more discussion of ethics on the campuses. (b) Remember, many of the young people of the sixties are the professors of today and they haven't changed their basic beliefs.

4. (a) A friend of mine, who is forty, had been a stock analyst on Wall Street fifteen years ago. (b) She married, had babies, raised her children, and now wanted to go back. (c) They said, "It doesn't matter what you did before."

5. (a) I would like to be chief of police. (b) I'll probably apply for jobs. (c) If nothing happens, I'll go to Cape Cod, build a house, and look at the waves.

6. (a) [My students] have learned how to take college tests. (b) They score high, especially in math. (c) They are quite verbal. (d) They give the impression of being bright. (d) Encouraged by their families, they come with the conviction that education is something they want, something they need. (e) But their definition of education is something else.

FOCUS **3**

▶ **Consistency in Tense Usage**

Being consistent in tense means keeping verbs in the same time frame.

EXAMPLES	EXPLANATIONS
Present Time Frame (a) Self-help groups **have become** very common all over America. (b) These groups **assist** people with everything from weight problems to developing confidence.	The tense may change within a time frame. For example, the tense may change from present perfect to simple present, as in sentences (a) and (b), but the time frame remains in the present.

Past Time Frame	Sometimes, however, it is necessary to change from one time frame to another, for example from past to present. A time-frame shift is usually signaled by a time marker (for example, *last week, currently, next year*.)
(c) Vera **graduated** from college last June.	
Present Time Frame	In example (d) *now* signals a shift from past to present time. Example (e) shifts to the present perfect, but remains in the present time frame.
(d) She now **works** for a law firm.	
(e) She **has worked** there for a month.	
Past Time Frame	If (e) had a past-time reference, as in (f), the verb would be ungrammatical because there is no explicit time marker to signal a time-frame shift. Nor is there any reason to depart from the present time frame, which has been established in (d).
(f) NOT: She **had worked** there for a month.	

EXERCISE 4

Each of the following passages has one sentence with an inappropriate verb tense. (1) Identify the time frame of the passage. (2) Identify the sentence that has the error and correct it. You may want to consult the time frame chart in Focus 1 for reference. Correction may involve changing the verb tense or using an explicit time marker to signal the shift in time frame. More than one verb tense can be correct in some cases.

▶ **EXAMPLE:**   (a) I am taking this coat back to the store. (b) Someone had burned a hole in it. (c) One button is missing too.

Time Frame: *Present*
Error: (b)
Possible Corrections: *Someone **has burned** a hole in it.*
OR *Someone **had burned** a hole in it **before I bought it**.*

1. (a) My music class is really interesting. (b) We have been studying the history of American jazz and blues. (c) I will have been taking this course for six weeks.

2. (a) Sula's in-groups include her softball team. (b) She had belonged to this team for three years. (c) Last year she played second base, but this year she is playing first base.

3. (a) Japanese researchers had demonstrated that a human virus can cause rheumatoid arthritis in mice. (b) The virus, HTLV-1, is capable of inserting its own genetic information into the genes of its host. (c) It causes leukemia and two rare nerve disorders.

4. (a) Although Elvis Presley has been dead for decades, his legacy lives on. (b) For example, there was a computer game "In Search of the King." (c) And the Jockey Club registry lists the following thoroughbred horses: Elvis Pelvis, Triple Elvis, Elvis' Double, Jailhouse Rock, Blue Suede Shoes, and Love Me Tender.

▶ Time-Frame Shifts in Written and Spoken Communication

In written and spoken communication, time-frame shifts sometimes occur, such as from present to past. These shifts will often be necessary when you move from statements that introduce a topic to ones that provide further information about the topic. There may or may not be explicit markers to signal time shifts.

Below are some reasons why you might change from one time frame to another, with examples given for each.

EXAMPLES	TYPE OF TIME-FRAME SHIFT	REASON FOR SHIFT
(a) The city of Wichita Falls **has** an interesting history. It *became* a town over a hundred years ago when the railroad started a route through that area. The land that was to become Wichita Falls *was* a prize in a poker game.	Present ⟶ Past	To explain or support a general statement with past description or elaboration on a topic.
(b) Our school **is helping** to conserve natural resources. We *recycled* tons of aluminum last year. We *started* using paper cups instead of styrofoam ones.	Present ⟶ Past	To support a claim about the present with examples from the past.
(c) The social connections of Americans **have changed** during the last century. In the past, individuals *depended* on their extended families and neighborhoods for social activities. Today many Americans live far from their extended families and often do not know many of their neighbors.	Present ⟶ Past	To support a general statement about change by comparing present and past situations.
(d) Last year our city **witnessed** an increase in the number of people who volunteered time for organizations helping those in need. Donations to these organizations also **increased**. We *need* to continue this assistance to others less fortunate than we are.	Past ⟶ Present	To express a comment or an opinion about a topic.

NOTE: The simple present and present perfect tenses often "frame" topics. We frequently use them to introduce topics, to make topic shifts, and to end discussion of a topic. These tenses often express general statements that the speaker believes to be true at the present time.

EXERCISE 5

Here are more passages from Studs Terkel's interviews in *The Great Divide*. Discuss the reasons for the verb tense shifts in each passage. Which passages change tenses within a time frame? Which passages change time frames? Which verb tenses are used to introduce topics in these passages?

▶ **EXAMPLES:** (a) Nothing is forever. (b) You always have to stay flexible, so you can change. (c) Five years ago, we were in the commodity business. (d) You bought and sold. (e) The customer was a farmer in Iowa. (f) Today he is a major New York Bank.

Reason for verb tense shift: The verb tense shifts from present to past to support a general statement about change by comparing present and past situations. This passage changes time frames. The present tense is used to introduce the topic.

1. (a) This kitchen is part of the old house. (b) My great-grandparents bought the place around 1895 or somewhere in there. (c) I'm fourth generation.

2. (a) I think the American dream for most people today is just survival. (b) When people came here from the old country, it was for a better life, not just survival. (c) I see that people that come over today seem to prosper faster than the ones who were born here. (d) Maybe it's because they know what it is to do without.

3. (a) The marketplace has changed in another way. (b) We have major class shifts in America. (c) The middle class, as traditionally known, is disappearing—being split. (d) You have a growing upper class.

4. (a) The role of the radio personality has changed greatly in the last decade. (b) Back then, we were given a pile of records and a few flip cards to read. (c) Keep the conversation to a minimum. (d) I once worked for a guy who had a stopwatch. (e) If you talked over eight seconds, you'd get in trouble. (f) Today, people want to hear what the individual has to say. (g) In the old days, we could squeeze in eight, ten records an hour. (h) Now I'm lucky if I get in two.

5. (a) I've been arrested five times. (b) I'm considered somewhat of a freak because I'm the police chief's wife. (c) I would march with my placard, hoping that the police wouldn't see me. (d) If I saw a policeman, I would hide behind my sign. (e) But they always saw me and they said, Aha, there she goes, the crazy wife of the police chief. (f) The police all hate my husband, so they think I'm exactly what he deserves.

Use Your English

You will hear two passages from the autobiography *I, Rigoberta Menchu*. Rigoberta Menchu is a young Guatemalan peasant woman who won the Nobel Peace Prize in 1992 for her work to ensure human rights and justice for Indian communities in Guatemala. These passages describe her peasant life in Guatemala. In each passage, there is one or more sentences that shift to a different time frame from the main time frame of the passage (for example, from the past to the present).

STEP 1 Listen to each passage once for content and note the main time frame: present, past, or future.

STEP 2 Listen to each passage again and write down the verbs that represent time-frame shifts and as much of the sentences they are in as you can recall.

STEP 3 Explain the reason for each time frame shift, with reference to Focus 4. Here is some vocabulary from the passage that will be helpful to know while listening:

finca—a Guatemalan farm or plantation where the Indian peasants are contracted to work by the landowners. Crops such as coffee, cotton and sugar are grown.

lorry—a truck that transports people from their villages to the *finca*

altiplano—the mountains

ACTIVITY 2: READING

Scan some comic strips in the newspaper to find ones that use a variety of verb tenses. In groups, discuss what the time frames are for each, and why tense changes occur. As a variation of this activity, cover up or blacken the verbs in comic strips. Then give another classmate the base forms of the verbs (the verb that comes after *to* in *to* + verb) and see if she or he fills in the same tenses as the original. Discuss any differences in choices.

ACTIVITY 3: READING

Select several paragraphs of something you find interesting from a textbook (for example, history, literature, or psychology) or some other book. Analyze the verb tense use in the paragraphs. What types of verb tense shifts or time-frame shifts occur? Analyze the reasons for tense or time-frame shifts.

ACTIVITY 4: READING

Look at a piece of writing you or a classmate has done recently, such as an essay or other type of paper. Analyze the types of verb tense shifts you see. Do you think verb tenses are used appropriately?

ACTIVITY 5: SPEAKING/WRITING

Prepare a brief talk or write an essay in which you compare one of the in-groups you belonged to when you were young that you no longer belong to with one that you belong to now. For example, you could compare two organizations, two schools, two neighborhoods, or two groups of friends.

UNIT 2

VERBS

Aspect and Time Frames

UNIT GOALS:

- To use simple verb tenses correctly
- To use progressive verb forms correctly
- To use perfect verb forms correctly
- To understand verb tense meanings and uses in present, past, and future time frames

▶ OPENING TASK
Insiders and Outsiders

In Unit 1, the Opening Task asked you to consider the groups to which you belong. At times the process of joining a new group can be uncomfortable. Most of us have experienced the sense of not belonging, of feeling like an outsider, when first joining a new group.

STEP 1   Read the two passages below on the theme of being an "outsider."

The first passage describes the sense of not belonging and confusion that many students experience when entering college, especially when they find themselves in large lecture classes.

> People are taking notes and you are taking notes. You are taking notes on a lecture you don't understand. You get a phrase, a sentence, then the next loses you. It's as though you're hearing a conversation in a crowd or from another room—out of phase, muted. The man on the stage concludes his lecture and everyone rustles and you close your notebook and prepare to leave. You feel a little strange. Maybe tomorrow this stuff will clear up. Maybe by tomorrow this will be easier. But by the time you're in the hallway, you don't think it will be easier at all.

>   From Mike Rose, *Lives on the Boundary*. New York: Penguin Books, 1990.

In the next passage, the fictional character Lindo Jong feels like an outsider when joining a new family through marriage. Upon marrying Tuan-Yu, she has moved in with his family and receives a cool reception from her mother-in-law, Huang Taitai:

> No big celebration was held when I arrived. Huang Taitai didn't have red banners greeting me in the fancy room on the first floor. Tuan-yu was not there to greet me. Instead, Huang Taitai hurried me upstairs to the second floor and into the kitchen, which was a place where family children didn't usually go. This was a place for cooks and servants. So I knew my standing.

> That first day, I stood in my best padded dress at the low wooden table and began to chop vegetables. I could not keep my hands steady. I missed my family and my stomach felt bad, knowing I had finally arrived where my life said I belonged.

STEP 2   For ten minutes, write your reaction to the passages. You could discuss one of the passages, or you might want to describe briefly a situation from your own experience or from something you have read that related to the theme of being an outsider. In small groups, take turns reading your reactions aloud.

▶ **R**eview of Simple Tenses

Simple tenses include the simple present, simple past, and simple future. They
have the following uses:

TIME FRAME	EXAMPLES	USE
Present	**(a)** Our in-groups **help** to define our values.	To express general ideas, relationships, and truths
Past	**(b)** Immigrants to America in the mid-nineteenth century **included** large numbers of Chinese.	
Future	**(c)** Families **will** always **be** important to most of us.	
Present	**(d)** Our family **visits** my grandparents after church every Sunday.	To describe habitual actions
Past	**(e)** Almost every year we **celebrated** my great aunt's birthday with a family picnic.	
Future	**(f)** The club **will collect** dues once a month.	
Present	**(g)** Kay **thinks** she has chosen the right profession.	To describe mental perceptions or emotions
Past	**(h)** People once **believed** the earth was flat.	
Future	**(i)** You **will love** our new puppy.	
Present	**(j)** Phil **has** three brothers.	To express possession or personal relationships
Past	**(k)** We **owned** a station wagon, but we traded it in for a compact car.	
Future	**(l)** By next month, Andrea **will have** a complete set of encyclopedias.	
Present	**(m)** The media **reports** that new evidence has been presented in the trial.	To establish the time frame and the moment of focus
Past	**(n)** When the United States **passed** the Chinese Exclusion Act in 1882, 100,000 Chinese were living in the United States.	
Future	**(o)** Phyllis **will call** you Thursday morning; I hope you will not have left for Omaha by then.	

EXERCISE 1

The following statements are from an Internet file called "Frequently Asked Questions" (FAQ). Each statement describes a contemporary myth or strange story. The news group that maintains the FAQ site tries to determine whether the statement is true or false.

For each statement: (1) identify the tense of the verbs in italics; (2) then state what use or uses each verb expresses; (3) discuss whether you think the statements are true or not. (Answers are given on page A-16.)

▶ **EXAMPLE:** The bubbles in plastic wrap *contain* a cheap but toxic gas.

Tense: *present*   Use: *To describe a general truth*
                              To express possession

(Not true)

1. It *is* acceptable to send coconuts through the mail without wrapping them.

2. A mime *had* a heart attack during his performance. People *thought* it was part of his act. He *died*.

3. A penny falling from the top of the Empire State Building *will embed* itself in the pavement.

4. Fast-food shakes that aren't marked "dairy" *have* no milk in them.

5. Albert Einstein *did* poorly in school.

6. Green M & M candies *are* an aphrodisiac.*

7. Contact lenses *will stick* to your eyeballs if you weld something while wearing them.

8. If mold grows on a Twinkie,** the Twinkie *digests* it.

Excerpted from "The Internet's Believe It or Not," *Harper's Magazine,* October 1994.

EXERCISE 2

Go back to Exercises 1 and 3 on pp. 3 and 5 in Unit 1. Find an example of a verb with each of the following uses. Write down your choices and prepare to discuss them in class.

▶ **EXAMPLE:** Waited (from the Examples, Exercise 1)
                   past habitual action.

1. past habitual action
2. present habitual action
3. past perception

4. future possession
5. past moment of focus

*An *aphrodisiac* is a drug or food which increases sexual desire.
**A *Twinkie* is a very sweet pastry; it is often referred to as "junk food."

▶ **Review of Progressive Verbs**

Progressive verbs include a form of *be* + a present participle (verb + *-ing*).

EXAMPLES	USES
(a) When Phil gets home from work, Andrea **is** often **studying.** **(b)** I **was driving** to the restaurant when I saw the meteor shower. **(c)** She **will be working** the night shift when I get home.	To describe actions already in progress at the moment of focus
(d) Eric usually goes out to eat on Fridays. This Friday, however, he **is cooking** at home. **(e)** The robins usually took up residence every spring in our old apple trees. One summer, though, they **were building** nests in some of the taller trees. **(f)** Most winters we spend our Christmas vacation at home. But this year we **will be going** to Vermont.	To describe actions at the moment of focus in contrast to habitual actions
(g) She **is** constantly **reminding** me to water the plants. **(h)** As a young boy, my brother **was** always **getting** into trouble. **(i)** Our math teacher **will be checking** our assignments each morning when class starts.	To express repeated actions
(j) Kendra works in the principal's office, but she **is helping** the new school nurse this week. **(k)** My father lived in Chile most of his life, except for two years when he **was living** in Argentina. **(l)** We'll live in a new home after the winter. Until then, we**'ll be renting** an apartment in the city.	To describe temporary situations in contrast to permanent states
(m) The final paper is due soon. I**'m finishing** it as fast as I can. **(n)** Yesterday the students discussed the projects they **were working** on this semester. **(o)** When they finish their projects, they **will be evaluating** each others' work for several days.	To describe periods of time in contrast to points of time
(p) Sara **is doing** volunteer work for the homeless this summer. **(q)** When I last saw Ali, he **was** still **planting** his vegetable garden. **(r)** I bet the baby **will** still be **sleeping** when we get home.	To express uncompleted actions

EXERCISE 3

Underline the progressive verbs in the passage below. State what additional information the progressive aspect expresses for each verb. (Refer to the uses presented in Focus 2.)

▶ **EXAMPLE:** (am sitting)

   to describe action in progress at the moment of focus

(a) I am sitting under a sycamore by Tinker Creek. (b) I am really here, alive on the intricate earth under trees . . . (c) What else is going on right this minute while ground water creeps under my feet? (d) The galaxy is careening in a slow, muffled widening. (e) If a million solar systems are born every hour, then surely hundreds burst into being as I shift my weight to the other elbow. (f) The sun's surface is now exploding; other stars implode and vanish, heavy and black, out of sight. (g) Meteorites are arcing to earth invisibly all day long. (h) On the planet the winds are blowing: the polar easterlies, the westerlies, the northeast and southeast trades.

From Annie Dillard, *Pilgrim at Tinker Creek*. New York: Bantam, 1974.

EXERCISE 4

In the following passage, a journalist describes virtual reality (VR) and her experience with it at Cyberthon, a twenty-four-hour marathon computer demonstration. Underline the progressive verbs. Then discuss why the writer uses them in the first paragraph and why she shifts from simple past tense verbs to past progressive verbs in the second and third paragraphs.

(1) Some architects are using VR (also called "cyberspace," a term coined by writer William Gibson, who dreamed up VR in his novel *Neuromance*) to show clients what a structure will look like before it's built. (2) Doctors are using it to practice surgery without making a single cut. (3) And, of course, NASA and the Defense Department (which hope to replace jet pilots with VR screens) have been following—and funding—VR since its inception.

(4) I waited in line impatiently for my turn at the Cyberhood, which focuses your eyes on a computer-generated 3-D image; you manipulate yourself, or "fly," by gripping a ball to the left of the machine. (5) The ball, Sense8* President Eric Gullichsen kept repeating to the users, is like your head; think of it as your head. (6) The trouble with that notion is that most people don't yank, twist, twirl, and push their heads, so most people were having trouble with the image: They were flipping it upside down, pulling their "head" back so far that the image became tiny and distant, hitting the floor with their wide-open eyeballs.

*Sense8 is a virtual reality company.

(7) The man in front of me, a shortish, plump guy in a blue shirt and jeans, was muttering to himself as he yanked at his "head." Finally he gave in and straightened up. (8) He turned out to be Robin Williams,** but no one paid much attention in this crowd — the machines were the celebrities.

EXERCISE 5

Decide whether a simple tense or progressive tense is appropriate for each blank and give the correct form of the verb in parentheses. The first one has been done for you.

1. Andre (a) (come) _comes_____ from Brazil and (b) (be) _____ a native speaker of Portuguese. Currently he (c) (study) _____ English at the University of Colorado. He (d) (take) _____ two courses: composition and American culture.

2. One of my most important in-groups (a) (be) _____ my church group. Right now we (b) (provide) _____ lunches for homeless people in the city park. Also, some of us (c) (tutor) _____ junior high students in math and English for the summer. Others in my group (d) (spend) _____ part of the summer doing volunteer work at senior citizen centers. We all (e) (feel) _____ that we (f) (gain) _____ a great deal ourselves by participating in these activities.

3. Next summer our family (a) (have) _____ a reunion during the July 4th holiday weekend. My uncle from Finland (b) (try) _____ to come, but he (c) (start) _____ a new business this year so it (d) (be) _____ difficult for him to get away. Another uncle (e) (spend) _____ the whole summer with us. He (f) (work) _____ at my mother's travel agency from June through August.

4. For many immigrants to the United States, their ethnic associations (a) (remain) _____ important in-groups long after they have left their home countries. Even while they (b) (learn) _____ a new language, many (c) (look to) _____ speakers of their native language as an in-group that (d) ((understand) _____ their struggles to adapt to a new way of life.

**A well-known American comedian and actor.

EXERCISE 6

Ask another classmate to tell you five things he or she does now as a result of in-group associations. Write a sentence for each, using present-time reference verbs, and report one or two of the ones you find most interesting to the rest of the class.

▶ **EXAMPLE:** *Martin plays the saxophone with a jazz band.*
As a student at Northwestern, he is majoring in environmental sciences.

▶ **R**eview of Perfective Verbs

Perfect verbs are formed by *have (has, have, had, will have)* + a past participle (verb -ed or irregular form).

EXAMPLES	USES
(a) *To date,* Mark **has taken** five days off from work for vacation.	To describe events that happen before the moment of focus.
(b) *When I last spoke to my mother,* she **had sent** me a letter, so she didn't want to repeat her news over the phone.	The time phrases and clauses in italics signal the moment of focus.
(c) *By this time tomorrow,* even more acres of the rain forest **will have been destroyed.**	
Continuing to present **Present Perfect** **(d)** My parents **have lived** in their house for forty years; this year they are remodeling the kitchen.	**Completed** **Simple Past** **(e)** My grandparents **lived** in their house on Tower Avenue until 1996.	To describe events that started in the past and continue to be true in the present, in contrast with completed events (which are related to the simple past).
(f) I **have finished** that chapter, so I can help you answer the questions. (My finishing the chapter is relevant to my ability to help now.) **(g)** I **had finished** the chapter before the soccer match started, so I was able to watch the whole match. (My finishing the chapter is relevant to having watched the match.) **(i)** I **will have taken** my last exam on the day you arrive here. (My completion of exams is relevant to your arrival date.)	**Contrast with:** **Simple Past** **(h)** I **finished** the chapter. Then I played video games. (Finishing the chapter and playing games are related only sequentially.)	To describe events that the speaker believes are relevant to the moment of focus. In (f), the moment of focus is the present; in (g), it is the past. (f) and (g) contrast with (h), which has a simple past verb.

EXERCISE 7

Underline the present perfect and past perfect verbs in the following passages. Explain what information is expressed by the perfective aspect for these verbs. What uses listed in Focus 3 are expressed? (A perfect verb can convey more than one kind of information.) The first has been done as an example.

▶ **EXAMPLE:** 1. (d) <u>had seen, heard, learned</u>—past perfect

Information: *describe events that happen before the moment of focus (Fatt Hing at the age of nineteen) and that are relevant to the moment of focus.*

1. (a) By 1851, in a matter of three years, there were 25,000 Chinese in California. (b) Fatt Hing was one of these 25,000. (c) His story is typical of the pioneer Chinese, many who came with him and many who came after him. (d) As a lad of nineteen, Fatt Hing had already seen and heard and learned more about the world than most of the men in his village, who had seldom set foot beyond the nearest town square. (e) For Fatt Hing was a fish peddler who went frequently from Toishan to Kwanghai on the coast to buy his fish to sell at the market. (f) Down by the wharves, where the fishing boats came in, Fatt Hing had often seen foreign ships with their sails fluttering in the wind. (g) He had seen hairy white men on the decks, and he had often wondered and dreamed about the land they came from.

2. (a) The dog has got more fun out of Man than Man has got out of the dog, for the clearly demonstrable reason that Man is the more laughable of the two animals. (b) The dog has long been bemused by the singular activities and the curious practices of men, cocking his head inquiringly to one side, intently watching and listening to the strangest goings-on in the world. (c) He has seen men sing together and fight one another in the same evening. (d) He has watched them go to bed when it is time to get up, and get up when it is time to go to bed. (e) He has observed them destroying the soil in vast areas, and nurturing it in small patches. (f) He has stood by while men built strong and solid houses for rest and quiet, and then filled them with lights and bells and machinery.

From James Thurber, *Thurber's Dogs, A Collection of the Master's Dogs, Written and Drawn, Real and Imaginary, Living and Long Ago.* New York: Simon and Schuster, 1955.

EXERCISE 8

Decide whether a simple form (present, past) or present perfect should be used for each verb in parentheses. The first has been done for you.

The Hotter'n Hell Hundred

(1) Near the Texas-Oklahoma border, where the wind never (seem) ___seems___ to stop, where the sun (broil) _____ the blacktop and (sap) _____ the strength, the cyclists (come) _____ each year. (2) They (come) _____ to Wichita Falls, Texas, by the thousands to ride in what (become) _____ the largest one-hundred-mile bicycle race in the world—the Hotter'n Hell Hundred. (3) The race (take) _____ place on Labor

Day weekend at the beginning of September, when temperatures regularly (soar) _____ past 100 degrees.

(4) The oddity of this race is that, with each passing year, it (become) _____ more and more a symbol of Wichita Falls, a city that, until recently, (be, hardly) _____ a cycling bastion. (5) In days past, the sight of a bicyclist (cause) _____ heads to turn in the pickup truck. (6) Tornadoes (be) _____ once more numerous than bicyclists in Wichita Falls.

(7) The Hotter'n Hell Hundred (start) _____ in 1982 when a postal worker (suggest) _____ a one-hundred-mile bike ride in 100-degree heat to celebrate Wichita Falls' one-hundredth birthday. (8) Today, the race (command) _____ the attention of almost the whole city as race weekend (approach) _____ .

Adapted with permission from J. Michael Kennedy, "It's the Hottest Little Ol' Race in Texas," *Los Angeles Times*, September 2, 1991.

EXERCISE 9

Decide whether a simple future or future perfect verb should be used for each verb in parentheses. The first one has been done for you.

(1) Our class has been discussing which in-groups we think (be) ___will___ or (be, not) _____ important to us ten years from now. (2) Hua says she knows her family (remain) _____ an

important in-group forever. (3) However, she thinks her associations with some campus groups, such as the French Club, (end) _____ by the time she graduates. (4) Kazuhiko thinks that he (be) _____ married for several years by that time. (5) He hopes he (have) _____ a few children of his own. (6) He believes his family (represent) _____ his most important in-group in the future. (7) Jose predicts that he (become) _____ a famous physicist by that time and that one of his important in-groups (be) _____ other Nobel Prize winners.

EXERCISE 10

With a partner, take the roles of Person A and Person B below. Each person should write five questions to ask the other person in an interview, based on the biodata information given. In your questions, use present, past, and future perfect verb forms. Use them in your responses when appropriate. Here are some patterns that may be useful for your questions:

Have you ever (done X)?

Had you (done X) before (Y)?

Do you think you will have (done X) before (Y)?

▶ **EXAMPLE:** Person A: *So you've taken piano lessons. Have you ever studied any other musical instruments?*

Person B: *Actually, yes. Before I took piano lessons, I had studied the violin for a year, but my playing was terrible!*

Person B: *I see you've lived in two other countries besides the United States. Which one did you live in first, and how long did you live in each one?*

Person A: *Well, I had lived in Peru for fifteen years before I moved to Madrid. I lived in Madrid for a little over three years.*

PERSON A	PERSON B
was on the track team in high school	took piano lessons as a child
lived in Peru	grew up in Korea
lived in Madrid	moved to the United States in 1992
traveled in Egypt and Africa	attended the University of Florida
parents live in New Mexico	attended Penn State
enrolled at the University of Texas	currently lives in New York
belongs to a health club	likes to watch basketball
loves old movies	loves to go to music concerts
is a sophomore	works at a television station
will graduate from college in three years	plans to move to Tokyo
plans to do a bicycle tour of Vietnam	will get a degree in broadcast journalism

▶ **Review of Perfect Progressive Verbs**

Perfect progressive verbs include present perfect progressive, past perfect progressive, and future perfect progressive. They are formed by *have (has, have, had, will have) + been* + a past participle (verb + *-ing*).

EXAMPLES		USE
Incomplete: Progressive	Complete: Nonprogressive	**USE**
(a) The jurors **have been discussing** the evidence. They still haven't reported their verdict.	(b) The jurors **have discussed** the evidence for a week. They are ready to report their verdict.	To express actions that have not been completed at the moment of focus, in contrast to actions that have been completed.
(c) Tam **had been listening** to the news when the explosion occurred.	(d) Tam **had listened** to the news before she left for work.	
(e) Jochen **will have been working** on his Master's degree for two years at the end of this month. He expects to finish in six months.	(f) Jochen **will have worked** at the bank for five years when he leaves for his new job in Quebec.	

EXERCISE 11

For each blank below, choose a simple past, present perfect, or present perfect progressive verb. The first one has been done for you.

(1) Alfredo (join) _____*joined*_____ the Friends of the Theater in his community five years ago and (be) _____ an active participant in this group ever since. (2) It (remain) _____ one of his favorite spare time activities even though he (stop) _____ trying out for roles in the plays last year because he (be) _____ too busy. (3) As a member, he (help) _____ promote the plays. (4) At times, he (look for) _____ costumes for the actors. (5) For last month's play, he (work) _____ with the props crew to get furniture and other props

for the stage sets. (6) He (find) _____ an antique desk to use for one of the sets, and he also (make) _____ a fireplace facade. (7) Most recently, he (try) _____ to get more businesses to advertise in the playbills.

EXERCISE 12

From Ms. H's choice of verb tense below, would you say that her "vowel affairs" have ended or not? Explain.

"All right! All right! If you want the truth, off and on
I've been seeing *all* the vowels—a, e, i, o, u. ...
Oh, yes! And *sometimes* y!"

▶ # **S**ummary: Present Time Frame

FORMS	EXAMPLES	USES	MEANINGS
SIMPLE PRESENT base form of verb or base form of verb + -s	**(a)** Children **need** social inter-action to develop language. **(b)** Kay **plays** on a volleyball team once a week. **(c)** Kay **considers** her Thai heritage an important in-group. **(d)** Andrea **has** a red bicycle.	timeless truths habitual actions mental perceptions and emotions possession	now
PRESENT PROGRES-SIVE *am/is/are* + present participle (verb + *-ing*)	**(e)** I **am completing** my Bachelor's degree in Spanish. **(f)** Andrea **is writing** an es-say. **(g)** Someone **is knocking** at the door. **(h)** Kay's brother **is staying** with her this summer. **(i)** Phil **is making** dinner.	actions in progress duration repetition temporary activities uncompleted actions	in progress now
PRESENT PERFECT *have/has* + past partici-ple (verb + *-ed* or irregu-lar form)	**(j)** Kay **has belonged** to the Sierra Club for four years. **(k)** Kay **has applied** to sev-eral hospitals for posi-tions; she is waiting to hear from them. **(l)** Andrea **has** just **finished** junior high school.	situations that began in the past, continue to the present actions com-pleted in the past but related to the present actions recently completed	in the past but related to now in some way
PRESENT PERFECT PROGRES-SIVE *have/has* + present par-ticiple (verb + *-ing*)	**(m)** Both Kay and Phil **have been playing** volleyball since they were teenagers. **(n)** This weekend Phil **has been competing** in a tournament which ends tomorrow.	continuous or repeated actions that are incomplete	up until and including now

EXERCISE 13

Choose simple present, present progressive, present perfect, or present perfect progressive for each blank. More than one answer could be correct; be prepared to explain your choices. The first one has been done for you.

(1) Ines (consider) ____considers____ her neighborhood in East Los Angeles to be one of her most important in-groups. (2) She (live) _____ in this neighborhood since birth, and she (know) _____ almost everyone in it. (3) Most of the people in the neighborhood (be) _____ from Mexico, but some (be) _____ from Central American countries. (4) Mr. Hernandez, who (live) _____ next door to Ines, always (insist) _____ that he (live) _____ the longest time in the neighborhood. (5) However, Mrs. Chavez, whom everyone (call) _____ "Tia," usually (tell) _____ him to stop spreading tales. (6) Mrs. Chavez (claim) _____ that *she* (be) _____ around longer than anyone. (7) Ines (watch) _____ many of the children younger than herself grow up, and she often (think) of them as her little brothers and sisters—the ones she (like) _____ , that is. (8) Just as her older neighbors (do) _____ for her, she now (help) _____ her younger neighbors keep out of trouble and (give) _____ them advice.

FOCUS **6**

▶ **Summary: Past Time Frame**

FORMS	EXAMPLES	USES	MEANINGS
SIMPLE PRESENT	**(a)** So on Friday, Terry **calls** Lila and **tells** her to be ready for a surprise.	past event in informal narrative	at a certain time in the past
SIMPLE PAST verb + -ed or irregular past form	**(b)** Kay **joined** the Girl Scouts when she **was** eight.	events that took place at a definite time in the past	at a certain time in the past
	(c) Phil **attended** Columbia University for two years as an undergraduate.	events that lasted for a time in the past	
	(d) Kay **went** to Girl Scout camp every summer until she entered high school.	habitual or repeated actions in the past	
	(e) Kay always **knew** that she wanted to be a doctor.	past mental perceptions and emotions	
	(f) Although she **did**n't **have** a car in college, Kay **owned** a motorbike.	past possessions	
PAST PROGRESSIVE was/were + present participle (verb + -ing)	**(g)** At midnight last night, Kay **was** still **making** her rounds.	events in progress at a specific time in the past	in progress at a time in the past
	(h) Kay **was talking** to one of the nurses when Phil called.	interrupted actions	
	(i) Andrea **was acting** in a community theater play for a month last year.	repeated actions and actions over time	
PAST PERFECT had + past participle (verb + -ed or irregular form)	**(j)** Before starting medical school, Kay **had taken** a long vacation.	actions or states that took place before another time in the past	before a certain time in the past
PAST PERFECT PROGRESSIVE had + been + present participle (verb + -ing)	**(k)** Andrea **had been studying** for two hours when her grandmother arrived to take her to the circus.	incomplete events taking place before other past events	up until a certain time in the past
	(l) Phil **had been working** at his computer when the power went out.	incomplete events interrupted by other past events	

EXERCISE 14

The comic strip below uses the following tenses: simple present, present progressive, simple past, past progressive, and past perfect. Find an example of each of these tenses in the comic strip. Then identify one verb phrase from the strip that expresses each of the following meanings:

1. event in progress
2. present situation
3. event completed in the past before another event
4. action completed at a definite point in the past
5. event in progress at a specific time in the past

Reprinted by permission of U.F.S. Inc.

EXERCISE 15

It is doubtful that any of the groups you belong to include trees; in the ancient Greek myths, however, more than a few family members ended up as flora of one sort or another. The following passage tells the story of the mythological character Dryope. For each blank, choose a simple past, past progressive, past perfect, or past perfect progressive form of the verb in parentheses. More than one choice could be possible. Be prepared to explain your choices. The first one has been done for you.

(1) One day Dryope, with her sister Iole, (go) ____went____ to a pool in the forest. (2) She (carry) _____ her baby son. (3) She (plan) _____ to make flower garlands near the pool for the nymphs, those female goddesses of the woodlands and waters. (4) When Dryope (see) _____ a lotus tree full of beautiful blossoms near

the water, she (pluck) _____ some of them for her baby.
(5) To her horror, drops of blood (flow) _____ from the stem;
the tree (be) _____ actually the nymph Lotis. (6) Lotis
(flee) _____ from a pursuer and (take) _____
refuge in the form of a tree. (7) When the terrified Dryope (try)
_____ to run away, she (find) _____ that her feet
would not move; they (root) in the ground. (8) Iole (watch)
_____ helplessly as tree bark (grow) upward and (cover)
_____ Dryope's body. (9) By the time Dryope's husband
(come) _____ to the spot with her father, the bark
(reach) _____ Dryope's face. (10) They
(rush) _____ to the tree, (embrace) _____ it, and
(water) _____ it with their tears. (11) Dryope (have) _____
time only to tell them that she (do) _____ no wrong intentionally. (12) She (beg) _____ them to bring the child often to the
tree to play in its shade. (13) She also (tell) _____ them to
remind her child never to pluck flowers and to consider that every tree and
bush may be a goddess in disguise.

From Edith Hamilton, *Mythology*. Copyright 1942 by Edith Hamilton. Copyright renewed 1969 by
Dorian Fielding Reid and Doris Fielding Reid. By permission of Little, Brown and Company.

EXERCISE 16

Retell Dryope's story in Exercise 15 in an informal narrative style. Use present
tense verbs instead of past tense verbs.

▶ **EXAMPLE:** *One day this woman named Dryope and her sister Iole* **go** *to a pool in
the woods. Dryope's* **carrying** *her baby son with her. . . .*

► **Summary: Future Time Frame**

FORMS	EXAMPLES	USES	MEANINGS
SIMPLE PRESENT	**(a)** Kay **completes** her residency next May. **(b)** After Kay **finishes** her residency, she will take a vacation.	definite future plans or schedules events with future time adverbials in dependent clauses	already planned or expected in the future
PRESENT PROGRESSIVE	**(c)** I **am leaving** at 7:00 a.m. tomorrow. **(d)** The family **is spending** the Christmas holidays in Boston.	future intentions scheduled events that last for a period of time	already planned or expected in the future
BE GOING TO FUTURE *am/is/are going to* *+ base verb*	**(e)** The movie **is going to start** in a few minutes. **(f)** I **am going to finish** this no matter what! **(g)** When you get older, you're **going to wish** that you had saved more money. **(h)** They **are going to travel** in India next summer.	probable and immediate future events strong intentions predictions about future situations future plans	at a certain time in the future
SIMPLE FUTURE *will + base verb*	**(i)** We **will** most likely **stay** at our beach cottage next summer. **(j)** I **will help** you with your homework this evening. **(k)** She**'ll be** very successful.	probable future events willingness/ promises predictions about future situations	
FUTURE PROGRESSIVE *will + be + present participle (verb + -ing)*	**(l)** Kay's parents **will be driving** from Chicago to Palo Alto next week. **(m)** Kay's family **will be living** in Palo Alto until she finishes her residency.	events that will be in progress in the near future future events that will last for a period of time	in progress at a certain time in the future

FORMS	EXAMPLES	USES	MEANINGS
FUTURE PERFECT *will + have* + past participle (verb + *-ed*)	**(n)** Kay's parents **will have left** Palo Alto before Andrea starts school.	before a certain time in the future	future events happening before other future events
FUTURE PERFECT PROGRESSIVE *will + have + been* present participle (verb + *-ing*)	**(o)** By the end of the year, Kay **will have been living** in California for four years.	up until a certain time in the future	continuous and/or repeated actions continuing into the future

EXERCISE 17

Choose an appropriate future-reference verb tense—simple present, present progressive, be going to, simple future, future progressive, or future perfect—to complete the dialogue below between Justin and his friend Patty. More than one verb tense might be appropriate for some blanks. Read the dialogue with a classmate. Discuss any differences in the choices you made.

Justin: My brother (1) (leave) ___is leaving___ tomorrow for his third trip to Europe this year!

Patty: What time (2) ___does he go/is he going___ (he, go)?

Justin: His plane (3) _____ (take off) really early—at 6 A.M., I think—so he (4) _____ (need) to get out of here by 4 A.M. or so. I (5) _____ (drive) him to the airport.

Patty: So why (6) _____ (he, go) to Europe again?

Justin: It's for his job. He (7) _____ (meet) his company's executives in Germany and then he (8) _____ (spend) a few days in Denmark. You know something? When I (9) _____ (finish) school and (10) _____ (get) a job, I (11) _____ (have) an exciting lifestyle too!

Patty: Oh, really? And what (12) _____ (you, do), if you don't mind my asking.

Justin: Not at all. Next summer, of course, after I (13) _____ (graduate), I (14) _____ (look) for a job for a while. With a little effort, I'm sure I (15) _____ (find) a very challenging and lucrative position in my field. Five years or so from now I (16) _____ (save) enough money to put a down payment on a penthouse condominium. By that time, I (17) _____ (make) enough to buy a flashy little sports car. I (18) _____ (put) away enough money by then to rent a beach vacation home every summer.,

Patty: It sounds as if you (19) _____ (live) the good life!

Justin: Well, I just said I (20) _____ (have) enough money to live like that. That doesn't mean I (21) _____ (do) it. Actually, now that I think about it, I (22) _____ (not, get) any of those things. At the end of the five years I (23) _____ (take) all that money I saved and (24) _____ (buy) the largest sailboat I can afford. I (25) _____ (quit) my job and (sail) around the world! Care to join the crew?

Use Your English

In *The Man Who Mistook His Wife for a Hat,* Dr. Oliver Sacks writes about his experiences treating unusual neurological disorders. You will hear a passage summarizing part of Dr. Sacks' true story of Dr. P., the man he refers to in the title.

STEP 1 Listen to the passage once for overall meaning.

STEP 2 On a separate piece of paper, make a chart like the one below.

STEP 3 Listen to the passage again. In the left-hand column of your chart, write down the past events that occurred before other past events. The first one has been done for you.

Earlier Past Event	Past event
1. He had been a singer	1. Later he became a teacher at the local school of music.

STEP 4 Listen to the whole passage one more time. In the right-hand column of your chart, write the past event that the earlier past event precedes, as in the example.

STEP 5 Compare your chart with a partner's and discuss the verb forms used in the column.

ACTIVITY 2: WRITING

Find a place that you think would be interesting to observe nature or people: a quiet place outdoors, a school cafeteria, an airport, or a busy restaurant, for example. Spend fifteen or twenty minutes in this place with a notebook to record observations of interesting sights and sounds. You might want to reread Annie Dillard's observations in Exercise 3. Read your observations to the rest of the class or in a small group without telling them where you were. Have your classmates guess the place you are describing.

ACTIVITY 3: WRITING/SPEAKING

Choose one person in the class. Describe what you think that person will be doing and how she or he will change in the next ten years or so. Read your descriptions to the class or in a small group to see if your classmates can identify the person.

ACTIVITY 4: WRITING

Reread the passage by James Thurber in Exercise 7. Think of another animal that might have some very different opinions about the human race than humans tend to have about themselves. The animal could be a house pet, such as a canary; another domestic animal, such as a pig; or a wild animal, such as a wolf. Write a description of how this animal has probably regarded the human race.

ACTIVITY 5: SPEAKING/WRITING

Gordon Allport used concepts of in-groups and out-groups to develop a theory about how prejudices are formed. The very nature of in-groups means that other groups are "out-groups." For example, if someone is Catholic, then non-Catholics would be "out-groups." Not all "out-groups" are at odds with each other. However, Allport believed that sometimes people treat certain out-groups as "the enemy" or as inferior to their group. As a result, prejudices towards those of other religions, races, or nationalities may form. Do you see evidence, in your school, community, or a larger context, of "out-groups" who are victims of prejudice? Working in groups, list some of the out-groups you think are discriminated against. Then describe the situation affecting one of these out-groups in an essay. State whether the situation has improved or gotten worse over time and whether you think it will have improved by end of the next decade or so.

SUBJECT-VERB AGREEMENT

UNIT GOALS:

- To identify the head noun in a subject
- To use correct verb forms for subjects with correlative conjunctions
- To know which kinds of nouns take singular or plural verbs
- To know how subject-verb agreement forms vary in formal and informal English

▶ OPENING TASK

What Are Your Reading Habits?

For over four decades, researchers for the Gallup Poll, which examines national trends, have been surveying Americans' reading habits and attitudes toward reading. They have asked people how often they read, what kinds of reading they do, and how reading compares with watching television as a leisure activity, among other things.

STEP 1 Take a poll of your class's reading habits. In pairs, take turns asking and answering the five questions below, which were used in the Gallup Poll. Write down your partner's responses. The response options are given in parentheses.

STEP 2 Pool the responses of all class members and tally the results. Convert the results for questions 1, 2, 3, and 4a to percentages, as shown in the Gallup results for Question 1.

STEP 3 Have one class member summarize the results. Then discuss them: Were any of the results surprising? For the first question, the Gallup results for three polling periods are shown for you to compare with your class's results. Some of the other results, taken from the 1990 poll, will be presented later in this unit.

Reading Habits

1. Are you reading any books or novels at the present time? (Yes/No)

2. When, as nearly as you can recall, did you last read any kind of book all the way through—either a hardcover book or a paper-bound book? (Within the last week/Within the last month/One to six months ago/Seven to twelve months ago/Over one year ago/Never)

3. During the past year, about how many books, either hardcover or paperback, did you read either all or part of the way through?(None/One to five/Six to ten/Eleven to fifty/More than fifty)

4. (a) Do you have a favorite author? (Yes/No)
   (b) If yes, who is it? (Any choice)

5. Which of these two activities—watching television or reading books—is:
   (a) The most relaxing for you?
   (b) The best way to learn for you?
   (c) The most rewarding for you?
   (d) The most enjoyable way to spend an evening for you?
   Your choices for (a)–(d) : Watching TV/Reading a book/Both/Neither

Gallup Results for Question 1

x	Yes	No
1990 Dec.	37%	63%
1957 March	17%	83%
1949 Jan.	21%	79%
	Yes	No
Class Results		

From *Gallup Poll Monthly*, February 1991.
Reprinted with permission from The Gallup
Organization, Inc., Princeton, New Jersey.

▶ **Overview of Subject-Verb Agreement**

EXAMPLES	EXPLANATIONS
	In English, certain verbs must show agreement in number (singular/plural) with the subjects of sentences:
(a) I **am** you/we/they **are** he/she/it **is**	• present-tense forms of *be*
(b) I/he/she/it **was** we/you/they **were**	• past-tense forms of *be*
(c) he/she/it **works**	• present-tense forms of third-person singular verbs
(d) One of the books that I **am** reading **has** been a bestseller for a year.	If the verb has more than one part, the first part agrees with the subject. Choosing the correct verb form is not always easy, even for native speakers of English. Some reasons for difficulties are the following:
Head Noun **(e)** (The main **reason** we decided to take a trip to the Rocky Mountains) **is** to learn geological history. **(f)** (That **novel** about alien invasions in several South American countries) **has been made** into a TV film.	• subjects with long modifying phrases following the head noun, as in (e) and (f)
(g) The **pair of scissors** you bought **is** really dull now. **(h)** **Every book** in the library **has been entered** in the new computer system.	• nouns and pronoun phrases whose number (singular/plural) may be confusing, as in (g) and (h)
Plural Noun **(i)** Those comic book**s** make me laugh. **Singular Verb** **(j)** That comic book make**s** me laugh.	• the *-s* ending in English as both a plural marker for nouns and a singular marker for third-person present-tense verbs, as in (i) and (j)

EXERCISE 1

To check for subject-verb agreement, (1) identify the subject of the sentence and then (2) find the noun that is the head of the subject. In each of the following sentences, underline the head noun of the subject. Then circle the correct form of the verb in parentheses.

▶ **EXAMPLE:** Many children's <u>parents</u> (begin/begins) reading to them when the <u>children</u> (is/are) less than three years old.

1. Young people today (is/are) just as likely to read for pleasure as older Americans.

2. The reading survey (finds/find) some good news for those who appreciate reading as a pastime.

3. Today's Americans (is/are) more likely to read to their children than their parents (was/were).

4. Reading to very young children (stimulates/stimulate) them to learn to read sooner.

5. The impact of reading to children at an early age (is/are) dramatic.

6. There (is/are) signs of a coming surge in reading in America.

7. Despite television and its influence, reading (seems/seem) to be coming back into favor.

Adapted from *The Gallup Poll Monthly*, February 1991, with permission of The Gallup Organization, Inc.

▶ **Identifying Head Nouns in Long Subjects**

EXAMPLES	EXPLANATIONS
(a) That **novel** about alien invasions in several southwestern states **has** recently **been made** into a TV movie. **(b)** All of the **characters** in that story written by our teacher **were** very believable.	When the subject head noun and the verb are separated from each other, it is harder to check for agreement. It can be especially troublesome when the head noun is singular but nouns in a modifying phrase are plural or vice versa.
Head Noun Prepositional Phrase **(c)** Another **poll** of Americans' reading and attitudes **was taken** in 1990. **Head Noun Compound Preposition** **(d)** The **library**, { together with / along with / as well as } bookstores, **provides** reading materials. **Head Noun with No*t* + Noun Phrase** **(e)** The **child**, not her parents, **was** an avid reader. **Relative Clause** **(f)** A **child** who likes to read **books** and whose parents encourage reading **does** better in school.	Here are strategies to find the head nouns: • If the subject has a prepositional phrase, locate the head noun to the left of the first preposition (for example, *of*). • Use the same strategy with subjects followed by compound prepositions, such as *together with, along with, and as well as*. • Locate the head noun before *not* + a noun phrase. • Similarly, look to the left of relative clauses (*who, which, that, whose* clauses) to identify the head noun.

EXERCISE 2

The following sentences summarize information about the Gallup Poll's 1990 reading survey. Put brackets [ ] around any modifying phrases following the head noun. Underline the head noun. Circle the appropriate forms in parentheses.

▶ **EXAMPLE:** The <u>library</u>, [along with bookstores], (provides/provide) reading materials.

1. The horror story writer Stephen King, together with romance novelist Danielle Steele, (was/were) the most popular of the authors named by the respondents.

2. One of the 1019 respondents to the survey (claims, claim) that (he or she/they) started reading at the age of one!

3. Some respondents, in answer to the question of who their favorite living author is, (gives, give) the name of a writer who has died many years ago.

4. According to Judy Fellman, the President of the International Reading Association, one reason so many parents are reading to their children (is/are) the abundance of children's literature.

5. A father whose own parents read to him when he was young (is/are) more likely to read to (his/their) children.

6. James Michener, as well as V.C. Andrews, (ranks/rank) third in author popularity among those surveyed.

7. A person who belongs to one of the higher income groups (tends/tend) to read more.

8. According to the poll, the college-educated female, not the college-educated male, (is/are) the most prolific (reader/readers), averaging eighteen books a year.

▶ **Agreement in Sentences with Correlative Conjunctions:**
*both . . . and; either . . . or;
neither . . . nor*

EXAMPLES	EXPLANATIONS
(a) Both **F. Scott Fitzgerald** and **Charles Dickens were** named as favorite authors in the 1990 reading poll.	**Both . . . and** When two subjects are connected by *both . . . and*, use a plural verb.
(b) Either the library or **bookstores have** current magazines. **(c)** Either bookstores or the **library has** current magazines. **(d)** Neither the book nor **the magazines discuss** this issue. **(e)** Neither the magazines nor **the book discusses** this issue.	**Either . . . or; Neither . . . nor** The traditional rule is that the verb should agree with the head noun after *or* or *nor*.
(f) Either Kay or **I am** going to the library this afternoon. **(g)** Neither the twins nor **he is** planning to go to the library. **(h)** Obviously, neither she nor **they are** interested in that topic.	This agreement rule also determines verb form when one or more of the subjects is a pronoun.

EXERCISE 3

Select the appropriate verb form and, in some cases, the correct noun phrase after the verb, for each sentence. In cases of *either . . . or* or *neither . . . nor*, use the rule in Focus 3 to select the verb.

▶ **EXAMPLE:** Neither the books nor the bookshelf (is/are) mine.

1. Either books or a magazine subscription (makes a nice gift/make nice gifts) for someone.
2. For a less expensive gift, both bookplates and a bookmark (is a good choice/are good choices).
3. Neither the Russian novelist Leo Tolstoy nor the Irish writer James Joyce (was/were) known to more than 50 percent of the 1990 Gallup Reading Poll respondents.
4. She said that either the reserved book librarian or the librarians at the main checkout desk (has/have) the information you need.
5. Both reading and writing (is/are) what we consider literacy skills.
6. Either you or I (am/are) going to present the first report.
7. In my opinion, neither the front page of the newspaper nor the sports pages (is/are) as much fun to read as the comics.
8. (Does/do) either the lifestyle section of the newspaper or the business section interest you?
9. I can see that neither you nor he (is/are) finished with your sections yet.
10. Both my brother and my parents (is/are) reading that new biography of Lyndon Johnson. Neither he nor they (has/have) read more than a few chapters, though.

EXERCISE 4

In groups of three, take turns sharing the responses you gave in the Reading Survey. Make up five statements summarizing the responses of your group using *both . . . and* or *neither . . . nor*. Report your findings to another group.

▶ **EXAMPLES:** *Neither* Mohammed *nor* Juanita has read more than five books this year.

Both Tomoyo *and* Gregorio have favorite authors. Tomoyo's is Toni Morrison and Gregorio's is Jorge Amado.

▶ **Agreement with Noncount Nouns, Collective Nouns, and Nouns Derived from Adjectives**

EXAMPLES	EXPLANATIONS
	Noncount Nouns
(a) The new gym **equipment has** just **been delivered**.	Noncount nouns in English include mass nouns and abstract nouns. These nouns take a singular verb.
(b) That **information is** very helpful.	
(c) My English **vocabulary has increased**.	**Mass Nouns** **Abstract Nouns**
(d) Your **advice is** always appreciated.	*equipment* *advice*
	furniture *behavior*
	grass *education*
	homework *information*
	machinery *knowledge*
	money *research*
	traffic *transportation*
	vocabulary *violence*
	Collective Nouns
(e) The **audience is waiting** patiently for the performance to begin.	Collective nouns define groups of people or animals:
(f) A **flock** of geese **is flying** overhead.	*audience* *group*
	class *herd*
	committee *the public*
	family *swarm*
	flock *team*
(g) The **class is going** on a field trip.	If the group is considered as a whole, use a singular verb. In most cases, collective nouns take singular verbs.
(h) The **team has been practicing** all week.	
(i) The **class have disagreed** among themselves about where they should go on their field trip.	If the group is considered as individual members, use a plural verb. This usage is less common in American English.
(j) The soccer **team have** differing opinions about strategies for the next game. Some think defense is the key, but others believe a more aggressive strategy is needed.	

EXAMPLES	EXPLANATIONS
(k) **The young want** to grow up fast and **the old wish** to be younger. **(l)** Is it true that **the rich are getting** richer and **the poor are getting** poorer?	**Nouns Derived from Adjectives** Noun phrases derived from adjectives that describe people, such as *the young*, *the rich*, and *the homeless*, take plural verbs.

EXERCISE 5

Take turns giving oral responses (between one and five sentences) to the following questions. Use the noun or nouns in bold print as the subject in at least one sentence. The first one is done as an example.

1. What kind of **transportation** do you prefer for getting to school?

▶ **EXAMPLE:** *Well, the **transportation** I prefer **is** driving my own car. But finding a parking space is difficult, so I take the bus most of the time.*

2. What is some good **advice** you've gotten during the past year from a friend, relative, or something you read?

3. What is some useful **information** you've learned in your English class?

4. What home office **equipment** do you think is the most helpful for you as a student?

5. Do you think **violence** is ever justified? Explain your opinion.

6. How would you describe your **knowledge** of sports? (Good? Fair? Poor? Does it vary according to particular sports?)

7. Do you think **the homeless** are being neglected in our society? What evidence do you have for your opinion?

8. Do you believe that **a college education** is necessary for everyone in our society? Who might not need a college education?

EXERCISE 6

The following sentences describe activities of groups. Circle the appropriate verb form for each.

▶ **EXAMPLE:** The group (has/have) just left.

1. The audience for the political rally (was/were) huge.

2. The audience (seems/seem) to have mixed reactions to the President's speech; some people are cheering wildly, while others are walking away, disgusted.

3. My family (celebrates/celebrate) birthdays with a special dinner.

4. The city government (is/are) ordering a reduction in water usage.

5. A swarm of bees (has/have) built a nest under the eaves of the roof. Look! The swarm (appears/appear) to be flying out in all directions from that spot.

6. The population of Phoenix (is/are) growing every year

7. The population of that country (has/have) disagreed among themselves for years about immigration policies.

8. The disabled (is/are) demanding more attention to their needs.

FOCUS 5

▶ **Subjects Requiring Singular Verbs**

Some types of subjects always take singular verbs.

EXAMPLES	EXPLANATIONS
	(Some common or proper nouns that end in -s:
(a) **Mathematics is** my favorite subject. Others: *physics, economics*	• courses
(b) **Measles is** no fun to have! Others: *mumps, arthritis*	• diseases
(c) **Leeds is** where my aunt was born.	• place names
(d) **The news** from home **was** very encouraging.	• *news*
(e) *Tracks* **was written** by Louise Erdrich.	• book and film titles
(f) *Dances with Wolves* **was awarded** an Oscar for the best movie.	
	Plural unit words of distance, time, and money:
(g) **Six hundred miles is** too far to drive in one day.	• distance
(h) **Two weeks goes** fast when you're on vacation.	• time
(i) **Fifty dollars is** a good price for that painting.	• money

EXAMPLES	EXPLANATIONS
	Arithmetical operations (addition, subtraction, multiplication, division):
(j) **Three plus seven equals** ten.	• addition
(k) **Four times five equals** twenty.	• multiplication
	Items that have two parts when you use the noun *pair*
(l) My **pair** of scissors **is** lost.	
(m) A **pair** of plaid shorts **was** on the dresser.	
(n) **My scissors are** lost.	
(o) **Those plaid shorts were** on the dresser.	Note, however, that you would use the plural verb if the noun pair is absent.
Subject	**Clause subjects:**
(p) **[What we need] is** more reference books.	The verb is singular even when the nouns referred to are plural.
(q) **[That languages have many differences] is** obvious.	
(r) **[Reading books and magazines] is** one of my favorite ways to spend free time.	Gerund (verb + *-ing*) and infinitive (*to* + verb) clauses also take singular verbs.
(s) **[To pass all my exams] is** my next goal.	

EXERCISE 7

Imagine that you are competing on a quiz show. For each definition below, you will be given three words, phrases, or numbers. You must choose the correct match and state the answer in a complete sentence.

▶ **EXAMPLE:** a film set in California (*Badlands, Down and Out in Beverly Hills, Star Wars*)

Answer: ***Down and Out in Beverly Hills*** *is a film set in California.*

1. the number of days in a leap year (364, 365, 366)
2. a disease that makes you look like a chipmunk (shingles, mumps, warts)
3. four (54 divided by 9, 100 divided by 20, 200 divided by 50)
4. a poem written by Geoffrey Chaucer (*The Canterbury Tales, Great Expectations, Guys and Dolls*)
5. a common plumber's tool (a pair of scissors, a pair of pliers, a pair of flamingoes)
6. a city in Venezuela (Buenos Aires, Caracas, Athens)
7. what you most often find on the front page of a newspaper (sports news, national news, entertainment news)
8. the study of moral principles (ethics, physics, stylistics)
9. the number of years in a score (ten, twenty, thirty)
10. a course that would discuss supply and demand (mathematics, economics, physics)

EXERCISE 8

What are your opinions and attitudes about each of the following topics? State at least two things that could complete each of the sentences below. Share some of your answers with the class.

▶ **EXAMPLES:** What this country needs <u>is health insurance for everyone and better education.</u>

1. What this country needs _____.
2. What I would like to have in five years _____.
3. Having a job while going to school _____.
4. That the rain forests are being destroyed _____.
5. What really irritates me _____.
6. What I find most frustrating about being in school _____.
7. Learning the rules of subject-verb agreement in English _____.

FOCUS **6**

▶ **Agreement with Fractions, Percentages, and Quantifiers**

With fractions, percentages, and quantifiers *all* (*of*) and *a lot of,* agreement depends on the noun or clause after these phrases.

EXAMPLES	EXPLANATIONS
(a) Fifty percent of the **book is** about poetry. **(b)** Half of **what he says is** not true. **(c)** All (of) our **information is** up-to-date.	Use a singular verb when the subject is: • a singular noun • a noun clause • a noncount noun
(d) One-fourth of the **students have** computers. **(e)** All (of) the **computers need** to be checked.	With plural nouns, use a plural verb.
(f) One-sixth of our **Spanish club has/have** relatives in Mexico. **(g)** A lot of my **family live/lives** in Pennsylvania.	With collective nouns, use either the singular or the plural, depending on your meaning.
(h) Each **book has** a code number. **(i)** Every one of the **students is** on time.	With quantifiers *each, every,* and *every one*, use a singular verb, whether the noun is singular or plural.
(j) A number of **students are** taking the TOEFL exam today. **(k)** The number of **students** taking the exam **is** 175. **(l)** None of the **advice was** very helpful. **(m)** None of the **magazines** I wanted **is** here.	With *a number of,* use a plural verb since the noun it modifies is always plural. *The number of,* however, takes a singular verb. With *none of,* use a singular verb in formal written English.

Summary: Form of the Verb Following Traditional Agreement Rules

	SINGULAR NOUN	NONCOUNT NOUN	PLURAL NOUN	COLLECTIVE NOUN
percentages	singular	singular	plural	singular/plural
fractions	singular	singular	plural	singular/plural
all (of)	singular	singular	plural	singular/plural
a lot of	singular	singular	plural	singular/plural
each, every	singular	singular	singular	
a number of			plural	
the number of			singular	
none of	singular	singular	singular	singular

EXERCISE 9

Summarize the information from the Gallup Poll below by writing five sentences about responses of the people surveyed. For subjects, you could use any of the following: *respondents, people surveyed, Americans, those who responded.*

▶ **EXAMPLE:** *Almost three-fourths of the respondents believe they spend too little time reading books for pleasure.*

Survey Question: Thinking about how you spend your nonworking time each day, do you think that you spend too much time or too little time . . .

	Too much	Too little	About right	No opinion
Watching television	49%	18%	31%	2%
Reading newspapers	8%	54%	35%	3%
Reading magazines	6%	65%	24%	5%
Reading books for pleasure, recreation	7%	73%	16%	4%
Reading books for work, school, etc.	9%	62%	19%	10%

Adapted from *Gallup Poll Monthly,* February 1991.

EXERCISE 10

Write three sentences that are true and three that are false about the members of your class, using the words in parentheses as the subjects. Read your sentences aloud to a classmate. Your classmate should decide which are true and which are false and should orally correct each false statement.

▶ **EXAMPLE:** *The number of female students in our class is twelve.*
     Response: False. The number of female students in our class is fourteen.

1. (The number of) _____ .
2. (Each) _____ .
3. (None) _____ .
4. (All) _____ .
5. (A lot of) _____ .
6. (A number of) _____ .

EXERCISE 11

Fill in each blank of the following radio news report with a *be* verb form that would be appropriate for formal English use.

▶ **EXAMPLE:** A number of reporters from other states _____ *are* _____ in town to cover news about the earthquake.

Here is the latest report on the aftermath of the earthquake. As most of you know, the earthquake has caused a great deal of damage and disruption to our area. A lot of the

houses near the epicenter of the quake (1) _____ badly damaged. A number of trees (2) _____ uprooted in that area also, so be careful if you are driving. All the electricity (3) _____ shut off for the time being. Water (4) _____ turned off also. None of the freeways in the vicinity (5) _____ currently open to traffic. Almost every side street (6) _____ jammed with drivers trying to get back home. The police (7) _____ directing traffic at major intersections. To date, the number of deaths resulting from the earthquake (8) _____ two. All people (9) _____ urged to stay at home if at all possible.

▶ **Exceptions to Traditional Agreement Rules**

Some of the agreement rules presented in this unit are observed mainly in formal English contexts, especially in formal written English. The following are cases where native speakers of English frequently do not follow the formal (traditional) rules, especially in spoken and less formal written English:

EXAMPLES	EXPLANATIONS
	***Either/Neither of the* + Noun Phrase**
	Formal rule: use a singular verb with *either* or *neither*.
(a) Either of the outfits **is** ⎫	Formal
(b) Either of the outfits **are** ⎬ appropriate.	Less formal
(c) Neither of the choices **is** ⎫	Formal
(d) Neither of the choices **are** ⎬ desirable.	Less Formal
	Either . . . or / Neither . . . nor
	Formal rule: the verb agrees with the closest subject noun.
(e) Either my parents or John **has** ⎫ the	Formal
(f) Either my parents or John **have** ⎬ car.	Less formal
(g) Neither you nor I **am** ⎫	Formal
(h) Neither you nor I **are** ⎬ convinced.	Less Formal
	***None* + Prepositional Phrase**
	Formal rule: use a singular verb.
(i) None of the magazines **is** ⎫	Formal
(j) None of the magazines **are** ⎬ here.	Less Formal
	***There* + *Be* (present tense) + Plural Noun**
	Formal rule: use *are* with plural nouns.
(k) There **are** ⎫ three books here you	Formal
(l) There**'s** ⎬ might like.	Less Formal

Note: Many less formal forms are becoming more common in all but the most formal written English contexts. *There are* is usually used with plural noun phrases in written English, however.

Summary: Form of the Verb with Formal versus Less Formal Usage

	FORMAL	LESS FORMAL
Either of the + (plural noun) *Neither of the* + (plural noun) *Either* (noun) *or* (singular noun) *Neither* (noun) *nor* (singular noun) *None of the* + (plural noun)	singular verb	singular or plural verb

EXERCISE 12

Decide which of the underlined verbs would be appropriate for formal written contexts and which would be acceptable in spoken English. Write "formal" or "informal" to indicate the usage.

▶ **EXAMPLES:** *Either of these economics courses <u>are</u> useful for my major.*
   Informal

1. Neither of those political surveys <u>are</u> valid because the sample was not random.

2. I am sure that either Professor Tori or Professor Kline <u>have</u> already addressed the issues you mention.

3. As far as we know, none of the experiment's results <u>has</u> been duplicated to date.

4. There<u>'s</u> some results that will surprise you.

5. Neither Dr. Gonzalez nor Dr. Vuong <u>are</u> presenting the findings of their studies until the results are checked again.

6. In conclusion, either of the textbooks I have reviewed <u>is</u> an excellent choice for an introductory chemistry course.

7. We have reviewed the report. None of the figures <u>seem</u> correct; they should be checked again.

8. Either of the reports submitted <u>are</u> useful for further study of this environmental problem.

9. Neither the campus medical center nor the library <u>is</u> safe should a strong earthquake occur.

10. Either you or I <u>are</u> responsible for this month's financial report; please let me know if I should submit it.

11. Neither of the claims Senator Holmes presented <u>is</u> justified.

12. There<u>'s</u> a number of errors in this report.

Use Your English

ACTIVITY 1: LISTENING

You will hear a summary of information from another Gallup survey. This one asked people questions about raising children.

STEP 1 As you listen to the summary, take notes on the information you hear.

STEP 2 At the end of the summary, you will hear eight statements based on the information in the survey. Listen to all the statements and decide whether each statement is true or false.

STEP 3 Listen to the statements again, pausing after each one. On a separate piece of paper, write T or F after you hear each statement. If a statement is false, write a correction using a complete sentence.

STEP 4 Listen to the summary again to check your answers and corrections.

ACTIVITY 2: SPEAKING

Below are some examples of spoken and written English that were found in the newspaper. Discuss the traditional rules of subject-verb agreement that have not been observed. How do they illustrate some of the troublesome cases of subject-verb agreement? (Why do you think the speaker or writer used a singular or plural verb in each situation?)

- "I have decided that everyone in these type of stories are rich." (Quoted statement by an actress in reference to a TV movie she appeared in)
- "Her expertise in the water as a lifeguard and her understanding of ocean currents, coupled with the fact that she is a strong swimmer, makes her a strong competitor." (Quoted comment about a champion swimmer)
- "I know there is going to be a major hassle with certain smokers, plus there is going to be a lot of attempts to bypass the regulation." (From a letter to the editor about no-smoking regulations)
- " . . . the chances of him coming back in the next eight years was very unlikely." (Quoted comment about a politician who ran for President)
- "In the Jewelry Center, All That Glitter Sure Is Gold" (Headline for a feature article)

ACTIVITY 3: RESEARCH/ SPEAKING/WRITING

Ask another class (or a group of teachers) to respond to the questions in the reading habits survey. Tally the results and write a survey report comparing them to your class's results.

ACTIVITY 4: RESEARCH/ SPEAKING/WRITING

Usage surveys have suggested that native speakers of English often use plural verbs with *either* when *of* plus a plural count noun follows *either*, as in sentences like this: *"Either of those times are okay with me for a meeting."* What do you think native speakers would choose in question forms: *"Are/Is either of those times okay with you?"*

STEP 1 In groups or with a partner, create a set of five questions with *either + of + plural noun* to test what verbs native speakers would choose. Here are some examples:

> **EXAMPLES:** 1. *Do/does either of you boys have a match?*
> 2. *Is/are either of you going to come with us to the movies?*
> 3. *Has/have either of your parents ever worked in a restaurant?*

STEP 2 Conduct a survey by giving your set of questions to at least ten native speakers of English. Ask them to choose the verb they would use.

STEP 3 Write a report of your results or give an oral report to the class.

ACTIVITY 5: WRITING

Write an essay expressing your views about society's treatment of one of the following groups of people: the poor, the disabled, or the elderly. You might want to compare how one of these groups is treated in the United States and in another country.

PASSIVE VERBS

UNIT GOALS:

- To know when to use passive verbs rather than active verbs
- To use correct forms of *be* and *get* passives
- To know the correct form and use of passives in descriptions
- To use passives correctly after *that* clauses and infinitive clauses
- To use passives to create connections in discourse

▶ OPENING TASK
A Short-Term Memory Experiment

Short-term memory describes the brain function in which information is retained temporarily, somewhere between thirty seconds and a few minutes. Numerous experiments have been conducted to test the recall of information stored in short-term memory, resulting in various theories about memory. One phenomenon believed to characterize short-term memory is called *the serial position effect*. In this task, you will be testing this effect. (You will find out later exactly what it means.)

STEP 1 With a partner, perform the following experiment to test the serial position effect. One person will take the role of researcher; the other will be the subject. A blank sheet of paper and a pen should be ready for the subject and the subject's book should be closed.

STEP 2 Researcher: Show the list of words on page A-17 to your subject. Ask him or her to study the list of words for one minute. After one minute has passed, close the book.

STEP 3 Subject: Immediately write down on the blank sheet of paper as many of the words as you can recall for one minute. You can write the words in any order. Then give the list to the Researcher. Note: It is important that you start writing immediately after the study time is up.

STEP 4 Read the explanation of the serial position effect on page A-17. Do the results of your experiment support or contradict this belief about short-term memory?

STEP 5 With your partner, write a brief report of the experiment, using the written list of words as your data. Assume that your reader has no previous information about your experiment. In your summary, describe the procedures and summarize the results. Use the model below to start the report.

Memory Experiment

This experiment was conducted to test the serial position effect on recalling information. One subject participated in the experiment. The subject was shown a list of thirty common words. . . .

STEP 6 Share your report with another set of partners. Then save the report for exercises later in this unit.

► **O**verview of Passive
versus Active Verb Use

EXAMPLES		EXPLANATIONS
ACTIVE VERBS	PASSIVE VERBS	We often use passive instead of active in the following contexts:
(a) **(Agent)** The brain **retains** **(Recipient)** information temporarily in short-term memory.	**(b)** **(Recipient)** Information **is retained** **(Agent)** temporarily by the brain in short-term memory.	• when we want to focus on the receiver of an action (recipient) rather than the performer (agent) of the action. We do this by making the recipient the grammatical subject. We may express the agent in a *by*-phrase following the verb.
(c) I **asked** the subject to look at the word list for one minute.	**(d)** The subject **was asked** to look at the word list for one minute.	• when the agent is less important than the recipient of an action. In reporting research procedures, for example, we do not need to refer to the researcher.
(e) The subject wrote down all the words she could remember. She **recalled** a total of thirteen words.	**(f)** The subject wrote down all the words she could remember. A total of thirteen words **were recalled.**	• when the agent is obvious from the context.
(g) It appears that something **is altering** the rats' brain cells.	**(h)** It appears that the rats' brain cells **are being altered.**	• when the agent is unknown.
(i) The researchers who did this study **have made** several major errors in analyzing the data.	**(j)** Several major errors **have been made** in analyzing the data.	• when we want to avoid mentioning the agent. For example, we may not want to say who is responsible for some wrongdoing or mistake.

EXERCISE 1

Provide a likely reason for each of the italicized passive verbs in the sentences below.

▶ **EXAMPLE:** *Two masterpieces of sixteenth century painting were taken from the museum.* The agent is unknown.

1. One method that is *used by* psychologists in research on memory is the relearning method.

2. In the relearning method, people have to relearn information that *was learned* earlier.

3. Sometimes when you *are introduced* to another person, you forget the person's name a few minutes later.

4. It seems that some misleading statements *were made* in advertising your auto repair services.

5. We have just received reports that a bomb *was set off* in the airport terminal shortly before midnight.

6. Construction of the Leaning Tower of Pisa *was begun* by Bonanno Pisano in 1173.

7. Small bits of information *are* often *remembered* by grouping the information into larger units, known as chunks.

8. Short-term memory *has been called* "a leaky bucket."

EXERCISE 2

Reread the paragraph introducing the Opening Task. Identify the sentences that have passive verbs and state why they are used.

EXERCISE 3

With your partner for the Opening Task, look at the report you wrote. If you used any passive verbs, identify the reasons for their use. If you didn't use any, find one or two sentences that you might change from active to passive based on the information in Focus 1. State what use each would reflect.

▶ **R**EVIEW OF **P**ASSIVE **V**ERB **F**ORMS

All passive verbs are formed with *be* + or *get* + past participle.

EXAMPLES	EXPLANATIONS
(a) That movie **is reviewed** in today's newspaper. **(b)** The garbage **gets picked up** once a week.	SIMPLE PRESENT *is/are* (or *get*) + past participle
(c) The possibility of life on Mars **is being explored.** **(d)** We **are getting asked** to do too much!	PRESENT PROGRESSIVE *is/are* + *being* (or *getting*) + past participle
(e) The butterflies **were observed** for five days. **(f)** Many homes **got destroyed** during the fire.	SIMPLE PAST *was/were* (or *got*) + past participle
(g) The Olympics **were being broadcast** worldwide. **(h)** She **was getting beaten** in the final trials.	PAST PROGRESSIVE *was/were* + *being* (or *getting*) + past participle
(i) Short-term memory also holds information that **has been retrieved** from long-term memory. **(j)** Did you hear he**'s gotten fired** from his job?	PRESENT PERFECT *has/have* + *been* (or *gotten*) + past participle
(k) This store **has been being remodeled** for six months now! I wonder if they'll ever finish. **(l)** It looks as though the tires on my car **have been getting worn** by these bad road conditions.	PRESENT PERFECT PROGRESSIVE *has* + *been* + *being* (or *getting*) + past participle
(m) The National Anthem **had** already **been sung** when we entered the baseball stadium. **(n)** He was disappointed to learn that the project **had**n't **gotten completed** in his absence.	PAST PERFECT *had* + *been* (or *gotten*) + past participle

EXAMPLES	EXPLANATIONS
(o) The horse races **will be finished** in an hour. **(p)** The rest of the corn **will get harvested** this week.	SIMPLE FUTURE *will* + *be* (or *get*) + past participle
(q) I bet most of the food **will have been eaten** by the time we get to the party. **(r)** The unsold magazines **will have gotten sent back** to the publishers by now.	FUTURE PERFECT *will* + *have* + *been* (or *gotten*) + past participle
(s) The election results **will have been getting tallied** by the time we reach the headquarters	FUTURE PERFECT PROGRESSIVE* *will* + *have* + *been* + *being* (or *getting*) + past participle
(t) A different chemical **could be substituted** in this experiment. **(u)** Don't stay outside too long. You **may get burned** by the blazing afternoon sun.	MODAL VERBS (Present Time Frame) modal (*can, may, should*, etc.) + *be* (or *get*) + past participle
(v) All of our rock specimens **should have been identified,** since the lab report is due. **(w)** The file **might have gotten erased** through a computer error.	MODAL VERBS (Past Time Frame) modal (*can, may, should*, etc.) + *have* + *been* (or *gotten*) + past participle

*Note: The *be* form of this passive tense is quite rare. Even the *get* form is not very common.

EXERCISE 4

Rewrite each sentence below to put focus on the recipients of action rather than on the performers (agents) of the action. Delete the agent if you do not think it needs to be mentioned. In some cases, you may want to restate the agent in a prepositional phrase beginning with *in* rather than with *by*.

▶ **EXAMPLE:**   The brain stores information.

   Information is stored in the brain.

1. A bundle of millions of fibers connects the brain cells.
2. In visual processing, the right hemisphere of the brain registers unfamiliar faces; the left hemisphere registers familiar ones.
3. The memory does not store an exact replica of experience.
4. The brain alters, organizes, and transfers information into one or more memory stores.

5. Psychologists have discovered certain facts that the multistore model of memory cannot explain.

6. Researchers are now investigating other ways in which we organize information in long-term memory.

7. Scientists have demonstrated the difference between recognition and recall in numerous experiments.

8. The researchers used case studies of stroke victims to learn more about information storage.

EXERCISE 5

Choose one or more of the following topics to discuss with a partner or in a small group.

1. What advice was given to you by friends or relatives when you did one or more of the following: (a) enrolled in a new school; (b) took up a new sport or hobby; (c) moved to a new place?

2. What is being done today to prevent or cure diseases?

3. What measures have been taken to help disabled people?

4. What improvements have been made recently in your school (facilities, new buildings, courses, etc.)?

5. What changes do you think will have been made in the way we communicate across distances by the middle of the next century?

FOCUS **3**

USE

Stative Passives in Contrast to Dynamic Passives

EXAMPLES		EXLANATIONS
DYNAMIC PASSIVES	STATIVE PASSIVES	Many verbs can be either dynamic or stative depending on their meaning. Dynamic passive verbs describe activities. Stative passive verbs do not report activities; they express states or conditions. Stative passive verbs do not have agents.
(a) The missing library book **was found** in the parking lot by a custodian.	(b) A map of Miami **can be found** on the Internet.	
(c) Our telephone line **is** finally **being connected** tomorrow.	(d) The transmission of a car **is connected** to the gearshift.	
(e) Stella **was called** for a job interview yesterday.	(f) The biological rhythm with a period of about twenty-four hours **is called** a circadian rhythm.	

EXERCISE 6

Each of the famous monuments or buildings below can be matched to two descriptions in a–j. (1) Match each landmark to the appropriate descriptions. (2) Rewrite each description as a sentence with a passive verb (or verbs) to put focus on the monuments and buildings as the main topics. (3) Delete the agents if they do not add much to the meaning or if they can be inferred from the context. (4) Make any other necessary changes.

EXAMPLE: *The Parthenon is considered to represent the peak of Greek architectural achievement.*

MONUMENTS AND BUILDINGS

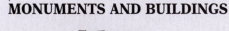

1. The Parthenon　　　　　2. Osaka Castle　　　　　3. Mount Rushmore

4. Ankor Thom　　　　　5. The Pyramids of Giza

DESCRIPTIONS

a. Workers wore out about four hundred drills a day to carve out the granite mountain.

b. The Cambodian god-king Suryavarman II intended it to be a funerary monument for himself.

c. Unlike in Europe, where builders used stone for castles, builders made this of wood.

d. People believe that workers constructed them using mounds or ramps to position the stone blocks.

e. Many consider it the peak of Greek architectural achievement.

f. In ancient times, a large complex of buildings surrounded them.

g. Located south of the Cambodian capital of Ankor Thom, people built it in the twelfth century.

h. Pericles had it built to celebrate Athens' victory over the Persians.

i. Guzton Borlum, the sculptor, designed it to symbolize American history and principles.

j. Historians regard it as the most formidable stronghold in Japan before people destroyed it in the early seventeenth century.

▶ Uses of Stative Passive Verbs

Stative passive verbs have a number of descriptive uses in discourse. Note that many of the stative passives in the examples below are followed by prepositions: *in, with, by, for,* etc.

EXAMPLES	USES
(a) The Amazon River **is located** in Brazil. **(b)** The ratel, a fearless animal, **is found** in Africa and India. **(c)** The Secret Service agents **were positioned** near the President.	• To describe location or position *Located* is often used in geographical description. *Found* typically describes plant and animal habitats. *Positioned* often suggests placement. Other verbs: *placed, situated, bordered (by), surrounded (by)*
(d) *The Daily Scandal* **is filled** with untrue stories. **(e)** The sea horse's body **is covered** with small bony plates.	• To describe characteristics or qualities This type of description is common in science.
(f) Temperature **is measured** in degrees. **(g)** The elements **are listed** according to weight.	• To describe manner or method This use is common in science and mathematics.
(h) France **is divided** into regions. **(i)** Geology **is made up** of many subfields, such as seismology and petrology.	• To describe part-whole relationships Other verbs: *composed (of), organized into*
(j) The Geiger counter **is used** for detecting radiation. **(k)** Greetings such as "How are you?" **are intended** to promote communication, not to get information.	• To describe purpose These verbs may be followed by *for* + gerund (verb + *-ing*) or an infinitive (*to* + verb). Other verbs: *designed, meant*
(l) Do you know the old song that begins: "The knee bone**'s connected** to the thigh bone"? **(m)** The two buildings **are joined** by an elevated walkway.	• To describe connection Other verbs: *attached (to), accompanied (by), separated (by, from)*

EXAMPLES	USES
(n) El Greco **is** best **known** for his religious painting. **(o)** Nagoya Castle **is considered** one of the greatest fortresses in the history of Japan.	• To describe reputation or association Other verbs: *regarded (as), thought to be, viewed (as)*
(p) The ratel **is** also **known** as "the honey badger." **(q)** Pants having legs that flare out at the bottom **are called** bellbottoms.	• To define or name Other verbs: *labeled, named, termed*

EXERCISE 7

Identify the stative passive verbs in each of the following sentences and state the use of each, based on the categories in Focus 4.

▶ **EXAMPLE:** Benin, a small country, *is situated* in West Africa.

Stative passive: *is situated*   Use: *to describe location*

1. As an infant, a person is in his mother's womb; grown up, the person is wrapped in custom; dead, the person is wrapped in earth. (Malay Proverb)

2. Hallucinations are often associated with abnormal mental conditions.

3. In the midwestern United States, soft drinks such as cola drinks or root beer are referred to as "pop."

4. Natural geysers, which are found in Japan, New Zealand, and the United States, are sometimes classified as renewable energy.

5. The Special Olympics is meant to give disabled people an opportunity to compete in athletic contests.

DO NOT WRITE IN THIS BOOK.

EXERCISE 8

(1) Match each numbered word or phrase in column A to the appropriate phrase in column B.

(2) Write a sentence for each, using a stative passive.

(3). Add other words or change word forms as necessary.

▶ **EXAMPLES:** 1,d. *Language **may be defined** as the spoken or written means by which people express themselves and communicate with others.*

*The spoken or written means by which people express themselves and communicate with others **is called** language.*

A

1. language
2. alcohol thermometers
3. the hand
4. monuments of unknown soldiers
5. human brain
6. Sigrid Undset

B

a. Belgium, Britain, France, Italy, Portugal, and the United States

b. three parts: the hindbrain, the midbrain, and the forebrain

c. the author of *Kristin Lavransdatter,* for which she won the Nobel Prize

d. the spoken or written means by which people express themselves and communicate with others

e. structural specialization at the end of the arm, enabling grip and fine motor tasks that characterize higher primates

f. measure low temperatures

FOCUS **5**

▶ **Complex Passives**

Complex passives are passive constructions followed by *that* clauses or infinitive clauses (*to* + verb).

EXAMPLES	EXPLANATIONS
(a) It **is believed** that primates first appeared on the earth about sixty-nine million years ago. **(b)** It **is said** that the number thirteen is bad luck. **(c)** It **was reported** that a hijacker was arrested this morning.	**Form:** Introductory *it* + passive verb + *that* clause **Use:** This form often serves to introduce a topic, since the new information comes at the end of the sentence.
(d) The topic of today's lecture is early primates. Primates **are believed** to have appeared on the earth about sixty-nine million years ago. **(e)** Many numbers are associated with superstitious beliefs. For example, thirteen **is said** to be an unlucky number. **(f)** A hijacker took over a jumbo jet flying to New York this morning. The hijacker **was reported** to have been demanding that the plane fly to South America.	**Form:** Subject (other than introductory *it*) + passive verb + *to* infinitive **Use:** This form could also be used to introduce topics, but it is especially appropriate after a topic has been introduced because the topic can then be put in the subject position.

EXERCISE 9

For each of the following numbered sentence groups, choose the sentence that best fits the context, using the principles of introducing or continuing topics as discussed in Focus 5. Consider each numbered group to be the beginning of a written article or spoken announcement.

1. Even today, some people believe that opening an umbrella in the house will bring bad luck. In parts of Asia, as early as the eleventh century,
   (a) it was considered to be an insult to open an umbrella inside a building.
   (b) opening an umbrella inside a building was considered to be an insult.

2. (a) It has been alleged that an employee of the museum is responsible for the theft of dozens of paintings.

(b) An employee of the museum is alleged to be responsible for the theft of dozens of paintings. Police are currently investigating the claim.

3. (a) It was reported this morning that a Pacific blacktip shark gave birth to three healthy pups at Sea World.

(b) A Pacific blacktip shark was reported to have given birth to three healthy pups at Sea World this morning. Officials commented that this marks the first documented birth of the species in captivity.

4. Of the comets that have been recorded, the least frequently returning one is Delavan's Comet, which appeared in 1914.

(a) This comet is not expected to return for twenty-four million years.

(b) It is not expected that this comet will return for twenty-four million years.

EXERCISE 10

The following actions or conditions and their results reflect superstitions in various parts of the world. Express each situation and result in sentences with two complex sentence structures: a *that* clause complex passive and an infinitive.

▶ **EXAMPLE:**   Action/Condition   Result

A picture falls in the house.   Someone will die.

1. *It is said that having a picture fall in the house will result in someone dying.*

    OR *It is said that if a picture falls in the house, someone will die.*

2. *Having a picture fall in the house is believed to cause someone to die.*

Action/Condition	Result
1. You enter a house with the left foot.	It will bring you bad luck.
2. You tie a red string around a finger of your left hand.	It will help your memory.
3. Say the word *abracadabra*.	It will ward off sickness.
4. You have a mole on your neck.	You will get money.
5. Tie knots in an apron.	It will protect you against accidents.

FOCUS **6**

▶ ## Contexts for the Use of Complex Passives

Complex passives are often used in journalism, in business, and in academic writing. Although not commonly used in informal spoken English, complex passives are frequent in formal spoken English (for example, news reports, speeches). Some of the most common uses follow.

EXAMPLES	USES
	To achieve an impersonal tone, avoiding the use of *I* or *we*:
(a) It **should be noted** that the results of our experiment cannot be generalized.	• in explanations and observations
(b) This product **is known** to be inferior.	
(c) It **is assumed** that all employees have completed the necessary hiring papers.	• in statements of desired or expected behavior
(d) All homework **is expected** to be turned in on time.	
(e) It **has been ruled** that the prisoner was unfairly convicted.	• in evaluations or judgments
(f) The house **was considered** to be vastly overpriced.	
(g) It **is believed** that baseball was being played in England in the early eighteenth century.	To express information that has not been verified as factual or true
(h) Mr. Blau **is alleged** to have stolen several car stereos.	
(i) In the nineteenth century, it **was thought** that personality traits and mental abilities could be detected by bumps on the head.	To describe past beliefs that are no longer regarded as true
(j) In ancient Greece, lightning bolts **were believed** to be weapons used by Zeus, the king of gods.	
(k) It **is assumed** that more and more species will become extinct if we continue to destroy the world's rain forests.	To express a general expectation about some future event
(l) The weather **is expected** to be warm and sunny all weekend.	

EXERCISE 11

The *Guinness Book of World Records* presents hundreds of fascinating facts about the superlatives of the world (and even of the known universe), whether they concern the biggest, the longest, the oldest, or the smallest. Imagine that you are a writer compiling facts for this book; your task is to rewrite the following information in complete sentences. Use the passive form of the verb given in parentheses. Change the phrasing of information and add words as needed. The first has been done as an example. Note that if an activity happened in the past (as in 1b), an infinitive verb expressing it must be perfective: *to + have +* past participle.

▶ **EXAMPLE:** **1.** (a) longest living fish: lake sturgeon (think)
   The longest living fish is thought to be the lake sturgeon.

   OR *It is thought that the longest living fish is the lake sturgeon.*

   the lake sturgeon is the longest living fish.

   1. (b) life span of one specimen of sturgeon: eighty-two years (report)
   It was reported that one specimen lived for eighty-two years.

   OR *One specimen was reported to have lived for eighty-two years.*

2. fastest flying insect: the American deer bot-fly (believe)

3. longest prison sentence: 10,000 years, imposed on a convicted murderer in Alabama, 1981 (say)

4. the longest United Nations speech: four hours, twenty-nine minutes, by Cuban President Fidel Castro on September 26, 1960 (know)

5. the smelliest living animal: the African zorilla (consider)

6. total number of active volcanoes: 850 (think)

7. Sirius A, the Dog Star: brightest of the 5776 stars we are able to see (presume)

8. the most baked beans eaten: 2780 by a British woman (allege) (Hint: use *a British woman* as your subject)

Using the Passive to Create Cohesion in Discourse

EXAMPLES	EXPLANATIONS
(a) For the first time, researchers have found **the remains of a mammal that has been entombed in amber. The remains,** including a backbone and ribs, **are estimated** to be eighteen million to twenty-nine million years old. Discovered in the West Indies, **these remains are believed** to be those of a tiny insect-eating mammal.	As explained in Focus 1, we put focus on a topic in English by making it the grammatical subject. Often a new topic is introduced at the end of a sentence. This topic then becomes the subject of the next sentence. As a result, a passive verb may be needed. Putting the topic in the subject position helps to create cohesion, making it easier for the reader or listener to understand the main ideas.
(b) Biologists have recently determined that **even the tiny brains of bees can recognize and interpret patterns. This feat was** once **thought** possible only through reason. In an experiment, bees learned to look for food only near **certain symmetrical or asymmetrical patterns. These patterns are reflected** in nature, such as blossoms of plants.	Often a synonym for the topic or a shortened form of the topic is used as the subject with a passive verb. (See Unit 6, Focus 2 for more information about these forms of reference.) This also helps to create cohesion. In some cases, it allows the writer or speaker to avoid using a subject with a long modifying phrase.
(c) Most theories of long-term memory **distinguish** skills or habits ("knowing how") from abstract or representational knowledge ("knowing that"). **This distinction is supported** by recent evidence that skill learning and the acquisition of knowledge are handled by different areas of the brain.	The subject of a passive verb may also be derived from the verb of a previous sentence.

EXERCISE 12

Circle the passive verbs in the following passages. Then explain why each passive verb is used.

▶ **EXAMPLE:** One of the world's largest pharmaceutical companies has recently fired its chairperson. The chairman *was suspected* of unethical accounting practices. Explanation: The passive verb *was suspected* is used in the second sentence to put focus on the topic, *the chairman*.

1. Researchers are studying the effects that physical stress and psychological factors have on the immune system. The immune system is designed to do two things: recognize foreign substances (antigens), such as flu viruses and tumors, and destroy or deactivate them.

Adapted from Carole Wade and Carol Tavris, *Psychology*, Harper and Row, 1987.

2. The ability of electric currents to float through certain materials completely untouched, without energy loss, is called superconductivity. This phenomenon was explained in a theory developed in 1972, an accomplishment that won the Nobel Prize. Superconductivity was thought to exist only at extremely cold temperatures, but in 1986, a scientist in Germany discovered a high-temperature superconductor.

3. The repeated eruptions of Mexico's Popocatepetl volcano have resulted in the growth of a lava dome to within fifty feet of the rim of the volcano. The dome is being fed by 20,000 cubic feet of fresh lava daily. If the lava overtops the rim, it could melt glaciers on the side of the mountain and create life-threatening mudflows.

4. In experiments to examine the ways in which infants form attachments to mothers or other caretakers, researchers separated infant chimpanzees from their mothers. Extended separations were found to result in abnormal social development.

5. A team of scientists have decoded the 1700 genes of a microbe living on the ocean floor. This microbe belongs to a class called arachae, a different class from the two most common branches of life—bacteria and eukaryotes, which include plants, animals, and humans. The existence of archaea was first proposed by Carl Woese and Ralph Wolfe at the University of Illinois. Archaea has some characteristics of other life forms but functions differently. About 500 species of archaea have been identified. The life form is thought to produce about 30% of the biomass on earth.

Adapted from "Decoding of Microbe's Genes Sheds Light on Odd Form of Life," *Los Angeles Times*, August 8, 1996.

EXERCISE 13

After each sentence or group of sentences, add a sentence with a passive verb to create cohesion, using the information given in parentheses.

▶ **EXAMPLE:** Any substance that is toxic to insects is known as an insecticide. (We use insecticides to control insects in situations where they cause economic damage or endanger health.)

Insecticides are used to control insects in situations where they cause economic damage or endanger health.

1. The ancient city of Troy was the setting of the legendary Greek siege described in *The Iliad*. (An earthquake destroyed the city around 1300 B.C.)

2. There are three types of muscle in humans and other vertebrates. One type is skeletal muscle. (Under a microscope, we see that this muscle is striped or striated.)

3. Most people associate the phrase "Survival of the fittest" with Darwin's Theory of Evolution. (However, a British philosopher, Herbert Spencer, first used the phrase, and Darwin later adopted it.)

4. The Great Wall of China served as a defensive wall between the old Chinese border with Manchuria and Mongolia. The first section was completed in the third century B.C. (The Chinese later extended it until it was 1400 miles long.)

5. Although the idea of submarines is an old one, the first submarine, made of wood and covered with greased leather, was not built until 1620. David Bushnell invented the first submarine used in warfare in 1776.

Use Your English

ACTIVITY 1: LISTENING/SPEAKING/WRITING

A famous psychology laboratory experiment conducted by Stanley Milgram in 1963 tested subjects' willingness to obey authority even when they believed they would be required to administer painful electric shocks to other subjects. In the taped passage, you will hear a description of the procedures and the results of this experiment. Take notes on the information you hear. With a partner, compare notes to get information you may have missed. Then write a summary of the experiment, using passive verbs where appropriate to put focus on recipients of action and to achieve coherence.

ACTIVITY 2: READING

Find a text that has a number of passive verbs. (Science texts, instruction manuals, and texts that define or classify are good sources). Analyze ten passives that you find. Are they dynamic passives or stative passives? Why did the writer use them?

ACTIVITY 3: WRITING/SPEAKING

In small groups, make up five sentences describing people, places, or things, but don't reveal who/what they are. In each sentence, use a stative passive verb. See if other groups can guess who or what you are describing. Here are some examples. Can you guess the answers?

▶ **EXAMPLES:**
1. *It is divided into nine innings.*
2. *It can be found in tacos, spaghetti sauce, and ceviche.*
3. *This famous British dramatist is known as the Bard of Avon.*
4. *They are also called twisters.*
5. *This country is bordered by Italy, Austria, Germany, and France.*

ACTIVITY 4: WRITING

Draw a diagram or map of one of the following:

- an area (your room, apartment or house, a neighborhood, or commercial district, for example)
- a machine or device
- an invention of your own creation (a machine that writes your papers for you? a device that gets you out of bed in the morning?).

In your diagram/map, label at least four or five objects, parts, buildings, or whatever would be found there. Then write a paragraph describing the locations of objects or the ways in which you have divided your diagram/map into parts. Use stative passives in your descriptions.

ACTIVITY 5: WRITING

As the manager of a large office-supply store, you have observed repeated inappropriate behavior among some of the employees. This behavior includes the following:

- showing up late for work and leaving early
- taking breaks longer than the fifteen minutes allowed
- eating snacks at the service counter
- talking to other employees while customers are waiting for service.

Write a memo to the employees to let them know what kind of behavior is expected of them while they are at work. Since you want to assume an impersonal tone, use complex passives.

ACTIVITY 6:
SPEAKING/LISTENING/WRITING

Interview a classmate about family or hometown history. Ask him or her to tell you about some events that are thought to be true but are not documented. The events might concern some long-ago period (for example, "Juan's great-grandfather was believed to have been born in Guatemala. The family is thought to have moved to Mexico in the early 1900s"). They could also include information about your classmate's youth as reported by his or her parents (for example, "Sonia is said to have been very good-natured as a baby.") Take notes during the interview. Then write up a report from your notes, using complex passives where appropriate to express some of the information. If time permits, present your report orally to the class.

ARTICLE USAGE

UNIT GOALS:

- To distinguish classification from identification meaning in articles
- To use definite, indefinite, and zero articles appropriately
- To distinguish particular from generic reference in articles
- To distinguish abstract generic from concrete generic meaning in articles
- To use the article in definitions of generic nouns
- To use the appropriate articles to correspond to body parts and illnesses

▶ OPENING TASK

Controversial Medical Practices

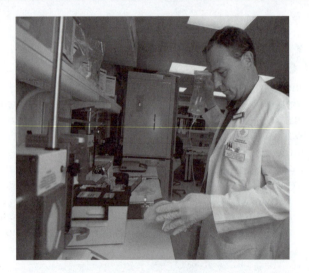

STEP 1 Read the following list of current or possible practices in the medical profession. Check whether you believe they are ethical or not ethical.

ETHICAL?

Yes	No		
☐	☐	a.	Researchers using animals (mice, cats, cows, etc.) to test the poison level of drugs or the effect of artificial organs that might be implanted into a human being.
☐	☐	b.	Drug companies bribing doctors with vacations and other perquisites ("perks") to prescribe new but less well-known drugs to their patients.
☐	☐	c.	Machines keeping alive severely injured people who are in a vegetative state.
☐	☐	d.	Childless couples using surrogate (substitute) mothers to bear children.
☐	☐	e.	Engineering genetic changes in embryos to prevent birth defects or diseases.
☐	☐	f.	Forcing birth control on a population that for religious or cultural reasons does not desire it.
☐	☐	g.	Parents conceiving a child in order to obtain a matching organ or tissue to save the life of another one of their children.
☐	☐	h.	Poor people selling their own organs in order to make a living.
☐	☐	i.	Requiring doctors to reveal the results if they have a positive AIDS test and to quit their active medical practices.

STEP 2 In small groups, discuss the pros and cons of several of these practices based on information you have heard or read about. Choose one member of your group to take notes on the discussion.

STEP 3 (Recorder) Summarize your group's discussion for the rest of the class. Which topics were the most controversial? Which opinions did your group agree on?

Classification versus Identification*
Meaning of Articles

EXAMPLES	EXPLANATIONS
	An indefinite article (*a/an* or Ø) classifies a noun and shows that it represents or reflects a type, group, or a class distinct from some other type, group or class. • singular nouns (*a/an*)
(a) What did you see yesterday? I saw **a** horror movie last week.	
(b) **An** earthquake (a natural disaster) struck at 7:10 A.M.	
(c) **A** gas (a type of gas) that can be deadly is carbon monoxide.	
(d) Ø Stars (celestial bodies)shine brightly.	• plural nouns (Ø)
(e) We expect Ø complications (additional problematic conditions) while she is sick.	
(f) Have you ever seen Ø traffic (passage of vehicles) like this?	• noncount nouns (Ø)
(g) Ø Mango juice (tropical fruit juice) can be made from Ø syrup (thick sweet liquid).	
	The definite article (*the*) can identify a noun and show that it has been singled out in some way. Generally, the speaker or writer knows the listener or reader is aware of the noun because it was previously mentioned or he or she can see it, has heard of it, has experienced it, has read about it, etc. • singular nouns (*the*)
(h) **The** movie (you heard about it) featured Dracula.	
(i) **The** earthquake (you know about it) destroyed many buildings.	
(j) **The** gas (you smell it) can be harmful.	
(k) **The** stars (we read about them) were discovered in 1952.	• plural nouns (*the*)

EXAMPLES	EXPLANATIONS
(l) **The** medical complications (you experienced them) were unexpected.	
(m) **The** traffic (we are riding in it) is dangerous.	• noncount nouns (*the*)
(n) Could you pass **the** maple syrup (you are near it)?	

*Adapted from P. Master, *Systems in English Grammar*. Englewood Cliffs, New Jersey: Prentice-Hall Regents, 1996.

EXERCISE 1

Look at the use of *a, an,* or *the* in each of the following cartoons.

STEP 1 Describe what is happening in each cartoon.

STEP 2 Discuss how the article classifies or identifies its corresponding noun.

▶ **EXAMPLE:** *Two children are pretending to be a doctor and a nurse to a teddy bear mother. The doctor is announcing the gender of a stuffed animal.*

• *"A" is used to classify the newborn as a male.*

It's a boy!

1.

Do you think Bob minds sitting in the back row?

2.

I told you it was an iron.

3.

I beat the eggs. Now what?

EXERCISE 2

Answer the following questions with noun phrases. Use *a/an, the,* or Ø to show that the noun is classified (shows kind, type, class, etc.) or identified (shows specific feature, aspect, characteristic, etc.)

▶ **EXAMPLES:** What part of a holiday dinner do you enjoy the most?
the stuffed turkey (identified)

What kind of meat do you like the most?
beef, a hot dog (classified)

1. What kind of movie is most exciting?
2. What feature of your classroom is unusual?
3. What kind of person is attractive?
4. What type of vegetables do you dislike the most?
5. What aspect of your English class was most interesting this week?
6. What type of clothing is usually made of wool?
7. What characteristic of rap music is unusual?
8. What class of animal gives birth to live young?
9. What part of a chicken do you like eating the most?
10. What aspect of your car or your friend's car is unusual?

EXERCISE 3

Fill in the following blanks with *a/an, the,* or Ø. In which blanks did you use *the* to refer to identifiable nouns?

On (1) ____the____ night of January 11, 1983, Nancy Cruzan,
(2) _____ healthy, twenty-five-year-old woman, lost control of her car
while driving in Jasper County, Missouri. As (3) _____ car overturned,
Nancy was thrown into (4) _____ ditch. When the ambulance reached
(5) _____ ditch, (6) _____ paramedics found her with no
(7) _____ detectable breathing or (8) _____ heartbeat. Today Nancy
lies in (9) _____ Missouri state hospital, in what is described all too
neatly as (10) _____ "persistent vegetative state." In reality, she lies in
(11) _____ bed in (12) _____ hospital, horribly contorted with
(13) _____ irreversible muscular and (14) _____ tendon damage.
She is fed through (15) _____ tube in her side.

EXERCISE 4

Fill in the following blanks with *the* or Ø. In which blanks, did you use the Ø to refer to classifiable nouns?

(1) ___The___ students entering our medical schools have
(2) _____ outstanding grade-point averages, and (3) _____
impressive scores on (4) _____ Medical College Admissions Test, and
(5) _____ glowing recommendations. There's no doubt that they have
(6) _____ capability to become (7) _____ good scientists and
(8) _____ good science doctors. But do they have (9) _____ makings
of humanists with (10) _____ commitment to treat everything from
(11) _____ broken bones to (12) _____ broken hearts? It is this
delicate balance between (13) _____ science and (14) _____ wisdom
that makes (15) _____ great physicians—(16) _____ ability to know
what to do with what has been learned.

Special Uses of the Definite Article

EXAMPLES	EXPLANATIONS
	Use *the*:
(a) **The sun** is very bright.	• with unique nouns
(b) **The most significant effect** occurred in June.	• before superlatives
(c) **The third component** was missing.	• before ordinals (*first, second, third*, etc.)
(d) **The main operator** was not on duty.	• before modifiers that make the noun that follows specific (*same, sole, chief, only, single, solitary, main*, etc.)
(e) Each of **the experiments** was successful.	• in phrases that refer to a specific part of a whole group
(f) Half of **the population** suffered greatly.	
(g) **The effect** of an earthquake can be felt for miles.	• with identifiable nouns that are followed by a modifying *of*-phrase
(h) We were uncertain about **the cause** of the fire.	
(i) **The beginning** of the movie was frightening.	
(j) A major urban problem is caring for **the poor** (people).	• before adjectives that represent groups of people
(k) "Heartbreak" is a song on **the radio.**	• with certain nouns, such as mechanical inventions and devices, to refer to a general example of something rather than a specific object the speaker/writer has in mind
(l) She got here fast because she took **the train.**	
(m) I went to **the barber** after classes.	• before locations associated with certain typical or habitual activities. The listener/reader may have no idea of the exact location to which the speaker/writer is referring.
(n) Have you been to **the beach** this summer?	
(o) She needs to pick up a few things at **the store.**	

EXERCISE 5

For each of the following sentences, circle the correct article in parentheses. Explain your choices to a partner.

▶ **EXAMPLE:** (A/the) sun is very bright today. I need to buy (a/the) cap at (a/the) store.

The sun is very bright. I need to buy a cap at the store.

Sun *is a unique noun; therefore,* **the** *is used.* **A cap** *is used because it refers to a type of hat, not to a particular one.* **The store** *is used because a location referring to a specific habitual activity (shopping) is being referred to.*

1. All civilizations of (a/the) world are enriched by trade and (a/the) stimulating impact of other cultures.

2. There are two main precursors to skin cancer. (A/the) first indication is spontaneous bleeding on some part of (a/the) skin. (A/the) second is the enlargement of a freckle or mole.

3. I'll be late for (a/the) meeting because I have to make (a/the) deposit at (a/the) bank.

4. (A/the) most significant effect of (an/the) earthquake was (a/the) destruction of many homes.

5. I read (a/the) wonderful story yesterday. (A/the) beginning of the story takes place in Vienna about (a/the) turn of (a/the) century.

6. In (a/the) past, (a/the) most important factor determining world power was (a/the) navy that could navigate (a/the) Mediterranean.

7. There were many reasons for (a/the) success of (a/the) project. (A/the) main reason was that at least half of (a/the) workgroup had Ph.D.s from around (a/the) globe.

8. (A/the) radio described several ways in which (an/the) elderly could obtain (a/the) best medical help.

9. In (a/the) next year, (an/the) exact mechanism by which cell receptors work will be better understood.

10. (A/the) last decade has been marked by (a/the) large increase in violence.

▶ **R**eview and Special Uses of Ø

EXAMPLES	EXPLANATIONS
	Ø is used when the following noun is non-specific. Use Ø with:
(a) Ø Flowers should be watered regularly.	• nouns that have general or generic reference (see Focus 4)
(b) I need to get Ø gas before we start for Seattle.	• nonspecific nouns that do not refer to a specific quantity or amount
	Also use Ø with:
(c) The children ran directly Ø home.	• certain nouns associated with familiar destinations
(d) They went Ø downtown after supper.	
(e) My grandmother walked to Ø school everyday.	
(f) He worked until Ø midnight.	• certain nouns of time (*night, dusk, noon, midday, midnight,* etc.)
(g) Ø Spring is a wonderful time of year.	• names of seasons (*spring, summer, fall, winter*)
(h) We had Ø lunch at a very good restaurant.	• names of meals (*breakfast, brunch, lunch, dinner,* etc.)
(i) The group arrived by Ø car.	• means of transportation (*by boat, by plane, on foot,* etc.)
(j) They came on Ø foot from the meeting.	
(k) We were informed by Ø mail that our subscription had been canceled.	• means of communication (*by phone, by mail, by telegram,* etc.)
	Certain idioms use Ø:
(l) They walked Ø arm in Ø arm down the aisle.	• phrases joined with *by, in,* or *and* (*day by day, week by week, side by side, arm in arm, neck and neck,* etc.)
(m) The ship was lost at Ø sea.	• participle + preposition + count noun (*wounded in action, lost at sea, missing in action, cash on delivery,* etc.)
(n) He put his heart and Ø soul into the project.	• phrases joined by *and* (*heart and soul, bread and butter, husband and wife,* etc.)
(o) Peter took Ø care of the details.	• verb + objects + preposition (*shake hands with, take care of, take advantage of, take part in, take notice of, take pride in,* etc.)

EXERCISE 6

Fill in the following blanks with *a/an, the,* or Ø. More than one answer may be appropriate.

It was (1) _____Ø_____ spring and (2) _____ young GI, returning
(3) _____ home from (4) _____ war, called his parents from
(5) _____ phone booth in (6) _____ bus station. His parents
had waited for a message by (7) _____ mail or (8) _____
telegram, but he had not gotten around to writing. On (9) _____ phone,
he told his parents that he would be coming by (10) _____ bus and that
he would be (11) _____ home by 5:00 that evening. But he hesitated
(12) _____ moment and then added that he was bringing
(13) _____ home (14) _____ friend, and he hoped that it
would be okay with them because his friend was handicapped. He had been
wounded in (15) _____ action and had no legs. He asked his parents'
permission. They told him that they felt very sorry for (16) _____ friend
but they were not really set up to cook (17) _____ breakfast,
(18) _____ lunch, and (19) _____ dinner for him—this was
not (20) _____ good time for him to come. The mother worked; there
were two floors in (21) _____ house; she would have to run up and
down; (22) _____ money was tight, etc., etc. As it turned out,
(23) _____ young man did not get off (24) _____ bus that
night, because he was (25) _____ handicapped soldier. It was their son
who had been wounded in (26) _____ action. The parents never saw
him again.

Particular versus Generic Reference of Articles

Generic reference relates to the general rather than the particular nature of something. Particular reference indicates one member of a class; generic reference indicates all or representative members of a class. Note in the following examples the particular and generalized meanings of *laser* in different contexts.

EXAMPLES	EXPLANATIONS
(a) Her doctor used a **laser** to treat her varicose veins.	• particular reference
(b) The **laser** cured Paul's cataract problem.	• particular reference
(c) The **laser** has been used in medicine since the 1960s.	• generic reference
(d) A **laser** can cut through soft tissue with a searing light.	• generic reference
(e) **Lasers** reduce the recovery period needed for ordinary operations.	• generic reference

EXERCISE 7

For each of the following pairs of sentences, circle the option that makes a general versus a particular reference about the italicized noun phrase. Note that different references are only sometimes marked by different articles.

▶ **EXAMPLE:** (a) An *immunity* is a resistance to infection.

(b) I have an *immunity* to small pox.

1. (a) You should take *the vitamins* on the counter.

(b) You should take *vitamins* in order to stay healthy.

2. (a) A *cholera epidemic* was started by contaminated food and water.

(b) *Cholera epidemics* kill many people every year.

3. (a) A *doctor* claimed to have discovered a miracle burn ointment.

(b) A *doctor* is trained to treat burns.

4. (a) *The motion picture industry* has created many movie idols.

(b) She is working for *the motion picture industry* in Los Angeles.

5. (a) There is no cure for *a cold*.

(b) I have had *a cold* for four weeks.

6. (a) *The mouse* used in the experiment was injected with morphine.

   (b) *The mouse* is an excellent research animal.

7. (a) The patient will sit in *the wheelchair* until her daughter arrives.

   (b) *The wheelchair* has improved the lives of the handicapped.

8. (a) Angela has been playing *the saxophone* for three years.

   (b) Angela has been playing *the saxophone* that was in the corner.

9. (a) *Some people* have been sitting in the waiting room since 11:00 A.M.

   (b) *People* kept alive only by machines should be allowed to die.

10. (a) *Water* from springs contains minerals.

    (b) *The water* from the spring cured my illness.

FOCUS **5**

USE

▶ ## *The* + Plural Nouns for General Reference

EXAMPLES	EXPLANATIONS
	Sometimes, *the* may be combined with plural nouns when referring generally to:
(a) The Sierra Club is intent on saving **the redwoods**.	• plant and animal groups that are the target of special attention
(b) We went to a fund-raising benefit for **the whales**.	
(c) **(The) Neo-Nazis** propagate discrimination and hate.	• social, political, religious, and national groups. (Note that *the* is optional here.) A few nationality words do not allow plural endings and require *the: the Swedish, the Danish, the Finnish, the Polish, the Swiss, the English, the French, the Dutch, the Irish, the Welsh, the British, the Chinese, the Japanese,* etc.).
(d) **(The) Republicans** have conservative values.	
(e) **(The) Jews** celebrate Passover.	
(f) **The Dutch** are very good at learning languages.	

EXERCISE 8

Match up the following associations with the corresponding types of people. (Some associations may apply to more than one group.) Select five statements and write them in complete sentences below.

▶ **EXAMPLE:** *(The) Italians eat a lot of pasta.*
Criminals commit serious crimes.

Association	**People**
1. face racial discrimination	a. Swiss
2. want equality in marriage	b. Muslim
3. know many languages	c. professor
4. like to dance	d. racist
5. eat a lot of pasta	e. politician
6. like to loan money at high interest	f. Brazilian
7. discriminate against different races	g. criminal
8. must "publish or perish"	h. feminist
9. forget campaign promises	i. laborer
10. pray to Allah	j. African American
11. want more than the minimum wage	k. Italian
12. commit serious crimes	l. banker

1. _____

_____

2. _____

_____

3. _____

_____

4. _____

_____

5. _____

_____

▶ **Abstract Generic versus Concrete Generic**

EXAMPLES	EXPLANATIONS
definite article = the laser indefinite article = a laser zero article = Ø lasers = Ø blood	The most common way to signal general reference in English is: • *the* + singular count nouns • *a/an* + singular count nouns • Ø + plural count nouns • Ø + noncount nouns
(a) **The dermatologist** specializes in skin care. **(b)** **The platypus** is an unusual creature. **(c)** The heaviest organ is **the skin**. **(d)** **The eucalyptus** is native to Australia. **(e)** What has revolutionized the workplace is **the computer**. **(f)** It is difficult to play **the harp**. **(g)** NOT: The towel absorbs water. **(h)** **An operation** is stressful to one's body. **(i)** Ø **Carriers** may pass infections on to others. **(j)** Ø **Ultrasound** can detect the sex of an unborn baby.	There are two types of generic reference:* • <u>Abstract generic reference</u> uses *the* with singular countable nouns and noncount nouns to refer to certain well-defined, entire classes of entities. These entities are humans, animals, organs of the body, plants, complex inventions, and devices that can often serve as agents of change. They are not simple inanimate objects. • <u>Concrete generic reference</u> pertains to each or all of the representatives of a class rather than to the whole class. It uses a greater variety of forms than abstract generic reference does. *a(n)* + singular count noun Ø + plural noun Ø + noncount noun
(k) **A police officer** carries **a gun**. **(l)** **A laser** directs **a beam of light** to make an incision. **(m)** **The/A dermatologist** uses a **special solution** to remove warts. **(n)** **The/A kangaroo** carries **its young** in a pouch. **(o)** NOT: An elephant is in danger of becoming extinct.	<u>Singular concrete generic nouns</u> with *a(n)* describe generalized instances of something. This means that the noun class is being referred to one member at a time and there may be references to other singular count nouns in the sentence. <u>Abstract generic nouns</u> may be preceded by *a(n)* if they are being referred to one member at a time.

*P Master, "Teaching the English Article System, Part II: Generic versus Specific." *English Teaching Forum*. July 1988.

EXERCISE 9

In each set, select one noun phrase that we can refer to with abstract generic *the*. Then, use that noun phrase in a general sentence. Note that descriptive words before and after nouns do not affect the use of generic *the*.

▶ **EXAMPLE:**   tattered flag/California redwood/stepbrother
The California redwood is older than other trees.

1. lining of the coat/apartment made of brick/African elephant
2. dust on the moon/illustration of the month/telephone for emergency communication
3. barbecue/artificial heart/Persian rug
4. free love/fin of a fish/French marigold
5. Hungarian embroidery/American automobile/Spanish tile
6. locksmith/key/door

EXERCISE 10

Check the sentences in which *the* could be substituted for *a(n)* to make a generic reference. Then explain why.

▶ **EXAMPLE:**   A transistor is used in computers.
*Because the transistor is a complex device, **the** is possible.*

1. An X-ray machine is used in radiotherapy.
2. A solar eclipse lasts about 7.5 minutes.
3. An octopus has eight legs.
4. A sprain is suffered when an ankle is wrenched.
5. A piano has fifty-two white keys.
6. A road is wider than an alley.
7. A human brain is larger than a bird brain.
8. A governor of a state (in the United States) has limited power.

EXERCISE 11

Read the following sentences that use *the* for abstract generic reference of a noun. Replace *the* with *a/an* and add singular noun phrases within a new sentence to show that you are talking about generalized instances of something.

▶ **EXAMPLE:**   The dog is man's best friend.
A dog needs its owner's attention every day.

1. The dragon only existed in fairy tales.

_____

2. The store manager needs good organizational skills.

_____

3. The plow is essential to farming.

_____

4. No shade tree is as beautiful as the weeping willow.

_____

5. One of the slowest animals is the snail.

_____

6. The cactus grows in warm climates.

_____

7. The piano is commonly found in American homes.

_____

8. The stomach is essential for digestion.

_____

9. The ophthalmologist examines eyes.

_____

10. The printing press was essential to mass communication.

_____

EXERCISE 12

Describe a usual or general tendency by completing the sentences below.

▶ **EXAMPLE:** A chocolate chip cookie is made of sugar, flour, butter, and chocolate chips.

1. A good party consists of _____

2. The Internet has changed _____

3. A healthy life includes _____

4. Builders name streets after _____

5. The police are needed for _____

6. Amnesia causes _____

7. Skillful architects create _____

8. A valuable education includes _____

▶ Definitions of Common Nouns

Standard definitions of generic nouns follow the pattern below. Generic nouns appear in the subject position of these definitions.

GENERIC NOUN	+ BE +	CLASSIFYING NOUN*	RELATIVE + PRONOUN +	VERB PHRASE
(a) **The dinosaur**	is	a prehistoric animal	that	scientists discovered through excavations.
(b) **A dinosaur**	is	a prehistoric animal	that	is now extinct.
(c) **Dinosaurs**	are	prehistoric animals	that	roamed the earth during the Mesozoic Age.

(d) **The chicken** is an animal that lays eggs.	Abstract generic nouns emphasize: • a class
	Concrete generic nouns emphasize:
(e) **A chicken** is an animal that lays eggs.	• an example, any members
(f) **Chickens** are animals that lay eggs.	• a group, all members
(g) **Chicken** is a meat that is very moist.	• all/any of something
(h) **The platypus** is a mammal that lays eggs.	Definitions can include: • classifications
(i) **A duck** is a bird that has webbed feet.	• attributes
(j) **Vultures** are birds that are larger than rats.	• comparisons
*See Focus 1.	

EXERCISE 13

Write incorrect definitions for the words provided below. Then, in pairs, take turns reading and correcting each other's definitions.

▶ **EXAMPLES:** bicycle

a) *A bicycle is a four-wheeled vehicle that you can sit on.*

b) *No, a bicycle is a two-wheeled vehicle that you can sit on.*

1. stethoscope	3. liver	5. palm tree	7. nail	9. honey
2. koala bears	4. spatula	6. eye	8. movie stars	10. violin

EXERCISE 14

Find the incorrect article (*a/an, the, Ø*) in the following definitions. Then, correct the error.

▶ **EXAMPLE:** The Universe is a system of galaxies that was created 10,000 million years ago.

1. The fashion design is a major that requires artistic talent.
2. A radio telescope is telescope that collects long-wavelength radiation.
3. Astronaut is a person who travels in space.
4. A neurosis is mental disorder that is relatively minor.
5. Dirge is a musical piece played at a funeral.
6. In many homes, prayers are said before meal.
7. The somnambulism is a word for a condition called sleepwalking.
8. The mercury is a white metallic element, which is liquid at atmospheric temperature.
9. Vaporization is the conversion of liquid into a vapor.
10. The blackboard is a surface that is used for writing.

FOCUS **8**

▶ # Articles with Names of Body Parts

EXAMPLES	EXPLANATIONS
	When generally referring to names of organs, parts of the body, or body fluids, we can use *the*:
(a) **The** heart can be transplanted. **(b)** Cancer of **the** bladder has been linked to cigarette smoking.	• singular body parts (*the* + noun)
(c) **(The)** blood carries nutrients to body tissues. **(d)** **(The)** skin is sensitive to ultra-violet rays.	• massive areas or fluids of the body (*the* + noncount noun)
(e) Excessive smoke inhalation damages **the lungs**. **(f)** Regular exams of **the teeth** will prevent serious dental problems. **(g)** **The veins** carry blood throughout the body.	• plural or paired body parts (*the* + noun + plural)

EXERCISE 15

Study the following diagram and write sentences describing the location or function of at least eight of the following body parts.

▶ **EXAMPLES:** a) The diaphragm is below the lungs.
b) The brain controls all muscular movements of the body.

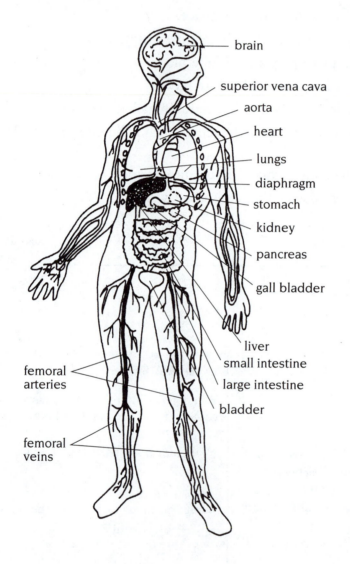

brain

superior vena cava

aorta

heart

lungs

diaphragm

stomach

kidney

pancreas

gall bladder

liver

small intestine

large intestine

bladder

femoral arteries

femoral veins

Articles with Names of Illnesses

The names of illnesses follow a range of noun patterns:

THE + NOUN	A/AN + NOUN		(THE) + NOUN + PLURAL
the flu	a cold	an ulcer	(the) bends
the gout	a hernia	a stroke	(the) mumps
the plague	a headache	an earache	(the) measles
	a heart attack	a sore throat	(the) hiccups

Ø + NONCOUNT NOUN		Ø + NOUN (WITH FINAL -S)
influenza	leukemia	diabetes
pneumonia	diarrhea	rabies
malaria	mononucleosis	herpes
arthritis	cardiovascular disease	AIDS
cancer	tuberculosis	

EXERCISE 16

Fill in a correct disease/illness that matches the information in the following blanks.

▶ **EXAMPLE:** __AIDS__ is caused by a blood-borne virus (HIV, Human Immunode-
ficiency Virus).

1. _____ is a disease that ravaged Europe between 1347–1351.

2. _____ is the bulging out of a part of any of the internal organs through a muscular wall.

3. _____ is a contagious disease that causes red spots to appear on the skin.

4. _____ is caused by a parasite, which is transmitted by a female mosquito.

5. _____ is a form of cancer that is marked by an increase in white blood cells.

6. _____ is an inflammation of the lungs caused by bacteria or viruses.

7. _____ is a decompression sickness experienced in the air or the water.

8. _____ consists of sores on the skin or internal parts of the body and is often caused by stress.

9. _____ is a common name for a cerebral hemorrhage.

10. _____ is a sound caused by contractions of the diaphragm.

EXERCISE 17

Review all of the rules in Unit 5. Locate ten article errors with *a/an, the,* or Ø in the following paragraph. The first one has been done for you.

(1) The gap between ^the rich and the poor, among countries and within countries, is widening. (2) Most of world's AIDS cases and HIV-infected people are in the developing countries. (3) Yet drug and hospitalization costs mean that "early intervention" is still meaningless concept in these countries. (4) Drug AZT remains too expensive for most of people who need it. (5) The industrialized world's total annual contributions to the AIDS in the developing world is estimated at $200 million or less. (6) The last year, the total expenditure for AIDS prevention and care in New York state alone was five times greater. (7) Total budget of the average national AIDS program in the developing world today is less than medical cost of caring for only fifteen people with AIDS in United States.

Adapted from J. Mann, "Global AIDS: Revolution, Paradigm, Solidarity." In O. Peterson, ed., *Representative American Speeches*, New York: The H.W. Wilson Co., 1991.

EXERCISE 18

Review all of the rules in Unit 5. Locate ten article errors with *a/an, the,* or Ø in each of the following blanks. Explain your choices to a partner.

(1) ___Ø___ insulin functions as (2) _____ indispensable middleman in (3) _____ metabolism. When we eat (4) _____ carbohydrate foods such as (5) _____ bread, (6) _____ vegetables, or (7) _____ fruit, (8) _____ simple sugar called (9) _____ glucose is usually (10) _____ end product of (11) _____ digestion,

and this sugar provides (12) _____ energy to each living cell;
(13) _____ insulin, in its turn, functions as (14) _____ doorman
to these cells, controlling (15) _____ access of (16) _____ glucose
molecules and other food sources such as (17) _____ protein and
(18) _____ fat across (19) _____ cell membrane and into each
cell's interior. With (20) _____ insulin, (21) _____ metabolism is
(22) _____ finely tuned feedback mechanism. Without it, only
(23) _____ trickle of (24) _____ fuel leaks into (25) _____
cells, hardly enough to stoke (26) _____ great human metabolic fur-
nace.

Adapted from S. Hall, *Invisible Frontiers*, New York: The Atlantic Monthly Press, 1987.

EXERCISE 19

Look at the underlined articles in the following paragraph. Explain the choice of
article in each case. Refer to rules in Unit 5.

▶ **EXAMPLE:**   Ø carrots
*Carrots are not particular but are a type of vegetable. Therefore, we
use Ø article.*

Some plants, such as (1) <u>Ø carrots</u>, will grow readily from (2) <u>Ø single
cells</u>; others, such as soybeans, will not. No one knows why. This reflects (3)
<u>an ignorance</u> at (4) <u>the fundamental level</u> of the regulation and (5) <u>Ø struc-
ture</u> of plant genes and of factors governing (6) <u>the growth</u> of plants. Gaining
such (7) <u>Ø knowledge</u> has the potential of quickening (8) <u>the rate</u> of breed-
ing new plants, raising (9) <u>Ø yields</u>, and extending (10) <u>Ø agriculture</u> to (11)
<u>Ø marginal lands</u>.

From: F. Bloom, "Introduction: Science, Technology, and the National Agenda." In A Report
by the Committee on Science, Engineering and Public Policy of the National Academy of
Sciences, National Academy of Engineering, Institute of Medicine, *Frontiers in Science &
Technology*, New York/San Francisco: W.H. Freeman and Co., 1983.

EXERCISE 20

Imagine that you have just taken notes on a lecture about the medical field.
Rewrite your notes in a paragraph, inserting articles where necessary.

▶ **EXAMPLE:**   medical field changed rapidly in lst century
The medical field has changed rapidly in the last century . . .

1. in past, family practitioner responded to all of family's medical
   needs (childbirths, surgeries, diseases, etc.)
2. doctor relied on natural remedies to alleviate pain

3. doctor's role was more of onlooker as "nature took its course"

4. today, doctors play more active role in healing

5. with their more specialized training, they are able to prescribe wonder drugs and perform surgeries on patients

6. prolonging life has always been ideal goal

7. sometimes lifesaving/enhancing procedures come in conflict with well-established social, religious, and moral values

8. thus, there is need for medical ethics

9. this is field that considers ethical implications of medical procedures and argues reasonable rights and limits doctors should have in making decisions about improving, prolonging, or saving lives

Use Your English

ACTIVITY 1: LISTENING/ WRITING

Listen to the minilecture about computers.

STEP 1 Take notes about the following items in the grid below.

STEP 2 Extend your notes to make as many sentences as you can, using the principles about article selection that you have learned in this unit.

▶ **EXAMPLE** abacus
An abacus was the earliest computing device used by the ancient Greeks and Romans.

1. use of the slide rule	
2. type of machine Gottfried Liebniz built	
3. invention of Charles Babbage	
4. mathematical theory of Alan Turing	
5. CPU	
6. memory	
7. VDU	
8. four ways computers can function	

ACTIVITY 2: RESEARCH/WRITING

The field of medicine can vary in different cultures. Do research at the library or conduct interviews with other students to learn about the practice of medicine in a place you are not familiar with. What are the medical training, medicine, and techniques associated with synthetic drugs, surgical technology, CAT scans, natural herbal drugs, acupuncture, homeopathy, massage, osteopathy, etc.? From your basic reading or interviewing, select one aspect of medical practice that interests you and write a short paper, incorporating correct use of the generic article.

ACTIVITY 3: READING/SPEAKING

Turn to pages 395–399. This activity presents special advice through runes, or alphabetic characters. Read each rune and accompanying advice. Underline all instances of nouns preceded by the. With a partner, discuss why *the* (instead of *a/an* or Ø articles) were chosen.

▶ **EXAMPLE** *You possess genuine power over events and you will find <u>the</u> solution to your problem within yourself.*
*__The__ is chosen because it describes an identifiable solution to a particular problem (versus a type of solution, in which case **a** would be used).*

ACTIVITY 4: READING/WRITING

Locate one chapter in an introductory science textbook (physics, chemistry, biology, etc.) that talks about general principles in that field. With a partner, read the first five paragraphs of the chapter. Make a list of abstract generic and concrete generic articles. Which type seems to be more frequent in this type of writing?

ACTIVITY 5: SPEAKING

Discuss which types of political, social, or religious groups would disagree most with each of the medical practices mentioned in the Opening Task. For example, would (the) Catholics be in favor of birth control? Would doctors be in favor of declaring positive AIDS tests results for themselves?

ACTIVITY 6: WRITING

Have you or anyone you've known suffered from any of the illnesses listed in Focus 9? If so, write a paragraph about your own or another's experience.

REFERENCE WORDS AND PHRASES

UNIT GOALS:

- To know the different reference forms in English
- To know the different uses of reference forms for linking ideas
- To use the appropriate reference forms for different contexts
- To avoid unclear reference by using appropriate forms

▶ **O PENING TASK**

Do Men and Women Communicate Differently?

People often use language differently based on differences in age, education, social status, gender, and so on. In her book *You Just Don't Understand: Women and Men in Conversation*, sociolinguist Deborah Tannen discusses how females and males differ in communication, drawing examples from American English speakers.

STEP 1 Divide into three groups. Each group should be assigned one of the three situations that follow. Using the questions below, discuss in your group what Professor Tannen says are typical female and male responses to the situation.

1. Do you agree that such responses are typical of men and women in the situations described?
2. Have you experienced any exceptions to these generalizations about male-female communication differences?
3. Do you think the gender-based communication differences described are common in cultures other than American culture?
4. Do you think that gender differences alone account for the different responses or could some other variables account for them? What might such variables be?

STEP 2 Have one person in each group present a brief summary of the group's discussion to the rest of the class.

Situation 1
TALKING ABOUT TROUBLES
Someone (male or female) has a personal problem. She or he is very upset and tells a friend about the problem.

If the friend is female: She empathizes by telling the person that she knows how it feels to have the problem. She may provide an example of the same problem or a similar one from her own experience.

If the friend is male: He offers advice about how to solve the problem.

Situation 2
EXPRESSING VIEWS
Someone expresses an opinion about a topic or presents his or her ideas on a topic.

If the listener is female: She expresses agreement with the speaker or, if she disagrees, asks for clarification or further explanation.

If the listener is male: He challenges the speaker's views and explores possible flaws in the argument or idea.

Situation 3
HAVING A CONVERSATION
A group of people at a social event, such as a party, are engaged in conversation.

If the group consists of females: They will tend to view conversation as a way of making connections and sharing experiences among participants. They will seek to use the conversation to establish common bonds among the group members.

If the group consists of males: They will tend to regard the conversation as a way to get attention or to impart information. More so than women, individual men will try to maintain center stage by delivering monologues, telling jokes or lengthy stories, or giving long explanations. They will typically be more concerned with asserting their own status than with establishing common bonds.

▶ **Review of Reference Forms**

EXAMPLES	EXPLANATIONS
Referent **(a)** Ruth enjoys talking about [gender-based language differences]. She finds **the topic** an interesting one.	Words and phrases that refer to information previously stated are called *reference forms*. The information that you are referring to is called a *referent*.
(b) Alma agrees that [men and women communicate differently in our society]. She believes **the observation** is true based on her personal experience.	**Reference Forms** • *the* + noun phrase
(c) Lin: Do you know much about [language variation]? Yumi: Not a lot, but I did read a little about **it** in my introductory linguistics course.	• Pronouns: *it*
(d) [Phonology and semantics] are areas of linguistics. **They** are concerned with language sounds and meanings, respectively. I studied **them** a few years ago.	*they, them*
(e) Our psychology professor says that [men tend to advise friends who come to them with troubles]. My experience supports { **this.** **this claim.**	• Demonstrative pronouns and determiners: *this; this* + singular/ noncount noun
(f) Fred: Do you think [men resist asking for directions]? Yani: I would agree with { **that.** **that generalization.**	*that; that* + singular/ noncount noun
(g) [Two of the gender differences] seem especially true to me. **These** **These differences** } will be the topic of my paper.	*these; these* + plural noun
(h) George: I know [people who constantly give advice when it's not requested]. Lily: **Those** **Those people** } are the ones that I avoid!	*those; those* + plural noun
(i) I read several studies about how [young boys are often encouraged to be aggressive and competitive]. I think **such an upbringing** would influence a boy's behavior when he gets older.	• Reference forms with *such such a/an* + singular noun
(j) I've never thought much about how [age, social class, and gender] influence the way we use language. However, I agree that **such factors** probably do affect greatly the ways in which we communicate.	*such* + plural or noncount noun

EXERCISE 1

Underline the reference forms (*the* + noun, *it, this,* etc.) that refer to information in previous sentences. Put brackets around the referents. There may be more than one reference form in a sentence.

▶ **EXAMPLE:**   Our group discussed [the responses to Situation 1].

We didn't always agree that <u>such responses</u> were typical.

1. According to our psychology professor, for women, talk is important for creating connections between people. For men these connections tend to be formed more through activities than talk.

2. Men and women sometimes experience frustration with each other because of their different communication styles. The frustration may be especially great between men and women who spend a great deal of time together.

3. Our professor notes that women have a tendency to make suggestions rather than give commands when they want something done. She thinks this tendency may reflect women's sense that they lack authority in certain situations.

4. Speakers use language differently depending on differences in age, education, social status, and gender. Such differences are of interest to linguists.

5. Pitch and volume are two aspects of speech. The way we use them in speech may affect how we are perceived by others in communication situations.

6. Women have higher pitched voices than men do. This can be a disadvantage when they are trying to assert authority.

7. In some business contexts, women may regard personal questions, such as how a fellow worker spent the weekend, as a way of showing friendliness. Men may consider the questions inappropriate in these contexts.

8. Some studies show that men tend to dominate conversation in groups including males and females. Based on your experience, do you agree with that?

9. I agree with the idea that men and women should try to understand each other's different communication styles. It makes sense to me.

10. We could accept the communication differences we have with the "other gender," or we could try to negotiate different ways of communicating that would be more productive and less frustrating. These are two possible approaches to our differences in communication styles.

EXERCISE 2

The following paragraph describes the common habit of worrying. Discuss what you think the reference is for each underlined reference form. Put brackets around each referent.

Worrying is the most natural and spontaneous of all human functions. It is time to acknowledge <u>this</u>, perhaps even learn to do <u>it</u> better. Man is the Worrying Animal. <u>It</u> is a trait needing further development, awaiting perfection. Most of us tend to neglect <u>the activity</u>, living precariously out on the thin edge of anxiety but never plunging in.

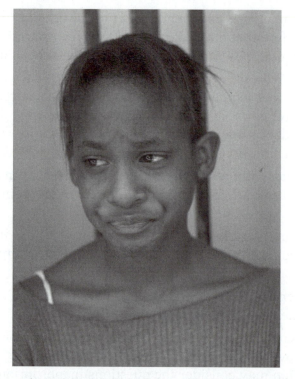

From Lewis Thomas, *The Medusa and the Snail.* New York: Bantam Books, 1979, p. 167.

EXERCISE 3

Write a paragraph stating your individual opinion in response to one of the questions (1–4) for any of the three situations in the Opening Task. Present evidence or an explanation to support your view. Exchange your paragraph with a classmate. Underline the reference forms and bracket the references in your classmate's paragraph.

▶ **R**eference Forms with *The* and Demonstrative Determiners

EXAMPLES	EXPLANATIONS
(a) I liked [the novels] very much. I might even reread some of them. I would recommend **the novels** to anyone who wants to know more about Chinese history.	**Complete Repetition** Reference forms may repeat all of the referent. We use this form more often as a later mention than as a second mention.
(b) Oh, look at [this book] in the children's section! My sisters and I must have read **it** a hundred times when we were young. **(c)** I read [two interesting studies about language variation between different age groups]. I have summarized $\begin{cases}\textbf{the two studies}\\\textbf{these two studies}\end{cases}$ in the introduction of my paper.	**Partial Repetition** Some reference forms repeat only part of the referent. We do not usually repeat a demonstrative determiner (*this, that, these, those*) + noun. Instead, we tend to us *it, them* or *the* + (noun phrase.) We do not usually repeat descriptive modifiers. In (c), only *two* and *studies* have been repeated for both example reference forms.
(d) I read [one study about language differences based on educational levels]. I did not, however, use $\begin{cases}\textbf{the article}\\\textbf{that article}\end{cases}$ in my paper.	**Synonym** A reference form can be a synonym of the referent. In (d), *article* is used as a synonym for *study* and the modifiers are not repeated.
(e) We went to see [*Hamlet*]. **The play** was performed outdoors at the city center. **(f)** I would like to take [South American literature and the history of jazz] next quarter. Several of my friends recommended **those courses.**	**Classifier** A reference form can also be a classifier of the referent. A classifier word or phrase describes a class or group that could include the referent. In (e), *Hamlet* can be classified as a play. In (f), *courses* classifies the two courses mentioned.

EXAMPLES	EXPLANATIONS
(g) Over the weekend [you should revise your essay and type it]. **The revised paper** should be turned in on Monday. **(h)** [The aerosol is sprayed into the chamber where the water vaporizes.] **This vaporization process** is repeated.	**Paraphrase** A reference form can also paraphrase a clause or sentence. We commonly use this form to refer to activities and the results of them: Activity: You revise an essay Result: *The revised paper* Paraphrases also refer to processes, as in (h). The reference form may repeat part of the referent as in (g) (*revise*), or it may use a classifying or describing word such as *process, effects,* or *results* as in (h).

EXERCISE 4

Underline reference forms with *the* and demonstrative adjectives in the second sentence of each sentence pair. Bracket the referents in the first sentence. To familiarize yourself with the different forms of reference, state what type of reference is used: (1) complete repetition of the referent, (2) partial repetition, (3) synonym, (4) classifier or (5) paraphrase. As a class, you may want to discuss why the various forms are used.

▶ **EXAMPLE:** Psychologists have distinguished [three dimensions of emotions]. These dimensions can be used to characterize differences in the ways cultures recognize and express emotions.

partial repetition: *It is not necessary to repeat the entire referent. We do not usually use complete repetition when there are modifiers.*

1. One dimension distinguishes between what are called the primary emotions and what are termed the secondary emotions. The primary emotions are considered universal by some psychologists.

2. The primary emotions are also considered to be biologically based. These feelings include anger, grief, joy, and disgust.

3. The secondary emotions are blends of the primary emotions. These emotions, such as contempt (a blend of anger and disgust), are not universal.

4. Another dimension of emotions distinguishes pleasant feelings from unpleasant ones. The positive emotions are ones such as love and joy, whereas the negative emotions are ones such as sorrow and shame.

5. The last dimension classifies emotions based on intensity. This classification of feelings can distinguish worry from terror and sadness from depression.

6. All societies have what are called display rules regarding emotions. These rules dictate how and when people may express certain emotions.

7. For example, in some cultures, people would express grief by crying. In other cultures, this emotion might be expressed by silence.

EXERCISE 5

Make up a sentence with a *the* reference or demonstrative reference to elaborate on ideas in each of the sentences below. The referent is underlined. Try to use a variety of the reference types discussed in Focus 2.

▶ **EXAMPLE:** *Anger* is a primary emotion.

This emotion is biologically based.

1. Everyone has negative feelings.
2. Psychologists note that the smile does not have universal meaning.
3. Facial expressions are important signals of emotion.
4. Fury is a very intense emotion.
5. Nonverbal signals such as posture, gestures, and eye contact also express emotions.

▶ **U**sing Personal Pronouns versus *The* Noun Phrases

EXAMPLES	EXPLANATIONS
(a) I like [that book] a lot. I read **it** last year. **(b)** Kip is taking [math and English]. **They** are his most challenging subjects, and he has homework for both of **them** almost every day.	Use the personal pronouns *it, they, them* when there is only one possible referent.
(c) Toni: There is evidence that [women tend to add more details to stories they tell than men do.] Ricardo: I believe **it**. **(d)** Tom: [Song's chances of winning a gold medal at the summer Olympics are getting better every day.] Lee: I don't doubt **it**.	Use *it*: • when the one possible referent is a clause • when the one possible referent is a sentence.
(e) I read [the book] before I saw the movie. **The book** was very interesting. **(f)** To Whom It May Concern: I am returning [the enclosed cassette recorder]. The volume control is jammed. Also, the sound quality does not seem very good. **The recorder** came with a one-year guarantee. **(g)** [Violence] is increasing in our society. **The problem** cannot be ignored. **(h)** This medicine should not be taken when you are driving because [it can make you sleepy or it may affect your vision]. **The adverse effects** are only temporary, but nevertheless, you need to be cautious.	Use *the* + noun phrase: • when there is more than one possible referent. In (e), *the book* and *the movie* would be possible referents if you used it. • when the referent might not be clear unless a noun phrase rather than a pronoun is used. In written English, this is often the case when the referent is several sentences before the reference form. • when you want to replace the referent with a classifier, a synonym, or a paraphrase. Sometimes you may want to replace a referent with a paraphrase because you cannot repeat the whole referent and a pronoun reference would not be clear. In (h), the referent is an entire clause. Using *they* for reference would be too vague.

EXERCISE 6

Decide whether *it*, *they*, *them*, or *the* + noun phrase is appropriate for each item below. (1) Identify the referent and bracket it. (2) If *the* + noun phrase should be used, choose a noun phrase that fits the context.

▶ **EXAMPLE:** Have you read [the book *Men Are from Mars, Women Are from Venus*]? ___It___ also discusses communication differences between men and women.

    (Only one possible referent, so *it* is appropriate.).

1. I have to write a paper for my class about the 1960s. I can't decide whether to write my paper about the Civil Rights marches in the early 60s or about the hippie movement in the late 60s. (a) _____ appeals to me because I'd like to find out more about the history of segregation in the South. (b) _____ are both interesting topics, however.

2. Sandro: Do you think it's true that men tend to be more direct about what they want than women do?
   Alicia: Oh yes, I'm convinced of _____.

3. I tried your suggestion to move the second paragraph of my essay to the beginning of the introduction. _____ is a good one; my teacher liked the revision also.

4. Plants break up water into hydrogen and oxygen with the help of sunlight. Sunlight that is caught by grains of chlorophyll in the plant splits the water molecules into hydrogen and oxygen. Most of the oxygen eventually passes out of _____.

5. Scientists believe that there are more than five senses. The organ for the sense of hearing is, of course, the ear. However, in addition, _____ has receptors that help us to create a sense of balance.

▶ **D**emonstrative Determiners and Pronouns

The forms of demonstrative pronouns and determiners *this, that, these,* and *those* tell the reader/listener whether a referent is singular or plural and whether the speaker/writer regards the referent as near or far.

	Singular	**Plural**
Near	this	these
Far	that	those

EXAMPLES	EXPLANATIONS
(a) Take **this chair** right here. **(b)** I'll get two of **these**, please. And one melon. **(c)** Can you see **that** tall **tower** in the distance? **(d)** **Those buildings** next to the tower are part of the new arts center.	The concept of distance (near or far) may involve the following: **Space** • Near: The speaker regards something as physically nearby. • Far: The speaker regards something as physically distant.
(e) Let's finish watching **this movie**. It's almost over. **(f)** **These** are difficult times because of the economy. **(g)** I'd like to see **that** again. It was one of my favorite musicals. **(h)** **Those** were called the golden years because prosperity was widespread.	**Time** • Near: There is a link to present time. • Far: Reference is to a time in the past not regarded as close to the present.
(i) [Age] is another factor affecting language use. **This influence** can be seen in the use of slang. **(j)** [The introduction to my thesis] provided background on my topic. It offered several hypotheses about language differences. **That section** also presented an outline of my thesis.	**Discourse Distance** • Near: The referent is close to the reference form in the text. • Far: The speaker or writer views the referent as distant. In (j), the writer regards the introduction as distant from the part being written.

EXAMPLES	EXPLANATION
(k) I believe [gun control laws are needed]. I feel very strongly about **this**.	**Psychological Distance** • Near: The referent is mentioned by the speaker herself or himself; and is something she believes.
(l) Hal: I think [gun control laws are needed]. Tori: I don't agree with **that**.	• Far: The referent is mentioned by another speaker. Tori disagrees with Hal's position.
(m) When Wilhelm Roentgen discovered the X-ray in 1895, he did not completely understand the nature of these new rays. He called them X-rays because the letter x stands for an unknown quantity in mathematics. **That** is how the X-ray came to be named.	Finally, we often use the demonstrative pronoun *that* in concluding statements to refer to an explanation or description we have given.

EXERCISE 7

Put an appropriate demonstrative form (*this, that, these,* or *those*) in each blank. If you think more than one might be appropriate, discuss the contexts (including speaker attitude) in which each might be used.

▶ **EXAMPLE:** In the middle of the nineteenth century, many American adventurers headed West to seek their fortunes. At ____that____ time, gold had been discovered in California and other states. (In referring to the middle of the nineteenth century, *that* indicates distance in terms of time.)

1. I spent my vacation last summer in Costa Rica and had a wonderful time. The people were really friendly, the scenery was beautiful and the weather was perfect. I also loved the food. You should visit _____ country sometime; you'd love it there, too.

2. Have you seen the entertainment section of the newspaper yet? There are a couple new movies at the theaters. (a) _____ movie based on one of Jane Austen's novels looks good. I think I'll pass on the new James Bond film, though. I've never really liked (b) _____ movies.

3. Erin: Did you know that the Pope will be in town (a) _____ weekend? Victor: No, I hadn't heard (b) _____ .

4. Dear Senator Rotrosen: I am writing (a) _____ letter to urge you to do something about cleaning up our polluted lake. (b) _____ situation is disgraceful; people are afraid even to go swimming. I know that some officials have suggested closing the beach to swimming, but (c) _____ is certainly not the answer to (d) _____ problem.

5. Have you ever wondered how and why fireflies produce their twinkling lights? (a) _____ lights are created by special glands. At night female fireflies sit on stems of grass while the males fly around flashing their lights. The females flash back and, after signals are exchanged a few times, the male finds the female. (b) _____ is how fireflies mate.

6. Enrique: I'm going to see some all-star wrestling matches tonight. Care to come along?

Soo: No thanks! You really like (a) _____ silly matches? I'd rather stay home and watch a video. Take a look at (b) _____ movies I just picked up. Maybe you'll change your mind.

Using Demonstrative Determiner + Noun Phrase for Clear Reference

EXAMPLES	EXPLANATIONS
(a) When you do strenuous exercise, you should wear proper clothing and [you should warm up first]. **This warm-up** will help prevent injuries.	Sometimes we need to use a demonstrative determiner + a noun phrase for clear reference.
(b) NOT: **This** will help prevent injuries.	In (b), *this* does not clearly signal the referent. *This* could be interpreted as both wearing proper clothing and warming up.
(c) Before writing your essay, you should try to [brainstorm some ideas and then put your ideas into categories]. **These prewriting techniques** can help you get started on your paper.	Like *the* + noun phrase reference, demonstrative determiner + noun phrase reference can help to describe or classify the referent.

EXERCISE 8

For the following contexts, use a demonstrative determiner and a classifying or descriptive noun to refer to the previous information that is in brackets.

▶ **EXAMPLES:** [Before making gravy, put the flour in a baking pan and bake it for about five minutes.] __This process__ will add to your preparation time, but it will keep your gravy from having a floury taste.

1. [Exciting. Suspenseful. Amusing.] _____ best describe the latest novel by Michael Rozinski.

2. If you spend too much time in the sun, you may get end up with [skin damage and dehydration]. _____ are not worth a sun tan.

3. We'll be hearing a lot from our elected officials about [whether or not taxes should be raised]. _____ continues to be a widely debated one.

4. [Smiles, frowns, raised eyebrows, and shrugs of the shoulder] all convey emotions. _____ may have different meanings in different cultures, though.

5. [Women] sometimes [think men are being unsympathetic] when they give advice about a problem rather than share troubles._____ stems from a difference between men and women in what they think is an appropriate reaction to such a situation.

FOCUS **6**

USE

▶ **Demonstrative Forms versus**
***The* and *It/Them* References**

EXAMPLES	EXPLANATIONS
(a) Oh, I've heard { **that joke** / **the joke** before. / **it**	In many contexts, you can use demonstrative, *the*, or *pronoun* reference forms. All would be acceptable.
(b) Moya told us { **the jokes.** / **those jokes.** / **them.**	The choice often depends on (1) the speaker's or writer's intentions, or (2) what the speaker/writer thinks the listener/reader knows.
	Emphasizing the Referent
(c) I heard [a speaker] on campus this afternoon.	Use demonstrative determiners or pronouns when you want to emphasize the referent.
(d) Less emphasis: **The speaker** was talking about the dangers of nuclear power.	Example (d) emphasizes the topic of nuclear power, not the referent.
(e) More emphasis: **This speaker** was the best I've heard regarding the nuclear power issue.	Example (e) emphasizes the referent more.
(f) I'm not sure if I'll [type my paper myself].	In example (g), *it* puts less emphasis on the referent, focusing on new information (the result of having to type without help). In example (h) placing *that* at the end of the sentence puts more emphasis on the referent *type my paper*.
(g) Less emphasis: If I do, **it** will probably take me all day!	
(h) More emphasis: I have more important things to do than **that**!	
	Avoiding Unnecessary Repetition
(i) I asked my instructor if I needed [to include a bibliography with my draft]. She told me **that** would not be necessary.	Use a demonstrative pronoun to avoid unnecessary repetition.
(j) Repetitious: She told me **[including the bibliography]** would not be necessary.	In example (j), the paraphrase with *the* + noun phrase gives too much information. We often use demonstrative pronouns when the referent is a clause or a sentence.
(k) [This paper] is one of the best I've written. I'm sure my classmates will enjoy **it.**	As mentioned in Focus 2, we do not usually repeat demonstrative phrases in second mention. We use some other reference form such as *it* or *the*.
(l) NOT: I'm sure my classmates will enjoy **this paper**.	

EXERCISE 9

Put an appropriate reference form in each blank. The referent is in brackets. Use one of the following forms: (1) *it*, (2) *the* + noun phrase, (3) demonstrative determiner (*this, that, these,* or *those*) + noun phrase, (4) demonstrative pronoun (*this, that, these,* or *those*). Use the notes in parentheses to guide your choice. For some blanks, more than one choice might be possible.

▶ **EXAMPLE:**   An article I read claims that [hot water freezes faster than cold water]. Were you aware of _____**that**_____ ? (Also possible: *that fact*)

1. I've just finished [a really good novel]. _____ was about an American woman who goes to live in India. (Put focus on the theme of the novel.)

2. I also read [a biography] last month. _____ was the most interesting one I have ever read. (Put focus on the subject of the sentence.)

3. I just found out that [Chinese, English, Spanish, Hindi, and Arabic are the most widely spoken languages]. I didn't know _____ before.

4. The Danish linguist Otto Jespersen described several theories on the origins of language. One is called the "ding-dong" theory. [The theory] proposes that speech arose as a result of people reacting to stimuli in their environment and making sounds to reflect it. _____ is not one that is believed by most linguists.

5. Another theory of the origins of language was termed [the "pooh-pooh" theory]. _____ maintains that speech started when people made instinctive sounds caused by emotions.

6. You can eat most vegetables either raw or cooked. [If you cook them], _____ may reduce the nutrients you get. (Emphasize the result.)

7. Nicholas is making sure that the spare tire for his car is well-inflated before he leaves for his business trip. During his most recent trip, [he got a flat tire and was stranded in the desert for hours]. _____ was the last thing he needed after a busy and exhausting week. (Emphasize the referent.)

8. We consulted the forest ranger as to whether we could [take our dog with us on our camping trip in the national park]. He said _____ would not be allowed.

9. [Five students] were singled out for awards at our end-of-the-year banquet. _____ had outstanding academic records and had participated in a number of community projects. (Emphasize the referent.)

FOCUS **7**

▶ **R**eference Forms with *Such*

EXAMPLES	EXPLANATIONS
(a) We need [a strong and honest leader]. **Such a person** is Mario Baretta.	The meaning of *such*, when referring to previous information, is similar to "like that" or "of that type of thing." In (a) *such a person* refers to a person belonging to the type "a strong and honest leader." In (b), *such responses* refer to responses that can be classified as "different for the same situation." With plural nouns, such phrases often follow a list or series of things as in (c).
(b) Men and women often have [different responses to the same situations]. **Such responses** may result from the ways they have been brought up.	
(c) You should try to eat more [fruits, vegetables, and whole grains]. **Such foods** are important for good health.	
(d) The police thoroughly investigated [the burglary]. They concluded that only experienced thieves could have accomplished **such a crime**.	**Structure forms with *such*:** • *Such* + singular noun Use *a* or *an* after *such*
(e) Did you hear [what he said]? I've never heard of **such an idea** before.	
(f) [Impatiens and fuchsia plants] need little sun. **Such plants** are good for shady areas of your garden.	• *Such* + Plural Noun
(g) I can't believe [the things]they told us about their neighbors. In my opinion, they shouldn't repeat **such personal information**.	• *Such* + Noncount Noun No article is used after *such* before a noncount noun.
(h) [Several students] have demonstrated superior performance in the field of mathematics. **One such student** is Ruby Pereda.	• (Number) + *Such* + Singular or Plural Noun Note that no article is used with *before student* in (h).
(i) Now more than ever we need reform-minded candidates for our city council. **Two such candidates** are Ben Ho and Ulla Teppo.	
(j) I admire **your attitude**. Such an attitude shows great respect for others.	**Referents of *Such* Phrases** The information that references with *such* refer to may be: • a phrase
(k) They said that **women should stay at home**. Such an attitude does not reflect the feelings of most Americans.	• a clause

EXAMPLES	EXPLANATIONS
(l) "The world owes me a living." Such an attitude will not get you very far, my father always tells me.	• a sentence
(m) **Girls should do all the housework. Women should serve the men in the family**. Such an attitude about the role of women is common in my culture, but it seems to be changing.	• more than one sentence

EXERCISE 10

Underline the *such* reference in each of the following groups of sentences or dialogues. Then state what the referent is. If you wish, you may paraphrase the referent.

▶ **EXAMPLE:** Men tend to view conversation as a way to assert status and to impart information. <u>Such attitudes</u> are not as common with women.

Referent: <u>Men's attitudes that conversation is for asserting status and imparting information</u>.

1. The Italian composer Guiseppe Verdi wrote one of his greatest operas, *Falstaff*, when he was eighty. To have created this brilliant musical work at such an advanced age is truly remarkable.

   Referent: _____

2. In the early decades of American film making, Asians were often portrayed as servants, launderers, cooks, gardeners, and waiters. Such stereotypes denied the many achievements of Asian Americans at that time.

   Referent: _____

3. Lightning never strikes in the same place twice. Rattlesnakes intentionally give warnings to their victims by rattling their tails. The sap of a tree rises in the spring. Such beliefs, although common, are not supported by scientific evidence.

   Referent: _____

4. Some people who pursue physical fitness with a passion fill up their homes with stationary bicycles, rowing machines, and stair climbers. Each time a new exercise machine appears on the market, they rush to their local sporting goods stores. However, such equipment is not needed to become physically fit.

Referent: _____

5. We are now faced with a number of serious problems in our metropolitan areas. One such problem is how to best help the thousands of homeless people.

Referent: _____

6. When you have just met someone, what types of personal questions should you avoid asking? The answer depends on what culture you are in. For example, in some cultures it might be acceptable to ask a woman how old she is, how much money she makes, or even how much she weighs, but in many cultures such questions are considered impolite.

Referent: _____

▶ *Such* versus Demonstrative Determiners

EXAMPLES	EXPLANATIONS
(a) When Mr. Clark came to our restaurant, he complained about the location of his table, criticized the menu, insulted the waiter, and failed to leave a tip. We hope we never again have to deal with . . . **Specific** **Type** **(a.1) this** person. **(a.2) such** a person	*Such* refers to a class or type of thing. Consequently, reference phrases with *such* have a more general meaning than *this, that, these,* or *those* before nouns. (a.1) refers to Mr. Clark. (a.2) refers to any person who would act the way Mr. Clark did.
(b) Two types of dinosaurs with bird-like hips were stegosaurs and ankylosaurs. **Specific** **Type** **(b.1) These** dinosaurs . . . **(b.2) Such** dinosaurs . . . were herbivorous.	(b.1) refers to stegosaurs and ankylosaurs. (b.2) refers to all dinosaurs with bird-like hips.
(c) In the United States, it has become common for the media to report every medical problem that the President suffers and every medical treatment, however minor, he receives. Does the public really need . . . **Specific** **Type** **(c.1) this** information? **(c.2) such** information?	(c.1) refers to information about medical problems and medical treatment. (c.2) refers more generally to information that is personal and unimportant in the context.

EXERCISE 11

Answer the following questions based on the examples in Focus 8.

1. Which words after *such* (*a/an*) (person, dinosaurs, information) repeat a word in the preceding sentence? Which do not? How can you explain this difference?

2. Can you think of words that might be substituted for those occurring after *such* (*a/an*) in the examples? Are they more general or more specific than the words in the examples? How do they change the meaning?

▶ **EXAMPLE:** *such a person—such a grouch*

(more specific; describes Mr. Clark negatively)

3. Often a modifier can be used to make a "class" word more specific. For example, *advanced* in "at such an advanced age" makes it clear that reference is to those ages late in life. In the examples in Focus 8, what modifiers could be added to define more specifically the words following *such* (*a*)?

EXERCISE 12

STEP 1 For each of the word pairs below, think of one or more categories that could be used to classify or characterize them.

▶ **EXAMPLE:** Word pair: football, hockey

Categories: *sports, spectator sports, violent sports, popular sports*

Word Pair	**Categories**
(a) love, anger	_____
(b) drug trafficking, murder	_____
(c) earthquakes, hurricanes	_____
(d) backgammon, chess	_____
(e) your choice (list-related words): _____	_____

STEP 2 Now select one of your categories for each word pair. Add to each pair other words or phrases that could be classified by this term.

▶ **EXAMPLE:** *Violent sports: soccer, boxing*

STEP 3 Write a statement (one or two sentences) for each topic above. Use *such* plus the category you selected. (The items could be the word pairs given or the words you added.)

▶ **EXAMPLE:** *I know many people who love to go to football and hockey games. However, I don t enjoy watching **such violent sports**.*

STEP 4 Discuss the difference in meaning that would result if you replaced *such* in each statement with a demonstrative determiner (this, that, these, those).

▶ **EXAMPLE:** *However, I don't enjoy **those** violent sports.*

*"**Such** violent sports" refers to any sports that are especially violent; "**those** violent sports" refers only to football and hockey.*

EXERCISE 13

Identify and correct the errors or inappropriate reference forms in each of the following sentences. There may be more than one way to correct errors.

▶ **EXAMPLES:** My friend suggested that I drop out of school and work for a while. I'm not sure what I think about such an advice.

Correction: *I'm not sure what I think about **such advice**.* (*Advice* is a noncount noun, so no article is used.)

1. What did you think about this research? I disagreed with this research.

2. Our math teacher gave us a surprise quiz. Can you believe he would be this unkind man?

3. Many modern cities have both buses and subways. Traffic congestion is certainly reduced by those public transportation.

4. This year I took both an English course and a Spanish course. It was quite easy for me because French is my native language and the two languages are similar.

5. I have a friend who likes to wear only two colors of clothing: blue and purple. She dresses in such colors every day.

6. One study says that male children do not pay as much attention to female children as they do to other males. What do you think about it?

7. Some people insist on giving advice even when it's not requested. Such an advice is generally not appreciated.

8. I am keeping the blue shirt I ordered from you. This shirt fits fine. However, I am returning the striped shirt because this was much too small.

9. In this paper, I plan to discuss two emotions that all cultures share. The two emotions that all cultures share are joy and grief.

10. Did you hear her boast that she never has to study for her courses? The student misses the point of what an education means.

Use Your English

ACTIVITY 1: LISTENING

You will hear two dialogues. Each dialogue illustrates a difference between male and female communication styles, according to Professor Deborah Tannen. After you have heard the dialogues, either discuss the following questions with a partner or write complete answers.

1. What communication differences do these dialogues illustrate?

2. Have you observed such differences in your own experience?

3. Can you think of exceptions to the generalizations that these dialogues illustrate?

ACTIVITY 2: WRITING/ SPEAKING/LISTENING

In teams, make up lists of statements that include both amazing facts and "untruths." Good sources for hard-to-believe facts are reference books such as *The Guiness Book of World Records* or *Ripley's Believe It or Not* as well as almanacs. Mix in with the amazing facts some of your own statements that are **not** true. Each team should then read their list of statements to another group. The listeners must agree on which ones they believe and which they don't believe. Score a point for each correct judgment as to whether a statement is true or not.

▶ **EXAMPLE:**   Team A: *The largest watermelon on record weighed 260 pounds.*

Team B: *We don't believe it.*

The statement is true. Team A gets the point.

ACTIVITY 3: SPEAKING/WRITING

Write a paragraph comparing the language use of different groups based on a variable other than gender. For example, consider differences you are aware of based on age, social status, occupation, geographical location, or education. When you have finished, identify the reference forms you used.

ACTIVITY 4: WRITING

Write a letter to either (a) a business to complain about unsatisfactory merchandise or (b) one of your political representatives (for example, a senator or the President) to voice your opinions about an issue that is important to you. Exchange your letter with another classmate. The classmate should check your use of reference forms to see if they are appropriate and then write a response to your letter, playing the role of the company or person to whom you addressed it.

ACTIVITY 5: WRITING

Choose one of the sentences below to develop a paragraph. Then write the rest of the paragraph, creating a context appropriate for including the sentence. (The sentence could occur anywhere in the paragraph after the first sentence.)

- Those subjects just aren't worth studying.
- Those TV programs should be taken off the air.
- Such advice should be helpful to anyone visiting _____ .
  (Choose a city or country to fill in the blank.)
- Such a person is to be avoided whenever possible.
- Such bad luck shouldn't happen to anyone.

ACTIVITY 6: READING

As you do reading for other courses or for your own interests, write down examples of *such* reference forms that you find in a notebook. Include the *such* phrase and the phrase(s) or sentence (s) to which each refers. Make a note of the context (for example, an explanation of a chemical process, a comment on people's behavior, a description of a product in an advertisement). At some point you may want to compare your findings with your classmates' to see the ways in which reference forms with *such* references are used in written texts.

RELATIVE CLAUSES MODIFYING SUBJECTS

UNIT GOALS:

- To use restrictive relative clauses to modify subjects
- To use restrictive relative clauses to make nouns more specific
- To know how to reduce restrictive relative clauses

▶ OPENING TASK
Trivia Challenge

STEP 1   The object of this game is to get the most answers right in a trivia game. Student A looks at page 127. Student B looks at page A-17.

STEP 2   To begin, Student A will create definitions of a person or thing, offering three options. Student B will listen and repeat the definition, completing the sentence with the correct word or phrase. If correct, he or she will receive one point.

STEP 3   Student B will now create definitions in the same way. The partner with the most points wins the game.

▶ **EXAMPLE:**   a person
explores and studies caves
Options: (a) transducer, *(b) spelunker,
(c) coanchor

Student A creates a definition:
*A person who explores and studies caves is called a (a) transducer, *(b) spelunker, or (c) coanchor*
(The correct answer is asterisked (*).)

Student B makes a guess:
A person who explores and studies caves is called a spelunker.
Congratulations to Student B.
He or she will be awarded one point for the correct answer.

Create a Definition:

1. an animal
   It mates for life.
   (a) seahorse, (b) boa constrictor, *(c) Canada goose

2. a book
   Its original title was changed six times.
   (a) *War and Peace* by Leo Tolstoy, *(b) *The Great Gatsby* by F. Scott Fitzgerald,
   (c) *Pride and Prejudice* by Jane Austen

3. an inventor
   Teachers gave him poor report cards.
   *(a) Thomas Edison, (b) Alexander Graham Bell, (c) Robert Fulton

4. a person
   He or she fits the interior parts of pianos.
   (a) mucker, (b) hooker inspector, *(c) belly builder

Guess the Correct Answer:

5. (a) dragonfly, (b) flycatcher, (c) firefly

6. (a) cornball, (b) impostor, (c) daytripper

7. (a) amphora, (b) amulet, (c) aspartame

8. (a) bodice, (b) causerie, (c) bloomers

►Overview of Restrictive Relative Clauses

- A restrictive relative clause modifies a noun phrase in a main clause. It is placed as close to the noun phrase as possible and is used to identify the noun.

Noun Phrase   **Relative Clause**

that

The contract (~~the contract~~ was signed yesterday) is now valid.

Main Clause

- There are four general types of restrictive relative clauses. They may modify main clause subjects or objects. Relative pronouns may be subjects or objects in their own clauses.

TYPES OF RELATIVE CLAUSES	NOUN PHRASE IN MAIN CLAUSE	RELATIVE PRONOUN IN RELATIVE CLAUSE
(a) **S** **S** *The contract* **that was signed yesterday** is now valid.	Subject	Subject
(b) **S** **O** *The contract* **that he signed yesterday** is now valid.	Subject	Object
(c) **O** **S** I have not read *the contract* **that was signed** yesterday.	Object	Subject
(d) **O** **S** I have not read *the contract* **that he signed** yesterday.	Object	Object

- This unit will focus on restrictive relative clauses that modify subjects in main clauses (like a and b). These clauses can have various relative pronouns, and the relative pronouns can fulfill various grammatical functions. *Whose* can function as a relative determiner.

EXAMPLES	SUBJECT BEING MODIFIED	RELATIVE PRONOUN	FUNCTION OF RELATIVE PRONOUN/ DETERMINER
(e) A person **who/that** sells houses is a realtor.	person	*who/that*	subject
(f) The secretary **whom/that** she hired is very experienced.		*whom/that*	direct object
(g) The employees **to whom** she denied a pay raise have gone on strike.		*whom*	indirect object
(h) The mansions **that/which** were sold last week were expensive.	thing or animal	*that/which*	subject
(i) The computer **that/which** they purchased operated very efficiently.		*that/which*	direct object
(j) The place **that/which** you spoke about is Denver.		*that/which*	object of a preposition
(k) Clerks **whose** paychecks were withheld are in trouble.	person, thing, or animal	*whose*	possessive determiner
(l) The division **whose** sales have reached a million-dollars will go to Hawaii.		*whose*	possessive determiner

EXERCISE 1

STEP 1 Here is a picture of a rather complex invention created by the artist Rube Goldberg. What do you think this device is used for?

From Charles Keller, *The Best of Rube Goldberg*, 1979.
RUBE GOLDBERG™ and © of Rube Goldberg Inc.
Distributed by United Media.

STEP 2 Reread the passage and underline all of the relative pronouns/determiners. Then, with your partner, identify and write down the function of the relative pronouns/determiners in each relative clause (subject, direct object, etc.). There may be more than one relative clause in a sentence.

▶ **EXAMPLE:** Sentence (1) *that* —*subject function in relative clause*

(1) A kerosene lamp that is set near the window has a high flame that catches on to the curtain. (2) A fire officer whom a neighbor calls puts out the flame with a stream of water that the officer shoots from outside the window. (3) The water hits a short man who is seated below the window. (4) He thinks it is raining and reaches for an umbrella which is attached to a string above him. (5) The upward pull of the string on one side of the platform causes an iron ball that is resting on the other side of the platform to fall down. (6) The ball is attached to a second string that wraps around a pulley and connects to a hammer. (7) The downward pull of the ball on the second string causes a hammer to hit a plate of glass. (8) The crashing sound of the glass causes a baby pup that is in a cradle to wake up. (9) In order to soothe the pup, its mother rocks the cradle in which the pup is sleeping. (10) The cradle, to which a wooden hand is attached, is on a high shelf above a stool. (11) A man who is sitting on the stool below the shelf and whose back is positioned in front of the wooden hand smiles as the wooden hand moves up and down his back.

STEP 3 Without looking at the sample passage, summarize the process shown in the picture.

EXERCISE 2

For each of the phrases below, write two sentences. Use a *who* relative clause for one and a *whose* relative clause for another.

▶ **EXAMPLE:** will not get a job

A person who is not skilled will not get a job.

A person whose interview skills are poor will not get a job.

1. will not pass the course
2. will be a good leader
3. will make a lot of friends
4. can never take a vacation
5. is prepared to take a test
6. should not drive a car

FOCUS **2**

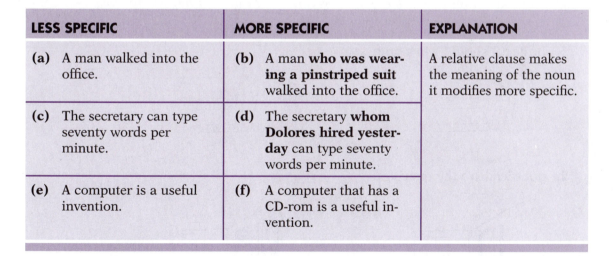

▶ **Making Noun Phrases More Specific with Relative Clauses**

LESS SPECIFIC	MORE SPECIFIC	EXPLANATION
(a) A man walked into the office.	(b) A man **who was wearing a pinstriped suit** walked into the office.	A relative clause makes the meaning of the noun it modifies more specific.
(c) The secretary can type seventy words per minute.	(d) The secretary **whom Dolores hired yesterday** can type seventy words per minute.	
(e) A computer is a useful invention.	(f) A computer that has a CD-rom is a useful invention.	

EXERCISE 3

Information Gap: Imagine that you are a new employee for a company. One of your co-workers has agreed to orient you to the new office. Ask a question about the objects or persons in each of the pictures in the left column while covering up the right column. Have your partner distinguish these objects or persons, explaining what he or she knows by looking at the pictures in the right column.

▶ **EXAMPLE:**

New Employee:
Ask about what you see
(cover up the right column)

Experienced Employee:
Tell about what you know
(cover up the left column)

box/contains file folders

New Employee: *Which box has the file folders?*
Experienced Employee: *The box that is sitting on the shelf has the file fold-ers.*

1. project/I should work on first

2. door/leads to the restroom

3. telephone number/belongs to the Moesler Corporation

Now switch roles with your partner

4. computer/has the Internet connection

5. light switch/illuminates the front of the conference room

 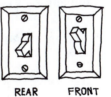

REAR   FRONT

6. book/our boss, Mr. Blake, wrote

▶ **R**eview of Reduced Relative Clauses

EXAMPLES	EXPLANATIONS
(a) The letter (**that**) he sent was never received. **(b)** The accountant (**whom**) he corresponded with was well qualified. **(c)** **NOT:** The accountant with (~~whom~~) he corresponded was well qualified.	We can delete relative pronouns if they function as objects in relative clauses. In examples (a) and (b), *that* and *whom* can be deleted. Relative pronouns cannot be deleted if they follow prepositions such as *with* or *to*.
(d) The conference room (**that is**) situated at the end of the hall is closed. **(e)** The water (**that was**) left in the pitcher evaporated. **(f)** The customer (**who is**) complaining to the manager is my aunt. **(g)** A child (**who had been**) playing on the equipment was asked to leave.	We can delete relative pronouns in relative clauses with auxiliary *be* in progressive or passive constructions. Both the relative pronoun and *be* are deleted.
(h) Chairs (**that are**) in the conference room cannot be moved. **(i)** A board member (**who was**) at the meeting decided to resign.	We can delete relative pronouns in relative clauses with *be* + preposition phrases. Both the relative pronoun and *be* are deleted.
(j) Clients **who are** interested will always return. **(k)** Interested clients will always return. **(l)** **NOT:** Clients interested will always return. **(m)** A girl **who was** beautiful stepped into the room. **(n)** A beautiful girl stepped into the room. **(o)** **NOT:** A girl beautiful stepped into the room	In relative clauses with *be* + adjective, we can delete the relative pronoun and *be*, but the adjective is usually moved before the noun in the main clause.
with **(p)** People (~~who have~~) credentials can be hired. **without** **(q)** The workers (~~who did not have~~) identification were asked to leave.	In relative clauses with *have* or *have not* (= possession or lack of possession), we can delete the relative pronoun and replace *have* or *have not* with *with* or *without*.

EXERCISE 4

Look again at the diagram in Exercise 1 and analyze the operation of the back scratcher. Look particularly at how the objects were affected during the process. Then, write a sentence containing a relative clause with an object relative pronoun. Put parentheses around the words that can be deleted.

▶ **EXAMPLE:** (B) The curtain __(that) the flame touched caught on fire.__

1. (C) The water _____
2. (E) The umbrella _____
3. (J) The hammer _____
4. (K) The plate of glass _____
5. (N) The cradle _____
6. (O) The wooden hand _____

EXERCISE 5

Read the following sentences. Identify relative clauses that can be reduced. Mark your suggested revisions directly on the text. Then explain your revisions to your classmates.

▶ **EXAMPLE:** (a) A person <del>who is assertive</del> can develop great self-confidence.
An assertive person

(b) A person <del>who has</del> self-confidence can do anything.
with

I changed (a) to "An assertive person can develop great self-confidence" because the relative clause contains "be" + adjective. I changed (b) to "A person with self-confidence can do anything" because the relative clause contains "have."

1. (a) It is easy to spot the person who is the decision maker in an American business meeting. (b) The decision maker is usually a person who is leaning toward the other members of the group and who is giving direct eye contact.

2. (a) Body language that is composed of many gestures can communicate 80% of a message. (b) A voice that is friendly, a posture that is relaxed, and a handshake that is firm all convey assertiveness.

3. (a) Anyone who has been working in the same position for a while will receive criticism at one time or another. (b) Criticism that is unfair needs to be countered. (c) Criticism that is constructive needs to be acknowledged.

4. (a) A person who is dressing for success in an American business setting should worry about the material, color, and style of his or

her clothing. (b) Generally, a suit that is coordinated and that is made of an expensive wool appears most authoritative. (c) Colors which are dark transmit more authority.

5. (a) If you are someone who feels unsatisfied with your personality, do not be discouraged. (b) Anyone who can develop a mental picture of what he or she wants to be can change. (c) Anyone who has the determination to keep this image in his or her mind on a day-to-day basis will see his or her new personality become a reality.

EXERCISE 6

Look at the pictures in Exercise 3 and write six sentences with reduced relative clauses that distinguish the objects. Share your sentences with your classmates.

▶ **EXAMPLE:** *The box with folders is sitting on the shelf.*

EXERCISE 7

Below you will find information about four homes that celebrities sold for various reasons. Write sentences about this information using as many relative clauses modifying subjects as you can. Put parentheses around words that can be deleted.

▶ **EXAMPLE:** *The mansion (that) the oil tycoon sold for $2,000,000 has three fireplaces.*

The penthouse whose owner was a world-renowned physician sold for $4,000,000.

VILLA
Owner: country western singer
Reason for sale: divorce
Price: $3,000,000

Enter through walled gates and find sophisticated hacienda. 2-acre home with horse corral. 6 bedrooms/8 baths. Pool, tennis, jacuzzi, spa.

PENTHOUSE
Owner: world-renowned physician
Reason for sale: death
Price: $4,000,000
Towering 20 stories above downtown. 3 bedrooms/4 bathrooms. Close to Music and Performing Arts Center. Modern design. 20 minutes from beach.

MANSION
Owner: oil tycoon
Reason for sale: bankruptcy
Price: $2,000,000

European chateau with hardwood floors. 50 miles from the coast. 4 bedrooms/ 4 bathrooms. 3 fireplaces. View of lake. Very private acre far from crowds.

BEACHHOUSE
Owner: corporate executive
Reason for sale: job move
Price: $5,000,000
On the beach. 3 acres + private 120 ft. of beachfront. Bright and spacious. Pool room. 3 stories. State-of-the-art sound/video system. 5 bedrooms/ 4 bathrooms. Greenhouse.

Use Your English

ACTIVITY 1: LISTENING

STEP 1 Listen to the taped segment of a lecture that explains various important business terms. On a separate piece of paper take notes about the terms introduced.

STEP 2 Use your notes to fill in the blanks of the following quiz.

1. The process in which someone decides how their property will be distributed after their death is called _____.

2. A term which means to substitute an inoffensive term for an offensive one is a/an _____.

3. A person who has died is referred to as a/an _____.

4. A term which means to die leaving a will is _____.

5. The action which describes someone dying without a will is _____.

6. The land and property which someone owns is called _____.

7. _____ is called "personal property."

8. _____ is called "a gift."

ACTIVITY 2: WRITING

Write a letter of complaint to a store or company about a defective item that you bought recently. Try to include at least two sentences with relative clauses modifying main clause subjects.

▶ **EXAMPLE:** *Dear Sir:*

The toaster that I bought in your store last week is defective. The selector lever that determines how dark the toast will be is stuck . . .

ACTIVITY 3: SPEAKING

Exercise 1 described an unusual invention—a back scratcher. Working with a partner, try to draw a similar diagram for another device. Then describe the various features of the device, following the format of Exercise 1. Choose one of the following ideas or one of your own. Explain to the class how your invention works.

fly swatter	cheese cutter
door opener	window washer
pencil sharpener	adjustable chair

ACTIVITY 4: WRITING

Find an outline, chart, or flow diagram that has various levels or interdependent steps in one of your textbooks or a magazine or newspaper. Describe the diagram using at least three sentences with relative clauses.

▶ **EXAMPLE:**

Unemployment

functional   cyclical   seasonal   structural

There are several types of unemployment. A person who is functionally unemployed has lost his or her job and is looking for another. A person who is a victim of a temporary downswing in the trade cycle is cyclically unemployed. A person who is seasonally unemployed means that he or she is not working during a particular season, e.g., the holiday season or the harvesting season. Someone who is permanently unemployed, and this is probably the most tragic, is a victim of a structural change in society which has made his particular field or skill obsolete.

After you have written your description, reduce all of the relative clauses that can be reduced according to the rules discussed in this unit.

ACTIVITY 5: SPEAKING/WRITING

Discuss the following business-related terms with a partner. Then write a definition for each term. Be sure to use a relative clause in each of your definitions.

▶ **EXAMPLE:**   per capita income
     The average annual income that a particular population earns is called "per capita income."

bankruptcy	gross national product	exchange rate
sales commission	prime rate	mortgage

ACTIVITY 6: WRITING/SPEAKING

Create your own "Trivia Challenge" game, like the one you played in the Opening Task.

▶ **EXAMPLE:** an animal

It doesn't carry its young in a pouch.

(a) seahorse, (b) kangaroo, *(c) ostrich

STEP 1 Work with a partner. Think of five items and definitions (you may use your dictionary for ideas).

STEP 2 Get together with another pair. See if they can guess the correct option. The team with the most correct guesses wins the game.

RELATIVE CLAUSES MODIFYING OBJECTS

UNIT GOALS:

- To use restrictive relative clauses to modify objects
- To use multiple restrictive relative clauses in a sentence
- To reduce relative clauses by deleting relative pronouns
- To choose appropriate relative clause forms for formal and informal communication

▶ **OPENING TASK**
Describing Inventions

You and a partner will work on this task together. Student A should look at the inventions and the invention dates on page 141, and B should look at the pictures and dates on page A-18. Take turns describing one of the inventions on your page without actually naming it. Your partner will guess what you have described.

▶ **EXAMPLE:** Student A: *I'm thinking of something that was invented in 1593 and that you use to measure the temperature.*

Student B: *Is it a thermometer?*

Student A: *Good guess!*

Thermometer
1593

▶ **EXAMPLE:** Student B: *I'm thinking of something that was invented about 1590 and that you can look through.*

Student A: *Is it glasses?*

Student B: *No, but it has a lens that you can look through to make small substances appear large.*

Student A: *Oh, it's a microscope.*

Student B: *That's right!*

Compound Microscope
About 1590

Student A

Jet Engine Aircraft
1939

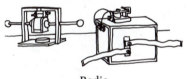

Polaroid Land Camera
1947

Telescope
1608

Zipper
1893

Radio
1895

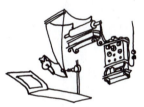

X-Ray Machine
1895

Safety Razor
1901

Air Conditioning
1902

Skyscraper
1885

▶ **T**ypes of Relative Clauses Modifying Objects

Relative clauses that modify objects can have various relative pronouns/determiners and different functions:

EXAMPLES	OBJECT BEING MODIFIED	RELATIVE PRONOUN	FUNCTION OF RELATIVE PRONOUN
(a) She knows a girl **who/that** can dance very well.	person	*who/that*	subject
(b) He looked for the banker **whom/that** he had met at the party.		*whom/that*	direct object
(c) He was angry at the person **whom/that** he had written a letter to.		*whom/that*	indirect object
(d) She talked to the students **whom/that** she was best acquainted with.		*whom/that*	object of a preposition
(e) **OR:** She talked to the students with **whom** she was best acquainted.		*whom*	object of a preposition (directly following preposition)
(f) I have noticed the trash **that/which** is piled on the street.	thing or animal	*that/which*	subject
(g) Did you see the apartment **that/which** he furnished himself?		*that/which*	direct object
(h) He patted the dog **that/which** he had given a bone to.		*that/which*	indirect object
(i) Toronto has a tall tower **that/which** you can get a great view from.		*that/which*	object of a preposition
(j) Toronto has a tall tower from **which** you can get a great view.		*which*	object of a preposition (directly following preposition)

EXAMPLES	OBJECT BEING MODIFIED	RELATIVE DETER-MINER	FUNCTION OF RELATIVE DETERMINER
(k) I need to find the man **whose** credit card has ex-pired.	person	*whose*	possessive determiner
(l) I was impressed by the trees **whose** branches seemed to touch the sky.	thing or animal	*whose*	possessive determiner

EXERCISE 1

Read the following story. Underline all relative clauses that modify objects. Circle the noun that is modified by each relative clause.

1) When my mother and I came to the United States, I experienced (a move) from which I felt that I would never recover. 2) My mother and I never got along very well. 3) She was a glamorous fashion model, but I looked like "a plain Jane" who was clumsy and overweight.

4) I was often left alone as my mother left for fancy parties at which she mingled with famous actors, artists, and musicians. 5) I desperately wanted to return to the country from which we had fled in Eastern Europe.

6) My mother was fortunate when she first arrived, for she got her first job through friends of a fellow countryperson who had married an American millionaire. 7) These friends immediately introduced her to everyone that they knew. 8) However, most of these friends were childless, and I had no one with whom I could share my loneliness and misery.

9) Not knowing where I could find happiness, I decided to begin copying the standards of style for which my mother was famous. 10) It had worked for her; perhaps it could work for me. 11) I followed numerous diets that would help me resemble a starved model. 12) Nothing delighted my mother more than the attempts that I made to become more like her. 13) I did not really believe in my new preoccupation with fashion. 14) It actually sent me into deep depressions which lasted weeks.

15) As the years went by, I went away to a prestigious college which provided me with many opportunities to travel abroad and meet famous people. 16) I always seemed to be looking for something that I had not obtained in my youth. 17) Finally, I met someone who could liberate me from all of the fashion nonsense.18) The love of my life turned out to be a scientist who liked to climb mountains and build things. 19) In fact, he built the first home that we lived in. 20) Believe it or not, this country cottage made possible the quiet life that I had always dreamed of as a teenager.

EXERCISE 2

Take turns asking and answering questions about the story in Exercise 1. In each response, use a relative clause that modifies an object.

▶ **EXAMPLES:**   Student A: *What kind of move did the author experience?*

Student B: *She experienced a move from which she felt that she would never recover.*

Student A: *How did the young girl look?*

Student B: *She looked like "a plain Jane" who was clumsy and overweight.*

FOCUS **2**

MEANING

▶ ## Using Relative Clauses to Modify Nouns

EXAMPLES	EXPLANATION
(a) The police caught a criminal **who had robbed three banks.** **(b)** He applied for work at companies **which his father recommended.**	A relative clause provides information that is necessary to identify or limit the noun it modifies. The clause specifies what type of thing(s) or person(s) is being described.

EXERCISE 3

STEP 1   A crime was committed at the Royal Restaurant.

In pairs, take the roles of a criminal investigator and a witness. The investigator demands that the witness give certain information from the left column below. The witness provides a response with a relative clause modifying an object using events, people, conditions, etc. in the right column below.

▶ **EXAMPLE:**   Investigator: *Tell me the name of the person whom you saw at the Royal Restaurant.*

Witness: *I don't remember the name of the person whom I saw at the Royal Restaurant.*

Investigator Information Required	Witness Experiences/Observations
1. Name of the man the witness saw at the Royal Restaurant.	You don't remember the name.
2. Name of a woman the man was with.	Nobody told you the name, but you think the name is Jones or Johnson.
3. Type of car the witness saw parked near the Billings Bank.	You saw a compact car. It had a scratch on the right side.
4. Type of tip the suspect left at the last meal.	He left a large tip. You found it under the salt and pepper shakers.
5. Name of the company. Its truck was seen across the street from the Royal Restaurant.	You forgot the name of the company.
6. Type of sound the witness heard near the restaurant.	You heard a scream. The scream startled you.
7. Type of button the witness picked up at the scene of the crime.	You picked up a gold button. You think it fell from the robber's jacket.
8. Sequence of events following the robbery.	You saw the man run down the stairs to a car. Its license plate was XXX 123.
9. Type of dog in the car.	You saw a small, black dog. It had one blue eye and one brown eye.
10. Name of a relative close to the female suspect.	You know she had a son. His name was Biffo.

STEP 2 Using some of the information obtained at the interview, write one paragraph about the Royal Restaurant crime. Include at least five relative clauses in your narrative.

▶ **Multiple Relative Clauses**

EXAMPLES	EXPLANATIONS
(a) Do you need a sleeping bag **which resists rain** and **which you can stuff into a pouch?** **(b)** She was wearing a hat **that my friend designed for a woman who had a funeral to attend.**	It is possible to use more than one relative clause in a sentence. These relative clauses may modify the same or different nouns.
(c) **AWKWARD:** Marissa wrote a letter. The letter complained about cosmetics. She had ordered cosmetics last week. **(d)** **BETTER:** Marissa wrote a letter **which complained about cosmetics that she had ordered last week.**	Multiple relative clauses are used in formal writing to be specific and concise. With multiple relative clauses, we can communicate more information using fewer words and/or sentences.

EXERCISE 4

The following patented inventions were never sold on a wide-scale basis. With a partner, describe for whom the inventions were probably made. Use two relative clauses modifying objects in each sentence.

▶ **EXAMPLE:** carry-all hat
The carry-all hat was probably invented for someone who does not want to carry a purse and who always needs her cosmetics nearby.

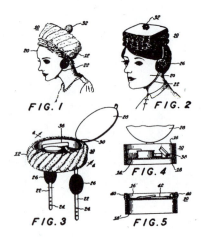

1. combination deer carcass sled and chaise lounge

2. eyeglass frame with adjustable rearview mirrors

3. power-operated pool cue stick

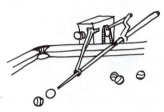

4. toilet-lid lock

5. baby-patting machine

EXERCISE 5

Combine the following groups of sentences into one sentence that contains two relative clauses modifying objects.

▶ **EXAMPLE:** Molly purchased a house. The house's former owner had made movies. The movies were box-office successes.

Molly purchased a house whose former owner had made movies which were box-office successes.

1. Students should be given scholarships. Scholarships cover all college expenses. College expenses include tuition and living expenses.

2. I am amazed at the invention. The man created the invention for some people. These people are disabled.

3. Most people did not buy chocolates. The youth were selling chocolates at a booth. The booth was located outside a supermarket.

4. Salespeople require an official contract. Clients have provided their signatures on the official contract. Their signatures are legible.

5. She admires one teacher. The teacher knew her subject area. The teacher was fair in grading.

6. A man was kidnapped by thugs. Their main interest was obtaining drugs. The drugs could be sold for thousands of dollars on the black market.

7. The women applauded the policy. The company instituted the policy for pregnant employees. The pregnant employees needed a three-month leave after their children were born.

8. The woman tightly clasped a locket. Her son had given her the locket before he left for an assignment. The assignment was in Saudi Arabia.

FOCUS **4**

▶ **D**eleting Relative Pronouns

EXAMPLES	EXPLANATIONS
(a) I sent a letter **(which)** he never received.	You can delete relative pronouns with the following functions: • direct object
(b) The faculty admired the student **(whom)** they gave the award to.	• indirect object
(c) Tom saw the movie **(which)** Sahib talked about.	• object of preposition
(d) They hope to find an apartment **(that)** is in a quiet area of town. **(e)** **NOT:** They hope to find an apartment is in a quiet area of town.	You can also delete relative pronouns that serve as subjects when the subject is followed by the *be*-verb. When you delete the relative pronoun, the *be*-verb must be deleted as well. The resulting sentences can have:
(f) I met the athlete (who was) **chosen** as "Player of the Year." **(g)** The child is delighted with the puppy (that is) **licking** her face.	• passive and progressive participles
(h) The realtor sold the home (which is) located **on Elm Street.**	• prepositional phrases
(i) She doesn't know anyone (that is) **smart enough** to pass the test.	• adjective phrases
(j) I do not want to be around a person **who has** the flu. **(k)** I do not want to be around a person **with** the flu. **(l)** Have you ever considered a job **that doesn't have** benefits? **(m)** Have you ever considered a job **without** benefits?	When the subject is followed by *have (not)* to indicate possession, you can substitute *with (without)* for the relative pronoun + *have (not)*.
(n) Could you recommend a book that appeals to all ages? **(o)** **NOT:** Could you recommend a book appeals to all ages?	You cannot delete relative pronouns if they are subjects of a relative clause that uses a verb other than *be* or *have*.

EXERCISE 6

With a partner, write descriptions of one or more sentences for the following pictures. Use at least one relative clause in each description. Then revise each description, deleting as many relative pronouns as possible. (Follow the rules in Focus 4.)

▶ **EXAMPLE:** A man brought flowers to a woman whom he admires.

Revision: *A man brought flowers to a woman he admires.*

1. _____

_____

3. _____

_____

2. _____

_____

4. _____

_____

▶ **R**elative Clauses in Formal and Informal Communication

EXAMPLES	EXPLANATIONS
Formal ↑ **(a)** I know the person **whom** he hired. **(b)** I know the person **who** he hired. **(c)** I know the person **that** he hired. ↓ **(d)** I know the person he hired. *Informal*	The use or omission of object relative pronouns may vary according to formality. *Whom* is used in formal writing but is often reduced to *who* or *that* in speaking. It can be omitted altogether in informal speech.
Formal ↑ **(e)** He saw the person **at whom** she laughed. **(f)** He saw the person **whom** she laughed **at**. **(g)** He saw the person **who** she laughed **at**. ↓ **(h)** He saw the person she laughed **at**. *Informal*	In formal written English, the preposition should always precede the object relative pronoun.

EXERCISE 7

Reread the story in Exercise 1. Mark word order changes and cross out relative pronouns that will make the story less formal.

▶ **EXAMPLE:** When my mother and I came to the United States, I experienced a move ~~from which~~ I felt that I would never recover. *from*
I was often left alone as my mother left for fancy parties ~~at~~
which she mingled with famous actors, artists, and musicians. *at*

EXERCISE 8

In pairs, read the following dialogue aloud. Then, edit the dialogue to create a less formal style. (Be sure to focus on relative clauses modifying objects and contractions.) Finally, reread the dialogue aloud, including the revisions that you have made.

▶ **EXAMPLE:**   **Luca:** Did you hear from the accountant to whom we talked last month?

Luca: Did you hear from the accountant to whom we talked last month?

Maya: No, I did not. Is he concerned about the bank account which we closed in January?

Luca: No, he is calling about personal taxes that *you* have not paid yet.

Maya: That makes another item that I do not need now—a reminder that I owe money.

Luca: I know what you mean. The accountant with whom I deal is always asking me if I have any earnings that I neglected to mention.

Maya: Well, this year has been especially bad for me. I bought a car for one of my daughters who has very expensive tastes. I came up short at the end of the year, and I still owe taxes on the book royalties that I earned in April and the horse race that I won in September.

Luca: Sometimes I wish the United States collected a tax which is a strict percentage of a person's salary. A lot of other countries collect this type of "flat" tax.

Maya: Well, until that happens, I guess I will have to deal with the accountant after all. Let me know if he calls again.

Use Your English

ACTIVITY 1: LISTENING/ WRITING

STEP 1 Listen to the tape and take notes on descriptive information about the following items. You may want to listen a second time to check your notes.

▶ **EXAMPLE:** an apartment building _____ *near the downtown* _____

1. braids _____
2. a joke _____
3. excuses _____
4. a ring _____
5. a model car _____
6. a writer _____
7. an engineer _____
8. colleges _____
9. a nurse _____
10. an artist _____
11. the hotel _____
12. a carnation _____
13. an unattractive man _____
14. a phone booth _____

STEP 2 Now describe how each item fits into the story. Create sentences using relative clauses modifying objects.

▶ **EXAMPLE:** *Kimi and Fred lived in the same apartment building which was located near the downtown of Los Angeles.*

STEP 3 What do you think will happen next? Write a short paragraph that describes your thoughts. Use at least one relative clause modifying an object in your paragraph.

ACTIVITY 2: SPEAKING

STEP 1 Find a partner

STEP 2 Each partner should draw a simple diagram without letting the other person see it.

STEP 3 Each partner should describe his or her diagram while the other partner tries to draw it on a piece of paper.

STEP 4 Each partner should compare his or her drawing with the original and note any differences between the two.

▶ **EXAMPLE:** *Draw a rectangle which is about 7 inches by 2 inches. Draw a diagonal line which extends from the upper left-hand corner to the lower right-hand corner. Draw an X with a circle around it in the top half. In the bottom half, draw a heart which has an arrow through it.*

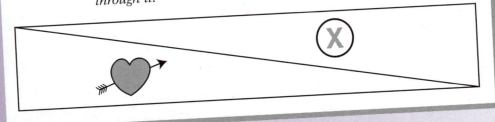

ACTIVITY 3: WRITING

Imagine that you are applying to a university that requires a formal letter of introduction about yourself. In your letter, describe academic and extracurricular activities that have shaped your life. Try to use a number of relative clauses modifying objects. You may want to describe some of the following ideas in your writing:

- a class that you especially enjoyed
- a talent that distinguishes you
- a book whose ideas inspired you
- a sport in which you excel
- a person whom you respect

▶ **EXAMPLE:** *My name is Nikita Korsu. There are many experiences about which I could write that have developed my character. My interest in academics appeared at a young age. In grade school, I had a teacher who inspired me to excel in mathematics . . .*

ACTIVITY 4: SPEAKING/WRITING

STEP 1 In pairs, look at the following picture and describe what you see.

STEP 2 Write a paragraph using at least five relative clauses modifying objects.

▶ **EXAMPLE:** *This picture depicts the dangers of pollution on the environment. Animals are standing in line on a beach which is littered with boxes and cans . . .*

NONRESTRICTIVE RELATIVE CLAUSES

UNIT GOALS:

- To distinguish restrictive from nonrestrictive relative clauses
- To use nonrestrictive relative clauses in definitions
- To use relative clauses to comment upon an entire idea
- To use nonrestrictive relative clauses with quantifying expressions

▶ OPENING TASK
The Class Reunion

Imagine that you and your classmates are attending your English class reunion ten years from today. As is the case at many class reunions, each of you will want to impress the others with your accomplishments and achievements over the past few years.

STEP 1 Jot down ideas in each of the following categories about what you have done and why it is so good. Be as creative as possible. Then, exchange your list of ideas with a classmate.

STEP 2 In groups of four, take turns bragging about your partner's accomplishments in the following categories, with each person in the group trying to outdo the others.

Category	What?	Why so good?
Your occupation		
Your family		
Your best vacation		
Your home		
Your _____		

▶ **EXAMPLES:** Occupation

A: *Now Chang is working for Rothwell International, which is one of the biggest engineering companies in the world.*

B: *Oh, really? Well, Carla works for Unifeat Studios, which is one of the most important motion picture studios in her home city.*

Family

A: *Mary's son, who is a tournament chess player, just won a competition.*

B: *Well, Barry's daughter, who just wrote a play about her hometown, also just received an award.*

▶ **Relative versus Nonrestrictive Relative Clauses**

EXAMPLES	EXPLANATIONS	
MEANING	**A restrictive clause . . .**	**A nonrestrictive clause . . .**
(a) I admire professors **who lecture well.**	• is necessary to identify the noun it describes (not all professors are admired, only the ones who lecture well).	
(b) I admire my professor, **who lectures well.**		• adds additional information; it does not help identify the professor in (b).
FORM		
(c) I prefer to fly on airlines **that have direct routes to major cities.**	• is not set off by commas.	
(d) When I return home to Chicago, I will telephone my mother, **who lives in Joliet.**		• is set off by one or more commas.
(e) Joliet, **which is a suburb of Chicago,** was a wonderful place to grow up.		
(f) My mother will pick me up at O'Hare (**which is the international airport near Chicago**).		• is sometimes set off by parentheses.
(g) She usually meets me at the baggage claim, **which exits onto the street,** rather than at the gate inside the building.		• uses *which* (not *that*) to describe places or things.
(h) **NOT:** She usually meets me at the baggage claim, that exits onto the street, rather than at the gate inside the building.		
(i) I always take the midnight flight, **(pause) which is never crowded.**		• is set off by a pause and a drop in intonation in speech.

EXERCISE 1

In the following pairs of sentences, add commas to the sentence that contains the nonrestrictive relative clause. Then explain to a partner why the clause is nonrestrictive.

▶ **EXAMPLE:**   (a) The smog that covers Mexico City is very unhealthy.

(b) Smog, which is a fog that has become polluted with smoke, is a pervasive problem in many large cities.

((b) *is nonrestrictive because it adds additional information to a general statement about all smog.*)

1. (a) The teacher who got married last year will not be returning this year.

(b) Your English teacher who has a thorough knowledge of English grammar can help you with your grammar problems.

2. (a) People who drink should not drive.

(b) People who require water to survive may someday run out of pure water.

3. (a) When I get to New York, I'm going shopping at a store which I heard about from a friend.

(b) When I get to New York, I'm going shopping at Saks Fifth Avenue which is located in downtown Manhattan.

4. (a) The world which is actually pear-shaped was once thought to be flat.

(b) The world which we live in today is very different from the world a century ago.

5. (a) Samuel Clemens who was a famous American author wrote *Tom Sawyer*.

(b) Samuel Clemens was the famous American author who wrote *Tom Sawyer*.

6. (a) Yesterday we went to "The City" which is how northern Californians refer to San Francisco.

(b) Yesterday we went to the city which is directly south of San Francisco.

EXERCISE 2

Reread your notes from the Opening Task on page 156. Write sentences from your notes with restrictive and nonrestrictive relative clauses. Write N next to the nonrestrictive relative clauses and R next to the restrictive relative clauses. Then, read your sentences aloud, inserting pauses with your nonrestrictive clauses.

▶ **EXAMPLE:** *I now live in Cartagena, which is the most beautiful resort city in Colombia.*   N

EXERCISE 3

Put brackets around all of the nonrestrictive relative clauses and circle the noun phrases they modify.

(1) (The Specialty Travel Index,) [which is well known to travel agents], should be consulted more often by the layman as well. (2) Anyone who is interested in traveling to rare or exotic places will enjoy thumbing through this volume. (3) Four hundred thirty-six tour operators advertise in this index. (4) Entries are organized by subject matter and geographical emphasis and are cross-indexed for your convenience. (5) For example, if you want to visit Mauritius, which is an island in the Indian Ocean, you only need to look under "M" in the geographical index, which is alphabetically organized. (6) If you would like a tour which specializes in "soccer," "solar energy," "space travel," or "spectator sports," you only need to look under "S" in the subject index. (7) "Chocolate tours," "whale-watching tours," "holistic health tours," and "military history tours" are just a few more of the some 176 special-interest tours that are listed in this index.

(8) Irma Turtle, who is one of the advertisers in *The Specialty Travel Index*, began her career in an interesting way. (9) Bored with her job in business, she decided to start a tour-guiding service. (10) Travelers on her first tour explored Algerian rock paintings, which had been discovered in the Central Sahara. (11) Today she leads other exciting tours. (12) For example, the tour of "Pantanal" of Brazil, which contains the world's largest wetlands, offers views of 600 species of tropical birds. (13) Another tour utilizes Berber guides to take travelers through the Atlas Mountains, which are in Morocco. (14) Finally, Jivaro Indians (whose ancestors were headshrinkers) now lead adventuresome tourists through the Ecuadorian Amazon.

(15) The next time you are planning a trip, don't forget to consult *The Specialty Travel Index*, which describes the unusual tours of Irma Turtle and other one-person travel operators.

Adapted from Arthur Frommer, *Arthur Frommer's New World of Travel*, 1988. Used by permission of the publisher: Frommer Books/Prentice Hall Press/A Division of Simon & Schuster, New York.

EXERCISE 4

Imagine you are a tourist visiting Vancouver, British Columbia, on your own. To entertain yourself, you took several tours of the city, which are listed below. Describe three tours you took in a letter to a friend. Use at least one nonrestrictive relative clause in each tour description.

▶ **EXAMPLE:** *Dear Owen,*

I've really been enjoying myself in Vancouver. I've already spent a lot of money on tours, but it has been worth it. First, I took the City of Vancouver Tour, which was a five-hour tour of important sights around the city . . .

Regards,
Your Name

Name: City of Vancouver Tour
Price: $35.00
Description: five-hour bus tour of important points of interest: Stanley Park, Queen Elizabeth Park, Capilano Suspension Bridge

Name: Dinner Theatre Evening
Price: $70.00
Description: bus transportation, six-course dinner, tip, and ticket to theatre "A Streetcar Named Desire"

Name: Victoria City Tour
Price: $75.00
Description: 12-hour bus ride to the capital of British Columbia, ferry toll included, world famous Butchart Gardens

Name: Whistler Resort
Price: $100.00
Description: one day of skiing at world-class resort, lunch, ski rentals not included

Name: Fishing Trip
Price: $175.00
Description: half-day of fishing on Pacific Coast, private boat, guide, tackle, bait, license, lunch

▶ **N**onrestrictive Relative Clauses in Definitions

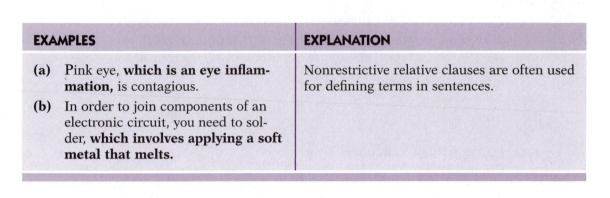

EXAMPLES	EXPLANATION
(a) Pink eye, **which is an eye inflammation,** is contagious.	Nonrestrictive relative clauses are often used for defining terms in sentences.
(b) In order to join components of an electronic circuit, you need to solder, **which involves applying a soft metal that melts.**	

EXERCISE 5

Imagine you are a world traveler who is getting ready for a long trip. Write sentences describing the items you always take with you. Look at the list below, and add two more of your own. Use a nonrestrictive relative clause to define each one.

▶ **EXAMPLE:** lap-top

I always bring a lap-top, which is a portable computer.

1. luggage cart
2. money belt
3. travel iron
4. adapter
5. travel calculator

6. Swiss army knife
7. book light
8. _____
9. _____

Using a Relative Clause to Comment on an Entire Idea

EXAMPLES	EXPLANATION
(a) Last week I returned from a three-week cruise, **which was a relief.** **(b)** I had eaten too much food, **which was a big mistake.**	Some nonrestrictive relative clauses comment on a whole idea in the main clause. These are used most often in informal conversation and always begin with *which*.

EXERCISE 6

STEP 1 Below are excerpts from letters you have written to friends and family about your travel mishaps. How would you explain these mishaps to your next-door neighbor in conversation? Use one of the following adjectives in your comments or one of your own:

disappointing   frightening   painful
exasperating   tiring   embarrassing
expensive   stressful   upsetting

▶ **EXAMPLE:** My brother and I were traveling in Mexico City. We got stuck in a horrible traffic jam in our taxi.

When my brother and I were traveling in Mexico City, we got stuck in a horrible traffic jam, which was very exasperating.

1. My friend and I wanted to save money in Venice. We walked from the train station all the way to our hotel.
2. I went hiking in the Sierra Nevada Mountains. I almost fell off a mountain trail.
3. I went on a bike tour of Canada. I fell down and broke my leg.
4. I left my traveler's checks in my hotel room. I did not have any way to pay my bill at an expensive Tokyo restaurant.
5. Last year I flew to Paris. I had to wait three extra hours to catch my return flight home.

6. I went on a ski trip and broke my wrist. I did not have health insurance so I had to pay for the X-ray myself.

7. I almost missed my flight to London. I had to run to the check-in counter with my suitcase and only had two minutes to spare.

8. I ate something in a restaurant that I had never tasted before. I got sick and could not sleep the entire night.

STEP 2 In groups of three, do the following:

First person: Tell about a travel mishap similar to the ones in Step 1.

Second person: Comment on the first person's travel mishap.

Third person: Summarize the mishap and comment on it using a relative clause.

▶ **EXAMPLE:** First person: *When I was in San Francisco, I took the wrong bus to Fisherman's Wharf.*

Second person: *That must have been frustrating.*

Third person: *When Kathy (first person) was in San Francisco, she or he took the wrong bus to Fisherman's Wharf, which was really frustrating.*

▶ # Quantifying Expressions with Nonrestrictive Relative Clauses

USE

EXAMPLES	EXPLANATION
(a) I have five phone calls to make, **all of which** should be done immediately. **(b)** I need three volunteers, **one of whom** must be strong.	Some nonrestrictive relative clauses comment on all of or some portion of a group of persons or things. To form this type of clause, combine a quantifier (such as *all of, most of, none of, many of, each of, two of*) with a relative pronoun.

EXERCISE 7

You are packing to go away to school. Comment on the items you intend to bring, filling in relevant information, using quantifiers, and providing a comma in each nonrestrictive relative clause.

▶ **EXAMPLE:** I have ___two___ pairs of shoes, _one pair of which must be repaired._

1. I'll need _____ shirts _____.

2. I want to take _____ sweaters _____.

3. I have to have _____ notebooks _____.

4. I'll bring _____ pens _____.

5. I must have _____ CD-roms _____.

EXERCISE 8

A group of teachers are traveling to Vietnam this summer; however, because of different travel interests, they will be arriving and departing at different times from the same three cities: Ho Chi Minh City (HCMC), Hue, and Hanoi.

Study the following schedule with the dates and times (morning or afternoon) of arrival. Then, fax a letter to a travel service in Vietnam that will arrange to pick up the teachers from the airport and deliver them to their hotels. The beginning of the letter appears below.

Name	City	Arrive	Depart	City	Arrive	Depart	City	Arrive	Depart
Peterson	HCMC	6/15 A.M.	6/20 A.M.	Hue	6/20 A.M.	6/21 P.M.	Hanoi	6/21 P.M.	7/30 P.M.
McGill	HCMC	6/18 A.M.	6/20 A.M.	Hue	6/20 A.M.	6/27 A.M.	Hanoi	6/27 A.M.	7/30 P.M.
Orselli	HCMC	6/15 P.M.	6/20 A.M.	Hue	6/20 A.M.	6/27 A.M.	Hanoi	6/27 A.M.	7/30 A.M.
Hopf	HCMC	6/18 P.M.	6/22 A.M.	Hue	6/22 A.M.	6/27 A.M.	Hanoi	6/27 A.M.	7/30 P.M.
Nguyen	HCMC	6/18 P.M.	6/22 A.M.	Hue	6/22 A.M.	6/27 P.M.	Hanoi	6/27 A.M.	7/30 P.M.

Date: _____   Time: _____

To: Vietnam Travel Service   Phone: _____   Fax: _____

From: _____   Phone: _____   Fax: _____

Number of Pages: __1__

Comments: _____

To Whom It May Concern:
A group of teachers will be coming to Vietnam for a visit. I would very much appreciate it if you could arrange airport transportation for the teachers, all of whom have slightly different schedules. Peterson and Orselli, both of whom will arrive at Ho Chi Minh City on June 15, must be picked up in the morning . . .

Use Your English

ACTIVITY 1: LISTENING/ WRITING

Listen to the following excerpts from tour guides of three different places. Take notes about the famous sights. Afterwards, summarize the tour or portions of the tour using nonrestrictive relative clauses.

	Sights	Characteristics
▶ **EXAMPLE:**	Lafayette Park	one of the best groomed parks in Washington, D.C.
	The White House	construction began in 1792
	Treasury Building	Andrew Jackson wanted to keep his eye on people handling cash.

First, they saw Lafayette Park, which is one of the best-groomed parks in Washington, D.C. Then, they saw the White House, whose construction began in 1792. Finally, they saw the Treasury Building, which Andrew Jackson wanted to watch carefully because it housed the money.

ACTIVITY 2: WRITING

You are preparing to be a tour guide of your hometown or the city you are presently living in. Think of five sights that are in a two-mile radius and write the script you would use, incorporating as many details as possible about the sight, such as historical origin, age, and unique aspects.

▶ **EXAMPLE:** *At the beginning of the tour, we will start with the most important place in my town, which is the Plaza Leon. The Plaza Leon, which is more than one hundred years old, is the gathering place for young people on Friday and Saturday nights and for parents and children on Sunday afternoons. Four streets extend out from the Plaza, which have wide sidewalks and are tree-lined. Hernandez Street, which was named after the first mayor of the city, contains all of the food stores—bakeries, fish markets, vegetable stands, etc. Fernando Street, which the first mayor named after his only son, is where all of the professional offices are housed. Via del Mar Street, whose pavement is made of cobblestone, is the only street which still has its original surface. Finally, two universities, one of which is the most famous university in my home country, are located on Horatio Street, which is my favorite street of all!*

ACTIVITY 3: WRITING/SPEAKING

STEP 1 In groups of three, name two facts that are common knowledge about the following people. Then, create one or more sentences that contain relative clauses about these individuals.

John Lennon	Princess Diana	Winston Churchill	Mother Teresa
Abraham Lincoln	Joan of Arc	Mahatma Gandhi	Fidel Castro

▶ **EXAMPLE:** John Lennon (*lead singer of the Beatles, born in Liverpool, England, was killed in New York*) John Lennon, who was the lead singer of the Beatles, was born in Liverpool, England.

STEP 2 Now think of another famous person you are familiar with. Present facts about this person to your classmates.

ACTIVITY 4: SPEAKING/WRITING

Interview several members of your class about various aspects of their native countries. Record that information below. Then, write several sentences, summarizing what you have learned using nonrestrictive relative clauses.

▶ **EXAMPLE:** *María, who is from Mexico, likes mariachi music. She also likes horchata, which is a popular milky white drink.*

Name	Native Country	National Foods, Sports, Dances, etc.
1.		
2.		
3.		

ACTIVITY 5: RESEARCH/SPEAKING

Visit a travel agency and bring in various travel brochures for places you would like to visit. In small groups, compare different destinations and places to stay.

▶ **EXAMPLE:** *I want to go to Hong Kong, which has many four-star hotels.*

ACTIVITY 6: WRITING

In one paragraph, describe the location, dates, people, and activities associated with a reunion you have attended. Use as many nonrestrictive relative clauses as possible.

▶ **EXAMPLE:** *Last summer I attended my family reunion, which was held on a ranch in Montana . . .*

RELATIVE ADVERB CLAUSES

UNIT GOALS:

- To know when relative adverbs can be used in place of relative pronouns
- To know the different patterns for using relative adverb clauses and use them correctly
- To know when to use the different patterns in speaking versus writing

STEP 1 Divide into small groups. Consult with your group members to see who can provide any of the following information about the city where you attend classes and the surrounding area.

History:

1. the year or decade when the city was founded (or century if the city is very old)
2. the reasons why people settled in the area, both in its earliest stages as a community and later during its development

Now:

3. the places where you think visitors would most like to go
4. the reasons why you think visitors would enjoy spending time in this city or area
5. the times when "rush hour" begins and ends if you live in a city with a lot of traffic
6. how most people get to work in the area (public transportation, car, bicycle, etc.)
7. the places where it's fun to go shopping
8. the places where you can go to hear live music or dance
9. the places where you can find peace and quiet outdoors
10. the restaurants where you can get the best food

STEP 2 Have one member of each group present some of the most interesting information the group discussed to the rest of the class.

Relative Adverbs versus Relative Pronouns

Relative adverbs *where, when, why* and *how* can replace prepositions + the relative pronoun which when these prepositions refer to place, time, reason, or manner.

Relative Adverb	Meaning
where	place
when	time
why	reason
how	manner

RELATIVE ADVERB	REPLACES PREPOSITION + WHICH
(a) (to which) A spa is a place **where** you go either to exercise or relax.	$\left.\begin{array}{l} to \\ at \\ from \\ in \end{array}\right\}$ *which*
(b) (during which) Summer is the time **when** many people take vacations.	$\left.\begin{array}{l} during \\ at \\ in \\ on \end{array}\right\}$ *which*
(c) (for which) A reason **why** some people move to large cities from small towns is to find jobs.	*for which*
(d) (the way in which) I don't understand **how** you solved this equation.	*(the way) in which*
(e) I like **how** you wrote your paper.	Note that when *how* replaces *in which* you must also delete the noun phrase *the way* before it.
(f) **NOT:** I like the way how you wrote your paper.	

EXERCISE 1

Substitute relative adverbs for preposition + *which* whenever possible. Make necessary deletions. In one sentence you cannot replace *which* with a relative adverb; explain why.

▶ **EXAMPLE:** The beginning of a new year is a time ~~during which~~ ^{when} many Americans decide to make changes in their lifestyles.

1. On January 1, the day on which resolutions for the new year are often made, we hear people vowing to lose weight, quit smoking, or perhaps change the way in which they behave toward family or friends.

2. Those who want to shed pounds may go to weight loss centers; these are places which offer counseling and diet plans.

3. Others may join a health club at which they can lose weight by exercising.

4. Still others choose a less expensive way to lose weight: They just avoid situations in which they might snack or overeat.

5. People who want to quit smoking may contact organizations that can help them to analyze the times at which they have the greatest urge to smoke and to develop strategies to break the habit.

6. Those who decide to change their behavior toward others may also seek professional help, to find out the reasons for which they act in certain ways.

7. Most people are sincere about their promises on the day on which they are made; however, by February, many New Year's resolutions are just a memory!

JANUARY						
Sun.	Mon.	Tue.	Wed.	Thur.	Fri.	Sat.
			1	2	3	4
5	6	7	8	9	10	11
12	13	14	15	16	17	18
19	20	21	22	23	24	25
26	27	28	29	30	31	

▶ **P**attern 1: Relative Adverb Clauses that Modify Nouns

EXAMPLES	EXPLANATIONS

Head Noun +	Relative Adverb +	Clause
a place	where	you can relax
a time	when	I can call you
a reason	why	you should attend

Relative adverb clauses often modify nouns. The noun is called a head noun because it is the head of the clause that follows.

Place

(a) A store **where** we can get cassettes is just around the corner.

Place

(b) Elba is the island **where** Napoleon was exiled.

The head noun is often a general word such as *place, time, or reason*, but it can also be a more specific word, especially for places and times.

Time

(c) I'll always remember the day **when** Neil Armstrong first landed on the moon: July 20, 1969. It was my birthday!

Time

(d) We read about the period **when** plagues spread throughout Europe.

Definite Noun	Indefinite Noun
the day when	**a day** when
the reason why	**one reason** why
	some reasons why
the place where	**places** where

The head noun can be definite (*the* + noun) or indefinite (*a, an, one, some*, or Ø modifier + noun). The head noun can also be singular or plural.

(e) Citizens of a country should learn
the way }
how } their government functions.

(f) NOT: Citizens of a country should learn **the way how** their government functions.

When you use *how*, you must delete the head noun. *How* adverb clauses have only two patterns: (1) *the way*; (2) *how*.

EXERCISE 2

Identify each of the head nouns in Focus 1. What other phrases could you substitute for these head nouns? Are your substitutions more general or more specific in meaning than the original ones?

▶ **EXAMPLE:**   A spa is a place where . . .
Head noun: a place

Substitution:
A spa is *a kind of health club* where . . .
More specific than *place*

EXERCISE 3

STEP 1   Match each of the time periods in the first column with an event in the second column. Then make sentences using an appropriate head noun + a relative adverb.

▶ **EXAMPLE:**   1887   Sir Arthur Conan Doyle wrote the first Sherlock Holmes story

1887 was <u>the year when</u> Sir Arthur Conan Doyle wrote the first Sherlock Holmes story.

1.	1961	**a.**	Whitcombe L. Judson invented the zipper
2.	August 10	**b.**	most people are fast asleep
3.	3 A.M.	**c.**	many couples get married in the United States
4.	Mesozoic Era	**d.**	Russian cosmonaut Yuri Gagarin orbited the earth
5.	1891	**e.**	Ecuadorians celebrate Independence Day
6.	June	**f.**	dinosaurs roamed the earth

STEP 2 Now match places with events. Again, make sentences using an adverb clause with an appropriate head noun. Try to use nouns other than *place* if possible.

▶ **EXAMPLE:** Florida, Missouri   Mark Twain was born here

Florida, Missouri is <u>the city where</u> Mark Twain was born. (Note that *here* is deleted.)

1. Ankara
2. the kidneys
3. New Zealand
4. basement
5. deli
6. caves

a. you can get a pastrami sandwich here
b. bats can often be found here
c. Turkey moved its capital here from Constantinople
d. Maori is spoken here
e. junk is often stored here
f. the water in your body gets regulated here

STEP 3 Match the following reasons to the statements in the second column. Again, give a sentence for each match.

▶ **EXAMPLE:** crime   many people move away from large cities because of this

Crime *is one reason why* many people move away from large cities.

1. aerobic exercise
2. surprise endings
3. the chance to "turn over a new leaf"
4. computer malfunctions
5. beautiful foliage
6. allergic reactions

a. people look forward to the New Year for this reason
b. some people avoid shellfish because of this
c. many love autumn for this reason
d. people enjoy the stories of Guy de Maupassant because of this
e. people take up jogging or bicycling to get this
f. students sometimes don't get papers in on time for this reason

STEP 4   Finally, match processes or methods in the first column to statements in the second. Make sentences for your matches using either the head noun *way* or the relative adverb *how*.

▶ **EXAMPLE:**   Adding *-ed* you do this to form the regular past tense in English

Adding -ed is the way you do this to form the regular past tense in English.

OR: *Adding -ed is how you form the regular past tense in English.*

1. studying history	**a.** you do this to teach a dog to lie down
2. journeying by covered wagon	**b.** you can do this to help prevent heart wagon disease
3. conducting an opinion poll	**c.** most early American pioneers traveled West by this method of transportation
4. repeating commands and giving rewards	**d.** the Greek orator Demosthenes did this to learn to speak clearly
5. eating healthy food and not smoking	**e.** people do this to survey the attitudes of large populations
6. talking with stones in his mouth	**f.** you can do this to prepare for a career as a lawyer

EXERCISE 4

Complete each of the blanks with appropriate words or phrases about yourself.

▶ **EXAMPLE:**   The shoreline is a place where I go to watch the birds.

Starting with my conclusion is the way I often begin to write a draft for a paper.

1. _____ was the year when I _____ .
2. _____ is the place where I _____ .
3. The reason why I don't like _____ is _____ .
4. The way I get to school/work is _____ .
5. _____ is a/the day when I _____ .
6. _____ is a reason why I _____ .
7. A _____ where I _____ is _____ .
8. _____ is how I _____ .

FOCUS **3**

▶ **Pattern 2:
Relative Adverbs
without Head Nouns**

EXAMPLES	EXPLANATIONS
Relative Adverb + Clause where — he lives when — the term starts why — I called how — she knows **(a)** This is **where** we will meet tomorrow. **(b)** That was **when** I decided to go to work. **(c)** **Why** she left is a mystery. **(d)** She explained **how** to change a tire.	A second pattern with relative adverbs has no head noun. As with Pattern 1, this pattern can express: • place • time • reason • manner

EXERCISE 5

Restate each of the sentences you made in Exercise 3 without the head nouns (except for the ones in Step 4 for which you used *how*).

▶ **EXAMPLE:** *1887 was when Sir Arthur Conan Doyle wrote the first Sherlock Holmes story.*

EXERCISE 6

Working with a partner or in a small group, decide whether each statement is true or false. If a statement is false, replace the phrase in italics with something that will make the statement true.

▶ **EXAMPLE:** *Spring* is when birds in the northern hemisphere begin their migration south.

Answer: *False.* **Autumn** *is when they migrate south.*

1. *New York* is where you can see the Lincoln Memorial.

2. *Late November* is when we celebrate the winter solstice.

3. *Religious persecution* is why many Europeans first settled in what became the United States of America.

4. *Majoring in mathematics* is how most undergraduate students prepare for a career in medicine.

5. *The 1970s* was the decade when Ronald Reagan was president.

6. *The drugstore* is where a bibliophile would go to add to her collection.

7. *Either July or August* is when a person born under the zodiac sign of Leo will celebrate his or her birthday.

8. *Using a meat barometer* is how you check to make sure meat is cooked well enough in the oven.

FOCUS **4**

FORM

▶ **Pattern 3: Head Nouns without Relative Adverbs**

EXAMPLES	EXPLANATIONS
<table><tr><td colspan="3">**Head Noun** + **Clause**</td></tr><tr><td>the place</td><td></td><td>we moved to</td></tr><tr><td>the time</td><td></td><td>I start school</td></tr><tr><td>the reason</td><td></td><td>they left</td></tr><tr><td>the way</td><td></td><td>you do this</td></tr></table>	
(a) Cook's is **a store** I go to for kitchen supplies.	A third pattern uses only the head noun and its modifying clause. This pattern can also express: • place
(b) November first is **the day** Catholics celebrate All Saint's Day.	• time
(c) **The reason** spiders can spin perfect webs is based on their instincts, not learned behavior.	• reason
(d) Public transportation is **the way** many city dwellers get to work.	• manner
(e) Dominic's is the restaurant I go **to** for pizza. **(f)** **NOT:** Dominic's is the restaurant I go for pizza. **(g)** Denver is the city I live **in**. **(h)** **NOT:** Denver is the city I live.	With specific head nouns that express place, you must often include a preposition of direction or position.
(i) Dominic's is the place I ⎧ **go** ⎫ for pizza. ⎩ **go to** ⎭	The preposition is often optional in informal English when *place* is the head noun.

Relative Adverb Clauses   **179**

EXERCISE 7

Make sentences using Pattern 3 (head nouns without relative adverbs) to provide information about yourself.

▶ **EXAMPLE:** where you live

Winnipeg, Canada is the city I live in.

1. where you were born
2. the date (month, day) when you were born
3. the way you make a certain food you like
4. the reason you are taking a specific course
5. the time of day (for example, morning, afternoon) best for you to get work done
6. a place you like to go to relax or have fun
7. a reason you like or dislike a course you are taking
8. the way people say "good luck" in your native language

▶ **C**ontexts for Relative Adverb Patterns

Here are some general guidelines for using the three patterns.

EXAMPLES	EXPLANATIONS
	Pattern 1: Head Noun + Relative Adverb + Clause We tend to use this pattern:
(a) Today is **a day when** all nations will want to join in prayers for peace in the world.	• to focus on or emphasize the time, place, reason, or manner.
(b) This is **the place where** most of my family lived at one time or another.	
(c) I know **a nursery where** you can get beautiful orchids.	• when the meaning of the head noun is specific.
(d) Barton's is **a store where** one can find expensive cameras discounted. (Less formal: Barton's is **where** you can get a fantastic deal!)	• when the context is more formal (such as written versus spoken English).
(e) **A place where** you can buy film is at the corner of Hammond and Belknap.	• when the head noun is the subject of a sentence rather than the predicate. In example (e), **a place** helps to introduce new information.
(f) The corner of Hammond and **Predicate** Belknap is **where** we usually meet.	
	Pattern 2: Relative Adverb + Clause We often omit the head noun:
(g) I know **where** you can find tomato sauce in this market.	• when the head noun has a general meaning (the time, the place) rather than a specific one.
(h) She told us **when** to show up.	
(i) Greece is **where** the Olympics started. (inferred: the country)	• when you can infer the head noun from the context or from general knowledge.
(j) 551 B.C. is **when** Confucius was born. (inferred: the year)	
Less formal	
(k) **Why** she did that is a mystery to me!	• when the context of speech or writing is informal.
	continued on next page

EXAMPLES	EXPLANATIONS
	Pattern 3: Head Noun + Clause
	This pattern tends to be used in contexts similar to ones for Pattern 1:
(l) Let us know **the day** you will arrive.	• when the head noun has a more specific meaning.
(m) Please state **the reason** you are seeking this position.	• when the context is more formal.

EXERCISE 8

Decide whether the form given in (a) or (b) would be more typical or appropriate for each context. Use the guidelines given in Focus 5. Explain your choices.

1. Ethel: Max! What did you just turn off that light for?
Max: Dear, if you'll wait just a minute, you'll find out . . .
(a) the reason why I did it.
(b) why I did it.

2. (a) The day I got married
(b) When I got married
. . . was one of the happiest days of my life.

3. (a) A place where you can get a great cup of coffee
(b) Where you get a great cup of coffee
. . . is right across the street.

4. Oh no! Can you believe it? I forgot . . .
(a) the place where I put my keys again.
(b) where I put my keys again.

5. (a) One reason many people feel stress
(b) Why many people feel stress
. . . is that they don't have enough spare time.

6. I would now like all of you in this audience to consider . . .
(a) the many times your families offered you emotional support.
(b) when your families offered you emotional support. It's hard to count them all, isn't it?

7. Let me show you . . .
(a) the way this CD player works.
(b) how this CD player works.

8. Ms. Cordero just told us . . .
(a) the time when we should turn in our papers.
(b) when we should turn in our papers.

9. Last year my family took a trip to see . . .
(a) the house where my great-grandfather grew up.
(b) where my great-grandfather grew up.

Use Your English

ACTIVITY 1: LISTENING

Form groups of three or four and compete in teams. The tape you'll hear will consist of twenty phrases that need to be identified with a place, time, reason, or manner. The phrases will use preposition + *which* clauses. Taking turns, each team needs to identify the phrase by using a sentence with a relative adverb clause. You may use any of the patterns discussed in this unit. If a team gives the wrong answer, the next team will have a chance to correct it. Award points for each correct answer.

▶ **EXAMPLES:** Tape: The continent on which the country of Rwanda is located.
  Answer: *Africa is the continent where Rwanda is located.*

  Tape: The month in which we celebrate both Lincoln's and Washington's birthdays.
  Answer: *February is the month when we celebrate both birthdays.*

  Tape: The way in which you say "Thank you" in French.
  Answer: *"Merci" is how you say "Thank you."*

ACTIVITY 2: WRITING/SPEAKING

How would you complete statements that begin as follows?
• I'd like to know the date (day, year, century, etc.) when . . .
• I'd like to find out the place (country, city, etc.) where . . .
• I wish I knew the reason(s) why . . .
• I am interested in finding out how . . .
Write a list of statements using each of the relative adverbs above (with or without head nouns) to express things you'd like to know. Use the patterns given to begin your sentences. Share your statements with others in your class to see if anyone can provide the answers.

ACTIVITY 3: WRITING

Did you know that some parts of your tongue can be more sensitive to certain tastes than other parts? The picture at the right shows sensitive areas for the four basic tastes: salty, bitter, sweet and sour. In a paragraph, describe the sensitivity location for each taste; use at least two relative adverb clauses.

▶ **EXAMPLE:** *Near the back of the tongue is where we have a sensitivity to-ward bitter tastes.*

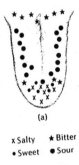

(a)

x Salty ★ Bitter
• Sweet ● Sour

ACTIVITY 4: WRITING/SPEAKING

Make lists of places and times/dates as are shown in Exercise 3, either individu-ally or in teams. Then present the items on your list one by one to others who must define or identify the word or phrase in some way with a relative adverb clause. (If you prefer to do this as a competitive game, you could set time limits for re-sponses and award points.) The following are a few examples of items and re-sponses.

Place/date/time	Possible response
February 14	That's a day when people exhange valentines.
Switzerland	It's a country in Europe where skiers like to go because of the Alps
trattoria	It's a restaurant where you can get Italian food.

ACTIVITY 5: SPEAKING/WRITING

With a classmate, take turns telling each other about dates and places that have been important or memorable in your lives. These could be times and locations of milestone events such as birth and graduation, but they could also include a few humorous incidents or dates/places that may not seem so important now but were when you were younger. (Examples: *1990 was the year when I broke my leg playing Frisbee; I'll never forget a trip to Florida, the place where I first saw the ocean*.) Take notes on your partner's events. Then report some of them orally to the class, using relative adverb clauses in some sentences. (In addition to *when* and *where*, you might also use the relative adverb *why* in giving reasons why a date or place was important.)

ACTIVITY 6: WRITING

Create a booklet providing information for tourists or new students about the city where you now live. Use some of the categories provided in the Opening Task as headings for your guide (for example: "Places Where You Can Go for Entertainment") and/or make up others you think would be useful (for example: "Places Where You Can Get the Best Pizza"). You could divide the project so that individuals or small groups would each be responsible for a section or two of the guide.

CORRELATIVE CONJUNCTIONS

UNIT GOALS:
- To use correlative conjunctions for emphasis
- To join phrases and clauses with correlative conjunctions
- To write sentences with parallel correlative constructions

▶ OPENING TASK
Planning a Course Schedule

Imagine that you would like to enter the New World Alternative College in order to earn an Associate's degree. The following list contains the classes that are offered and the number of required courses and electives in each category to obtain a degree.

NEW WORLD ALTERNATIVE COLLEGE
Course Offerings, Requirements, and Electives

English Course (1 course)
Expository Writing
Technical Writing

Humanities (2 courses)
Linguistics
Philosophy
Religious Studies

Social Sciences (2 courses)
Anthropology
Communication Studies
Economics
Geography

Physical Sciences (2 courses)
Geology
Astronomy
Physics

Mathematics (1 course)
General Mathematics
Computer Science

Life Sciences (2 courses)
Psychology
Biology
Microbiology

Environmental Studies (4 courses)
The Greenhouse Effect
Air Pollution
Garbage Disposal
Hazardous Waste
Acid Rain
Endangered Wildlife

History (1 elective)
U.S. History
World History

Foreign Language (1 elective)
Chinese
French

STEP 1 In the following table, write in two courses from each category that you would be interested in taking. In some cases, there are only two courses to choose from. These are written in for you.

COURSES I WOULD LIKE TO TAKE	#1	#2
English Composition	Expository Writing or Technical Writing	X
Humanities		
Social Sciences		
Physical Sciences		
Mathematics	General Mathematics or Computer Science	X
Life Sciences		
Environmental Sciences		
History	U.S. History or World	X
Foreign Language	Chinese or French	

STEP 2 Discuss your choices in groups of four.

STEP 3 Summarize the results of your discussion.

▶ **EXAMPLES:** *All of us must take either expository writing or technical writing.*
Maria is interested not only in Geology but also in Astronomy.
Neither Tom nor Gustaf would like to take Garbage Disposal.

MEANING

Correlative Conjunctions for Emphasis

EXAMPLES		EXPLANATIONS
Coordinating Conjunctions	**Correlative Conjunctions**	Coordinating conjunctions and correlative conjunctions can be used to show different types of relationships:
and	*both . . . and not only . . . but also*	• additive
or	*either . . . or*	• alternative
nor	*neither . . . nor*	• negative
		In general, the correlative conjunctions are more emphatic.
		Additive Relationships
(a) A: I hope Pablo **and** Karl come to the party next Saturday.		• less emphasis
B: You're in luck! **Both** Karl **and** Pablo are coming.		• more emphasis
(b) C: I hope Pablo is coming to the party next Saturday.		• even greater emphasis (*not only* usually comes before already known information, and *but* introduces new or surprising information)
D: Guess what? **Not only** is Pablo coming, **but** Karl is **also.**		
		Alternative Relationships
(c) A: Can you come on Wednesday **or** Thursday?		• less emphasis
B: Yes, I can come on **either** Wednesday **or** Thursday.		• more emphasis
		Negative Additive Relationships
(d) A: Milly doesn't eat candy, **nor** do I.		• less emphasis
B: You mean **neither** you **nor** Milly has a sweet tooth?		• more emphasis

EXERCISE 1

Answer the following questions with correlative conjunctions for emphasis. Write your answers below.

▶ **EXAMPLE:** Spain doesn't border on Portugal or France, does it?

Yes, it borders on both Portugal and France.

1. President's Day and Valentine's Day aren't in February, are they?
2. Cameroon and Algeria are in South America, aren't they?
3. Honey or sugar can be used to sweeten lemonade, can't it?
4. Whales and dolphins are members of the fish family, aren't they?
5. Niagara Falls is situated in Brazil and Uruguay, isn't it?
6. Martin Luther King, Jr. and Jesse Jackson were prominent black lawyers, weren't they?
7. You can travel from California to Hawaii by boat or airplane, can't you?
8. Ho Chi Minh City and Saigon refer to different places in Vietnam, don't they?

EXERCISE 2

Using the information in parentheses, respond to the following statements with *not only . . . but also.*

▶ **EXAMPLE:** I heard that Samuel has to work on Saturdays. (Sundays)

*Samuel has to work **not only** on Saturdays **but also** on Sundays.*

1. Shirley Temple could dance very well. (sing)
2. The language laboratory is great for improving pronunciation. (listening comprehension)
3. Nola should exercise twice a week. (go on a diet)
4. Becky has to take a test on Friday. (finish a project)
5. Thomas Jefferson was a great politician. (inventor)
6. The dictionary shows the pronunciation of a word. (part of speech)
7. The International Student Office will help you to locate an apartment. (get a part-time job)
8. It rained all day last Tuesday. (last Wednesday)

Joining Phrases and Clauses
with Correlative Conjunctions

EXAMPLES	EXPLANATIONS
(a) **Neither** the pedestrian **nor** the bicyclist saw the car approaching. **(b)** Mary will **not only** complete her coursework **but also** write her Master's thesis by June. **(c)** Mrs. Thomas was **both** surprised **and** jubilant that her daughter was awarded a scholarship. **(d)** Mark usually eats **either** at home **or** on campus.	All four correlative conjunction pairs can join phrases.
(e) **Either** the teacher has to slow down the lecture pace **or** the students need to take notes faster. **(f)** **Not only** was Mr. Jones strict **but** he was **also** unfair.	Only two of the correlative conjunction pairs can join clauses.
(g) **Not only is she** taking physics **but** she is **also** taking biology. **(h)** **NOT:** Not only she is taking physics but she is also taking biology.	In combinations with *not only . . . but also,* the position of the subject following *not only* is inverted with the first auxiliary verb, *be,* or *do.*

EXERCISE 3

Using the information you obtained in the Opening Task on page 186, write sentences about your classmates' preferences.

▶ **EXAMPLES:** *Natasha may take either U.S. History or World History.*

She wants to enroll in microbiology and either psychology or biology.

EXERCISE 4

Think of a couple you know who have lived together for a long time. Fill out the grid with information about the couple. Then, with a partner, discuss the couple's appearance, preferences, habits, or other features of their lives together. Use as many correlative conjunctions as you can.

▶ **EXAMPLES:**   Appearance: *Both Chau and George have black hair.*

Preferences: *On weekends Chau and George like to go either out to eat or to the movies.*

Habits: *Chau and George neither smoke nor drink.*

	Name #1:	Name #2:
Appearance		
Preferences		
Habits		

FOCUS **3**

▶ **Parallelism; Being Concise**

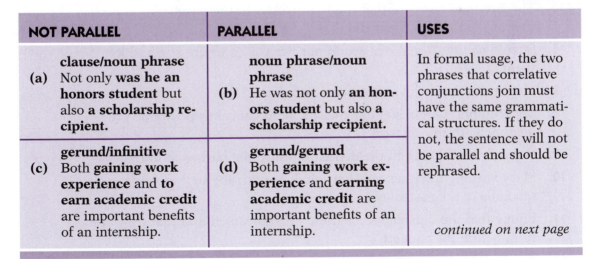

NOT PARALLEL		PARALLEL		USES
(a)	**clause/noun phrase** Not only **was he an honors student** but also **a scholarship recipient.**	(b)	**noun phrase/noun phrase** He was not only **an honors student** but also **a scholarship recipient.**	In formal usage, the two phrases that correlative conjunctions join must have the same grammatical structures. If they do not, the sentence will not be parallel and should be rephrased.
(c)	**gerund/infinitive** Both **gaining work experience** and **to earn academic credit** are important benefits of an internship.	(d)	**gerund/gerund** Both **gaining work experience** and **earning academic credit** are important benefits of an internship.	*continued on next page*

NOT CONCISE	CONCISE	USES
(e) She knew either **that she needed an A** or **that she needed a B** to pass the course.	**(f)** She knew that she needed **an A** or **a B** to pass the course.	In addition, parallel structures should be concise, without unnecessary repetition.
(g) Not only was **John disqualified because of poor attendance** but **Betty was also disqualified for poor attendance.**	**(h)** Not only **John** but also **Betty** was disqualified because of poor attendance.	

EXERCISE 5

Read each sentence. Write OK next to sentences that are well-formed, parallel, and not repetitious. Rephrase the rest for concise, formal style. The first two have been done as examples.

1. I cannot stand to eat either liver or raw fish. OK
2. Not only is Maria tired but also sick. *Maria is not only tired but also sick.*
3. Not only *The New York Times* carried but also *The Los Angeles Times* carried the story of the train disaster in Algeria.
4. Juanita will both major in English and in sociology.
5. The Boston Red Sox either made the finals in the baseball competition or the Detroit Tigers did.
6. Suzuki neither found her watch nor her wallet where she had left them.
7. The Smith family loves both cats and dogs.
8. Mr. Humphrey thinks either that I should cancel or postpone the meeting with my advisor.
9. Not only am I going to the dentist but also the barber tomorrow.
10. Mary is going to either quit her job or is rearranging her work schedule to take astronomy.
11. I hope that the musicians are both well-rehearsed and that they are calm before the concert.
12. Todd neither saw or talked to his roommate, Bill.
13. Both bringing a bank card and cash is necessary for any trip.
14. Nor my two daughters nor my son wants to take an aisle seat on the airplane.

EXERCISE 6

The following paragraphs have some nonparallel, inconcise structures with correlative conjunctions. Identify and rephrase them for formal usage.

(1) In the last forty years, family life trends have changed dramatically in the United States. (2) In the past, it was expected that everyone would get married in their early twenties. (3) Now having to choose either between a family or a career, many are opting for the career and remaining single. (4) Others are postponing first marriages until their thirties or forties.

(5) If and when couples decide to marry, many are deciding to limit their family size. (6) Not only couples are having fewer children but they are also deciding to have no children at all. (7) On the other hand, some singles are either deciding to raise their own or adopt children by themselves. (8) In addition, many same-sex partners are not only choosing to form binding relationships but also to become parents.

(9) In the past, women worked either for personal satisfaction or to earn extra money for luxuries. (10) Today both husband and the wife must work in order to survive. (11) Because of this, husbands and wives do not always adhere to traditional sex roles. (12) Now either the husband might do the cooking and cleaning or the wife might do the cooking and cleaning.

(13) Both because of the greater stress of modern life and the greater freedom that each partner feels, divorce is becoming more and more common. (14) Neither the rich are immune nor the poor. (15) In some states, the divorce rate approaches fifty percent. (16) Marriage cannot be all bad, though. (17) Not only many people get divorced but these same people also get remarried one or more times throughout their lifetimes.

Use Your English

ACTIVITY 1: LISTENING

You will listen to a dialog between a college advisor and a student. Listen to the taped conversation, and fill in the grid as the student responds to the advisor's questions.

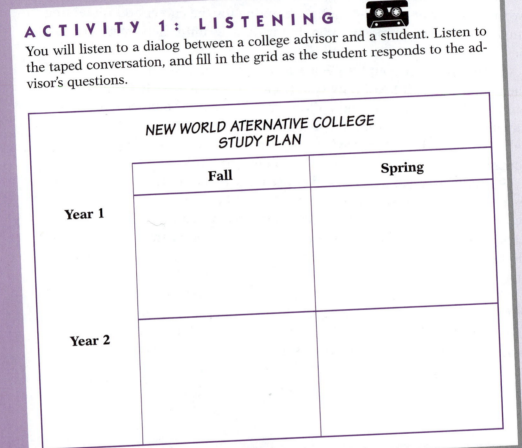

NEW WORLD ATERNATIVE COLLEGE STUDY PLAN

	Fall	Spring
Year 1		
Year 2		

ACTIVITY 2: WRITING

Imagine that you are a supervisor for a company that allows fairly flexible hours for its part-time employees. Your boss recently called you to find out which day and time would be most convenient for each employee's evaluation conference. In order to help you in your decision, you asked the four workers you are supervising to indicate on the following blank schedule forms which hours they are available. An "A" indicates that a worker is available during a particular hour.

Conference Availability Charts

Pepita

	M	T	W	Th	F
9–10	A		A		A
10–11	A	A			
11–12		A	A	A	
12–1					
1–2			A		A

Tuan

	M	T	W	Th	F
9–10					
10–11					
11–12		A	A	A	
12–1	A	A	A	A	A
1–2			A		A

Tom

	M	T	W	Th	F
9–10					
10–11	A	A			
11–12			A		
12–1	A	A	A	A	A
1–2		A		A	

Laleh

	M	T	W	Th	F
9–10	A		A		A
10–11					
11–12			A		
12–1					
1–2		A		A	

Now write a memo to your boss, detailing who is and who is not available at various times for their evaluation conferences. Try to use the words *both*, *either*, or *neither* in your writing.

▶ **EXAMPLE:**

Memo

Dear Mr. Masters,
Both Pepita and Laleh are available from 9 to 10:00 on Monday, but neither Tuan nor Tom can come at that time.

L. A. T. C. Mission College
3000 Mission College Blvd.
Santa Clara, CA 95054
(408) 855-5095

ACTIVITY 3: SPEAKING

Imagine that you have two children and both you and your spouse have to work outside the home, which leaves little time for running a household. In the chart below, choose which chores you would like to do and which chores you would like your spouse to do by marking an "X" under the appropriate column. If you feel that any of the tasks should be shared, write "B" (for both) under each column. Discuss your choice of respective duties with a classmate, using as many of the expressions you have learned in this unit as possible.

▶ **EXAMPLE:** *Both my spouse and I should share cooking meals because we both work.*

	My Chore	My Spouse's Chore
cook meals	B	B
wash dishes		
vacuum floors		
dust furniture		
decorate the house for holidays		
care for the yard		
bring in the mail		
shop for food		
shop for clothes		
get the car repaired		
pay bills		
clean toilets and fixtures		
do laundry		
take out garbage		
get the children dressed		
give the dog a bath		
take care of a child who is sick		

ACTIVITY 4: LISTENING/ WRITING/SPEAKING

Listen carefully to a television program (for example, a cooking program or a sports program) and jot down the statements you hear that contain *both/and, not only/but also, either/or,* or *neither/nor.* Bring your notes to class and discuss which types of correlatives were used more often and whether they were used to show emphasis or not.

▶ **EXAMPLES:** *You can use either butter or margarine in the recipe.*
Not only did he strike out but he also got hit by a flying bat.

ACTIVITY 5: WRITING/SPEAKING

THE CORRELATIVE GAME

Preparation for the Game

STEP 1 Divide into two teams. Each team should create a set of eighteen cards that contain difficult True/False statements, which will hopefully stump the other team. You should pattern these statements after the structures you have learned in this lesson. For example:

▶ **EXAMPLE:** *Neither South Africa nor Argentina has a northern seaport. (T)*

STEP 2 On a second set of cards, each team will write the names of team members on the opposite team, using the following constructions:

Either *Mary* or *Sam* (six cards with other names)
Both *Tony* and *Maria* (six cards with other names)
Neither *Thanh* nor *Vivian* (six cards with other names)

Rules of the Game

STEP 1 Teams should exchange sets of cards. Each team will have eighteen True/False Cards and eighteen Name Cards.

STEP 2 One member of the first team reads the name card first, for example:

"Either Mary or Sam" — This means that only one of these two students can answer the question.
"Both Tony and Maria" — This means that both Tony and Maria can help each other answer.
"Neither Thanh nor Sam" — This means that Thanh or Sam cannot answer the question, but the rest of the members of the team can.

If the first card is chosen, Mary or Sam decides who will take a guess. For the sake of example, presume Mary decides to try.

STEP 3 The member of the first team reads the True/False statement. If Mary can answer it correctly, she gets one point and the game continues. If she answers it incorrectly, it is the other team's turn.

STEP 4 The team with the most points at the end of the stack of True/False cards wins the game.

SENTENCE CONNECTORS

UNIT GOALS:

- To understand the differences between conjunctions and sentence connectors
- To use appropriate sentence connectors to express various logical meanings
- To choose appropriate sentence connectors for formal and informal contexts
- To use correct punctuation for sentence connectors in writing

▶ **O PENING TASK**

How Things Came to Be

Cultures all over the world have creation myths, which explain how life on earth came to be.

STEP 1 Read the two creation myths from Finland and Micronesia that are summarized below. They describe how the earth, the sky, and the first people on earth came to exist.

STEP 2 Write a paragraph describing the similarities and differences between the two creation myths. In comparing the stories, consider the following questions:

1. What existed at the beginning of creation?
2. In what order were things created?
3. How were the earth and sky created?
4. Who was responsible for creating the first people and how were they created?

From Finland:

In the beginning there was only Water, Air, and Air's daughter, Ilamatar. Ilamatar spent her time wandering around the world. One day Ilamatar sank down to rest upon the ocean's face as she was very tired. When she lay down, the seas rolled over her, the waves tossed her and the wind blew over her. For seven hundred years, Ilamatar swam and floated in the sea. Then one day while she lay floating with one knee up out of the water, a beautiful duck swooped down and landed on her knee. There it laid seven eggs. As the days went by, the eggs grew hotter and hotter until Ilamatar could no longer endure the heat and pulled her knee into the water. Because of this, the eggs rolled into the ocean and sank to its bottom. Eventually, one of the eggs cracked. From the lower half of its shell, the earth was formed. From the egg's upper shell, the sky formed over the land and sea. From the yolk of the egg, the sun rose into the sky. From the white of the egg, the moon and stars were created and took their place in the heavens. Later, Ilamatar gave birth to the sea's child, whom she called Vainamoinen. For seven years Vainamoinen swam the seas. Then he went ashore and became the first person on earth.

From Nauru, Micronesia:

In the beginning there was only water and the creator, Areop-Enap, who lived in a mussel shell in the sea. It was very dark in the sea and also in the shell; as a result, Areop-Enap couldn't see very well. He could, however, feel around in the dark. Thus it was that he discovered a large snail and a small snail who were occupying the shell with him. Areop-Enap used his power to change the small snail into the moon and put it at the top of the shell. Then, by the light of the moon, Areop-Enap spotted a worm in the shell. He got the worm to separate the upper and lower parts of the shell. The lower part became the earth, while the upper part became the sky. Because of all this work, the poor worm died of exhaustion. His sweat, dripping into the lower shell, became the salty sea. After the sky and the earth had been created, Areop-Enap placed the big snail into the sky to be the sun. Finally, from stones he made the first people to hold up the sky.

(Adapted from Maria Leach, *The Beginning: Creation Myths around the World*, New York: Funk & Wagnalls, 1956.)

▶ **Connectors**

There are many types of meaning relationships that can exist between two ideas. Words or phrases that express these relationships are called connectors. The chart below shows some of these relationships.

EXAMPLES	TYPES OF RELATIONSHIPS	EXAMPLES WITH CONNECTORS
(a) Areop-Enap created the moon. He put it at the top of the shell.	time sequence	**After** Areop-Enap created the moon, he put it at the top of the shell.
(b) Areop-Enap lived in a mussel shell. Two snails lived there.	added idea	Areop-Enap lived in a mussel shell. Two snails lived there **as well.**
(c) In the Finnish myth, the heavens were created from an egg. The sun was formed from the yolk of the egg.	example	In the Finnish myth, the heavens were created from an egg. The sun, **for example**, was formed from the yolk of the egg.
(d) In the Finnish myth, the earth did not exist in the beginning. In the Micronesian myth, at first there was only the sea.	similarity	In the Finnish myth, the earth did not exist in the beginning. **Similarly,** in the Micronesian myth, at first there was only the sea.
(e) In the Micronesian myth, the sun was a snail. In the Finnish myth, the sun came from an egg yolk.	contrast	In the Micronesian myth, the sun was a snail, **whereas** in the Finnish myth the sun came from an egg yolk.
(f) Ilamatar was very tired. She lay down on the ocean's face.	result	Ilamatar was very tired, **so** she lay down on the ocean's face.
(g) Creation myths are universal. They are found throughout the world.	clarification	Creation myths are universal. **That is**, they are found throughout the world.

Types of Connectors

EXAMPLES	EXPLANATIONS
Independent Clause **(h)** Ilamatar kept the eggs on her knee, **Independent Clause** **but** eventually they got too hot.	There are three main types of connectors: coordinating conjunctions, subordinating conjunctions, and sentence connectors. • **Coordinating conjunctions** connect the ideas in two independent clauses. The coordinating conjunctions are *and, but, for, or nor, so,* and *yet.* In written English, we usually write these clauses as one sentence, separated by a comma.
Dependent Clause **(i)** **After** Areop-Enap put the snail in **Independent Clause** the sky, he made people. **Independent Clause** **(j)** Areop-Enap put the snail in the sky **Dependent Clause** **before** he made people.	• **Subordinating conjunctions** connect ideas within sentences. They show the relationship between an idea in a dependent clause and an idea in an independent clause. Common subordinating conjunctions include: **Time** *after, before, once, since, until, when, whenever, while* **Reason** *as, because, since* **Result** *in order that, so that, that* **Contrast** *although, even though, though, whereas* **Condition** *if, even if, provided that, unless* **Location** *where, wherever*
Independent Clause **(k)** Areop-Enap discovered two snails living in the shell with him. **Independent Clause** **In addition,** a worm inhabited the shell, as he later found out. **Independent Clause** **(l)** Ilamatar could not endure the heat from the eggs; **consequently,** **Independent Clause** she put her knee back into the water.	• **Sentence connectors** usually express relationships between two or more independent clauses. The independent clauses may be separate sentences, as in (k). They may also be in the same sentence, separated by a semicolon, as in (l). The remainder of this unit is concerned with the third type of logical connector, sentence connectors.

EXERCISE 1

For each of the sentence pairs below, state what the relationship of the second sentence is to the first: time sequence, added idea, example, similarity, contrast, result, or clarification.

▶ **EXAMPLE:** Ilamatar's child swam the seas for seven years. He went ashore.

Relationship: *time sequence*

1. The myths of many cultures include a god of thunder. The Mayan god of thunder was Chac.

2. In Greek mythology, Ares, the god of war, was often violent and belligerent. The goddess Athena was a peacemaker.

3. Myths entertain us. They help us to understand human behavior.

4. Ancient civilizations did not know the scientific explanations for natural phenomena such as storms. They made up stories to explain these events.

5. In North American Indian cultures, cosmogony is a major theme in myths. These myths explain how the world was created.

6. In a Chinese creation myth, a man named Pan Gu lived in an egg for eighteen thousand years. He woke up and chopped the egg in two with an ax.

7. In many African folktales, the village represents a place of order. The bush, or jungle, represents a place of mystery and destructive forces.

8. Jason, the leader of the Argonauts in Greek mythology, went on a long sea voyage to get the Golden Fleece. The Greek hero Odysseus embarked on a long voyage.

9. In an Indonesian myth, the first woman in the world cursed a great flood that washed away her garden. She was punished with a malformed child who had only one eye, one arm, and one leg.

10. A common animal in many myths and folktales is the trickster. In Asia, the trickster is often a rabbit or a monkey.

FOCUS **2**

▶ **Addition Connectors**

Simple Addition

CONNECTORS	EXAMPLES	MEANINGS
also	**(a)** You can pay your fees by credit card. You can **also** write a check.	These connectors express simple addition. They have the meaning of *too* or *also*.
in addition	**(b)** Ming has to register for classes today. **In addition,** he has to pay his course fees.	
furthermore	**(c)** This plant requires sun all day. **Furthermore,** it needs rich soil.	
moreover	**(d)** As your mayor, I promise to make this city safe for all. **Moreover,** I will create new jobs.	

Emphatic Addition

CONNECTORS	EXAMPLES	MEANINGS
what is more (informal: *what's more*)	**(e)** We have succeeded in cleaning up the river. **What is more,** we have made it the cleanest in the entire state.	Emphatic connectors signal an idea that stresses some aspect of what has been previously stated. Their meaning is similar to: "Not only *that* (what I just said), but also *this* (what I am saying now)."
as well	**(f)** Ricardo won the award for athletic achievement. He received academic honors **as well.**	
besides (THIS)*	**(g)** My brother goes to school full-time. **Besides this,** he manages to work twenty hours a week.	

*In this example and others in the unit, THIS means what has been previously mentioned. THIS will often be a demonstrative pronoun (*this, that, these,* or *those*) or a demonstrative determiner + noun phrase (for example: as well as *this fact*).

Simple Addition versus Emphatic Addition

EXAMPLES	MEANINGS
(h) I think I would be an excellent person for this job. My background in computers is extensive. **Simple Addition** **(i)** I **also** have excellent writing skills. **Emphatic Addition** **(j)** I have excellent writing skills **as well.**	We often use simple addition and emphatic addition in the same contexts. The emphatic connector simply stresses the added information more than the simple connector does.

Intensifying Addition

CONNECTORS	EXAMPLES	MEANINGS
in fact	**(k)** Spokane has a lot of rain lately. **In fact,** it has been raining all week.	Intensifying connectors show that an idea will strongly support another one.
as a matter of fact	**(l)** You can take the rest of the pie with you. **As a matter of fact,** I wish you would since I'm on a diet.	
actually	**(m)** Gretchen has never cared for the color magenta. **Actually,** it's one of her least favorite colors.	

Intensifying Addition versus Emphatic Addition

EXAMPLES	EXPLANATIONS
(n) This weekend is going to be very busy. I have a lot of schoolwork to do. **Emphatic addition** **(o)** **Besides that,** I have to finish moving to my new apartment. **Intensifying addition** **(p)** **In fact,** I have to write three papers.	We use emphatic connectors when we add a related idea. (o) adds another activity that will be accomplished. We use intensifying connectors to elaborate an idea. (p) supports the idea of having a lot of schoolwork.

EXERCISE 2

Use an appropriate sentence connector from the list below to show the kind of addition relationship expressed in the last sentence of each pair or group of sentences. More than one connector could be appropriate for most contexts. Try to use each connector in the list once.

also	*moreover*	*besides*
in addition	*what is more*	*in fact*
furthermore	*as well*	*as a matter of fact*
		actually

▶ **EXAMPLE:** Leonardo Da Vinci was a painter and sculptor. He was an architect and a naturalist.

He was an architect and a naturalist as well.

(Other possible connectors: all simple and emphatic addition connectors)

1. The poinsettia is a beautiful plant, but be careful with it around animals. It is poisonous.

2. Jerry has plenty of sunscreen if you'd like to use some when we go to the beach. He has four different kinds.

3. I can't go skating because I have to work on Saturday. I need to get a new pair of skates.

4. The Aztec deity Quetazlcoatl was the god of the sun and the air. He was the god of wisdom and a teacher of the arts of peace.

5. Ladies and gentlemen of the jury: I will show you that the defendant could not possibly have committed this crime. This is an innocent man before you! I will reveal who really should be on trial today.

6. Our teacher asked us if we had ever read *El Cid*. I hadn't. I had never even heard of it.

7. Gina is very talented musically. She plays the flute with the symphony orchestra. She occasionally plays bass violin with a jazz group.

8. Potassium maintains fluid balance in body cells. It controls nerves and muscles.

9. You have an error in article usage in the third paragraph of your report. You need to correct a spelling error in that paragraph.

10. Well, I admit I ate a lot of the cookies that were in the kitchen. I probably had about a dozen.

EXERCISE 3

Make up two sentences for each of the following instructions. Use an addition connector to link ideas between sentences. An example has been given for the first one.

1. Give two reasons why you enjoy something you often do in your spare time.

▶ **EXAMPLE:** *I enjoy volunteer work with children at the hospital because I like children. Besides that, it gives me work experience for my future career in medicine.*

2. Give two reasons why you like one movie or television show you've seen better than another.

3. State two advantages of flying over driving when a person goes on a long trip.

4. State two uses for computers.

5. Give two reasons why people tell stories about themselves.

6. Give two reasons why you would want to improve your English grammar skills.

7. State two differences between English and your native language.

8. Give two reasons why someone should visit a particular city or country.

9. Give two reasons why someone should get to know you.

10. State two things that you are very good at doing.

▶ **Alternative Connectors**

CONNECTORS	EXAMPLES	MEANINGS
on the other hand *alternatively*	**(a)** I may work this summer. **On the other hand,** I may take a long vacation. **(b)** You could take the history course you eventually need this semester. **Alternatively,** you could complete your schedule with a science course.	These connectors indicate a possibility in addition to the one just mentioned. *On the other hand* and *alternatively* have similar meanings. *Alternatively* is a more formal connector. It is used mainly in written English.
✓	**(c)** Washington, D.C., might be fun to visit this summer. Other Possibility Part Changed in (c) **(d)** **On the other hand,** it might be too crowded. fun **(e)** **On the other hand,** Minneapolis might be a better city to visit in the summer. Washington, D.C. **(f)** **On the other hand,** it might be better to go there in the fall. this summer	The "other possibility" could be various parts of a previously mentioned idea. Here are some alternative statements that might follow example (c).

EXERCISE 4

Add a statement after each sentence below that would express another possibility. Use *on the other hand* or *alternatively* to signal the connection.

▶ **EXAMPLE:**   I could get a job this summer.

       On the other hand, I could take a few courses in summer school.

   1. I could stay home this weekend.

   2. You might want to get a cat for a pet.

   3. The theory of the Big Bang, explaining the origins of the universe, could be correct.

4. If you're looking for a used car to buy, you could check the classified ads in the newspaper.

5. Legalizing heroin in the United States could help decrease crime.

6. Parents who are upset with the violence that their children see every day on television could write letters to the television stations.

EXERCISE 5

Form small groups. Read each of the statements below. Then take turns forming alternative statements for each one. Each person must focus on a different part of the statement. Use *on the other hand* or *alternatively*.

▶ **EXAMPLE:**   It could be fun to get a job making pizzas this summer.

    On the other hand,

      it could get boring after awhile.
      (focus: fun)

      it might be more interesting to get work at a television studio.
      (focus: a job making pizzas)

      it would probably be more fun to eat the pizzas!
      (focus: making)

1. Hong Kong might be a good place to go for our winter vacation.

2. Advanced Composition could be a good course for me to take next quarter.

3. It might be fun to go shopping on Saturday.

4. We might want to explore this cave tonight.

5. You could call your family this weekend.

Exemplifying, Identifying, and Clarifying Connectors

EXEMPLIFYING CONNECTORS	EXAMPLES		MEANINGS
for example	**(a)**	Reactions to bee stings can be severe. **For example,** a person could experience breathing difficulty.	These connectors introduce examples of what has been mentioned.
for instance	**(b)**	Some sports involve considerable body contact. Take, **for instance,** football.	*For example* and *for instance* introduce a typical member of a group or a typical instance.
especially	**(c)**	Violence in movies seems to be increasing. Action films **especially** appear to be getting more violent.	*Especially* and *in particular* introduce an important member of a group or an important instance.
in particular	**(d)**	Learning the rules for article usage in English can be difficult. **In particular,** the use of articles with generic nouns may be confusing.	
to illustrate	**(e)**	The steps for saving your computer file are quite simple. **To illustrate,** we will save the file you have just created.	*To illustrate* and *as an example* often introduce a lengthy example such as a process or narrative.
as an example	**(f)**	Many great composers have had their share of misery. **As an example,** consider the life of Mozart.	

IDENTIFYING CONNECTORS	EXAMPLES		MEANINGS
namely	**(g)**	There is a very important issue before us; **namely,** we need to decide how to reduce the budget by one-fourth.	These connectors identify something either previously mentioned or implied. They introduce a more specific or detailed elaboration.
specifically	**(h)**	I have a question about connectors. **Specifically,** when do you use *in fact?*	

CLARIFYING CONNECTORS	EXAMPLES		MEANINGS
that is	**(i)**	The garlic should be minced; **that is,** you should chop it into very small pieces.	These connectors signal that something will be rephrased or clarified.
in other words	**(j)**	You can't go on with this hectic lifestyle. **In other words,** you need to learn to relax.	We use *that is* and *in other words* in both spoken and written English. *I mean* is less formal; we generally do not use it in formal academic English to clarify a statement.
I mean	**(k)**	I can't go to that play. **I mean,** seventy dollars is just too much for me to spend in one evening.	

EXERCISE 6

Use an exemplifying, identifying, or clarifying connector from the list below that would be appropriate for each blank. The first has been done as an example.

for example	*especially*	*to illustrate*	*that is*
for instance	*in particular*	*as an example*	*in other words*

1. Many words in English have origins in Greek myths. *Chaos,*
   _____for example_____, is a word the Greeks used to describe the un-
   ordered matter that existed before creation.

2. Some natural objects have English names that
   derive from Roman words for mythological characters. Planets, _____ , have been
   given such names. _____ , here are
   a few of them. Jupiter is named after the god of
   he sky. Neptune, in Roman mythology, was the
   god of springs and rivers. And Saturn was one of
   the gods of agriculture.

3. Some names for metals in English also derive from myths. The
   metal uranium, _____ , comes from the Latin *Uranus*
   (the god of the sky). The metal tellurium comes from the Latin
   Tellus (the goddess of the earth).

4. Sometimes we may refer to an idea as *chimerical;* _____ , it is un-realistic or fanciful. This word comes from the name for a Greek monster, the Chimeaera, which had a lion's head, a goat's body, and a dragon's tail.

5. Some English names for bodies of water also derive from Greek words. This is true _____ in the case of oceans. The name for the Arctic Ocean, _____ , comes from the Greek word for *bear: arkto.* The name for the Atlantic Ocean derives from *Atlantides,* who were sea nymphs. And the word ocean itself comes from *Oceanus,* the oldest member of the mythological race, the Titans.

6. Some governments are known as *plutocracies;* _____ , they are governments run by the wealthy. The word *plutocracy* comes from *Plutus,* the god of wealth.

EXERCISE 7

Add an identification statement after each of the following sentences to further specify information conveyed. Use *namely* or *specifically* to indicate its relationship to the sentence before it.

▶ **EXAMPLE:**   There is one thing I really like about you.

Namely, you never blame other people when something is your fault.

1. I'd like to know a few things about you.
2. I have one bad habit I wish I could break.
3. There are several things you might do to improve your financial situation.
4. There are two movies I'd like to see.
5. There are a few things about my future I often wonder about.
6. There is one thing I would like to have accomplished by this time next year.

EXERCISE 8

Following is a list of words along with their definitions. Make up one sentence using each word. Then for each, add an independent clause that explains the word. Use *in other words, that is,* or *I mean* to signal the relationship between the clauses. Use a semicolon to punctuate them.

▶ **EXAMPLE:**   intractable   difficult to manage or get to behave

Our new labrador puppy is intractable; in other words, it is hard to make him behave.

1. ichthyologist   (noun)   someone who specializes in the study of fishes
2. polychromatic   (adj.)   having many colors

3.	terriculous	(adj.)	living in the ground
4.	carnivore	(noun)	meat-eating animal
5.	digress	(verb)	to stray from the main topic in speech or writing
6.	captious	(adj.)	tending to find fault with things and to make petty criticisms
7.	xenophobic	(adj.)	having a fear or dislike of strangers or foreigners
8.	equivocate	(verb)	to avoid making a direct statement about something

FOCUS **5**

MEANING
USE

▶ Similarity Connectors

CONNECTORS	EXAMPLES	MEANING
similarly	**(a)** The lungs of vertebrates absorb oxygen from the air. **Similarly,** gills, the respiratory organs of many aquatic animals, take in oxygen from water.	These connectors signal that two or more ideas or situations are alike.
likewise	**(b)** If you study, you will probably do well on the exam. **Likewise,** if you write in a journal every day, you will probably become a better writer.	
in the same way	**(c)** Learning to play a musical instrument well requires practice. **In the same way,** learning to speak a second language fluently cannot be accomplished without practice.	

Using Similarity Connectors

EXAMPLES	EXPLANATIONS
(d) Blake likes to collect stamps. **Likewise,** this has been one of Karen's favorite hobbies for years. **(e)** NOT: Blake likes to collect stamps. **Likewise,** Karen likes to collect stamps.	Paraphrase the information after the connector. Don't just repeat the previous information word for word.
(f) Football players try to carry a football across their goal line. **Similarly,** soccer players try to kick a soccer ball into a goal.	The comparison often involves several different terms: FOOTBALL SOCCER *players* ←——→ *players* *carry* ←——→ *kick* *football* ←——→ *soccer ball*
(g) Patrice bought some new clothes when we went shopping. **Likewise,** Mira bought a few new outfits. **(h)** The spots on leopards help to camouflage them in the jungle. **Similarly,** spots on fawns help to hide them in the woods.	*Likewise* and *in the same way* often suggest greater similarity, or sameness, than *similarly* does.
(i) Dogs may get disturbed during an electrical storm. Cats may react **in the same way.** **(j)** A man in the audience started to heckle the speaker. Others behaved **similarly.**	You can use similarity connectors at the end of sentences when you are expressing the point of similarity in a verb phrase.

EXERCISE 9

The chart below gives information about myth and folklore spirits in western Europe. Imagine that you are a folklorist, and that you have been asked to write a summary of the ways in which these spirits are similar. As preparation for your summary, use the information in the chart to make at least five pairs of sentences expressing similarity. Use a similarity connector with the second sentence of each pair.

▶ **EXAMPLE:** *Pixies enjoy playing tricks on humans; elves,* **likewise,** *enjoy fooling people.*

Name of Spirit	fairy	pixie	brownie	elf
Where found	Ireland, England, Scotland	England	Scotland	Scandinavian countries
Typical residence	forests, underground	forests, under a rock	humans' houses, farms	forests
Appearance	fair, attractive, varied size	handsome, small	brown or tawny, small, wrinkled faces	varied: some fair and some dark
Visibility to humans	usually invisible; visible by use of a magic ointment	usually invisible	usually invisible	usually invisible; visible at midnight within their dancing circle
Clothing color	green, brown, yellow favorite: green	always green	brown	varied
Favorite pastime(s)	dancing at night	dancing at night; playing tricks on humans	playing tricks on humans	dancing at night; playing tricks on humans
Rulers	fairy king and queen	pixie king	none	elf-king

Contrast and Concession Connectors

CONTRAST CONNECTORS	EXAMPLES	MEANINGS
however	**(a)** In some creation myths, the sun exists before people do. In others, **however,** people create the sun.	These connectors show that two ideas contrast.
in contrast	**(b)** The characters in legends may be based on people who actually lived. **In contrast,** the characters in fables, often animals, are fictional.	
on the other hand	**(c)** The proposed new hotel complex will benefit our city. **On the other hand,** it will create serious problems with increased traffic.	
though	**(d)** This lake is not very good for fishing. It's great for swimming and water skiing, **though.**	
in fact	**(e)** Early civilizations thought *the earth was the center of the universe.* **In fact,** *the earth revolves around the sun.*	These connectors signal that the following statement is contrary to something previously stated. The contrary parts are shown in italics.
however	**(f)** Some people think that *whales are fish.* **However,** *these animals are actually mammals.*	

CONCESSION CONNECTORS	EXAMPLES	MEANINGS
even so	**(g)** New York has many urban problems. **Even so,** it is still a great city.	These connectors signal a reservation about something. The first statement is true, but the second statement is also true or needs to be considered.
however	**(h)** Most of my meal was excellent. The vegetables, **however,** were slightly overcooked.	
nevertheless	**(i)** Native Americans have often had difficulty preserving their traditions. **Nevertheless,** they have been able to pass down old stories about their culture to the new generations.	The second statement may also express surprising or unexpected information.
nonetheless	**(j)** I know mountain climbing can be dangerous. I'd like to try it **nonetheless.**	
despite (THIS)	**(k)** Chifumi has to get up at 5 A.M. to get to school on time. **Despite this,** she has never missed a class.	
in spite of (THIS)	**(l)** The day was cold and rainy. **In spite of the inclement weather,** we decided to take a hike.	
on the other hand	**(m)** Learning a new language can be fun. **On the other hand,** it can be frustrating.	

EXERCISE 10

Use the information in the chart from Exercise 9 to make up five sentence pairs expressing differences between the various European folklore spirits.

▶ **EXAMPLE:** *The favorite pastime of fairies is dancing at night. Brownies, in contrast, enjoy playing tricks.*

EXERCISE 11

The chart below gives information about people who have made remarkable achievements in the face of adversity. Use the information to make up sentence pairs linked by a concession connector.

▶ **EXAMPLE:** *Helen Keller was deaf and blind. In spite of these difficulties, she became an eloquent communicator.*

Person	Difficulty	Achievement
Helen Keller	was deaf and blind	became an eloquent communicator
Martin Luther King, Jr.	encountered racial prejudice	preached nonviolence toward adversaries
Beethoven	became deaf	continued to write symphonies
Charles Dickens	grew up in poverty	became a famous novelist
Stephen Hawking	is confined to a wheelchair by Lou Gehrig's disease	became an internationally acclaimed physicist
Jim Abbott	had only one arm	played professional baseball as a pitcher

EXERCISE 12

As you have seen in this unit, some sentence connectors may signal more than one meaning relationship. These include *on the other hand* (alternative, contrast, concession), *in fact* (intensifying addition, contrast), and *however* (contrast, concession). Review these connector meanings in Focus 2, Focus 3, and Focus 6. Then write down which relationship each signals in the sentences below.

▶ **EXAMPLE:**   You could drive to Denver if you have time. On the other hand, you could consider flying there.

Relationship: *alternative*

1. The mechanic told me the fuel pump needed to be replaced. In fact, the fuel pump was fine.
   Relationship:

2. Your essay is very good. It could use some more variety in vocabulary, however.
   Relationship:

3. I might take biology next quarter. On the other hand, I may take geology.
   Relationship:

4. In the distance, the next city looked fairly close. However, as it turned out, it wasn't very close at all.
   Relationship:

5. That television set is expensive. In fact, it costs triple what my old one cost.
   Relationship:

6. The weather forecast predicted heavy rain all weekend. On Saturday, however, there was not a cloud to be seen anywhere.
   Relationship:

7. This soup has a good flavor. On the other hand, it could use a little salt.
   Relationship:

8. Nylon is a very light material. It is, however, very strong.
   Relationship:

9. I'm having a hard time following these directions. In fact, it seems impossible to figure them out.
   Relationship:

Connectors Expressing Effects/Results and Purposes

EFFECT/RESULT CONNECTORS	EXAMPLES	MEANINGS
accordingly	**(a)** Rain is an important theme in many African religions. **Accordingly,** their rituals often focus on rain-making and rain-stopping.	These connectors signal that a statement is an effect or result of something. They differ mainly in their degrees of formality. We use *as a result (of)*, *because of*, and *due to* in both spoken and written English. We use *therefore, consequently, thus,* and *hence* more in written English. *Thus* and *hence* are the most formal connectors.
as a result	**(b)** English spelling rules can be confusing. **As a result,** some have proposed simplified spelling.	
as a result of **(THIS)**	**(c)** Some people suffer from acrophobia. **As a result of this phobia,** they avoid heights.	
because of **(THIS)**	**(d)** Canvas is strong material. **Because of its strength,** it is used for tents.	
due to (THIS)	**(e)** A megaphone is a hollow cone. **Due to its shape,** it can amplify sound.	To express cause-effect or reason-result relationships in conversation, speakers tend to use subordinating conjunctions like *because* and *since* as in (**j**), more than sentence connectors.
consequently	**(f)** John couldn't get to the library. **Consequently,** he wasn't able to finish his research.	
therefore	**(g)** The plot of this book is not very original. The ending, **therefore,** is easy to predict.	
thus	**(h)** Spring water is filtered through permeable rocks. **Thus,** it is usually fairly clean.	
hence	**(i)** Fluorocarbons have stable carbon-fluorine bonds; **hence,** they are inert and heat resistant.	
	(j) The ending of this book is very easy to predict **because** the plot isn't very original.	

PURPOSE CONNECTORS	EXAMPLES	MEANINGS
in order to (DO THIS)	**(k)** We'll test your cholesterol to-morrow. **In order to check it,** we must ask you not to eat any-thing for four hours.	Purpose connectors also express causal relation-ships.
with this in mind	**(l)** Catherine needed to go to the market after work. **With this in mind,** she took her grocery list with her.	
for this purpose	**(m)** The candidate for mayor needed to increase her campaign funds. **For this purpose,** her manager scheduled several fund-raising dinners.	Of the connectors shown here, *for this purpose* is the most formal.

EXERCISE 13

The two charts below give information about various characters from myths and legends. Use the information from Chart A to make sentence pairs ex-pressing reason-result relationships. Use Chart B to make sentence pairs ex-pressing purpose relationships. For all sentence pairs, use an appropriate sentence connector.

▶ **EXAMPLES:** *The Norse Gods believed nothing could harm Balder, the sun god. Consequently, they thought it fun to hurl weapons at him.*

Robin Hood wanted to help the poor. For this purpose, he robbed the rich.

Con

Chart A

Character(s)	Event/Situation	Result
1. Norse gods	believed nothing could harm Balder, the sun god	thought it fun to hurl weapons at him
2. Con, relative of Pachacamac, Incan god of fertility	was defeated in battle by Pachacamac	left Peru and took the rain with him
3. Gonggong, Chinese god of the waters	had his army destroyed by Zhurong, god of fire	fled in disgrace to the west and smashed into a mountain pillar holding up the sky
4. Paris, Trojan hero	wanted the beautiful Helen of Troy for his wife	gave the goddess Aphrodite a golden apple to win her favor

Chart B

Character(s)	Action/Event	Purpose
1. Robin Hood	robbed the rich	help the poor
2. Haokah, Sioux god of thunder	used the wind as a drumstick	create thunder
3. The Pied Piper of Hamlin	played his musical pipe so the rats would follow him out of town	rid Hamlin Town of rats
4. Momotaro	left his Japanese village and made the dangerous journey to Oni Island	conquer the horrible Oni ogres and bring back the priceless treasures they had stolen

Punctuation of Sentence Connectors

Many sentence connectors can be used at the beginning, the middle, or the end of a sentence or independent clause. The punctuation surrounding a sentence connector depends on where it appears in a sentence.

EXAMPLES	EXPLANATIONS
(a) Apollo is the god of the sun in Greek mythology. **Similarly,** Balder is the sun god in Norse myths.	If the connector begins a sentence, use a period before it (ending the previous sentence) and a comma after it.
(b) Balder was much loved by the other gods; **however,** he was accidentally killed with a mistletoe dart by one of them.	If the connector begins an independent clause after another independent clause in the same sentence, use a semicolon before it and a comma after it.
(c) Many mythological characters have more than one name. Some, **in fact,** have several name variations.	If the connector is in the middle of a sentence or an independent clause, we usually separate it from the rest of the clause with commas.
(d) Aphrodite is the Greek goddess of love. She is **also** the goddess of beauty.	We do not usually use commas with *also* when it is in the middle of a sentence.
(e) Balder died from his dart wound. His wife Nanna died **as well,** having suffered a broken heart.	We do not use commas before *as well* when it follows a verb.
(f) The gods were grief-stricken when Balder died. The mortals reacted **in the same way.**	If the connector comes at the end of the sentence, punctuation is usually not necessary except for two connectors: *however* and *though*.
(g) Tu, known in Polynesian myths as the angry god, was quite belligerent. He could sometimes be very kind, **however.**	

EXERCISE 14

As a review of the connectors in this unit, go back to Exercise 1. Rewrite the second sentence in each numbered pair, adding an appropriate sentence connector and punctuation where needed.

Use Your English

ACTIVITY 1: LISTENING/ WRITING

There are a number of Greek myths that explain how certain flowers came to be. Like many myths, different versions exist of these stories; they usually have common elements but vary in some details of the story. You will hear two versions of the Greek myth of Echo and Narcissus, which tells how the Narcissus flower came to be. Listen once to both versions to get a general idea of how they are similar and how they differ. Listen a second time and take notes on each version. When you have finished, briefly collaborate with two or three classmates to fill in any details you might have missed. From your notes, write a description of the similarities and differences of the two versions. Use a variety of contrast and similarity sentence connectors.

ACTIVITY 2: WRITING

In groups, create a list of ten facts or opinions on different topics. Below each fact, leave several spaces. Then pass the list to another group. The members of that group have to add another fact to each statement, using an addition sentence connector to signal the relationship. When they are finished, they should pass the list to another group who will do the same thing until several groups have added sentences to each list.

▶ **EXAMPLES:**   Group 1: *Tomatoes are very good for you.*
Group 2: *In fact, they are a good source of vitamins.*
Group 3: *In addition, they taste good.*
Group 4: *Furthermore, you can use them in a lot of different ways, such as in making sauces or salads.*
Group 1: *San Francisco is a beautiful city.*
Group 2: *It also has great restaurants.*
Group 3: *It's a book lover's city as well.*
Group 4: *What's more, you can go sailing in the bay.*

ACTIVITY 3: WRITING/RESEARCH

STEP 1 Make a list of five words that you think others in the class might not be very familiar with. Use a dictionary if necessary. Try to find words that could be useful additions to someone's vocabulary.

STEP 2 Exchange lists with one of your classmates. Each of you should look up the words you have been given in the dictionary to see its range of meanings. Then write one sentence using the word in a context and add a statement defining the word, using one of the clarification sentence connectors (*that is* or *in other words*) as was done in Exercise 8. If you wish, you can connect the sentences with a semi-colon to show their close relationship.

▶ **EXAMPLE:** *Some folktales are moralistic; in other words, these stories instruct people on how to behave.*

STEP 3 Give your sentences to your partner; check each other's sentences for correctness.

ACTIVITY 4: WRITING

"Turning point" is a term we sometimes use to describe an event that has changed or influenced someone in an important way. Consider three turning points in your life. Write an essay in which you explain how each turning point has changed your life. Use reason-result sentence connectors in your explanations.

▶ **EXAMPLE:** *One of the major turning points in my life was when my family left Laos for the United States. Because of this, we had to start a new life and adjust to an entirely different culture. . . .*

ACTIVITY 5: SPEAKING/ LISTENING/WRITING

STEP 1 Pair up with another classmate. Your task is to find out six things that you have in common and six things that are different about you. The similarities and differences should not be things that are apparent (for example, not similarities or differences in physical appearance, the similarity of both being in the same class). Consider topics such as goals, hobbies, travels, language learning, families, and various likes and dislikes (foods, sports, courses, books, movies, etc.).

STEP 2 As you discover the similarities and differences, make a list of them. Then, each of you should write six sentence pairs expressing your discoveries, using similarity and contrast connectors. Divide the task equally so that each of you states three similarities and three differences. Share some of your findings with your classmates.

▶ **EXAMPLES:** *Sven started learning English when he was twelve.* **Similarly,** *I first started taking English courses when I was thirteen.*

Wenxia loves to read science fiction. **In contrast,** *I read mostly nonfiction books.*

I love math. Tina, **on the other hand,** *hopes she never has to take another math course in her life.*

ACTIVITY 6: RESEARCH/WRITING

Creation myths from around the world often have similarities; for example, in many myths, the earth and sky are formed by dividing an egg. Find two more creation myths from different cultures. Write an essay in which you summarize each myth and describe similarities and differences between the two myths.

MODAL PERFECT VERBS

UNIT GOALS:

- To use the correct forms of modal perfect verbs
- To choose correct modals to express judgments, obligations, and expectations
- To choose correct modals to make deductions and guesses
- To choose correct modals to express results of past conditions and to make predictions

▶ **OPENING TASK**
Mr. Retrospect's Hindsight and Advice

Mr. Retrospect is an advice columnist who specializes in telling people what they should have done after the fact.

STEP 1 Read the following letter sent to Mr. Retrospect and his reply.

Dear Mr. Retrospect:

A few weeks ago I asked a woman out to dinner. She seemed pleased with the invitation, but when my mother and I arrived at her house to pick her up she looked dismayed and said that she suddenly felt ill and couldn't go with us. She didn't look sick to me. She must have changed her mind. What could the reason have been? I must say, I'm a rather handsome guy, so I don't think it was my appearance.

Henry

Dear Henry:

From what you have described, I'd guess that this woman must have had a different idea of your plans for the evening. Frankly, it's rather un-usual for mothers to accompany their sons on dates. You could have taken your mother out to dinner on another night.

Mr. Retrospect

STEP 2 Write a response to one of the following letters.

Dear Mr. Retrospect:

On a recent trip, I visited a relative I don't know very well, one of my great aunts. She lives in a very rural area; the nearest large city is three hundred miles away. I'm her only nephew, so she was really looking forward to my visit. Everything was fine until we sat down to eat. When I asked her what was in the stew she had just served, she announced, "Possum and squirrel," I was so shocked that I refused to eat anything and had to leave the table. I'm afraid that I hurt my great aunt's feelings even though later I said I was sorry. Now I am wondering what I could have said to be more polite.

Wild animal lover (well, squirrels anyway)

Dear Mr. Retrospect:

My hairdresser recently talked me into a new hairstyle that makes me look like a porcupine. I hated it! Unfortunately, he thought it was the perfect style for me. After he finished styling my hair he proclaimed "It's you!" I didn't know what to say. How do you think I should have responded?

Sally

STEP 3 In small groups, share the response you wrote.

► **R**eview of Modal Perfect Verbs

Although modal perfect verbs have a number of meanings, the forms are fairly simple.

EXAMPLES	EXPLANATIONS
(a) You **should have seen** that film. **(b)** They **must have come** from miles away.	**Active voice:** modal + *have* + past participle
(c) That concerto **should have been played** slowly. **(d)** His house **must have been built** during the last century.	**Passive voice:** modal + *have* + *been* + past participle
(e) I **must have been dreaming!** **(f)** We **could have been playing** tennis instead of having to clean up after the rainstorm.	**Progressive:** modal + *have* + *been* + present (*-ing*) participle
(g) The game **might** not **have ended** yet. **(h)** You **may** not **have read** that carefully enough.	**Negative:** In negative forms, *not* comes after the modal.

Summary of Modal Perfect Forms

	subject + modal (*not*) + *have*	*been*	past participle	present participle
ACTIVE		—	gone.	
PASSIVE	He could (not) have +	been	gone.	
PROGRESSIVE		been	—	going.

NOTE: There is also a passive progressive form for perfect modals: modal + *have* + *been* + *being* + past participle: *The old school building* **must have been being demolished** *the week that we were gone.* This verb form, however, is not very common in either spoken or written English.

EXERCISE 1

Complete each blank with a modal perfect verb using the cues in parentheses. The first one has been done as an example.

(1) My friends and I discussed the letters Mr. Retrospect received and the responses we would make to them. (2) Josef thought that Henry (must/be born) __must have been born__ on another planet. (3) Inna agreed and added that his mother (not/could/know) _____ much about dating etiquette either. (4) Takiko thought Henry's date (might/call) _____ him later and (tell) _____ him what the problem was. (5) For a response to his letter, we (would/inform) _____ Henry that his date (may/be) _____ a bit surprised to find out that Mom was chaperoning and that next time Mom should stay home. (6) As for the Wild Animal Lover's dining experience, we all agreed that we (not/could/eat) _____ that dinner either, but we (not/might/want) _____ to hurt the great-aunt's feelings. (7) I suggested that he (might/say) _____ he was allergic to squirrel or possum. (8) That excuse (not/would/stray + -ing) _____ too far from the truth since he probably (would/get) _____ sick from eating it. (9) Finally, concerning the last letter, we disagreed about how Sally (should/respond) _____ to her hairdresser. (10) Rosa thought Sally (could/ask) _____ the hairdresser to restyle her hair. (11) Marty said she (might/suggest) _____ to him that her spiked hair could hurt someone. (12) We all concurred that Sally (should/find out) _____ what her hairdresser planned to do before he styled her hair. (13) We also agreed that the hairdresser (must/think + -ing) _____ only of his own preferences at the time and that Sally should look for a new stylist.

USE

Expressing Judgments about Past Situations: *Should Have, Could Have, Might Have*

EXAMPLES	EXPLANATIONS
(a) You **should have gone** to bed earlier. (But you didn't.)	The modal forms *should have* (and negative *should not have*), *could have*, and *might have* express judgments about something that did not happen.
(b) They **shouldn't have spent** so much money. (But they did.)	
(c) The teacher **could have warned** us that we would have to know all the math formulas for the test. (But she didn't.)	
(d) Robert **might have written** us that he was coming. (But he didn't.)	
(e) You **shouldn't have taken** the day off from work. It created a burden for everyone else.	These modals can express a variety of attitudes: • *Should have* and *should not have* with second- or third-person subjects often imply criticism.
(f) Carmelita **should have treated** her sister better. It created a burden for everybody else.	
(g) I **shouldn't have taken** the day off from work. Now I'm even more behind.	• With *I* or *we* as the subject, *should have* and *should not have* may express regret.
(h) We s**hould have treated** our sister better. Now she won't even talk to us, and it's all our fault.	
(i) You **could** } **have called** us when **might** you were in town. We didn't even know you were here.	• *Should have, could have,* and *might have* can all express irritation, anger, or reproach. In certain contexts, they may express the speaker's judgment that someone has shown a lack of thoughtfulness or courtesy.
(j) You **might have asked** me if I wanted some dessert before you told the waiter to bring the bill.	
(k) Ian **could have offered** to contribute to the cab fare. He certainly had the money to do so.	• *Could have* also expresses capability more directly than *should have* and *might have* do.

EXERCISE 2

Make a statement expressing a judgment about each of the following situations. Use *should have, could have,* or *might have* + verb in your response. Examples are given for the first one.

▶ **EXAMPLES:** A friend failed a test yesterday.

> She **could have spent** more time studying.
> She **might have asked** her teacher for help before the test.

1. One of your classmates returned a paperback book to you with the cover torn. When you gave it to him, the book was new.
2. A manufacturing company was charged with pouring chemicals into the river.
3. You were stopped by the police while driving your car. Your license plates had expired.
4. A neighbor locked herself out of her apartment and didn't know what to do. So she just sat down on the front steps and waited for someone to notice her.
5. A friend wanted to get a pet but her roommates didn't like cats or dogs. So she moved out of the house she shared with them.

EXERCISE 3

The following story describes the unfortunate experiences of the Park family—Seung, Eun Joo, and their daughter Anna—at a hotel where they recently spent a vacation. For each situation, state what you think the hotel staff or the Parks should have, could have, or might have done.

▶ **EXAMPLES:** When the Parks arrived at the hotel, the front desk clerk was talking on the phone to her boyfriend and ignored them.

> *The clerk could have at least acknowledged their presence.*
> *The Parks should have looked for another hotel!*

1. When the clerk got off the phone, she told the Parks that their rooms had been given to someone else. However, other rooms would be available in four hours.
2. The Parks decided to have lunch in the hotel restaurant. Their waiter, who had a bad cold, kept coughing on their table as he took their orders.
3. When the food arrived, Eun Joo's soup was so salty she could feel her blood pressure rising by the second. Seung's pork chop was about as edible as a leather glove. Anna's spaghetti looked like last week's leftovers and it tasted worse.
4. When the Parks were finally able to check into their rooms, the bellhop forgot one of their bags in the lobby. Instead of getting it, he rushed off, explaining that he had to catch a train. Mr. Park ended up bringing the bag up by himself, which made him quite angry.

Expressing Obligations and Expectations: *Be Supposed to Have, Be to Have*

Be supposed to have and *be to have* are perfect forms of phrasal modal verbs. Their meanings depend somewhat on the tense of the *be* verb.

EXAMPLES	EXPLANATIONS
(a) We **were supposed to have taken** our exam on Friday, but our teacher was sick.	We use the past tense of *be supposed to have* + past participle to refer to something that was planned or intended but that did not happen.
(b) We **are supposed to have made up** the exam by next week.	We use a present tense form of *be supposed to have* when we expect something to be completed in the future.
(c) I **was to have graduated** in June, but I need to take two more courses for my degree. **(d)** Governor Carroll **is to have submitted** his resignation by next Friday.	*Be to have* expresses similar meanings as *be supposed to have. Be to have* is more common in formal English. Like *be supposed to have, be to have* refers to a past event that did not occur when *be* is past tense. It refers to a future expectation when *be* is present tense.

EXERCISE 4

Complete the sentences to make statements about yourself.

▶ **EXAMPLE:** I was supposed to have <u>transferred to another college</u> this year, but <u>I needed more financial aid than I was offered</u> .

1. I was supposed to have _____ this year, but _____ .
2. In my _____ class, I was supposed to have _____ by (put in a day or date here) _____ , but _____ .
3. I was to have _____ last (insert time phrase: weekend/ month, etc.) _____ , but _____ .

EXERCISE 5

Interview a classmate to find out three things that she or he was supposed to have done during the last few months but didn't do. Report at least one of them to the class.

▶ **EXAMPLE:** *Fan was supposed to have gone to the mountains last weekend but her car broke down before she even got out of town.*

Inferring/Making Deductions from Past Evidence: *Must (Not) Have, Can't Have, Should (Not) Have, Would (Not) Have*

Modal perfect verbs can express two kinds of past inference: We may infer that something (1) almost certainly did or did not happen or (2) probably did or did not happen.

EXAMPLES	EXPLANATIONS
(a) Myla: Our chemistry experiment failed. We **must have followed** the procedures incorrectly. (We **must not have done** it the right way.)	**Inferring Near Certainty** We use *must have* when we infer that something almost certainly happened.
(b) Alberto: We **can't have performed** the procedures incorrectly! I read every step carefully before the experiment and checked each one afterwards, too.	*Can't have* is the opposite of *must have*. We use it to express a belief that something is almost impossible or unbelievable. These examples express strong inferences, not facts. Since both (a) and (b) refer to the same event, one of them must be wrong.
(c) If the test tubes aren't here, Brian **must have taken** them.	Unlike *must have, should have* does not express an inference that something almost certainly happened.
(d) **NOT:** If the test tubes aren't here, Brian **should have taken** them.	
(e) Let's check on our second experiment. The powder **should have dissolved** by now.	**Inferring Probability** We use *should have* to express an expectation about a past event. We may infer that something happened, but we don't know for sure.
(f) We **should have gotten** a chemical reaction when we heated the solution, but nothing happened. I wonder what went wrong.	Sometimes we use *should have* to express an expectation about a past event that we know did not occur.
(g) If our observations are correct, the burglary **would have occurred** shortly after midnight.	*Would have* may also express an inference that something probably happened. We use it to speculate about what happened if we accept a certain theory or if we assume certain conditions. Sometimes the condition is stated in an *if*-clause as in (g).
(h) About one hundred seconds after the big bang, the temperatures **would have fallen** to one thousand million degrees.	The condition may be implied rather than directly stated. In (h), the implied condition is: if we accept the big bang theory as a model of how the universe began. The writer uses *would have fallen* instead of *fell* because the big bang theory is hypothetical.

EXERCISE 6

According to one model of how the universe began, between ten and twenty thousand million years ago the density of the universe and the curvature of space-time became infinite; this point in space-time was termed the "big bang." The following passage describes what some physicists believe probably happened after the big bang. Underline or write down the modal perfect verbs that express probability. Why does the author use these forms instead of simple past tense?

(1) Within only a few hours of the big bang, the production of helium and other elements would have stopped. (2) And after that, for the next million years or so, the universe would have just continued expanding, without anything much happening. (3) Eventually, once the temperature had dropped to a few thousand degrees, and electrons and nuclei no longer had enough energy to overcome the electromagnetic attraction between them, they would have started combining to form atoms. (4) The universe as a whole would have continued expanding and cooling, but in regions that were slightly denser than average, the expansion would have been slowed down by the extra gravitational attraction. (5) This would eventually stop expansion in some regions and cause them to start to recollapse.

From: Stephen Hawking, *A Brief History of Time: From the Big Bang to Black Holes*, Bantam, 1990.

EXERCISE 7

The following sentences express some hypothetical statements about how native languages are learned. Fill in the blanks, using *must have, can't have,* or *should have* and the correct form of the verb in parentheses.

▶ **EXAMPLE:**   *Researchers believe children <u>can't have</u> learned their first languages just by memorizing words.*

1. Since the number of possible sentences in any language is infinite, we (learn) _____ our native languages by simply storing all the sentences we heard in a "mental dictionary."

2. Children (develop) _____ their ability to speak their native languages by learning rules from adults because adults are not conscious of all grammar, pronunciation, and meaning rules either.

3. A child (acquire) _____ his or her native language by the age of five; if not, we suspect that something is physically or psychologically wrong.

4. When a native English-speaking child says words like *ringed* and *doed*, this shows that she or he (apply) _____ a familiar rule for the past tense.

5. Similarly, if a child says words like tooths and childs, we speculate that she or he (overgeneralize) _____ the rule for regular plurals.

▶ **Expressing Guesses about Past Situations:** *May Have, Might Have, Could Have, Can Have*

We use certain modal perfects to make statements about the past when the speaker is not sure what happened.

EXAMPLES	EXPLANATIONS
(a) The movie **may have** already **started**. There are only a few people in the lobby. **(b)** I **might have gotten** an A on the test. I think I knew most of the answers.	*May have* and *might have* indicate that the speaker doesn't know if an event has occurred but has reason to believe that it has.
(c) I **may have met** him a long time ago. Both his name and face are very familiar. **(d)** I **might have met** him a long time ago, but I doubt it. He doesn't look at all familiar.	From the speaker's viewpoint, *might have* sometimes expresses less possibility of a past event having occurred than *may have* does.
(e) I don't think insects killed our strawberry plants. We **could have used** the wrong kind of soil. Or maybe we didn't fertilize them enough.	*Could have* often expresses one possible explanation among others. The speaker may imply that other explanations are possible.
(f) **Might** Carol **have been** the one who told you that? **(g)** **Could** too much water **have killed** the plants? **(h)** **Can** that **have been** Tomás on the phone? I didn't expect him to call back so soon.	*Might have, could have, can have* (but not *may have*) are also used in questions. *Might have* and *could have* in questions express guesses about a past event. We use *can have* only in questions. Usually a form of *be* is the main verb. The first sentence of (h) can be paraphrased: *Is it possible that Tomás was on the phone?*

EXERCISE 8

Each numbered group of statements below expresses certainty about the cause of a situation. For each, give an alternate explanation, using a perfective modal that expresses possibility. Can you think of any others?

▶ **EXAMPLE:** Look! The trunk of my car is open! Someone must have broken into it!

Alternate explanation: *You may have forgotten to shut it hard and it just popped open.*

1. Rebecca made a lot of mistakes on her economics assignment. She must not have studied the material very carefully.

2. Our English teacher didn't give us back our papers today. She must have been watching TV last night instead of reading them.

3. We invited Nora and Jack to our party but they didn't come. They must have found something better to do.

4. Carlos usually gets off of work at five and is home by six. It's now eight and he's still not home. He can't have left work at five.

5. Christopher Columbus went looking for India and ended up in North America. He must have had a poor sense of direction.

EXERCISE 9

To review the uses of perfect modals so far, return to the letters at the beginning of this chapter. Which of the letters in the Opening Task on pages 226 and 227 has a modal expressing advisability? Which has an inference modal? Which one includes a modal expressing possibility? Identify the perfective modals the letter writers used. Did you use these same modals in your answers? If you did, share some of your answers with the class. If not, give a one sentence answer to each now using these modals in perfective forms.

FOCUS **6**

▶ **Expressing Results of Unreal Conditions:** *Would Have, Could Have, Might Have*

EXAMPLES		EXPLANATIONS
(a)	**Unreal Condition** If Jung had arrived before noon, **Hypothetical Result** he **would have seen** us.	*Would have, could have,* and *might have* express hypothetical results of conditions that did not happen (unreal conditions).
(b)	**Actual Condition** Jung arrived after noon, **Actual Result** so he missed seeing us.	
(c)	If I had been at that intersection ten minutes earlier, I **would have seen** the accident.	The following modals express different degrees of probability of the results: • high probability
(d)	If the car had stopped for the light, the accident **could have been avoided.**	• capable of happening
(e)	If Dorothea had been wearing her seat belt, she **might have escaped** injury.	• a chance of happening

We also use these modals in statements that only imply the condition rather than state it directly. These statements may express a missed opportunity or a rejection of one option for another.

EXAMPLES	IMPLIED UNREAL CONDITION	IMPLIED FACT
(f) Tim **would have been** a great father.	if he had been a father.	He is not a father.
(g) I **could have gone** to medical school.	if I had wanted to go to medical school	I did not go to medical school.
(h) Hannah **might have made** the debate team.	if she had tried out for the debate team	She did not try out for the debate team.

EXERCISE 10

For each sentence, give two result modals (would have, could have, or might have) that would be appropriate, using the verb in parentheses as the main verb. For each, explain the difference in meaning and/or use between the two modals you choose.

▶ **EXAMPLES:** If the weather had been nicer, they (stay) _____ longer at the beach.
(1) *would have stayed*
(*They definitely wouldn't have left so early; they had intended to be there longer.*)
(2) *could have stayed*
(*It would have been possible to stay longer; this form might be used if cold or rainy weather forced them to leave.*)

1. If Sam had been prepared for the interview, he (get) _____ the job.

2. If you had let me know you needed transportation, I (drive) _____ you to your appointment.

3. If we had been more careful about our environment, we (prevent) _____ damage to the ozone layer.

4. The chairperson (call off) _____ the meeting if she had known so many committee members would not be here today.

EXERCISE 11

Make up three hypothetical results to follow each condition. Use *would have, could have,* and *might have*. Explain your choices of modal based on the degree of probability of each result.

▶ **EXAMPLE:** If I had lived in the nineteenth century, *I would have owned a horse instead of a car. I could have learned how to make ice cream instead of buying it from the supermarket. I might have wanted to be a farmer instead of going into business.*

Explanation: *It is quite likely that I would have owned a horse rather than a car. It is somewhat probable that I would have learned to make ice cream. It's possible, but not very likely, that I would have wanted to be a farmer.*

1. If I could have picked any city to grow up in,

2. If I had been the ruler of my country during the last decade,

3. If I could have been present at one historical event before I was born,

4. If I had been born in another country,

5. If I had been able to solve one world problem of this past century,

EXERCISE 12

What might be an implied condition for each of the following hypothetical statements? Write down a few of your answers for each sentence.

▶ **EXAMPLE:**   I could have won the race.
Possible implied conditions:
If I had just run a little faster at the beginning . . .
If I had trained harder . . .

1. Rob could have been a fluent Spanish speaker.
2. Xavier might have been the class valedictorian.
3. You could have come with us to the planetarium.
4. Kenneth Chen would have been the best candidate for that office.
5. I might have considered being a (*state a career or profession here*).

EXERCISE 13

Seven of the modal perfect verbs in the sentences that follow express unreal conditions. The others do not. Write down the modals expressing unreal conditionals. Then write which meaning each of these modals has: (a) expectation or obligation, (b) result of a stated condition, or (c) result of an implied condition. (See the summary in Focus 8, p. 241.)

1. This essay you wrote is rather brief. You could have developed your ideas more.
2. Would you see if the mail is here? It should have come by now.
3. Anita should have gone to law school. She would have been a good lawyer.
4. Seth could have turned in your assignment for you yesterday if you had let him know you wouldn't be able to attend class.
5. The conference was supposed to have started on Friday, but it was postponed until next month.
6. Elena might have asked me before she took my dictionary. I needed it to write my English paper.
7. I could have told you that the swimming pool would be closed today. You should have asked me before you drove over there.
8. Scientists believe that life on earth could have begun more than 3.4 billion years ago.
9. If that lecture had gone on any longer, I would have fallen asleep.
10. We could have gone out of town for our vacation, but we decided to stay home and remodel the kitchen instead.

▶ **Predicting the Completion of a Future Event:** *Will Have, Shall Have*

Will have and *shall have* are future perfect modal forms. They express the completion of a future event before another future time.

EXAMPLES	EXPLANATIONS
(a) By the time you get this postcard, I **will have left** Portugal.	Possible meaning: You will get this postcard in a week or so. I'm leaving Portugal tomorrow.
(b) At the end of this week, **I'll have been** in Athens for four months.	In spoken English, *will* is often contracted.
(c) By this date next year, we **shall have reduced** our air pollution by thirty percent.	*Shall have* has the same meaning as *will have*. American English speakers rarely use this form in everyday English. Some types of formal English, such as speeches or legal documents, use *shall have*.

EXERCISE 14

Use the information in the first and second columns of the chart below to express what will have most likely happened by the time period in the third column. You may want to add an *if* or *unless* clause to your sentence if you think it is needed. The first has been done as an example.

▶ **EXAMPLE:** *By July, the Changs' store **will have been** open for seven months.*

Time Period 1	Event of Time Period 1	Time Period 2
1. December	the Changs will open their computer software store	July
2. 2000	Larry will complete all the requirements for his college degree	2001
3. May 1995	Patty Schwartz and Roger Peterson got married	May 2045
4. July	Brina will visit Alaska, the only U.S. state that she's never been to before	August
5. September 1	Winnie has vowed to learn ten new words every day	October 1
6. 1964	laser first used for eye surgery	2014

▶ **S**ummary of Modal Perfect Verbs

EXAMPLES	MODAL PERFECT VERBS	IMPLIED FACT	MEANING/ USE
(a) You **should have** told me.	*should have* *could have* *might have*	You didn't tell me.	Judgment of past situation
(b) We **were supposed to have left** before Thursday.	*be supposed to have* *be to have*	We didn't leave.	Expectation, obligation
(c) Our professor **must have cancelled** class today.	*must have* *can't have*	—	Inferring near certainty about past situations
(d) The film I dropped off **should have been developed** yesterday.	*should have* *would have*	—	Inferring probability about past situations
(e) She **may have missed** the bus. I don't see her anywhere.	*may have* *might have* *could have* *can have*	—	Expressing guesses about past situations
(f) He **would have written** if he had known you wanted him to.	*would have* *could have* *might have*	He didn't write.	Result of stated unreal condition
(g) You **could have stayed** with us.	*would have* *could have* *might have*	You didn't stay with us.	Result of implied real condition
(h) By next month, they **will have finished** the first stage of the project.	*will have* *shall have*	—	Predicting completion of a future event.

Use Your English

You will hear two telephone conversations. The first is between friends; the second is a business conversation. Each conversation elicits some type of advice or judgment from one of the speakers.

STEP 1 Listen to the two conversations once to get the meaning.

STEP 2 You will hear each conversation a second time. At the end of each one, take the role of the person who offers advice or makes a judgment. Provide an appropriate response to the person asking for your advice or opinion. Use a perfect modal verb. Write down your responses; then compare them with those of some of your classmates.

ACTIVITY 2: WRITING

Write three brief scenarios that describe thoughtless, rude, or somehow inappropriate behavior. Exchange scenarios with a classmate and write at least one judgment about each of the situations your classmate has written, using *could have*, *might have*, or *should have*. Use a variety of modals in responding. Afterwards, if time permits, share a few of your situations and responses with the class.

▶ **EXAMPLE:** *You were riding a subway train to school. You were standing up because it was very crowded, and suddenly the train stopped. A woman next to you spilled her diet soda all over your new jacket.*

Judgments:
She shouldn't have been drinking a soda on the train.
She could at least have offered to pay for dry cleaning the jacket.

ACTIVITY 3: WRITING

Write five sentences stating things that you would (could, might) have done or not done, or situations that would (could, might) have happened in the past if circumstances had been different. Choose one of your sentences to explain in more detail. Write one or two paragraphs based on the sentence you selected.

▶ **EXAMPLE:** *If my family had not moved to the United States, I might not have learned English.*
If my parents had not helped me so much, I couldn't have gone to college.

ACTIVITY 4: READING/SPEAKING

Find an article in a book, newspaper, or magazine that describes an unsolved or unexplained situation: a crime, an unusual occurrence, strange weather patterns, etc. Have a class discussion in which students take turns summarizing the unexplained events to the rest of the class and classmates offer probable or possible explanations using *must have, can't have, may have, might have,* and *could have.*

ACTIVITY 5: RESEARCH/WRITING/SPEAKING

Be an amateur detective! The next time you are in a supermarket, observe the items that the person checking out in front of you has in his or her cart or basket. (This is one time when you might want to get behind someone who has a lot of groceries!) Try to note as many items as you can, but don't let the person know that you are doing it. Afterwards, in a classroom oral presentation, briefly describe the person and then state deductions and guesses about him or her based on the items, using perfective modals expressing inference and possibility.

▶ **EXAMPLE:** *He had a case of soda and lots of chips and dip in his cart; he might have been getting ready for a Super Bowl party.*

ACTIVITY 6: WRITING

Imagine what the person in this photograph was like. What do you think his life might have been like? Write a paragraph describing your impressions. Include deductions and guesses using perfect modal verbs.

Discourse Organizers

UNIT GOALS:

- To know how discourse organizers help listeners and readers understand information
- To use appropriate connectors to introduce, organize, and summarize topics
- To use *there + be* appropriately to introduce topics that are classified
- To use rhetorical questions to introduce and change topics and to focus on main points

▶ O P E N I N G T A S K
Analyzing Issues

What global, national, or local issues interest you most?

STEP 1   With a partner, choose one of the following topics. Each of you will be writing a paragraph about some aspect of the topic.

- pollution
- the problems of the homeless
- teenage pregnancy
- AIDS awareness
- the right to end one's own life if terminally ill
- censorship on the Internet
- crime prevention
- immigration policies
- drug abuse

- safety from terrorism on airplanes
- the English-only movement in the United States
- a social or political problem in the area where you live
- something that needs to be changed at your school or campus (course requirements, needed facilities, etc.)

STEP 2   With your partner, explore the topic by writing five questions about it. Here is an example for the topic of overpopulation:

1. Is overpopulation becoming a more serious problem?
2. How should the problem of overpopulation be dealt with in developing countries?
3. Does anyone have the right to tell others how many children they should have?
4. What are the religious, cultural, and individual factors we need to consider in addressing the population problem?
5. Can we ever solve the problem of overpopulation?

STEP 3   After you and your partner have written the questions, select one question for the issue you chose and write a paragraph answering the question to the best of your knowledge.

STEP 4   When you have finished, exchange paragraphs. Each of you should try to guess the question the other has answered. Save the questions and the paragraphs you wrote for exercises later in this unit.

▶ **O**verview of Discourse Organizers

This unit presents structures that speakers and writers use to signal or emphasize the organization of discourse. These structures help the listener or reader follow the discourse, focus on main points, and understand how parts are related. The following are uses of the discourse organizers covered in this unit.

EXAMPLES	EXPLANATIONS
(a) **First,** we need to examine the root causes of crime in our city, such as lack of education.	**Use:** to show the sequence of topics or main points
(b) **After that,** the existing laws and programs should be evaluated.	**Form:** sequential connectors
(c) **Finally,** we need to determine who will pay for new programs.	
(d) **There are** many reasons why crime is increasing in our cities.	**Use:** to introduce topics
(e) **Is crime really increasing as much as everyone thinks it is?** The answer to this question may surprise you.	**Forms:** *there + be,* rhetorical questions
(f) So far, we have considered the positive side of general education requirements. **Next,** let's look at some of their drawbacks.	**Use:** to signal topic shifts
(g) Lack of education may be one cause of crime. **But what about parental responsibilities in cases of juvenile crime?**	**Forms:** sequential connectors, rhetorical questions
(h) **To summarize**, the statistics just presented indicate that air quality has been steadily improving during the last decade.	**Use:** to introduce a summary of what has been or will be discussed
(i) This paper examines the contributions of recent immigrants to the state economy. **Overall**, my research will show that immigrants have played a significant role in economic development.	**Form:** summary connectors
(j) **Should we be paying more tuition when we cannot even get the courses we need to graduate on time?**	**Use:** to emphasize key points, especially in argumentative discourse **Form:** rhetorical questions

EXERCISE 1

Match each of the sentences containing discourse organizers in the first column with topics in the second column. Then identify the form of discourse organizer in each and its apparent use. More than one use might be possible. The first has been done as an example.

▶ **EXAMPLE:** 1. i. (kinship systems); Form: *there + be*; Use: *to introduce a topic*

1. There are two types of family relatives I will discuss today: those involving blood relations and those resulting from marriage.

2. What does your clothing reveal about your identity?

3. To summarize, I have described several types of behavior that are typically regarded as masculine.

4. So far I have discussed the benefits of regular exercise. But what about people who become obsessed with workouts and spend half their lives at the sports club?

5. Lastly, I will talk about adrenaline, which is produced by the adrenal gland and raises blood pressure in stress situations.

6. Is there any reason why women and minorities should earn less than white males in comparable jobs?

7. To start with, we will describe one of the most widely used services, known as e-mail. After that, we will discuss news bulletin boards.

8. Thirdly, let's consider programs that feature real-life police on patrols dealing with violent criminals.

9. There are two main types of theories that can categorize most of modern cosmology: evolutionary theories and continuous creation theories.

10. In summary, my presentation today will provide several compelling reasons why our campus needs more space for cars.

a. How the universe was created and evolved

b. Basics of the internet

c. Violence on television

d. Parking problems on campus

e. Gender roles

f. How people express themselves through their style of dress

g. Major hormones in the human body

h. Starting a physical fitness program

i. Kinship systems in anthropology

j. job equality

L. A. T. C. Mission College
3000 Mission College Blvd.
Santa Clara, CA 95054
(408) 855-5095

Sequential Connectors: Chronological and Logical

EXAMPLES	EXPLANATIONS
	Sequential connectors may be chronological, logical, or both:
(a) **At first,** the lake seemed very cold. **Later,** after we had been swimming for a while, it seemed warmer.	Chronological connectors signal the sequence of events in time, such as the events of a story or the steps of a procedure.
(b) I have several items of business to share with you at this meeting. **First,** I will report on our latest expenditures. **Then,** I will present a proposal for our next ad campaign. **Lastly,** I will tell you about holiday party plans.	Logical connectors organize the sequence of events in a text, such as the parts of a speech or an essay. They are especially common in formal, spoken English contexts, such as presentations and academic lectures.

Chronological

EXAMPLES	CONNECTORS	USES
(c) **At first,** Frederick didn't like his new neighbor.	*at first*	Beginning
(d) Eva was running slowly in the race at first. **Eventually** she pulled ahead, though.	*eventually*	Continuation
(e) Our first destination was Seoul, Korea. **Subsequently** we went to Bangkok, Thailand.	*subsequently*	
(f) **At last** they reached Vancouver, where they planned to spend the night.	*at last*	Conclusion
(g) **In the end,** both our hero and his adversary die.	*in the end*	

Chronological or Logical

CHRONOLOGICAL	LOGICAL	CONNECTORS	USES
(h) **First,** turn on the ignition. **(j)** **First of all,** check the gas level.	**(i)** **First,** let's consider the main issues. **(k)** **First of all,** I will discuss the arguments against building the new subdivision.	*first* *first of all*	Beginning
(l) **To start with,** open a new file and save it. **(n)** **To begin with,** Matt went to Costa Rica.	**(m)** **To start with,** the developers have not done an environmental impact study. **(o)** **To begin with,** let's look at the effects of air pollution in the valley.	*to start with* *to begin with*	Beginning
(p) **Next,** he flew to Venezuela. **(r)** **Then,** he traveled to Brazil. **(t)** **After that,** he visited a friend in Argentina.	**(q)** **Next,** I will explain my opponent's stand on this issue. **(s)** **Then,** I will summarize the main points of the debate. **(u)** **After that,** I will evaluate the various arguments.	*next* *then* *after that*	Continuation
(v) **Finally,** he spent a few weeks in Chile. **(x)** **Lastly,** check the oil level.	**(w)** **Finally,** I will present the implications of my position. **(y)** **Lastly,** new jobs are needed.	*finally* *lastly*	Conclusion

Logical

EXAMPLES	CONNECTORS	USES
(z) **The first type of pollution** I'd like to discuss is that caused by automobiles.	*the first* + noun	Beginning
(aa) **One cause of prejudice** is ignorance.	*one* + noun	
(bb) **In the first place,** we need to get more legislation to help the disabled.	*in the first place*	
(cc) **Secondly,** we also have a problem with noise pollution.	*secondly*	Continuation
(dd) **The second point** concerns the issue of whether. . . .	*the/a second* (*third, fourth,* etc.) + noun	
(ee) **A second question we might ask** is who should take responsibility for the homeless?		
(ff) **In the second place,** we need to change our attitudes.	*in the second place*	
(gg) **The last reason** is one I am sure everyone is aware of.	*the last* + noun	Conclusion
(hh) **A final question** might be how we will fund our project.	*a final* + noun	
(ii) **To conclude,** pollution is obviously getting worse in our city.	*to conclude*	
(jj) **In conclusion,** parents must take a more active role in schools.	*in conclusion*	

EXERCISE 2

Make up a sentence with a beginning sequential connector that could follow each of the sentences below. Try to use a variety of connectors.

▶ **EXAMPLE:** *My family is very special.* **In the first place,** *my father and mother have worked very hard to provide all of us an education.*

1. My family is very special.
2. Learning to do word processing is simple.
3. I appreciate many of the things my friends do for me.
4. Smoking can cause a lot of health problems.
5. We need to start taking major steps to save our planet.
6. When I started learning English, I encountered many difficulties.
7. A person who has really had an influence on my life is (*put person's name here*).

EXERCISE 3

For five of the sentences below, write a list of ideas that could follow, using beginning, continuation, and concluding sequential connectors in your list. Try to use a variety of connectors.

▶ **EXAMPLE:** I can think of several things I don't have that I'd like to have. *To start with, I'd like to have a really good camera. Next, I wouldn't mind having a new car. Lastly, I'd love to have my own house.*

1. There are several things I'd like to do on my next vacation.

2. Our school could use a few improvements.

3. I have a few gripes about _____ . (You pick the topic.)

4. I think I have made progress in several areas during the past few years.

5. My home (apartment/room) is a comfortable place for several reasons.

6. Several world problems seem especially critical to me.

7. I have several goals for my future.

EXERCISE 4

Exchange the paragraph you wrote for the Opening Task with either your partner for that task or another classmate. Did your classmate use any sequential connectors in the paragraph? If so, which ones? If not, would any of the connectors in Focus 2 be appropriate to organize ideas in the paragraph? Discuss your analysis with your classmate.

FOCUS **3**

▶ *There* + *Be* as a Topic Introducer

There + *be* often introduces a topic that the speaker or writer has classified into different parts.

EXAMPLES	EXPLANATIONS
(a) **There are** three ways to get to the freeway from campus. **(b)** **There were** four principal causes for the recession. **(c)** **There could be** several explanations for this child's behavior.	The *be* verb can be any tense and can follow a modal verb such as *can, could,* or *may.*
(d) There are { three / a few / several / many / a number of } { aspects / causes / effects / factors / methods / principles / reasons / rules / stages / steps / strengths / theories / ways } to consider.	Noun phrases that come after the *be* verb often include a number or a quantifier (for example, *four, several*) and an abstract general noun (for example, *aspects, reasons*).
(e) There are **three kinds of** rhetorical questions. **(f)** There are **several types of** students.	Classifying phrases such as *kinds of* or *types of* often follow *there + be.*
(g) There are many driving rules to keep in mind when you get behind the wheel. **The first** rule of the road is to be courteous to other drivers. **(h)** There are five stages in this process. **In the first stage**, water is drawn through a tube.	You may use sequential connectors, as shown in Focus 2, to organize topics that follow an introduction with *there + be.*

Beginning	Continuing	Ending
first	*second, third,* etc.	*last*
first of all	*secondly*	*finally*
to start with	*next*	*lastly*
the first + noun	*the second, the third,* etc. + noun	*the last* + noun
one	*a second, a third,* etc.	*the last*
one + noun	*a second* + noun, etc.	*a final* + noun
in the first place	*in the second place*	*finally*

The sequential connectors in this chart are most often used for subtopics after *there + be* introducers.

Composition books often caution writers against overusing *there + be.* This is good advice to avoid wordiness; keep in mind that this is not the only way to introduce a topic.

EXERCISE 5

Fill in the blanks with appropriate words or phrases from Focus 3. Use different forms of connectors for each passage. Add commas where needed.

▶ **EXAMPLE:** <u>There are</u> two <u>kinds</u> of twins. <u>The first</u> is called identical. <u>The second</u> is called fraternal.

1. (a) _____ three (b) _____ of extrasensory perception, or ESP, that I will be discussing in today's lecture. (c) _____ I will talk about telepathy, perhaps the best known and most researched area. (d) _____ I will explain telekinesis, which concerns the ability to move a distant object through will power alone. (e) _____ I will describe the phenomenon of precognition, which involves knowing ahead of time about an event.

2. If you have pollen allergies, (a) _____ a number of (b) _____ that you might try to avoid pollen. (c) _____ stay in an air-conditioned room. (d) _____ when you drive, keep your windows up and your air conditioning on. (e) _____ shower as soon as you go inside after being exposed to a lot of pollen. (f) _____ get an air-filter system in your home. (g) _____ if you live in the United States, move to Europe! That continent does not have the ragweed pollen that plagues people in the United States.

3. (a) _____ three main (b) _____ in the process of making rayon, a fabric produced from soft woods and other vegetable materials. (c) _____ the material is pulped. (d) _____ it is treated with caustic soda, nitric acid, and other substances until it turns into a liquid. (e) _____ it is forced through tiny holes in metal, forming liquid filaments which solidify into threads.

4. (a) _____ of pasta, with a great variety of shapes.
   (b) _____ is macaroni, which is a curved tube.
   (c) _____ is fettuccine, which looks like a thin ribbon.

Capelletti is (d) _____ ; it is shaped like a hat. (e) _____ is ravioli; it is square-shaped and stuffed with cheese or meat. (f) _____ is rotelle, which has a corkscrew shape. And these are only a few of them!

EXERCISE 6

Write a sentence with *there + be* to introduce a classification for each topic below. Then write at least two or three sentences that could develop the topic.

▶ **EXAMPLE:** *There are three grammar points we will cover this week. One is relative clauses. A second is generic articles. The last is the conditional form of verbs.*

1. Types of books you like the best
2. Things that you think make a good movie or TV program
3. Topics that you are covering in a particular class for a specific amount of time (a week, a quarter, a semester)
4. Steps for performing a procedure that you know how to do (replacing a printer cartridge, solving a math problem, studying for an exam, parallel parking)
5. Professions or careers that would be good for someone who likes people
6. A topic of your choice

EXERCISE 7

Look again at the paragraph you wrote for the Opening Task on page 245. Did you use a *there + be* introductory phrase? If so, read your sentence to the class. If not, make up a sentence that might be used to develop one of your questions, using *there + be* as an introducer.

DO NOT WRITE IN THIS BOOK

USE

▶ **Summary Connectors**

Summary connectors also help to organize discourse. Some of these connectors signal that the ideas expressed summarize what has been said before.

EXAMPLES		CONNECTORS	USE
(a)	**In summary,** drug abuse is a major problem today.	*in summary*	General summary
(b)	**To summarize,** we should all exercise our right to vote.	*to summarize*	
(c)	**As has been previously stated,** many people did not consider AIDS a serious problem at first.	*as (has been) previously stated/ mentioned*	Review of main idea

Some summary connectors can be used either for introductions—summarizing what is to be presented—or for conclusions, summarizing what has already been stated.

LINK TO FOLLOWING DISCOURSE (INTRODUCTION)		LINK TO PRECEDING DISCOURSE (CONCLUSION)		CONNECTORS	USE
(d)	I have been asked to report on our recent experiments. **All in all,** they have been very successful.	(e)	From the presentation I have just given, I hope you will agree that, **all in all,** our experiments have been successful.	*all in all*	Summary of points
(f)	**Overall,** the quality of television appears to be declining. For example, the news is becoming more and more like entertainment.	(g)	From the evidence I have presented in this essay, it appears, **overall,** the quality of television is declining.	*overall*	
(h)	**Briefly,** the arguments for gun control can be summed up in the following way.	(i)	**Briefly,** so far I have discussed three of the arguments for gun control.	*briefly*	Condensation of points
(j)	**In short,** the arguments against euthanasia, which I will discuss next, are mostly religious ones.	(k)	**In short,** as I have shown, the arguments against euthanasia are mostly religious ones.	*in short*	

EXERCISE 8

Choose three of the sentences or brief passages below. Write a summary statement for each. Use the summary connector indicated in parentheses. In small groups, compare the summary statements you wrote with those of your classmates.

▶ **EXAMPLE:**   My paper will discuss the problem of overpopulation. (briefly)
Summary statement: *Briefly, overpopulation is a serious threat to the survival of all life on earth.*

1. Today, I'd like to talk about something I know every one of you is concerned about. (briefly)

2. By hooking a computer into a national electronic system, you can communicate and get information in a number of ways. For example, you can send and receive messages from others who have subscribed to the system or get the weather report for the day. You can take courses or play computer games. You can make travel reservations or look up information in an encyclopedia. (all in all)

3. Without iron, the body wouldn't have hemoglobin, which is an essential protein. Hemoglobin, found in red blood cells, carries oxygen to the rest of the body. A deficiency of iron can cause headaches and fatigue. (in short)

4. Good friendships do not develop easily; they require effort. You need to make time for your friends. You should be prepared to work out problems as they arise, since things will not always go smoothly. You shouldn't expect perfection from your friends. (in summary)

5. So far I have discussed several of the causes and effects of divorce. (as has been previously mentioned)

6. There are several things to keep in mind if you want to train a dog to obey you. First, you need a lot of patience. Secondly, you should not punish your dog for misbehaving but rather correct the inappropriate behavior. You should never hit a dog unless it is threatening to bite someone. Finally, remember to praise your dog for behaving properly. (all in all)

7. Fellow classmates: We have finally reached this proud moment, when we will receive our diplomas as testimony of our many achievements. In my speech to you this afternoon, I would like to stress what I believe is one of the most important purposes of education. (briefly)

8. In many American cities, it's difficult to get much real news from the local television news programs. For example, the local news on a typical hot summer day might feature interviews with people who are complaining about the weather and perhaps a look at this season's swimwear fashions. You may find out how much money a blockbuster movie made at the box office over the weekend. Another "news" segment might tell you about some new product that you can buy. (overall)

FOCUS 5

▶ Rhetorical Questions to Introduce and Shift Topics

Rhetorical questions, unlike other questions, are not used to ask for information. Two uses of rhetorical questions are to introduce a topic and to shift from one topic to a new one.

EXAMPLES	EXPLANATIONS
(a) How does nitrogen circulate? **(b)** What are the most common causes of fatigue? **(c)** Is aggression a part of human nature? **(d)** Can Congress save the budget?	The form of a rhetorical question may be either a *Wh*-question (*who, what, when, where, why*) or a *yes/no* question.
(e) "What Is a University?" by John Henry Newman **(f)** "Are Women Human?" by Dorothy Sayers **(g)** "Were Dinosaurs Dumb?" by Stephen Jay Gould	Titles of books, articles, and speeches also use rhetorical questions to introduce topics.
(h) Remember the great health care debate?* **(i)** So far, we have looked at some of the causes of teenage gangs. But what are the effects on the communities in which they live?	Rhetorical questions may introduce background information about a topic. We also use rhetorical questions to signal a shift from one subtopic to another.

*Note that this question leaves off the first two words, *"Do you,"* of the full question form for an informal, conversational tone.

EXERCISE 9
The excerpts below are from the beginning paragraphs of books, articles, or essays. For each, predict what the rest of the text might be about.

1. What do we know about the universe, and how do we know it? Where did the universe come from, and where is it going? Did the universe have a beginning, and if so, what happened before then? What is the nature of time? Will it ever come to an end?

2. Are you as white knuckled as I am when traveling as an air passenger? What's it worth to save a buck?

3. Do you believe that the more you diet, the harder it is to lose weight because your body adapts and turns down your rate of burning calories—your metabolism?

4. Why is it that when newspapers are confronted with a story that has anything to do with sex, they often screw it up?

▶ **R**hetorical Questions to Focus on Main Points

Another kind of rhetorical question focuses the listener/reader on the main points of a topic and emphasizes the speaker/writer's viewpoint. It is sometimes called a "leading question."

EXAMPLES	SPEAKER/WRITER VIEWPOINT	EXPLANATIONS
(a) Haven't we had enough wars?	We have.	Leading rhetorical questions seek agreement from the listener or reader. They imply a *yes* answer. In other words, from the writer's or speaker's viewpoint, a negative answer is not possible.
(b) Don't divorced fathers as well as mothers have rights?	They do.	
(c) Isn't English hard enough to learn without all those different article usage rules?	It is.	
(d) We've had enough wars, haven't we?	We have.	Leading questions have the same meaning as negative tag questions that seek agreement (falling tone in spoken English).
(e) What kind of solution is that to our problem?	It is a bad solution.	Another type of rhetorical question that focuses on main points implies a response in the negative. In other words, the speaker/writer will not take *yes* for an answer.
(f) How much longer can we ignore the signs of global warming?	We can't ignore them any longer.	
(g) Who was more committed to nonviolence than Gandhi?	No one was more committed.	

EXERCISE 10

Write a leading rhetorical question to express each of the following opinions. More than one form is possible, and some ideas need to be rephrased, not just transformed into a question. State the positive implication of each in parentheses.

▶ **EXAMPLE:** Opinion: We've gone far enough in the space race.
Possible questions and implications:
Isn't it time to stop the space race? (It is.)
Haven't we gone far enough in the space race? (We have.)
Shouldn't we consider stopping the space race? (We should.)

1. Our senior citizens deserve more respect.
2. We need to start thinking more globally.
3. Our school already has too many required courses.
4. Women deserve the same job opportunities as men.
5. All people should have a place to live.

EXERCISE 11

State the writer's viewpoint for each of the following rhetorical questions. Then state what you think is the thesis (the main point) of each text that follows. Discuss which of the questions you find most effective in making their points.

▶ **EXAMPLE:** How many Americans can afford a $45,000 Mercedes-Benz? Should auto safety be reserved only for the wealthy?
Writer's viewpoint: *Not many Americans can afford a Mercedes and auto safety should not be reserved for only the wealthy.*
Thesis: *Auto safety devices should be put on all cars, not just expensive cars.*

1. Fair-minded people have to be against bigotry. How, then, can fair-minded people ignore, condone, or promote discrimination against divorced fathers—100 percent of whom are men—and make believe it isn't discrimination?

2. I am, I hope, a reasonably intelligent and sensitive man who tries to think clearly about what he does. And what I do is hunt, and sometimes kill . . . Does the power that orchestrates the universe give a deer more importance than a fly quivering in a strip of sticky tape?

3. One of the more popular [comic book] characters is Wolverine, a psychopath with retractable metal claws embedded in his hands and a set of killer instincts that makes him a threat to friend and foe alike. This is a proper role model for children?

4. In 1977 the federal government spent twice as much on dental research as it did on alcoholism research. How many murders and fatal accidents are accounted for by impacted wisdom teeth or unsightly overbite?

5.

EXERCISE 12

The following excerpts from an essay by Isaac Asimov use six rhetorical questions to develop an argument about the need for population control. Identify the rhetorical questions. Then discuss how the author uses them to develop his ideas. What is the overall effect of the questions? Discuss which ones you think are most effective in emphasizing key points and introducing subtopics.

LET'S SUPPOSE . . .

Suppose the whole world became industrialized and that industry and science worked very carefully and very well. How many people could such a world support? Different limits have been suggested, but the highest figure I have seen is twenty billion. How long will it take before the world contains so many people?

For the sake of argument, and to keep things simple, let's suppose the demographic growth rate will stay as it is, at two per cent per annum. . . . At the present growth rate our planet will contain all the people that an industrialized world may be able to support by about 2060 A.D. . . .

Suppose we decide to hope for the best. Let us suppose that a change *will* take place in the next seventy years and that there will be a new age in which population can continue rising to a far higher level than we think it can now. . . . Let's suppose that this sort of thing can just keep on going forever.

Is there any way of setting a limit past which nothing can raise the human population no matter how many changes take place?

Suppose we try to invent a real limit; something so huge that no one can imagine a population rising past it. Suppose we imagine that there are so many men and women and children in the world, that altogether they weigh as much as the whole planet does. Surely you can't expect there can be more people than that.

Let us suppose that the average human being weighs sixty kilogrammes. If that's the case then 100,000,000,000,000,000,000,000 people would weigh as much as the whole Earth does. That number of people is 30,000,000,000,000 times as many people as there are living now.

. . . Let us suppose that the population growth-rate stays at 2.0 percent so that the number of people in the world continues to double every thirty-five years. How long, then, will it take for the world's population to weigh as much as the entire planet?

The answer is—not quite 1600 years. This means that by 3550 A.D., the human population would weigh as much as the entire Earth. Nor is 1600 years a long time. It is considerably less time than has passed since the days of Julius Caesar.

Do you suppose that perhaps in the course of the next 1600 years, it will be possible to colonize the moon and Mars, and the other planets of the solar system? Do you think that we might get many millions of people into the other world in the next 1600 years and thus lower the population of the Earth itself?

Even if that were possible, it wouldn't give us much time. If the growth-rate stays at 2.0 percent, then in a little over 2200 years—say by 4220 A.D.—the human population would weigh as much as the entire Solar system, including the Sun.

From Isaac Asimov, *Earth: Our Crowded Spaceship*, Fawcett, Greenwich, CT, 1974.

Use Your English

You may at times have wished you had a photographic memory—that is, one that remembers everything it receives as input—especially when you need to study for an exam. However, not being able to forget anything can be detrimental, as case histories in abnormal psychology have shown. You will hear a brief psychology lecture on the benefits of forgetting. Listen for the discourse organizers (sequential connectors, *there + be*, summary connectors, rhetorical questions) that the speaker uses as cues to introduce topics and focus on the main points. Take notes on the main ideas of the lecture on a separate sheet of paper. Then, listen to the tape one more time and write down the discourse organizers the speaker used to organize the lecture. Compare your notes and the list of discourse organizers with several classmates.

ACTIVITY 2: READING/WRITING

Are you familiar with the saying "It's as American as baseball, motherhood, and apple pie"? The apple pie reference probably means eating it rather than making it, but here's a chance to test your knowledge of American cooking. The recipe below explains how to make an apple pie. The directions, however, are not in the proper sequence. In small groups or with a partner, rewrite the steps of the recipe. Add sequential connectors to some of the sentences to help organize the text.

APPLE PIE

- Stir the mixed ingredients with the apples until the apples are well coated.
- Dot the top of the pie with ½ tablespoon of butter before putting on the top crust.
- Line a 9-inch pie pan with a pie crust; put aside while you prepare the apple filling.
- Cover the pie with a top crust and bake it in a 450-degree oven for 30 minutes.
- Peel, core, and cut 5 to 6 cups of apples into very thin pieces.
- Place the coated apples in layers in the pie shell.
- When the pie comes out of the oven, sprinkle 1 cup of grated cheese on top and put it under a broiler to melt the cheese.
- Combine and sift over the apple slices ½ cup of brown sugar, ⅛ teaspoon of salt, 1 tablespoon of cornstarch, and ¼ teaspoon of cinnamon.

ACTIVITY 3: WRITING/READING/SPEAKING

Think of a topic that can be classified into parts or aspects (kinds of things, steps in a process, etc.), choosing something that your classmates would know something about. Write a sentence for the topic using *there are*.

▶ **EXAMPLES:** *There are lots of things you need to be aware of when you're driving.*
There are several ways to get from campus to the airport.
There are many kinds of students at this school.

Exchange papers with another classmate and write one thing/way/kind etc. that could develop the topic. When you are through, exchange again with a different student and add something to another paper. Use appropriate connectors. Continue exchanging papers until each has at least three or four sentences that develop the topic. Read some of the results aloud.

ACTIVITY 4: SPEAKING OR WRITING

Expand one of the following topics into a short talk, using discourse organizers. Present your talk to the class or in small groups.
- *There are a number of things a new student to this campus should be told when he or she gets here.*
- *There are several (or many) goals I have for the future.*
- Choose one of the topics mentioned in the Opening Task, focus boxes, or exercises in this unit.

ACTIVITY 5: READING/WRITING/SPEAKING

Look through magazines and newspapers for evidence of rhetorical questions in advertisements. Discuss the kinds of questions that are used to sell products. Then create your own ad for a product, either a written one that might be used in a magazine or a script that could be used for a TV or radio commercial. Share your creations with the class; if possible, perform the commercials.

ACTIVITY 6: WRITING

Choose one of the topics from the Opening Task on page 245 or another issue that interests you. Write a persuasive essay in which you express an opinion on the topic. Try to convince your readers of the validity of your viewpoint. Use appropriate discourse organizers in developing your essay.

UNIT 15

CONDITIONALS

Only, If, Unless, Even Though, Even If

UNIT GOALS:

- To know the different kinds of conditional sentences in English
- To use *only if, unless, not unless,* and *if not* correctly to express conditions
- To know the difference between *even though* and *even if* and use them correctly
- To use conditional forms to give advice

▶ OPENING TASK
When They Were Young

"When I was young, we went out to eat only if it was a special occasion."

"When I was a child, we were lucky if we went to the movies a few times a year!"

"When I was your age, we couldn't leave the table unless we asked permission."

Do these comments sound familiar? Part of the process of growing up is listening to your parents, grandparents, or other older relatives tell you how things were different "back then" or "when we were your age."

STEP 1 In many societies, life in the past was more difficult than it is now, and children had less freedom than they do today. Consider what your older relatives (parents, grandparents, etc.) have told you about the way life was for them when they were younger. List some of the rules, restrictions, and hardships they have described.

STEP 2 In small groups, write down some of the things your older relatives could not do as a result of the rules, restrictions, and hardships. Here are some examples:

▶ **EXAMPLES:** *Bertha's mother couldn't drive a car even after she got her license unless one of her parents went with her.*

Antonio's great aunt could go out on dates only if one of her older brothers went along.

To support his family, Hyung's grandfather took a job as a grocery store clerk in the United States even though he had owned his own business in Korea.

STEP 3 Report some of your group's most interesting descriptions to the rest of the class. Discuss whether you think your older relatives would enjoy being young now. Explain why or why not. Give some examples of things that they would probably like or things they would dislike.

FOCUS **1**

▶ **Review of Conditional Sentences with *If***

EXAMPLES	EXPLANATIONS
General Truth **(a)** If you **are** sixty-five or older, you **qualify** for senior citizen discounts.	**Factual Conditionals** One common type of factual conditional describes general truths. This type of conditional is often used in the sciences to describe physical laws.
Habitual Present **(b)** If my great-grandmother **comes** over, we usually **go** to the park. **Habitual Past** **(c)** When my mother was young, if relatives **visited** on Sunday, they **stayed** all day.	Another common type of factual conditional refers to habitual events. The event may be present or past.
Inference: Explicit **(d)** If that **was** grandmother on the phone, she **must have missed** the train. **Inference: Implicit** **(e)** If that **is** grandmother on the phone, she **is** still in Connecticut.	A third type of factual conditional infers something. The inference may be explicit or implicit. In explicit inference, the main-clause verb includes the modal *must* or *should*.
(f) If my great-grandmother **comes** tomorrow, we **may go** to the park.	**Future Conditionals** These conditionals describe future events.
Present Hypothetical **(g)** If we **lived** closer to our grandparents, we **would see** them more often. (We don't live close to our grandparents; we don't see them as often as we would like to.) **(h)** If my great-grandmother **were** alive today, she **might** not **approve** of the tattoos that many young people have.	**Hypothetical Conditionals** The present hypothetical conditional describes conditions that are untrue or hypothetical.
Past Hypothetical **(i)** If my great-aunt **had been born** about fifty years later, she **might have been** a doctor instead of a nurse.	Past hypothetical conditionals describe conditions and results that were unreal or untrue in the past.

266 UNIT 15

Summary of Verb Tenses Used With Conditional Sentences

TYPE OF CONDITIONAL	IF-CLAUSE	MAIN CLAUSE
Factual: general truth **Factual: habitual**	simple present simple present simple past	simple present simple present simple past
Factual: inferential	simple present simple past *will* *be going to* } + base verb	various tenses
Future	simple present	*will* *could* *may* *might* *be going to* } + base verb
Hypothetical: Present	simple past or subjunctive *were*	*would* *could* *might* } + base verb
Hypothetical: Past	past perfect (*had* + past participle)	*would have* *could have* *might have* } + past participle

EXERCISE 1

To review verb tenses for conditional tenses, complete each of the blanks by writing the appropriate form of the verb in parentheses. The first has been done as an example.

1. If my aunts and uncles (go) _____ *go* _____ out for dinner, they always (eat) _____ *eat* _____ at the same Italian restaurant.

2. My mother has two older sisters. She told me that if she (be) _____ the oldest in the family, her parents (expect) _____ her to do much of the housework, so she was glad that she was the youngest child.

3. If my brother (come) _____ for a visit from Ecuador next summer, he (bring) _____ his entire family, including two dogs and a parrot.

4. I (telephone) _____ my family this weekend if I (stay) _____ in town.

5. If my family and I (have) _____ the time, we (make) _____ videotapes of all of our older relatives to create a family history. We never seem to have much free time, though.

6. If that package we just got (be) _____ from Uncle Carlos, it (must, be) _____ my birthday present.

7. If family members (disagree) _____ about values, they (should, remember) _____ that it is natural for different generations to think differently.

8. Gretchen (spend) _____ the whole year with her grandfather in Berlin if she (finish) _____ her senior project before June.

9. Could you see who's at the door? If that (be) _____ my sister, she (have) _____ the charcoal for the barbecue.

10. We're not going on vacation until next month. If we (go) _____ now, we (miss) _____ seeing my cousins, who are touring the east coast this summer.

EXERCISE 2

With a partner, take turns asking and answering the following questions about the school or schools you have attended. Answer each question with a complete conditional statement. If necessary, think of a particular class in a school you attended.

▶ **EXAMPLES:** What happened if a student got into a fight at your school? Possible answers:

In my elementary school, if a student got into a fight, the principal called up the parents.

If a student got into a fight in my high school, he or she was suspended for a few days.

In junior high school, if a student got into a fight, he or she had to meet with the school counselor.

What happened in one of your classes in elementary, junior high, or high school if:

1. a student walked in twenty minutes late to class?
2. a student didn't turn in the homework assignment?
3. a student cheated on an exam?
4. a student constantly interrupted the teacher?
5. a student broke a rule such as not chewing gum in class, not talking out of turn, etc.?
6. a student gave the wrong answer?
7. the students strongly disliked a teacher?

EXERCISE 3

Complete each of the following past conditional statements. First complete the conditional statement with any other information you want to add; then express a hypothetical past result.

▶ **EXAMPLES:** If my elementary school had. . . .
   If my elementary school had offered English classes, I would have learned English more easily.
   If my elementary school had been less strict, I would have enjoyed it more.

1. If I had had a chance to . . .
2. If my parents (or mother or father) had lived . . .
3. If my grandparents had been able . . .
4. If my family had been . . .
5. If my English teacher had given . . .

EXERCISE 4

Add a condition to each of these past hypothetical statements.

▶ **EXAMPLE:** I would have studied more
   If I had known I was going to get a C in my biology course last quarter, I would have studied more.

1. I would have worked harder
2. I would have been happier
3. my last year in school would have been easier
4. my parents would have been upset with me
5. my life would have been less complicated

▶ **Exclusive Conditions:**
Only If and *Unless*

We use both *only if* and *unless* to express the only condition under which an event will or should take place.

EXAMPLES	EXPLANATIONS
(a) **Main Clause: Affirmative** As a girl, my grandmother went shopping **Condition** **only if** she had finished her assigned chores.*	Use *only if* when the main clause is affirmative. It means "only on the condition that."
(b) **Main Clause: Negative** As a girl, my grandmother didn't go **Condition** shopping **unless** she had finished her assigned chores.	Use *unless* when the main clause is negative. It means "except on the condition that."
(c) **Main Clause: Affirmative** As a girl, my grandmother stayed home **Condition** on Saturday **unless** she had finished her homework.	You can also use *unless* when the main clause is affirmative. The implication, however, is negative. In (c), the implication is that Grandmother didn't go anywhere on Saturday if she hadn't finished her homework.
(d) Nowadays, my grandmother would spend the day shopping **only if** she **were** bored.	For hypothetical present, use the subjunctive form *were* in formal written English, just as with other hypothetical conditionals.

*In spoken English, native speakers often separate *only if*, placing *only* before the main verb and *if* after it. As a girl, my grandmother *only* went shopping *if* she had finished her chores, she would *only* spend the day shopping now *if* she were bored.

EXERCISE 5

Decide whether *if, only if,* or *unless* should be used in each blank. The first one has been done for you.

In the Old Days . . .

As each generation matures, it tends to judge the younger generations as somehow not quite measuring up to those of the past: the new generation may be regarded as a bit lazier, less disciplined or less imaginative. My family was no exception.

"Drive to school!" my father would exclaim to my siblings and me. "Why, when we were your age, we walked everywhere (1) _____unless_____ there was a severe snowstorm. And if we couldn't walk, we went by car (2) _____ the buses weren't running." The meal options were generally fewer for my parents' generation also: (3) "_____ we didn't like what was served for dinner," my mother would remind us, "we had to eat it anyway." According to my parents, entertainment was more active before television watching became the main leisure pursuit, and obligations more strictly followed. As children, they usually played games outside (4) _____ the weather was dreadful. And that, of course, was allowed (5) _____ all homework had been completed. Later, dating in high school wasn't permitted (6) _____ grades were acceptable, and then (7) _____ the parents had met the potential date.

Perhaps people shouldn't talk about the past (8) _____ they promise not to make the present sound so much worse than the past. Or they could make comparisons (9) _____ they admit that some aspects of the past weren't so great. On the other hand, glorifying the past and complaining about the present may be an inalienable right of the older generations.

EXERCISE 6

Make each of the following a negative condition by using *unless* instead of *only if* and making other changes as necessary.*

▶ **EXAMPLE:** When I was your age, we went to the movies only if it was a holiday.
When I was your age, we *didn't go* to the movies *unless* it was a holiday.

1. Back in the old days, we locked our houses only if we were going on a vacation.

2. We could have ice cream for dessert only if it was a special occasion.

3. We could go out after dinner only if we had cleaned up the kitchen.

4. In high school, we were permitted to stay overnight at our friends' houses only if all the parents had met each other.

5. We were allowed to go to house parties only if they were chaperoned by adults.

*In spoken English, native speakers often separate *only if*, placing *only* before the main verb and *if* at the end of the verb phrase.

▶ Fronted *Only If* and *Not Unless* Clauses

EXAMPLES	EXPLANATIONS

(a) **Only if** our parents approved
    Verb Subject Verb
    could we   go out on a date.
 	
(b) **Not unless** a party was chaperoned
    Verb Subject   Verb
    did my parents **allow** me to attend.
	You can use *only if* or *not unless* at the beginning of a sentence to emphasize a condition. Invert the subject and the first verb in the main clause. The first verb may be an auxiliary (*be, have, do*), a modal verb (*will, could, may*, etc.), or main verb *be*.

(c) **Unless** he finishes his chemistry project,
    Subject Verb
    he   **is** not **going** on the weekend trip.
	Do not invert the subject and first verb when you begin a sentence with *unless*. Separate the condition from the main clause with a comma.

EXERCISE 7

Add an *only if* or *not unless* conditional clause to the beginning of each of the following statements to emphasize a condition. Make other changes as needed.

▶ **EXAMPLE:** It's fun to do calculus problems.
Only if you love mathematics is it fun to do calculus problems.

1. Most snakes will try to bite a person.
2. Going bungee jumping is fun.
3. Learning the conditional forms in English is easy.
4. Spiders make great pets.
5. It is worth spending ten years to get a Ph.D.
6. Watching MTV is the best way to spend your free time
7. I will get up at 4 A.M. tomorrow.

▶ *If . . . Not versus Unless*

EXAMPLES	EXPLANATIONS
Future Main Clause **(a)** Juana will take a math course . . . **Future Conditional Clause** . . . if it does not conflict with her work schedule. . . . unless it conflicts with her work schedule. **Future Main Clause** **(b)** She won't take a science course . . . **Future Conditional Clause** . . . **if** it does **not** satisfy a requirement. . . . **unless** it satisfies a requirement.	**Future or Hypothetical Conditions** In statements that express future or hypothetical events, subordinators *if . . . not* and *unless* have roughly the same meaning. They describe the negative conditions under which something will or may happen.
Main Clause: Contrary to Fact **(c)** Violeta couldn't have passed her Latin exam . . . **Condition: Contrary to Fact** . . . **if** she had**n't** had a tutor. **Main Clause** **(d)** Violeta couldn't have passed her Latin exam . . . **Condition** . . . **unless** she'd had a tutor.	**Past Conditions** In statements that express past conditions, use *if . . . not* to express a condition that is contrary to fact when the main clause is also contrary to fact. The meaning of (c) is that Violeta **did** pass the exam and she **did** have a tutor. Two meanings are possible when we use *unless* to state the condition. In (d) the most probable meaning is the same as example (c): Violeta **did** have a tutor; she **did** pass the exam. However, another possible meaning is that Violeta **did not** pass the exam and that only tutoring might have kept her from failing.
(e) Wen and Temu wouldn't have so much homework **if** they were **not** taking calculus. **(f)** **NOT:** Wen and Temu wouldn't have so much homework **unless** they were taking calculus.	**Present: Contrary to Fact Main Clause** To express a statement that is contrary to present fact, use *if . . . not* to state the condition. In (e), Wen and Temu **are** taking calculus; they **do** have a lot of homework. We do not use *unless* for this meaning.
(g) Thanks for helping me get my new job. **If it weren't for** you, I would still be working at that horrible place. **(h)** **If it hadn't been for** the encouragement of her English-speaking friends, Pham wouldn't be so fluent in English. **(i)** **NOT: Unless** it were for you . . . **(j)** **NOT: Unless** it had been for the encouragement of her English-speaking friends . . .	We also use the expressions *if it weren't for* + noun and *if it hadn't been for* + noun to express conditions with main clauses that are contrary to present fact. In (g), the speaker is not working at the horrible place; in (h), Pham is fluent in English. The conditions have made these present facts possible. We do not use *unless* as shown in (i) and (j).

EXERCISE 8

Complete each of the blanks by forming a negative conditional statement with the cues in parentheses. The cues describe conditions that are contrary to fact. Use *if . . . not* or *unless* as appropriate. In cases where both are possible without a change in meaning, give both. Add any words or phrases you think are needed.

▶ **EXAMPLE:** Sandy needs two more courses in chemistry to graduate. He's glad now that he took a chemistry course last year. <u>If he hadn't completed</u> <u>Chemistry I, he wouldn't have been able to enroll in Advanced Chemistry</u> <u>this term.</u>
<u>Unless he had completed Chemistry 1, he wouldn't have been able to enroll</u> <u>in Advanced Chemistry this term.</u>
(not complete Chemistry I/not be able to enroll in Advanced Chemistry this term)

1. Roberto's advisor was concerned that Roberto had decided not to take a typing class. Roberto explained that _____ _____ . (not drop the typing class/not be able to work at the pharmacy last month)

2. Earl has been complaining all term about the amount of reading he has to do for his courses. He says that the history class is the worst. In fact, _____ _____ . (not take a history course/have only light reading right now for his classes)

3. Leila is glad that she tape-recorded her grandfather talking about his child- hood. _____ . (not record his reminiscences/not know about this part of her family history.)

4. Natasha took a TOEFL preparation course. She told me that _____ _____ . (not take the course/be much more worried about the exam)

EXERCISE 9

Complete the following sentences with a statement about yourself.

▶ **EXAMPLE:** If it hadn't been for my parents, I *might not have gone to college.*

1. If it hadn't been for my parents,
2. If it weren't for my friends' support,
3. If it weren't for (name)_____ 's good advice,
4. If it hadn't been for my knowledge of _____ ,

▶ *Even Though* and *Even if*

Both even though and even if emphasize conditions. However, their meanings are different.

EXAMPLES	EXPLANATIONS
(a) My uncle walked to work **even though Actual Condition** his job was five miles away. (His job was five miles away; nevertheless, he walked to work.)	*Even though* is an emphatic form of *although*. It means "despite the fact that." The condition after *even though* expresses a reality.
(b) My uncle will walk to work **even if Real or Not Real Condition** it is raining. (He walks when it rains as well as when it doesn't rain.)	Even if is an emphatic form of *if*. It means "whether or not." The condition after *even if* may or may not be a reality.
(c) My uncle $\begin{cases} \text{walks} \\ \text{used to walk} \end{cases}$ to work **even if it** $\begin{cases} \text{rains.} \\ \text{was raining.} \end{cases}$	*Even if* can mean "even when" with habitual present conditions and past tense conditions. We can paraphrase (c): He walks to work even when it rains; he used to walk to work when it was raining.
(d) **Even if** I have to stay up all night, I will finish this paper.	***Even* versus *Even If* and *Even Though***
(e) **NOT: Even** I have to stay up all night, I'll finish this paper.	*Even* cannot be used as a substitute for *even though* or *even if. Even* is not a subordinator. In your writing, you should check any uses of *even* to make sure that you don't mean *even if* or *even though*.
(f) **Even though** it was late, we stayed up to find out who had won the election.	
(g) **NOT: Even** it was late, we stayed up to find out who had won the election.	

EXERCISE 10

Choose the correct form, *even though* or *even if,* for each blank.

▶ **EXAMPLE:** The children bought their mother a special gift last Mother's Day ___even though___ they didn't have much money.

1. Fran's mother was never without a car. However, she would often walk three miles to the market _____ she could have driven if she had wanted to.

2. _____ Duane's grandfather had a daytime job, he also worked every evening for many years.

3. Our family had a rule for dinner: We had to eat at least a few bites of each kind of food. _____ the food was something we had tried before and didn't like, we still had to eat a mouthful.

4. Last Christmas Eve, _____ the temperature dropped to below zero, my father insisted we take our traditional stroll through the neighborhood singing Christmas carols.

5. We'd love for you to spend the holidays with us. It would be wonderful if you could stay at least a week. But _____ it's only for a day or so, we hope you'll plan to come.

EXERCISE 11

Complete each of the blanks below with information about your efforts to achieve current goals and your dreams for the future. Share your responses with your classmates.

1. Even though I don't like to _____, I do it anyway because _____.

2. I try to _____ even if _____.

3. Even though _____, I hope I can _____.

4. Even if I never _____, I still _____.

5. I would like to _____ even though _____.

▶ **G**iving Advice

EXAMPLES	EXPLANATIONS
(a) Don't make reservations at the Four Seasons restaurant **unless** you're prepared to spend a lot of money.	We often use connectors such as *unless, only if, even if,* and *even though* in statements that offer advice.
(b) Take a foreign language course **only if** you're willing to do homework faithfully every day.	
(c) You should pay your taxes on time **even if** you have to borrow the money.	
(d) Be sure to take a trip to the waterfall **even though** it's a long drive on a dirt road. It's well worth the trouble!	
(e) Don't go to see the movie *Last Alien in Orlando* **unless** you need a nap. (Implication: The movie is really boring!)	We sometimes use humorous conditions with advice statements to make a point indirectly. The advice in (e) and (f) has an ironic tone; the conditions are not meant to be taken literally.
(f) Take English 4 **only if** you have nothing to do on the weekends. (Implication: The class is difficult; you'll have a lot of homework.)	

EXERCISE 12

Make advice statements by combining information in the Condition and Advice columns. First match each condition with an appropriate piece of advice. Then make a full statement, using an appropriate conjunction: *if, only if, unless, even if, even though.* Make any changes necessary. The Conditions statements can either begin or end your sentences.

Condition	Advice
you have plenty of water	take a hike in Death Valley

Unless you have plenty of water, don't take a hike in Death Valley.
Take a hike in Death Valley only if you have plenty of water.

Condition		Advice	
1.	you don't have a wetsuit to keep you warm	**a.**	order the Kung Pao chicken
2.	you are in Cody, Wyoming	**b.**	take a riverboat cruise on the Mississippi River
3.	you have exact change for the busfare	**c.**	walk to the top of the cathedral in Seville, Spain
4.	you love spicy food	**d.**	get on a bus in New York City
5.	the doorman at your hotel calls a cab for you	**e.**	treat yourself to a good meal in Paris
6.	you like slow-moving leisurely trips	**f.**	don't go swimming off the Oregon Coast in winter
7.	you don't mind climbing a lot of stairs	**g.**	be sure to visit the Buffalo Bill Museum of the Wild West
8.	your budget is limited	**h.**	don't forget to tip him

EXERCISE 13

Working with a partner, make up sentences that offer advice for at least five of the following situations using an *only if* or a *not unless* clause.

▶ **EXAMPLE:** What to do or not to do in the city where you live
Don't plan to go out for dinner at a restaurant in my hometown unless you can get there before 10 P.M.

1. How not to get lost at a particular place (your campus, a shopping mall, a city)
2. What to wear or what not to wear for a night on the town where you live
3. When *not* to do something where you live
4. A place someone shouldn't shop at because of high prices or poor quality
5. A course or subject not to take at your school
6. A movie someone should not waste their time to see
7. A book someone should not bother to read

EXERCISE 14

The paragraph below has five errors involving the conditionals focused on in this unit. Identify and correct them.

HOW TO EVALUATE HEALTH NEWS

(1) These days we are constantly hearing and reading about biomedical studies concerned with factors that affect our health. (2) Even these studies often present results as general "facts," the conclusions are not always true. (3) Only if multiple studies have been done it is wise to generalize results to a larger population. (4) Furthermore, you shouldn't be too quick to believe a study unless the number of subjects involved isn't large, because generalizations cannot be made from a small sample size. (5) Even the sample size is big enough, the results may not be statistically significant. (6) In other words, a statistical difference between two factors may be important only the difference could not happen by chance.

Use Your English

ACTIVITY 1: LISTENING

You will hear two brief passages providing advice about health and safety issues. After each one you will hear three statements. Only one is a correct paraphrase of an idea in the passage. Choose the correct paraphrase. Compare your answers with those of your classmates.

1. a b c   2. a b c

ACTIVITY 2: WRITING/SPEAKING

Consider some of the family or school rules that you, your siblings, and your friends had to follow when you were younger. Create a list of rules that could be expressed with *if, unless,* or *only if* conditions. Use the categories below for ideas. In small groups, compare your lists. If possible, form groups that include different cultural backgrounds and discuss some of the cultural similarities and differences revealed by your lists.

- Mealtime etiquette
- Eating snacks
- Watching television or playing computer games
- Having friends over or staying at friends' houses

- Dating
- Going out with friends at night
- Making long distance phone calls
- Classroom rules
- School cafeteria rules

▶ **EXAMPLES:** *In my elementary school in Taiwan, we were allowed to speak in class only if we raised our hand and the teacher gave us permission.*

When I was in high school, I couldn't have any of my friends over to visit unless one of my parents was home.

ACTIVITY 3: WRITING/SPEAKING

Most of us have some strong opinions or beliefs about things that we would never do or that we would be very unlikely to do. For example, a person might believe that she would never accept a job that she hated or would never live in a very cold climate.

STEP 1 Make a list of five things that you believe you would be very unlikely to do. For each item on your list, imagine a circumstance under which you might change your mind or be forced to behave differently and write it down as a possible exception. Use either *unless* or *only if*.

▶ **EXAMPLE:** *I wouldn't live in a very large city.*

Exception: *I would do it only if I could be chauffeured wherever I wanted to go.*

STEP 2 Compare your responses with those of your classmates.

ACTIVITY 4: WRITING

Here's a chance to share your knowledge. Either individually or as a collaborative project with some of your classmates, create a brief guide for one of the following topics. Your guide could be intended as a Web page for the Internet or a poster.

- A guide that informs students which courses at your school to avoid or which to take only under certain conditions
- Advice about what to do or not to do in your hometown or country
- A travel guide to some place you've been that you like
- A guide explaining the basics of how to use the Internet or some specific aspect of it
- A guide for women on understanding men
- A guide for men on understanding women
- A guide of your choice

For as many items as possible, use condition statements with *only if, unless, even if,* or *even though*. Your conditions could be humorous or serious.

ACTIVITY 5: WRITING

Imagine that you could be in charge of your school or city for a year. You could make any rules or laws you wish, and everyone would have to obey them. Make a list of the regulations you would enforce, using conditional statements where they might be needed.

▶ **EXAMPLE:** Rules for School:
The teachers cannot assign homework unless it truly promotes learning.

Students can arrive late to class only if they have a written excuse or a small gift for me.

ACTIVITY 6: SPEAKING/WRITING

Write an essay describing the life of one of your older relatives or friends from information you have heard about him or her. If possible, interview the person. Use at least a few conditional statements in your description.

UNIT 16

REDUCING ADVERB CLAUSES

UNIT GOALS:

- To know how to reduce adverb clauses of time and cause
- To position and punctuate reduced adverb clauses
- To reduce adverb clauses with emotive verbs
- To avoid dangling participles in writing

▶ OPENING TASK
The Lone Traveler

On one of your hiking trips to Mills Landing, you found an old diary with a few notes scrawled in it. Apparently, a lone traveler had kept a record of his travels about one hundred years ago.

Jan. 30: Discouraged by poor crops. No cash. Left Springton by wagon in search of work.

Feb 4: Today searched for job in Powtown. No luck. All jobs require skills I don't have.

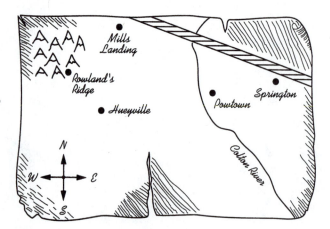

March 15: Crossed the Colton River but raft turned over. Lost everything except diary and watch. Walked to Hueyville.

March 18: No work in Hueyville. Met kind woman there. Told me about vacant house abandoned by miners near Rowland's Ridge.

March 21: Sold my watch for supplies. Hiked to Rowland's Ridge. Found shack and moved in.

March 27: Days and days of rainy weather. Decided to fix up place. Borrowed tools to fix roof, walls, and floors.

March 29: Hammering floorboards. Saw red bag. Opened it. Eureka! A bag full of money. I am rich.

April 8: Guilty conscience. Worry about possible owner. Hiked to Mills Landing and asked Sheriff what to do. Says the money is mine because money left long ago. No one will ever claim.

STEP 1   Using your map (provided on previous page), trace the traveler's steps with a partner.

STEP 2   With your partner, write a brief article for the local newspaper about the lone traveler's story. Describe the traveler's route and what occurred along the way.

▶ **EXAMPLE:**

100-Year-Old Diary of Traveler Found

Yesterday a diary was found which tells the story of a former resident of the area. Apparently, one hundred years ago, a lone traveler, discouraged by poor crops and having no cash, had left Springton in order to find work. Searching for a job in Powtown, the traveler . . .

▶ **R**educing Adverb Clauses of Time

We can reduce adverb clauses of time that contain the words *before, after, while, when,* and *since.* To do this, the subject of the main clause and the adverb clause must be the same. These reduced clauses are called participle phrases and use verb + *-ing.*

FULL ADVERB CLAUSE	REDUCED ADVERB CLAUSE*	TIME MEANING
(a) **While we are hiking/were hiking/hiked,** we admire/admired the scenery around us. *are/were* V + *-ing* ⟶ V + *-ing*	(b) **(While) hiking,** we admire/admired the scenery around us.	A time happening at the same time as the time expressed in the main clause
(c) **Since he has/had been living in Paris,** he has/had learned to speak French quite well. *has/had been* V + *-ing* ⟶ V + *-ing*	(d) **(Since) living in Paris,** he has/had learned to speak French quite well.	A time occurring before and up to the point of the time expressed in the main clause
(e) **After we have/had hiked around the canyon,** we are/were exhausted. *have/had* V + *-ed* ⟶ *having* + V + *-ed*	(f) **(After) having hiked around the canyon,** we are/were exhausted.	A time occurring before the time expressed in the main clause
(g) **When they are/were being searched,** they feel/felt nervous. *are/were* + *being* + V + *-ed* ⟶ *being* + V + *-ed*	(h) **(When) being searched,** they feel/felt nervous.	A time occurring at the same time or immediately after the time expressed in the main clause
(i) **When Sam gets tired,** we will leave.	(j) **NOT:** Getting tired, we will leave.	The subject of the main clause and the subject of the adverb clause are not the same. The adverb clause cannot be reduced.

*For some of these reduced adverb clauses, you can either keep or leave out the adverb, as in (b), (d), (f), and (h) above.

EXERCISE 1

Complete the following sentences about the out-of-doors. Give advice, using *should* or *shouldn't*.

▶ **EXAMPLE:** After getting lost in the woods, <u>you should look for familiar</u> <u>landmarks such as hills or trees</u>.

1. While walking along a narrow ridge, _____.
2. When hiking in an area with poisonous snakes, _____.
3. After having fallen into icy water,_____.
4. Before entering a meadow filled with deer, _____.
5. When washing dishes in the wilderness, _____.
6. Before lighting a fire in the woods, _____.
7. Before being attacked by mosquitoes, _____.
8. After having spotted a bear, _____.

EXERCISE 2

Read the following story. Reduce the full adverb clauses of time where possible.

(1) Since ~~he graduated~~ (*graduating*) from high school, Juan has been working and studying very hard. (2) While he attends classes at a community college, he works part-time at a bank. (3) After he graduates from the community college, he would like to attend a four-year university in order to become an architect. (4) Some day Juan would like to get married and have a family. (5) However, before he gets married, he is planning to take a trip to Europe. (6) When he is traveling through Europe, he hopes to see the great architecture of France and Spain.

EXERCISE 3

Reflect on your last month of activities and write at least five sentences containing reduced adverb clauses of time like those shown in Focus 1.

▶ **EXAMPLE:** *After having taken my biology exam, I had to take a nap.*

▶ **R**educing Adverb Clauses That Show Cause

We can also reduce adverb clauses containing *because, since,* and *as* to *-ing* phrases. Again the subject in the main clause must be the same as the subject in the adverb clause.

FULL ADVERB CLAUSE	REDUCED ADVERB CLAUSE*	CASUAL MEANING
(a) **Because we take/took/are taking/were taking the bus,** we save/saved a lot of money.	(b) **Taking the bus,** we save/saved a lot of money.	The participle phrase contains the cause or reason. The main clause contains the result. The participle phrase can refer to present and past time as was shown in Focus 1.
(c) **Since I have/had been rehearsing every day,** I am/was ready to perform.	(d) **Rehearsing every day,** I am/was ready to perform.	
(e) **As I have/had never gone skiing,** I want/wanted to take lessons.	(f) **Never having gone skiing,** I want/wanted to take lessons.	In the reduced form, a negative word like *never* or *not* can precede the auxiliary verb. This means that the action did not occur.
(g) **Because he is/was not being watched by the police,** he is/was free to move.	(h) **Not being watched by the police,** he is/was free to move.	

*These reduced clauses do not include the adverb. That is, it is not possible to say "Because taking the bus, we saved a lot of money."

EXERCISE 4

Tony and Maria have had several mishaps on their camping trip. Suggest a cause for each mishap by adding a reduced adverb clause to each sentence below. Compare your completed sentences with a partner.

▶ **EXAMPLE:** They got lost on their hike.
Not having brought a map, they got lost on their hike.

1. Tony was bitten by mosquitoes.
2. They were very thirsty.
3. They were very hungry.

4. Maria jumped in fright.
5. Maria was shivering.
6. Tony developed a blister.

EXERCISE 5

Imagine that you have received a letter from a friend who is having a difficult time adjusting to life at a university in the United States. She is making excuses for several of her actions. Write a piece of advice for each problem, using a reduced causal adverb clause.

▶ **EXAMPLE:** Because I arrived at my first class late, I waited outside the room and missed the entire lecture.
Having arrived to the class late, you should have quietly entered the room and sat down.

1. Because I have no computer, I do not type my papers.
2. Since I watched a lot of TV, I did not do my homework.
3. As I have not understood my instructor, I have stopped going to class.
4. Because I do not know anyone, I sit alone in my room for hours.
5. Since I hate the food on campus, I go out for dinner every night and now I'm almost broke.
6. As I am embarrassed by my accent, I do not speak to many people.
7. As I am very shy, I do not ask questions about my assignments in class.
8. As I got a D on my last test, I am planning to drop my class.
9. Because I made expensive long distance calls to my family every other night, I ran up a huge phone bill.
10. Since I did not have enough time to write my research paper, I copied most of the information from an encyclopedia.
11. Because I was put on academic probation, I have felt very depressed.
12. Since I do not speak English very well, I speak my native language with friends from my native country.

FOCUS **3**

► **Position and Punctuation of Reduced Adverb Clauses**

EXAMPLES	EXPLANATIONS
(a) **Hiking alone in the mountains,** Diane always carries water and a compass. (b) The doe, **having been frightened by the noise,** disappeared from the clearing. (c) The trackers waded across the river, **holding tightly to the reins of their horses.**	Reduced adverb clauses (participle phrases) may appear at the beginning, middle, or end of a sentence.
(d) The trackers waded across the river **while holding tightly to the reins of their horses.**	Commas are needed in all positions, except the sentence-final position with the adverb included, as in (d).

EXERCISE 6

Insert commas where needed in the following story.

(1) Tiffany was a very lucky girl. (2) Being born into a very wealthy family she always got everything she wanted. (3) She was given a pony before celebrating her eighth birthday. (4) After turning ten years old she had a tutor to teach her anything she wanted to learn. (5) Enjoying sports she learned how to sail, ski, and scuba dive. (6) Turning twelve her interests changed to travel. (7) Enjoying traveling she decided to have her sixteenth birthday on a ship. (8) For a whole weekend, she and her friends were eating, playing games and dancing while cruising to Mexico.

(9) Tiffany's luck began to change, however, on her eighteenth birthday. (10) Her parents promised her a shiny red sports car, but they told her that she would have to pay for the insurance herself. (11) Not having a well-paying job she avoided buying insurance and drove her car anyway. (12) One night, speeding along a winding road she saw another car coming towards her. (13) She beeped loudly, but the car did not move over. (14) She swerved her car to the right barely missing the other car as it drove by. (15) Her car hit a tree, but she was not hurt. (16) Arriving on the scene a police officer asked to see her driver's license and her insurance identification. (17) Lucky Tiffany's luck ran out when she told him that she had no insurance. (18) Unfortunately, she had to pay for the damages to the car out of her own pocket not having followed her parents' advice.

EXERCISE 7

Match the following main clauses and participle phrases. Try placing the participle phrases in different positions, using commas as necessary.

▶ **EXAMPLE:** *Praising its taste, Marco Polo drank tea during his visit to China.* (7-f)

Participle Phrases

1. Having healed numerous individuals from malaria

2. Conquering American tropical lands

3. Sold either as fresh fruit or made into juice

4. Upsetting the natural order of climate and ecology

5. Prompting explorers to leave on long voyages

6. Grown almost year-round

7. Praising its taste

8. Extracting the sweet juice from the sugar cane

9. Dried

Main Clauses

a. agriculture and industry have ruined tropical lands.

b. bananas are available in every season.

c. the natives sucked on the tender green shoots.

d. pineapple has been an important cash crop.

e. pepper was a prize commodity in the Middle Ages.

f. Marco Polo drank tea during his visit to China.

g. the Spaniards were introduced to cocoa and chocolate.

h. quinine is a very useful medicinal plant.

i. cinnamon rolls up into small sandy-brown cigarette shapes.

FOCUS **4**

▶ **R**educed Adverb Clauses with Emotive Verbs

EXAMPLES	EXPLANATIONS
Emotive Verbs: *amuse confuse frustrate please* *annoy embarrass interest puzzle* *bewilder excite intrigue shock* *bore frighten irritate surprise* *captivate*	Reduced adverb clauses often contain emotive verbs (verbs that express feelings or emotions).
(a) **Amused** by the movie, Tony laughed out loud. **(b)** **Frightened** by the noise, Donna left to investigate.	If we use the *-ed* participle, the focus is on the person experiencing the emotion.
(c) The clown stood on his head, **amusing** the spectators. **(d)** Two students whispered in the back of the room, **annoying** the teacher.	If we use the *-ing* participle, the focus is on the person or thing causing the emotion.

EXERCISE 8
Circle the correct option.

▶ **EXAMPLE:**   Nick jumped, _____ by the lightning.
        (a) frightened   (b) frightening

1. The hikers, _____, gazed at the lovely waterfall.
   (a) surprised and bewildered   (b) surprising and bewildering

2. _____ by mosquitoes, Miko could not sleep.
   (a) Bothered   (b) Bothering

3. The movie, while _____ and sensational, was inappropriate for children.
   (a) intrigued   (b) intriguing

4. _____ that the bears had invaded the camp, the family left.
   (a) Irritated   (b) Irritating

5. _____ by the lecture, many students fell asleep.
   (a) Bored   (b) Boring

6. _____ in Indian artifacts, Martin collected arrowheads.
   (a) Interested   (b) Interesting

7. They walked north instead of east, _____ their directions.
   (a) confused   (b) confusing

8. The play, while _____ and funny, did not keep us awake.
   (a) amused   (b) amusing

9. The children walked away with their heads down, _____.
   (a) embarrassed   (b) embarrassing

10. The trapeze artist did a double flip in the air, _____ the audience with her performance.
   (a) excited   (b) exciting

FOCUS **5**

MEANING

▶ Avoiding Dangling Participles

A dangling participle occurs if the subject of the main verb is not the same as the implied subject of the participle phrase. To avoid this error, both participle and main verb should relate to the same subject in a sentence.

DANGLING PARTICIPLES	MEANING AS WORDED
(a) The path was more visible **carrying a flashlight**.	The path was carrying a flashlight. **Reword:** Carrying a flashlight, I could see the path.
(b) **Using binoculars,** the pond was clearly defined.	The pond was using binoculars. **Reword:** Using binoculars, I could see the pond clearly.
(c) **Enclosed in a waterproof can,** the hikers kept the matches safe.	The hikers were enclosed in a waterproof can. **Reword:** Enclosed in a waterproof can, the matches were kept safe by the hikers.

EXERCISE 9

While hiking in the woods in some parts of the world, a person may encounter a skunk and be unexpectedly sprayed. The following sentences relate to Jane's experience with this, but some of them contain dangling participles. Identify which sentences are incorrect, explain why they are humorous as they are presently stated, and reword the main clause to make each sentence correct.

▶ **EXAMPLE:** Hiking in the woods, a skunk crossed Jane's path.
This sentence is humorous because it suggests that the skunk, not Jane, was hiking in the woods. The appropriate form would be "While Jane was hiking in the woods, a skunk crossed her path."

1. Having been sprayed by a skunk, she screamed loudly.
2. Frightened and humiliated, we walked Jane back to the campground.
3. Having returned to the campground, we looked for some catsup.
4. Applying a thick coat of catsup all over her body, the skunk smell was neutralized.
5. Soaking her clothing for thirty minutes in vinegar and water, the smell diminished.
6. Having been victimized by a skunk, we were informed by Jane that she will think twice about hiking in the woods again.

EXERCISE 10

Rewrite these sentences to correct the participle errors. There may be several ways to correct a sentence.

▶ **EXAMPLE:** After having been bitten by mosquitoes, the ointment felt soothing to her skin.

After having been bitten by mosquitoes, she rubbed a soothing ointment onto her skin.

1. James pet the dog, while barking.
2. While having a bath, water leaked over the sides of the tub.
3. The hurricane terrified people, being driven from their homes.
4. Slithering along the path, I spied a snake.
5. Nearly suffocated by the heat, the room was packed with people.
6. The canned fruits and jams helped the family survive, having prepared for the winter.
7. Sobbing and wailing, the search party was able to locate many survivors.
8. Sitting on the beach, the waves seemed huge to Martin.
9. After spending two hours in the waiting room, the nurse finally called his name.
10. Convicted of the murder of her two sons, the judge sentenced the woman to death.
11. Having achieved so much in so little time, Cecelia's award was well deserved.
12. Since being relocated in Philadelphia, his homesickness grew stronger.

Use Your English

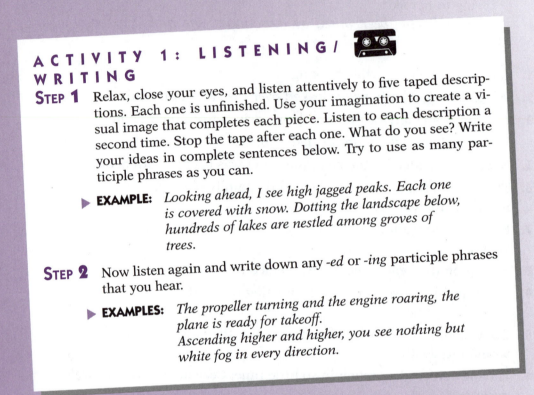

ACTIVITY 1: LISTENING/ WRITING

STEP 1 Relax, close your eyes, and listen attentively to five taped descriptions. Each one is unfinished. Use your imagination to create a visual image that completes each piece. Listen to each description a second time. Stop the tape after each one. What do you see? Write your ideas in complete sentences below. Try to use as many participle phrases as you can.

▶ **EXAMPLE:** *Looking ahead, I see high jagged peaks. Each one is covered with snow. Dotting the landscape below, hundreds of lakes are nestled among groves of trees.*

STEP 2 Now listen again and write down any *-ed* or *-ing* participle phrases that you hear.

▶ **EXAMPLES:** *The propeller turning and the engine roaring, the plane is ready for takeoff.*
Ascending higher and higher, you see nothing but white fog in every direction.

ACTIVITY 2: WRITING

We often use reduced adverb clauses to give directions for carrying out some procedure. Consider something you know how to do very well that requires several motions (for example, making beef jerky, changing a tire, operating a video camera). Then, write the directions to do this activity, using at least two reduced adverb clauses.

▶ **EXAMPLE:** *Before making beef jerky, purchase three pounds of lean beef. Cut strips of the beef about one-half-inch thick. Then, hang these strips on a wood framework about four to six feet off the ground. After building a smoke fire, allow the meat to dry in the sun and wind.*

ACTIVITY 3: READING/LISTENING/WRITING

The Old West has been a popular theme of many books, movies, and television programs. Action-packed scenes show men and women of the frontier fighting against excessive temperatures, hunger, wild animals, and outlaws. Read a western story or watch a western show on TV or at a theater and try to summarize an impressive scene. Use at least four reduced adverb clauses in your summary.

▶ **EXAMPLE:** *Hearing that fifty head of cattle had disappeared from the Parker Ranch, the sheriff organized a tracking party to try to recover the animals. Twelve men, chosen for their riding skill and speed, were assembled. Rising early in the morning, the tracking party began their search. Following the tracks of the cattle, the men located all fifty head at the base of a ravine before noon. They also located the three rustlers who had stolen them. Riding back to the Parker Ranch, the trackers were relieved that the outlaws had been captured.*

ACTIVITY 4: LISTENING/WRITING

Imagine you are a sports announcer for a local TV station. Watch five minutes of a sports event, e.g., basketball, baseball, or football, and take notes on what happened. Write a paragraph describing the players' activities.

▶ **EXAMPLE:** *Crossing second base, Tony Evans was tapped by another player. Running to third, he tripped and fell . . .*

ACTIVITY 5: LISTENING/SPEAKING

Check out a "Books on Tape" novel (for example, Charles Dickens' *A Tale of Two Cities*, Mark Twain's *Huckleberry Finn*, Willa Cather's *O, Pioneers*) from your local library or video store. Play the tape and identify one or two descriptive passages. Within these passages, listen for examples of reduced adverb clauses. Share these examples with your classmates.

PREPOSITION CLUSTERS

UNIT GOALS:

- To use verbs with the correct preposition clusters
- To use adjectives with the correct preposition clusters
- To use common multiword preposition clusters
- To use preposition clusters to introduce a topic or identify a source

▶ **OPENING TASK**

New Arrivals

STEP 1 Look at the following pictures and captions describing immigrants and refugees from around the world.

Somalian refugees in a refugee camp.

Italian immigrants deplaning in Australia.

STEP 2 Now think about one group of refugees or immigrants that has recently settled in your native country or in a country you are familiar with. Think about the circumstances surrounding the group's departure from their homeland and present living conditions in the new country. Jot down notes about these circumstances in the chart below.

Immigrant or Refugee Group = _____	
1. Why they departed from their country	
2. What they hope for in their new country	
3. What group (if any) they are at odds with in the new country	
4. What aspects of life they are unaccustomed to in the new country	
5. Who they associate with in the new country	
6. What jobs they are good at in the new country	
7. How their contributions result in a richer cultural heritage for the new country	

STEP 3 Discuss the results of your brainstorming with your classmates.

▶ **Verb + Preposition Clusters**

EXAMPLES	EXPLANATION
(a) Refugees **differ from** immigrants in that they have not chosen to leave their homeland.	Verb + preposition clusters must be followed by noun phrases or gerunds.
(b) Refugees usually **plan on** returning to their homeland as soon as the hostilities are over.	

> **Other examples of verb + preposition clusters are:**
> | | |
> |---|---|
> | *consist of* | *count on* |
> | *hope for* | *deal with* |

EXERCISE 1

There are four verb + preposition clusters in the chart prompts in the Opening Task. Can you identify them? Now, use your notes from the chart and write four sentences about the immigrant or refugee group you described, using verb and preposition clusters.

▶ **EXAMPLE:** *The Vietnamese departed from Vietnam in order to find better economic and political conditions.*

EXERCISE 2

The following incomplete sentences contain verb + preposition clusters. Complete them in two ways, with a noun phrase and with a gerund.

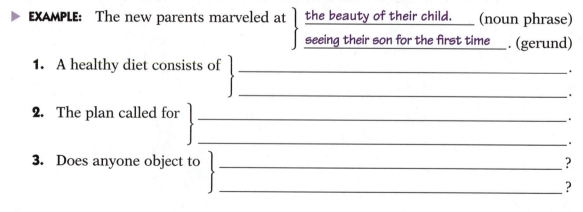

▶ **EXAMPLE:** The new parents marveled at 〉 <u>the beauty of their child.</u> (noun phrase)
<u>seeing their son for the first time</u> . (gerund)

1. A healthy diet consists of 〉 _____ .
_____ .

2. The plan called for 〉 _____ .
_____ .

3. Does anyone object to 〉 _____ ?
_____ ?

4. Ever since I was a child, I have counted on } _____.

_____.

5. As it is very late, you can dispense with } _____.

_____.

6. After the accident, Jaime withdrew from } _____.

_____.

7. Will the president succeed in } _____?

_____?

8. The protesters were demonstrating against } _____.

_____.

9. Why can't she distinguish between } _____?

_____?

10. I don't agree with the politician who believes in } _____.

_____.

FOCUS 2

▶ **Verb + *With* Clusters**

EXAMPLES	EXPLANATION
(a) The laborers **consulted with** their union. (b) They decided not to **cooperate with** management.	Verb + *with* clusters show association between or among people.

> **Other examples of verb + *with* clusters are:**
> *associate with*   *join with*   *unite with*
> *deal with*   *side with*

EXERCISE 3

Ask and answer *should* questions with a partner. Use the words from the three columns below for ideas.

▶ **EXAMPLE:** *Should homeowners deal with realtors to sell their homes?*
No, they shouldn't deal with realtors; they should try to sell the houses themselves.

	Subject	Verb + Preposition	Object
1.	homeowners	associate with	their children
2.	criminals	cooperate with	students
3.	the rich	consult with	ophthamologists
4.	parents	deal with	the police
5.	patients	join with	realtors
6.	young people	side with	gangs
7.	teachers	unite with	the poor

▶ **V**erb + *From* **Clusters**

EXAMPLES	EXPLANATION
(a) The garage was **detached from** the house. **(b)** Rice pudding **differs from** bread pudding.	Verb + *from* clusters imply separation.

Other examples of verb + *from* clusters are:

abstain ⎫
desist ⎪ *from*
detach ⎪
deviate ⎭

differ ⎫
dissent ⎪ *from*
emerge ⎪
escape ⎭

flee ⎫
recede ⎪ *from*
recoil ⎪
retire ⎭

separate ⎫
shrink ⎪ *from*
withdraw ⎭

EXERCISE 4

Fill in one of the verbs + *from* from Focus 3 in each blank below. You may need to change the verb form in some examples.

1. Certain groups follow restrictive dietary laws. For example, Orthodox Jews
   (a) _____ pork and shellfish. Sometimes these and other groups
   who (b) _____ the status quo or (c) _____ the norm
   are considered strange by outsiders but extremely religious by those from
   within the same community.

2. Refugees come to a foreign country to live for many different reasons. They
   want to (a) _____ persecution, war, disaster, or epidemics.
   Certain Southeast Asians have (b) _____ tragic conditions in their
   native lands but have become successful in their new homes around the
   world.

3. Some newcomers to a country go through culture shock. This
   phenomenon makes some people (a) _____ social relationships.
   Because of depression, they also sometimes (b) _____ responsibilities. They may even (c) _____ psychological help because they
   are not used to dealing with doctors for psychological problems.

4. Mr. Johnson is getting older. His hair (a) _____ his forehead. Next
   year he plans to (b) _____ his job.

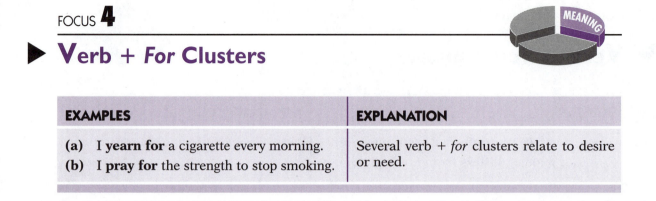

▶ **V**erb + *For* Clusters

EXAMPLES	EXPLANATION
(a) I **yearn for** a cigarette every morning. **(b)** I **pray for** the strength to stop smoking.	Several verb + *for* clusters relate to desire or need.

Other examples of verb + *for* clusters are:				
ask for	*thirst for*	*hope for*	*wish for*	*long for*

EXERCISE 5

Select one or two of the sets of preposition clusters below. Create short paragraph(s) with the verb + preposition clusters and then share the results with your class.

▶ **EXAMPLE:** rebel at, shudder at, jeer at

*The people held up their fists and **jeered at** the tanks as they moved into the city. They had been **rebelling at** following the central government for the past twenty-five years. They **shuddered at** the thought of military rule in their own quiet neighborhoods.*

1. talk of, think of, disapprove of
2. listen to, object to, reply to
3. plan on, embark on, live on
4. believe in, persist in, result in
5. look at, laugh at, point at

EXERCISE 6

Study the chart on the next page about immigration movements to the United States. Use different verbs + *for* to describe why the different groups came to the United States.

▶ **EXAMPLE:** Cubans *The Cubans longed for freedom in a non-Communist country.*

1. Irish
2. Germans
3. Norwegians
4. Poles
5. Jews
6. Austrians
7. Italians
8. Mexicans
9. Haitians
10. Vietnamese

What other immigrant groups are coming to the United States today? Why?

Major Immigration Movements to the United States

Group	When	Number	Why
Irish	1840s and 1850s	About 1½ million	Famine resulting from potato crop failure
Germans	1840s to 1880s	About 4 million	Severe economic depression and unemployment, political unrest, and failure of liberal revolutionary movement
Danes, Norwegians, Swedes	1870s to 1900s	About 1½ million	Poverty; shortage of farmland
Poles	1880s to 1920s	About 1 million	Poverty; political repression; cholera epidemics
Jews from Eastern Europe	1880s to 1920s	About 2½ million	Religious persecution
Austrians, Czechs, Hungarians, Slovaks	1880s to 1920s	About 4 million	Poverty; overpopulation
Italians	1880s to 1920s	About 4½ million	Poverty; overpopulation
Mexicans	1910 to 1920s 1950s to 1990s	About 700,000 About 2 million	Mexican Revolution of 1920; low wages and unemployment Poverty; unemployment
Cubans	1960s to 1990s	About 700,000	Communist takeover in 1959
Dominicans, Haitians, Jamaicans	1970s and 1990s	About 900,000	Poverty; unemployment
Vietnamese	1970s and 1990s	About 500,000	Vietnam War 1957 to 1975; Communist takeover

Source: U.S. Immigration and Naturalization Service

► **Adjective + Preposition Clusters**

EXAMPLES	EXPLANATION
(a) The house stands **adjacent to** the river. **(b)** The town is **dependent on** fishing.	Adjective + preposition clusters
(c) We are **burdened with** high taxes. **(d)** Miwa **is accustomed to** eating three meals a day.	*Be* + adjective (*-ed*) + preposition clusters

---

Other examples of adjective + preposition clusters are:

free		*eager*		*compatible*	
immune	*from*	*homesick*	*for*	*unfamiliar*	*with*
safe		*sorry*		*content*	
expert		*proficient*		*careless*	
good	*at*	*rich*	*in*	*happy*	*about*
swift		*successful*		*enthusiastic*	
ignorant					
afraid	*of*				
proud					

EXERCISE 7

Create your own questions for the following answers, using two different adjective + preposition phrases from Focus 5.

▶ **EXAMPLES:**   A healthy mathematician
*Who is **free from** disease and **good at** math?*

A sloppy executive
*Who is **careless about** his appearance and **successful in** his job?*

1. A calm athlete
2. A claustrophobic politician
3. An anxious addict
4. A clean mechanic
5. A weary worrier
6. A joyful seamstress
7. A repentant runner
8. Your suggestion

EXERCISE 8

Discuss what the following organizations are *interested in, concerned about, accustomed to, committed to, dedicated to,* and/or *preoccupied with.*

▶ **EXAMPLE:**   The World Bank
The World Bank is interested in aiding the world's poor.

1. Greenpeace
2. European Community
3. The Peace Corps
4. The United Nations
5. The Red Cross
6. UNICEF
7. The Fulbright Program
8. Amnesty International
9. Your suggestion
10. Your suggestion

FOCUS **6**

FORM

▶ # Multiword Preposition Clusters

Some preposition clusters consist of three or more words.

EXAMPLES	EXPLANATIONS
(a) Some refugee groups are **at odds with** immigrants from other countries.	Multiword preposition clusters follow this pattern: *preposition + (article) noun + preposition*
(b) **In case of** an emergency, please call campus security.	Many clusters use *in* or *on* as the first preposition and *of* as the second preposition

Common multiword clusters:			
in + noun + *of*	*on* + noun + *of*	*in* + *the* + noun + *of*	*on* + *the* + noun + *of*
in case of	*on account of*	*in the course of*	*on the advice of*
in charge of	*on behalf of*	*in the event of*	*on the basis of*
in place of	*on top of*	*in the habit of*	*on the part of*
in lieu of	*on grounds of*	*in the name of*	*on the strength of*
in favor of		*in the process of*	*on the face of*

Less regular combinations:

by *means of*	*in return for*	*at odds with*	*with the exception of*
with respect to	*in addition to*	*for the sake of*	

EXERCISE 9

Write *in* (*the*) or *on* (*the*) in the following blanks.

▶ **EXAMPLE:** _____On the_____ basis of the evidence, the defendant was acquitted.

1. _____ case of an emergency, duck under your desks and cover your heads.

2. _____ account of his great skill, he completed the task with ease.

3. _____ advice of my physician, I must take these pills and get plenty of rest.

4. I have decided to buy the warehouse _____ strength of expert opinion.

5. _____ event of an earthquake, do not panic.

6. She wants a divorce _____ grounds of mental cruelty.

7. He will pay the bail _____ lieu of staying in jail.

8. She is _____ habit of joking when she should be serious.

9. _____ behalf of the committee, I would like to thank you for all of your work.

10. _____ course of the evening, everyone laughed and had a good time.

EXERCISE 10

Working with a partner, fill in the following blanks with the expressions below. Compare your answers with those of your classmates.

in the habit of	with reference to	for the sake of
as a consequence of	with the purpose of	in lieu of
for lack of	with an eye to	
on account of	in addition to	

▶ **EXAMPLE:** <u>With reference to</u> your question, many Afghans are living in Pakistan and Iran.

1. The United States is _____ turning back many Mexicans from its southern border.

2. Bulgarians of Turkish descent are emigrating from Bulgaria _____ reuniting with their families in Turkey.

3. European Jews and North American Jews have inhabited Israel _____ recreating a Jewish homeland.

4. _____ the bloodshed in Sri Lanka, many Tamils have left Sri Lanka and gone to England.

5. One reason some Vietnamese have been turned back to Vietnam from Hong Kong is _____ space.

6. Nicaraguans have fled to the United States _____ escaping war.

7. After 1975 many Cambodians escaped into Thailand _____ humane treatment.

8. _____ Moroccans and Tunisians, Senegalese have immigrated to Italy to find work.

9. _____ starvation, Nigerians, Ugandans, Sudanese, and Chadeans have fled to other African countries.

10. _____ staying in Romania, many Romanians of Hungarian descent are moving to Hungary.

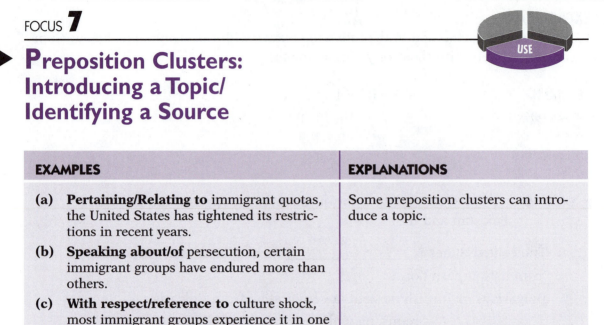

Preposition Clusters: Introducing a Topic/ Identifying a Source

EXAMPLES	EXPLANATIONS
(a) **Pertaining/Relating to** immigrant quotas, the United States has tightened its restrictions in recent years.	Some preposition clusters can introduce a topic.
(b) **Speaking about/of** persecution, certain immigrant groups have endured more than others.	
(c) **With respect/reference to** culture shock, most immigrant groups experience it in one form or another.	
(d) **Based on/upon** immigration statistics, more men than women emigrate from their native countries.	Other preposition clusters can identify a source.
(e) **According to** Professor Herbert, many immigrants decide to return to their native countries after a few years.	

EXERCISE 11

Complete the following sentences.

▶ **EXAMPLE:** Based on the weather report, _____*it will rain tomorrow*_____.

   1. According to scientists, _____.

   2. With respect to our solar system, _____.

   3. With reference to recent political events,_____.

   4. Speaking about discrimination,_____.

   5. Relating to my last conversation with my family,_____.

   6. Based upon my own observations, _____.

   7. According to the dictionary,_____.

   8. Pertaining to the death penalty, _____.

   9. With respect to the students in this class,_____.

  10. Speaking of good movies,_____.

EXERCISE 12

Supply the appropriate prepositions for the blanks in the following passage adapted from John Crewdson's *The Tarnished Door* (New York: Times Books, Inc., 1983, pp. 96–97).

The reforms of the McCarran Act of 1952 limited annual immigration to the United States to 290,000, with 120,000 of the immigrants coming (1) _____from_____ Western Hemisphere countries and the other 170,000 coming (2) _____ Eastern Hemisphere countries. Preference was given (3) _____ the reunification of families by reserving three-quarters of each year's visas for relatives of resident aliens and citizens of the United States. Thus, most immigrants over the 290,000 were family members who were exempted (4) _____ the numerical limits of the preference system. Because one-fifth of the visas were reserved (5) _____ persons with needed talents or skills, many of those who did get visas were unsuited (6) _____ all but the most menial work. The year the law was passed, the United States admitted 113,000 immigrants from Europe and only 71,300 from Asia, Mexico, Africa, and Latin America. By 1977 the number of European immigrants had fallen (7) _____ 70,000 while the number of Asians, Africans, Mexicans, and Latin Americans had risen (8) _____ 231,000.

In 1976, in an effort to increase the equitability of visa distribution still further, the 20,000 annual ceiling on immigrants from each Eastern Hemisphere nation was also imposed (9) _____ all Western Hemisphere countries, including Mexico, which until then had by itself accounted (10) _____ about half the Western Hemisphere's quota of 120,000 visas a year.

Use Your English

ACTIVITY 1: LISTENING/ WRITING

Listen to the following tape and take notes about President John F. Kennedy's administration. After listening to the tape, answer the following questions, using preposition clusters in each response.

▶ **EXAMPLE:** What is one positive cause that JFK contributed to?

He contributed to the establishment of the Peace Corps.

1. What was Kennedy's administration known for?
2. How did he unite with Americans of all colors and religions?
3. What were the elderly happy about?
4. Speaking about school segregation, what did Kennedy do?
5. Who cooperated with local technicians to build roads in Tanganyika, Africa?
6. Who did the United States join with to form the Organization for Economic Cooperation and Development?
7. What were the Latin Americans enthusiastic about in 1962?
8. Why did the United States and Russia consult with each other?

ACTIVITY 2: RESEARCH/WRITING

The following terms relate to intercultural contact or movement from, to, or within a country. Find definitions of the following terms from dictionaries, encyclopedias, textbooks, classmates, your teacher, etc. Give definitions of these terms while citing your sources, using the expression *according to.*

▶ **EXAMPLE:** *According to the World Book Encyclopedia, a refugee is any uprooted person who has a well-founded fear of persecution for reasons of race, religion, nationality, membership in a particular social group, or political opinion.*

1. refugee
2. emigrant
3. guest worker
4. brain drain
5. multiculturalism
6. political correctness
7. melting pot
8. xenophobia

ACTIVITY 3: WRITING

The Statue of Liberty in New York Harbor has a plaque at its base that states the following:

Give me your tired, your poor
Your huddled masses yearning to breathe free,
The wretched refuse of your teeming shore.
Send them, the homeless, tempest-tossed to me,
I lift my lamp beside the golden door!

Do you believe it is possible for countries such as the United States to have an open-door policy? Should all people who desire it be allowed to freely immigrate and settle in the United States? What, if any, limits should be put on immigration? Should there be quotas? What obligation would the new country have to support the immigrants? Write a short composition on this topic, incorporating at least five preposition clusters you have learned in this unit.

ACTIVITY 4: WRITING/SPEAKING

Form two teams. Have each team create a set of eight cards that contain various types of preposition clusters with one or more prepositions missing. For example:

| hint _____ | _____ reference _____ |
| elegible _____ | _____ favor _____ |

Exchange cards with another team. See which team is most accurate at producing sentences with *because* clauses and the preposition cluster on the card.

▶ **EXAMPLES:** 1. *I like to **hint at** what I want for my birthday because my family never knows what to buy.*

   2. *I was **eligible for** the grand prize because I had entered the contest.*

   3. *In **reference to** his request, I do not feel that we should grant it because he is very irresponsible.*

ACTIVITY 5: LISTENING/WRITING

Watch fifteen minutes of a nature TV show or video that describes the life cycles, migration patterns, communication habits, etc. of an animal (for example, polar bear, bumblebee, salmon, jack rabbit, Canada goose). Jot down examples of preposition clusters that you hear.

▶ **EXAMPLE:** *Canada geese depart from their homes in the north and fly south for the winter.*

ACTIVITY 6: WRITING/SPEAKING

The suffix -ism refers to a doctrine, practice, system, quality, or theory. For example, "terrorism" is a practice of using terror to accomplish a particular end. Below you will find an explanation of terrorism that utilizes adjective + preposition phrases. Create more sentences that explain other "isms," using the same adjective + preposition phrases or others of your choice. Then present these explanations to a small group or the class.

▶ **EXAMPLE:** *Terrorism is often **associated with** hijacking. It is usually **accompanied by** violence. It is **based on/upon** perceived injustices among groups. It is **dependent on** people willing to risk their own lives. It is **harmful to** innocent bystanders.*

- commercialism?
- internationalism?
- capitalism?

- racism?
- socialism?
- feminism?

- communism?
- nationalism?
- _____

ACTIVITY 7: LISTENING/ WRITING/SPEAKING

As a class, brainstorm several controversial topics. These can be social issues, legal problems, or political debates. Then, form groups of three. Assign a different role to each group member: Interviewer, Respondent, and Notetaker. Have the Interviewer ask the Respondent his or her opinion about one of the social, legal, or political issues suggested. (The Interviewer should ask the Respondent to be specific about what aspect of the issue he or she agrees or disagrees with and what source or evidence he or she has used to support this position.) The Notetaker will jot down examples of preposition clusters that are heard in the conversation and later share these notes with the other two group members.

▶ **EXAMPLE:** affirmative action

Interviewer: How do you *feel about* affirmative action?
Respondent: In general, I am *in favor of* it.
Interviewer: How about in the university setting?
Respondent: There I feel that it is essential.
Interviewer: Why do you say that? Could you give me an example? . . .

GERUNDS AND INFINITIVES

UNIT GOALS:

- To identify the functions of gerunds and infinitives in a sentence
- To use a variety of gerund and infinitive structures correctly
- To distinguish gerunds from infinitives
- To use *for* with infinitives and *'s* with gerunds
- To use gerunds as objects of prepositions and phrasal verbs

▶ OPENING TASK
Skills and Qualifications

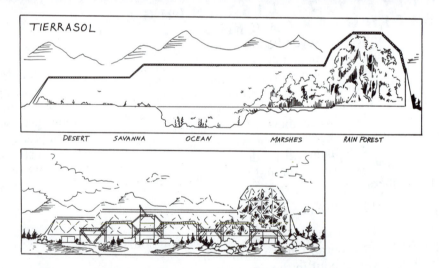

TIERRASOL

DESERT   SAVANNA   OCEAN   MARSHES   RAIN FOREST

STEP 1 You and a partner have been asked to consider the strengths and weaknesses of the following ten applicants for "Tierrasol," an experimental space station in the Arizona desert. This glass-and-steel station will test on Earth how well human beings could survive in a space station on Mars. Those selected will enter the structure and not leave for two years. The station is airtight and has:

- a greenhouse-like structure
- miniature deserts, marshes, oceans, savannas, and rain forests
- plants typical of various regions
- insects, fish, fowl, and small mammals
- individual apartments and laboratories for each Tierrasolian
- a library, a computer center, and communications facilities for all Tierrasolians
- the capability to receive newspapers, mail, and television broadcasts

STEP 2 In pairs, jot down ideas about why you think each person in the chart that follows might like to be a candidate. Think about why he or she would want to be part of the experiment and what positive skills or characteristics he or she could bring to the project.

Candidate	Rationale
Computer Engineer female, 25 years old	She probably wants to participate because her husband might participate. Having good computer skills could help the team communicate from Mars to Earth.
Microbiologist husband of computer engineer, 35 years old	
Police Officer male, 45 years old	
Waste Management Specialist wife of police officer pregnant, 41 years old	
Former Peace Corps Health Worker female, 52 years old, single	
Medical Intern female, 24 years old, single	
Farmer male, 43 years old, widowed	
Ecologist male, 23 years old, single	
Astronaut female, 36 years old, married	
Politician male, 58 years old, divorced with three children	

STEP 3 Share the results of your brainstorming with your classmates.

FOCUS **1**

▶ **O**verview of Gerunds and Infinitives

EXAMPLES	EXPLANATIONS
	Infinitives (*to* + verb) or gerunds (verb + *-ing*) can have various functions in a sentence:
(a) **Speaking English** is fun. **(b)** **To travel to Mars** would take months. **(c)** It would take months **to travel to Mars.**	**Subject:** Gerunds and infinitives can function as subjects. However, it is more common for infinitives that are subjects to move to the end of the sentence with *it* as the new subject.
(d) His dream was **to sail around the world.** **(e)** Her hobby is **weaving baskets.**	**Subject Complement:** A subject complement follows *be* and refers back to the subject of the sentence.
(f) I don't understand the need **to take a ten-minute break.** **(g)** The instruction **to wear safety goggles** has saved many people's eyes.	**Noun Complement:** Noun complements explain the nouns that they refer to. The infinitive can be a complement to certain abstract nouns (for example, *advice, decision, desire, fact, opportunity, order, plan, possibility, proposal, request, refusal, requirement, suggestion, way, wish*). (See Unit 21, Focus 1 for a more extensive list of abstract nouns.)
(h) I am sorry **to inform you of the delay.** **(i)** They were pleased **to meet you.**	**Adjective Complement:** Certain adjectives can be followed by infinitives. These include: *afraid disappointed pleased* *amazed eager proud* *anxious eligible ready* *apt (un)fit reluctant* *ashamed fortunate sad* *bound glad shocked* *careful happy sorry* *certain hesitant sure* *content liable surprised* *delighted likely upset* *determined*
(j) Paco hopes **to see the play.** **(k)** Carol remembered **mailing the package.**	**Direct Object:** A direct object follows a verb. Depending upon the verb and accompanying meaning, the object may be an infinitive or a gerund.
(l) **By studying hard,** you can enter a good school. **(m)** Thank you **for helping me.** **(n)** **NOT:** He lost the deal because of wait too long.	**Object of Preposition:** Gerunds, not infinitives, are objects of prepositions.

EXERCISE 1

Read the following text and underline all gerunds and infinitives. Then identify the function of each one.

(1) Alan Loy McGinnis in his book *Bringing Out the Best in People* (Augsbur Publishing House, Minneapolis, 1985) describes twelve important principles or rules for helping people to perform to the best of their ability. (2) The first rule is to expect the best from the people you lead. (3) A true leader needs to drop the role of "watch-dog" and to display a positive attitude toward everyone who works under him or her. (4) The second principle is to make a thorough study of the other person's needs. (5) Walking a mile in another person's shoes will allow a leader to truly understand someone he or she is working with. (6) The third rule is to establish high standards of excellence. (7) Many people have never learned the pleasure of setting high standards and living up to them. (8) The fourth rule is to create an environment where failure is not fatal. (9) People who expect to succeed all of the time often cannot rise from a failure. (10) An effective motivator needs to know how to help people deal with their failure.

(11) "Climbing on other people's bandwagons" is the fifth principle that McGinnis suggests. (12) A good leader needs to identify the beliefs and causes of the people that he or she works with. (13) By using these good ideas, he or she can encourage them to pursue as many of these goals as possible. (14) Employing models to encourage success is the sixth rule. (15) Everyone loves hearing about true success stories of others to build confidence and motivation. Recognizing and applauding achievement is the seventh rule. (16) A good leader tries to look for strengths in people and catch them "doing something right" so that he or she can compliment them.

(17) The eighth rule is to employ a mixture of positive and negative reinforcement. (18) Using praise is only one of many methods used to motivate. (19) Sometimes a person does his or her best because he or she is afraid to be punished. (20) The ninth and tenth rules relate to appealing sparingly to the competitive urge and placing a premium on collaboration. (21) Some competition is good; however, the decision to work with other people creates good morale and allows the job to be completed more efficiently.

(22) The eleventh principle is to learn how to deal with troublemakers in a group. (23) A leader who does not learn how to handle a problematic person will never learn how to stay in difficult situations and solve them. (24) Finally, the twelfth rule is to find ways to keep the motivation of the leader, himself or herself, high. (25) Renewing oneself through sports, reading, going to a restful spot, etc. are all necessary for the good leader to become energized and to successfully perform the other eleven principles.

Which functions of gerunds and infinitives are most common in this selection? Is the "*to*-verb" structure always a complement? What other meaning can it have? (Hint: review sentences 15 and 18.)

FOCUS **2**

▶ **Infinitives and Gerunds in Perfective, Progressive, and Passive**

EXAMPLES	EXPLANATIONS
(a) Eva's plan has always been **to return** to her homeland.	simple infinitive (*to* + verb)
(b) She hoped **to have earned** an Olympic gold medal by the time she was twenty.	perfective infinitive (*to* + *have* + past participle)
(c) Their goal is **to be working** by March.	progressive infinitive (*to* + *be* + present participle)
(d) We wanted **to have been swimming** by now.	perfective progressive infinitive (*to* + *have* + *been* + present participle)
(e) The suggestion **to be seen** by a surgeon was never followed.	passive infinitive (*to* + *be* + past participle)
(f) They were happy **to have been chosen** for the award.	perfective passive infinitive (*to* + *have* + *been* + past participle)
(g) Part of the problem is not **knowing** enough.	simple gerund (verb + *-ing*)
(h) She was excited about **having watched** the race from start to finish.	perfective gerund (*having* + past participle)
(i) **Being appointed** to the board of directors is a great responsibility.	passive gerund (*being* + past participle)
(j) **Having been selected** for the experiment gave her career a boost.	perfective passive gerund (*having been* + past participle)

EXERCISE 2

With a partner, discuss the following topics using infinitives and gerunds in simple, perfective, progressive, and passive forms. Give reasons for your responses.

▶ **EXAMPLE:** A movie you enjoyed seeing

I enjoyed seeing "Star Wars I" because I like science fiction.

1. a holiday food you like to eat
2. a present you would like to be surprised with
3. a sport you enjoy playing
4. a place you are excited about having seen
5. another name you would like to have been named
6. a job you would like to be doing right now
7. a famous person in history you would like to have met
8. a topic you would like to have been studying by now
9. a story you liked being told as a child
10. a feeling you had after having been recognized for something

EXERCISE 3

A woman received a $1000 prize for winning a short-story writing contest. Her acceptance speech appears below. Fill in the appropriate gerund or infinitive. In some cases, more than one answer may be correct.

It is a great honor (award) __to be awarded__ this generous prize tonight. (1) _____ (present) an award for something that I enjoy doing anyway thrills me. (2) _____ (say) that I am indebted to my parents would be an understatement. (3) _____ (have) parents who were trained as teachers gave me an important start. From the time I was very young, (4) _____ (study) four hours every day after school was required. It was a frequent sight (5) _____ discussing main points and rehearsing the answers to problems. (6) _____ (scold) by our parents for not paying enough attention to our work would have been the greatest shame.

Besides doing my homework for school, (7) _____ (read) fiction and nonfiction books took up much of my leisure time. (8) _____ (read) so many types of books by the time I got to college proved to be a marvelous advantage. (9) _____ (see) so many good written models allowed me to creatively and effortlessly produce my own work for my university English classes.

Today, it requires more discipline for me (10) _____ (be) a good writer. (11) _____ (marry) with three children leaves less time to write. It requires initiative (12) _____ (arise) every day at 5:00 A.M. to write. (13) _____ (write) in this manner is the only way that I have been able to produce several short stories and a few poems. (14) _____ (not receive) very good marks on my essay pieces in college, I have left essay writing to some other writer! Well, I can see that my time is up. It has been an honor (15) _____ (select) as the winner of this contest and I thank my parents, family, and all of you for your recognition today.

EXERCISE 4

Fill in the following blanks with appropriate infinitives. More than one answer may be possible.

▶ **EXAMPLE:** The requirement _____to wear_____ a spacesuit is essential protection for the astronaut.

1. Few people have made the decision _____ an astronaut.

2. The proposal _____ expendable rockets with rockets that could return to Earth saved a great deal of money for the tax-payer.

3. The space program strictly heeded the advice _____ the astronauts for eighteen days after their flight to the Moon in order to assure their good health.

4. The suggestion _____ a "moon base" would allow much useful scientific research.

5. A precaution _____ after every spaceflight includes isolating lunar samples until the scientific team is satisfied that no risk of contamination remains.

6. The decision _____ space-walks occurred in 1964 with Project Mercury.

7. The first words _____ by Neil Armstrong as he stepped on to the surface of the moon were "That's one small step for a man; a giant leap for mankind."

8. The next challenge _____ is a mission to Mars.

EXERCISE 5

With a partner, take turns asking and answering the following questions. Use an adjective complement in each of your responses.

▶ **EXAMPLE:** What are you bound to do after you finish your schooling?
I am bound to get a job as a computer technician.

1. What type of food are you hesitant to eat?
2. What are you apt to do in the next few weeks?
3. Which clubs here or in your native country are you eligible to join?
4. What sport are you reluctant to try?
5. What movie are you likely to see in the next few weeks?
6. Which country would you be delighted to visit?
7. Which student in your class is most liable to be successful?
8. What are you sure to do after your class today?
9. Which friend are you most happy to know?
10. What movie star or musical star would you be ready to meet?

FOCUS **3**

MEANING

▶ **Gerunds versus Infinitives**

Certain types of verbs (verbs of emotion, verbs of completion/incompletion, and verbs of remembering) can be affected by the choice of infinitive or gerund.

EXAMPLES	EXPLANATIONS
(a) **To eat** too much sugar is not healthy. (b) **Eating** too much sugar is not healthy.	Infinitive and gerunds as objects and subjects sometimes have equivalent meanings.
(c) **ACTUAL:** For the time being, I **prefer** *being* a housewife. (d) **POTENTIAL:** When my children are grown, I would **prefer** *to get* a job outside the home. (e) **ACTUAL: Playing** golf every day is boring. (f) **POTENTIAL: To play** golf every day would be my idea of a happy retirement.	In other cases, we choose an infinitive or gerund by the meaning of an action. We often use gerunds to describe an actual, vivid, or fulfilled action. We often use infinitives to describe potential, hypothetical, or future events.

Verbs of Emotion

ACTUAL EVENT	POTENTIAL EVENT
(g) Did you **like** *dancing* that night? You seemed to be having a good time.	**(h)** Do you **like** *to dance*? I know a good nightclub.
(i) Tim **hates** *quarreling* with his wife over every little thing.	**(j)** Tim **hates** *to quarrel* with his wife. It would be the last thing he would want to do.
(k) I **preferred** *studying* astronomy over physics.	**(l)** I **prefer** *to study* physics next year.

Verbs of Completion/Incompletion

ACTUAL EVENT	POTENTIAL EVENT
(m) **I started** *doing* my homework. Question #1 is especially hard.	**(n)** Did you **start** *to do* your homework?
(o) Did you **continue** *watching* the program yesterday after I left?	**(p)** Will you **continue** *to watch* the program after I leave?
(q) He **began** *speaking* with a hoarse voice that no one could understand.	**(r)** He **began** *to speak*, but was interrupted by the lawyer.
(s) She **stopped** *listening* whenever she was bored.	**(t)** She **stopped** *to listen* to the bird that was singing. (Note: *to* means "in order to".)
(u) They **finished** *reading* the book.	**(v)** I will **finish** *reading* this book before I go shopping. (Note: *Finish* always requires a gerund.)
	(w) **NOT:** I will finish to read the book.

Verbs of Remembering

EXAMPLES	TIME SEQUENCE	EXPLANATION
(x) Tom **remembered** *closing* the door.	First: Tom closed the door. Then: Tom remembered that he did so.	Besides the real event and potential event meanings, *remember, forget,* and *regret* signal different time sequence meanings when we use a gerund or an infinitive.
(y) Tom **remembered** *to close* the door.	First: Tom remembered that he needed to close the door. Then: Tom closed the door.	

EXERCISE 6

In the Opening Task on pages 316 and 317, you and your classmates considered the candidates for Tierrasol. At the last minute, the media released new information about the candidates based on several confidential interviews. Read and select the correct verb in each of the quotes that follow. In some cases, both verbs may be correct. If so, explain why.

▶ **EXAMPLE:** Microbiologist: I would like (<u>to go</u>/going) only if my wife could go.
*(**To go** is preferred because the situation is hypothetical.)*

1. Microbiologist: (To live/living) in Tierrasol without my wife would be dreadful.

2. Computer engineer: I love (to smoke/smoking). As a matter of fact, I smoke three packs of cigarettes a day.

3. Police officer: (To carry/carrying) a gun is a necessity. In fact, I don't go anywhere without it.

4. Waste management specialist: I mean (to stay/staying) in Tierrasol only until the baby is born.

5. Former Peace Corps health worker: I hated (to work/working) under stressful conditions. That's why I returned early from my assignment.

6. Medical intern: (To pass/passing) the Medical Boards Exam this fall is my intention. Unfortunately, I have already failed it twice.

7. Farmer: I loathe (to live/living) in closed spaces. I have claustrophobia.

8. Ecologist: I regret (to inform/informing) the committee in my application that I was a water quality expert because I actually have limited knowledge of this area.

9. Astronaut: I will continue (to benefit/benefiting) from this experience in future space missions, even after Tierrasol.

10. Politician: Did I remember (to tell/telling) you that funding for future Tierrasol projects will be one of my major campaign issues once this project is finished?

Gerunds and Infinitives as Direct Object

EXAMPLES	EXPLANATIONS
	Another way to predict the form of a direct object complement (either gerund or infinitive) is by the choice of verb in the base sentence.
(a) Scientists **appear** to be getting close to an explanation. **(b)** **NOT:** Scientists appear being getting close to an explanation.	• An infinitive must follow *want, need, hope, promise,* and *appear* (and other verbs in List A on pages A-8). Notice here that many of these verbs (although not all) signal potential events, a meaning of infinitives discussed in Focus 3.
(c) Juan **hates** (for) **Isabel** to worry.	• Some verbs from List A (*desire, hate, like, love* and *prefer*) may optionally include *for* with the infinitive complement when the infinitive has an explicit subject.
(d) Einstein **convinced other scientists** to reject Newtonian physics. **(e)** **NOT:** Einstein convinced to reject Newtonian physics. **(f)** **NOT:** Einstein convinced other scientists rejecting Newtonian physics.	• *Advise, convince, invite* and *warn* (and other verbs in List B on page A-9) are followed by infinitive complements with explicit subjects.
(g) Einstein **risked** introducing a new theory to the world. **(h)** **NOT:** Einstein risked to introduce a new theory to the world.	• *Appreciate, enjoy, postpone, risk,* and *quit* (and other verbs in List C on pages A-9 and A-10) take only gerunds. Notice that many of these verbs (although not all) signal actual events, a meaning of gerunds discussed in Focus 3.

EXERCISE 7

Read the following text. Underline all direct object infinitives, and circle all direct object gerunds. (Not every sentence may have one.)

Then, make a list of the verb + infinitive or gerund combinations that you find.

▶ **EXAMPLE:** **Verb** + **Infinitive** **Verb** + **Gerund**
learn *to speak* *prefer* *saying*

EINSTEIN'S EARLY EDUCATION

(1) Albert Einstein was born in Ulm, Germany, in 1879. (2) Because he learned <u>to speak</u> at a late age, his parents feared that he was retarded. (3) Modern observers prefer (saying) that he was a daydreamer. (4) When he was five years old, Einstein began to attend a Catholic school. (5) One instructor was especially critical of his abilities and told his parents that it did not matter what field young Albert chose because he would not succeed in it. (6) In 1889, Einstein transferred to a very strict German school called the Luitpold Gymnasium. (7) The rigid structure forced Einstein to distrust authority and become skeptical.

(8) At age twelve, Einstein picked up a mathematics textbook and began teaching himself geometry. (9) By 1894, Einstein's father's business had failed to prosper, and the family moved to Italy. (10) Einstein, however, remained behind and began feeling lonely and unhappy. (11) Consequently, he paid less attention to his studies and was finally asked by one of the teachers to leave. (12) He joined his family in Italy but was not able to matriculate at a university because he did not have a diploma. (13) When he heard that a diploma was not necessary to enter at the Swiss Polytechnique Institute in Zurich, he decided to apply.

(14) Einstein traveled to Switzerland but did not pass the entrance examination. (15) He was not prepared well enough in biology and languages, so he enrolled in the Gymnasium at Aarau to prepare himself in his weaker subjects. (16) Albert enjoyed studying in Aarau more than at the Lietpold Gymnasium because the teachers wanted to teach students how to think. (17) He took the exam again and was finally permitted to matriculate into a four-year program. (18) Einstein did not excel during these years at the Institute. (19) In fact, he rarely attended the lectures. (20) He read his books at home and borrowed his classmates' notes to pass tests.

(21) When Einstein graduated in 1900, he failed to obtain a position at the Institute. (22) His professors did not intend to reward Einstein's lackadaisical attitude toward classes with a position. (23) Because he did not get an academic appointment, he worked at the Swiss Patent Office. (24) He worked there for several years until he was offered an appointment as Associate Professor of Physics at the University of Zurich. (25) It was there that Einstein's revolutionary theories of space-time began to take hold and threatened to destroy the reputations of other colleagues who had built their careers on Newton's ideas of a clockwork universe.

What meaning does the "*to*-verb" structure have in sentences 15 and 20?

EXERCISE 8

Complete the following sentences based on the passage in Exercise 7. Use an infinitive or gerund. The first one has been done for you.

▶ **EXAMPLE:** As a baby, Einstein appeared _____ *to be* _____ retarded.

1. As a young child, he failed _____ his teachers.

2. At age twelve, Einstein decided _____ himself geometry.

3. Einstein neglected _____ his homework.

4. When Einstein's family left for Italy, he quit _____ .

5. Because of this, one teacher advised him _____ school.

6. Without his family, he couldn't help _____ lonely.

7. He didn't mind _____ his family in Italy.

8. Unfortunately, he couldn't begin _____ at a university without a diploma.

9. He tried _____ the Swiss Polytechnique but could not pass the entrance exam.

10. He regretted _____ the entrance exam the first time.

11. Professors at the Polytechnique declined _____ Einstein a position because of his lackadaisical academic performance.

12. As a clerk at the Swiss Patent Office, he continued _____ about physics.

13. The University of Zurich invited Einstein _____ a faculty member.

14. Many professors couldn't help _____ Einstein's unusual ideas.

15. Soon he began _____ well-established professors with his revolutionary theories.

EXERCISE 9

Look back at the notes you made for the Opening Task on page 317 and additional information you learned in Exercise 16. Assume that only five of the applicants can be chosen for the two-year experiment in the Tierrasol structure.

STEP 1 In pairs, rank order the applicants from 1 (= most desirable) to 10 (= least desirable). Consider what might be the appropriate mix of males and females, whether married couples or singles are preferable, what skills and abilities are most essential, what compatibility factors should be considered, etc.

STEP 2 As a whole class, come to a consensus about which five applicants would be most desirable.

STEP 3 After this discussion, answer the following questions.

1. Who has the class chosen to be the top five finalists?

2. Was there any candidate that you personally regretted eliminating?

3. Did any of your classmates persuade you to select someone that you had not originally selected?

For with Infinitives and *'s* with Gerunds

EXAMPLES	EXPLANATIONS
(a) **(For people)** to see is a wonderful gift. (b) **(Your)** neglecting your teeth will cause an earlier return to your dentist.	The subject of an infinitive or a gerund is often not stated but can be implied from context. It will either have a general reference or a specific one that can be determined from other references in the sentence or paragraph.
(c) **For a Russian** to be the first man in space was commendable. (d) Her desire was **for them** to take a trip around the world.	When an infinitive functions as a subject or a subject complement, any stated subject of the infinitive should be preceded by *for*. If a pronoun follows *for*, it must be in object form.
(e) They hoped **for her** to be able to attend the concert. (f) I expected **(for) him** to be there when I finished. (g) We advised **the couple** to postpone their marriage.	When the infinitive functions as a direct object, its stated subject should take object form if it is a pronoun and may or may not be preceded by *for*. Three options are possible depending upon the verb. (See Focus 4.)
(h) **Their denying the allegation** was understandable. (i) I didn't like **the dog's barking** all night.	When the subject of a gerund is stated, it takes the possessive form.

EXERCISE 10

Read the descriptions of problem situations. Following each description is a statement about the problem. Fill in the blank with *for + noun/pronoun* or a possessive construction to complete each sentence.

▶ **EXAMPLE:** Sue went to a party. Ralph did not speak to her all evening. Sue disliked _____Ralph's_____ ignoring her at the party.

1. Burt did not get enough sleep last night. He ended up yelling at Mrs. Gonzalez, his boss. _____ yelling at his boss was a big mistake.

2. Mrs. Sutherland warned students to do their own work during the test. Sue got caught cheating. _____ to get caught cheating was shameful.

3. Tony did not watch where he was going and ran into the rear end of the car in front of him. The driver of the car resented _____ hitting her car.

4. Nina always goes to bed at 9:00 P.M. Her friend, Nathan, forgot and called her house at 11:00 P.M. Nina was very angry. Nina expected _____ to call at an earlier hour the next time.

5. Bill's grandmother mailed him a birthday package, which arrived a week before his birthday. Bill couldn't wait and opened the package early. Bill's mother was upset about _____ opening the present before his birthday.

6. Ursula left the house when it was still dark. When she got to school, she noticed that she was wearing one black shoe and one brown shoe. _____ to leave the house without checking her shoes was very silly.

7. Mrs. Lu has several children who make a lot of noise everywhere they go. All of her neighbors are very upset. _____ to let her children run wild angers the neighbors.

8. Michelle has asked Than to go to the movies several times. Than always tells her that he can't because he has to watch a TV show, do his homework, call his mother, etc. Michelle is tired of _____ making excuses.

EXERCISE 11

Read the following sentences. Write C beside correct sentences and I beside the incorrect sentences and make all necessary corrections. Be sure to refer to Focuses 3, 4, and 5 to review the rules.

▶ **EXAMPLE:** _____I_____ He agrees ^to^ speak at the convention.

1. _____ I expected him to see me from the balcony, but he didn't.

2. _____ They intended interviewing the ambassador the last week in November.

3. _____ I regretted to tell her that she had not been sent an invitation to the party.

4. _____ Patty has chosen attending the University of Michigan in the fall.

5. _____ Have you forgotten to fasten your seat belt again?

6. _____ Terry getting married surprises me.

7. _____ Would you please stop to talk? I cannot hear the presenter.

8. _____ Did he suggest us go to a Japanese restaurant?

9. _____ She can't stand to do her homework with the radio turned on.

10. _____ Mr. and Mrs. Hunter forced their daughter's joining the social club against her will.

11. _____ For they to be traveling in Sweden is a great pleasure.

12. _____ Please remember working harder.

13. _____ Mary tends to exaggerate when she tells a story.

14. _____ I don't mind Tai to arrive a little late to the meeting.

15. _____ Would you care have a drink before we eat dinner?

16. _____ John avoided go to the dentist for three years.

17. _____ They can't afford taking a trip to the Caribbean this year.

18. _____ She coming late to the appointment was a disappointment.

Gerunds as Object of Prepositions and Phrasal Verbs

EXAMPLES	EXPLANATIONS
(a) The Tierrasol committee could not **agree to** the farmer's **being** on the list of finalists. **(b)** The members **argued about keeping** the police officer and the Peace Corps worker as well.	Gerunds generally follow verbs + prepositions, such as *agree to, look at, worry about,* etc.
(c) The teacher **asked for the committee to make** a decision within twenty minutes. **(d)** She **hoped for them to make** their announcement by 4:00.	An exception to this is when the preposition is *for* with such prepositional verbs as *ask for, ache for, care for, hope for, long for,* etc. In this case, use an infinitive with a "subject."
(e) The inhabitants will be able to **carry on eating** at regular mealtimes. **(f)** I can't **put up with listening** to so much rap music. **(g)** They will **look forward to returning** to regular eating patterns once the experiment is over.	Phrasal verbs and phrasal verbs followed by prepositions (*put up with, cut down on, stand up for,* etc.) always take the gerund (versus infinitive) form. Note that the first *to* is not an infinitive marker in (g) but is a part of the phrasal verb + preposition *look forward to*.
(h) Church authorities were not **accustomed to thinking** that the sun was the center of the universe. **(i)** These theories made the Catholic Church **suspicious of** Galileo's **being** a loyal Christian.	We also use gerunds following adjective + preposition combinations such as *content with, surprised at, annoyed by.*

EXERCISE 12

Since the beginning of time, human beings have tried to understand who they were and where they came from through religious beliefs, theories, and rituals. Write general statements about these ideas, using the prompts below. Include a gerund or infinitive in each response.

▶ **EXAMPLE:** people   believe in   (human beings evolved from apes)
Some people believe in human beings' having evolved from apes.

1.	religions	insist on	(God has created living things)
2.	cultures	call for	(people have dietary restrictions)
3.	cultures	think about	(their ancestors are pleased or displeased with them)
4.	people	hope for	(relatives are reunited in an afterlife)
5.	members	wait for	(God returns to the chosen people)
6.	believers	complain about	(other people don't believe)
7.	religions	argue about	(priests have proper authority)
8.	members	agree to	(their children are baptized)

EXERCISE 13

Read the following notes about important figures in scientific history. Write sentences about each person, using one of the following expressions: *celebrated for, famous for, good at, proficient in, renowned for, skillful in,* or *successful in.*

▶ **EXAMPLES:** Aristotle, Greek philosopher, laws of motion
Aristotle was a Greek philosopher who was famous for developing theories about motion.

1. Ptolemy, Egyptian philosopher and astronomer, made charts and tables from an observatory near Alexandria, Egypt

2. Descartes, French philosopher, developed a theory of knowledge by doubting, believed intuition was the key to understanding

3. Copernicus, Polish astronomer, concluded that the sun was at the center of the universe

4. Kepler, German astronomer and mathematician, realized that planets travel in ellipses rather than circles

5. Galileo, Italian astronomer and physicist, improved the telescope; wrote *The Starry Messenger,* which refuted the prevailing theory of an earth-centered universe

6. Newton, English mathematician, determined general laws of motion and the laws of gravity

7. Einstein, German physicist, published the Special Theory of Relativity and the General Theory of Relativity, introduced the concepts of gravitational fields and curved space

EXERCISE 14

Fill in the following blanks with a gerund or infinitive.

After taking off on the last Mercury mission, Gordon Cooper settled in for a good night's sleep halfway through his journey. Compared with most of the duties of spaceflight, it seemed (1) __to be_____ (be) an easy enough undertaking. But Cooper ended up (2) _____ (have to wedge) his hands beneath his safety harness to keep his arms from (3) _____ (float around) and (4) _____ (strike) switches on the instrument panel.

Since Cooper's flight, (5) _____ (sleep) in space has become a routine matter—maybe too routine. When carrying out an especially boring or tiring task, some astronauts have nodded off—only they didn't really nod: they simply closed their eyes and stopped (6) _____ (move). There are none of the waking mechanisms that we would expect (7) _____ (have) on earth—one's head (8) _____ (fall) to one side or a pencil (9) _____ (drop) to the floor.

Space crews have also found that they don't need handholds and ladders to get around; they quickly learn (10) _____ (push off) with one hand and float directly to their destinations. (11) _____ (eat), use a computer, or do some other stationary task, astronauts now slip their stockinged feet into loops or wedges attached to the floor. Similarly, a single Velcro head strap suffices (12) _____ (keep) sleeping astronauts from (13) _____ (drift out) toward the ventilation ducts.

A favorite recreation in space is (14) _____ (play) with one's food. Instead of carrying food all the way to their mouths with a utensil, some experienced astronauts like (15) _____ (catapult) food from spoons. Although (16) _____ (drink) coffee seems like the most natural thing on Earth, in space it won't work. If you tried (17) _____ (tip) the cup back to take a drink, the weightless coffee would not roll out. One astronaut offers the following advisory: "Don't let your curiosity tempt you into (18) _____

(explore) a larger clump of liquid than you're prepared

(19) _____ (drink) later." If you don't start

(20) _____ (drink) your blob with a straw, it eventually attaches itself to the nearest wall or window.

   Although spaceflight has its irritations, these are necessary if astronauts are to soar. The whole idea of airborne testing is to make

(21) _____ (live) and (22) _____ (work) in

weightlessness easy and unremarkable for ordinary folk.

Adapted from: D. Stewart. "The Floating World at Xero G." *Air and Space.* August/September 1991, p. 38.

Use Your English

ACTIVITY 1: LISTENING

Listen to a story about a famous unsolved mystery. Use information from the tape to complete each sentence below. Use a phrase containing an infinitive or a gerund based on what you have heard.

▶ **EXAMPLE:** Cullen was not good at _____conversing_____.

1. _____ describes Priscilla's fashion tastes.

2. Cullen finished _____.

3. _____ was one indication of Cullen's violence.

4. Priscilla and Cullen decided _____.

5. Priscilla allowed various characters _____.

6. Cullen probably resented Priscilla's _____.

7. Beverly Bass and her friend "Bubba" Gavel tried _____.

8. Soon after the crime, the police succeeded in _____.

9. _____ was "Racehorse" Haynes' best talent.

10. "Racehorse" Haynes convinced the jury _____.

11. The prosecutors failed _____.

12. The jurors admitted _____.

ACTIVITY 2: WRITING

Imagine that you are a newspaper journalist and you have just witnessed the takeover of a small island nation by a totalitarian regime. Three weeks of intensive investigation has uncovered a complete story of what happened. Write a short objective article summarizing events and answering the following important questions. Use at least five noun complements in your writing.

▶ **EXAMPLE:** *At 6:00 A.M. Caribbean time, Dimiti Island was peacefully taken over by a military junta who have been struggling for power for the past ten years. On Thursday, President Martin made the appeal to the United Nations* **to help his small island nation;** *however, the request* **to send peace-keeping troops** *was refused.*

1. Who made an appeal to the United Nations to help the country?
2. What happened to the request to send peace-keeping troops?
3. Who made the suggestion to call another meeting for negotiation?
4. Why was the reminder to continue negotiations ignored?
5. Why did the military resist the advice to wait another month?
6. Who gave the order to enter the palace grounds?
7. Who gave permission to enter the gates of the presidential palace?
8. Why can't the President make an appeal for the people to fight against the military?
9. Who has the motivation and ability to stop the intruders?
10. Why is there a tendency for small island governments to be overtaken in this manner?

ACTIVITY 3: WRITING

You are a news reporter called to interview a visitor from another planet. Although this creature looks very much like a human being and speaks English, you find that she has some very different characteristics. Describe what you learned from the alien as a result of your interviews. You might include some information about what the alien is accustomed to, annoyed at, capable of, concerned about, desirous of, incapable of, interested in, suited for, susceptible to, sympathetic toward, and weary of. Use at least five gerund complements in your report.

▶ **EXAMPLE:** *The alien has a very unusual diet. She is used to eating tree bark and grass.*

ACTIVITY 4: SPEAKING

According to Einstein's special theory of relativity, astronauts who make a round-trip journey to a nearby star at a speed near the speed of light might age only a year or so. However, when they return to earth, they would find everyone else a great deal older. This type of "time travel" to the future is possible. Would you consider volunteering for such a mission? What would be the consequences of doing so? When you returned, would you continue to love your spouse or partner even though you would no longer be the same ages? What would you arrange to do on your first day back? Would you enjoy accepting future space mission assignments? Discuss these questions with your classmates.

ACTIVITY 5: SPEAKING/WRITING/READING

With a partner, write a fifteen-item quiz which you can give to another pair of classmates to test their knowledge of gerunds and infinitives.

▶ **EXAMPLE:** 1. *I am interested in* _____ *(fly) to Tahiti.*
2. *The teacher needs Tom* _____ *(ask) his parents for permission.*

ACTIVITY 6: WRITING

You have decided that you would like to be included in the Tierrasol project. Write a letter to the Tierrasol selection committee, explaining why you feel you are qualified for the project. Try to be as persuasive as you can while using at least two gerund complements and four infinitive complements in your writing.

ACTIVITY 7: LISTENING/SPEAKING

Listen to a video or a taped TV drama or romance. Jot down at least ten examples of infinitives or gerunds that you hear. Share your results with the class.

ACTIVITY 8: WRITING/SPEAKING

STEP 1 Imagine that you have an entire day free and you have limitless energy to enjoy the many activities that your town or city has to offer. Make a list, being fairly specific about where you want to go, what you want to see, what you want to eat, etc.

▶ **EXAMPLE:**
1. *Eat an omelet for breakfast at the restaurant "Beach Cafe."*
2. *Go shopping for three hours at the Silverstone Shopping Center.*
3. *Eat lunch and watch a noon performance of "Guys and Dolls" at the Searchlight Pavilion.*
4. *Go swimming at the public pool for two hours.*
5. *etc.*

STEP 2 Share your plans with a partner.

▶ **EXAMPLE:** *In the morning, I want to eat an omelet at the Beach Cafe. Then, I'd like to go shopping for two hours at the Silverstone Shopping Center. . . .*

STEP 3 Now imagine that you are visiting a town or city for just one day and a travel agent has just given you this same list of ideas as suggestions. Comment on your partner's recommendations using as many structures covered in this unit as possible.

▶ **EXAMPLE:** *The plan/recommendation/suggestion to eat an omelet at the Beach Cafe sounds wonderful.*

It would be nice/a thrill/interests me to go shopping for three hours at the Silverstone Shopping Center.

I can't stand/detest/don't like seeing musicals, so I'd like to do something else besides watching "Guys and Dolls."

PERFECTIVE INFINITIVES

UNIT GOALS:

- To use the correct forms of perfective infinitives
- To use perfective infinitives to express ideas and opinions about past events
- To use perfective infinitives to express emotions and attitudes
- To use perfective infinitives to express obligations, intentions, and future plans
- To use perfective infinitives with *enough* and *too*

▶ OPENING TASK
Time Travel to the Past

Have you ever wished you could go back in time and meet famous people from past eras, see things that no longer exist in the world, or participate in exciting historical events?

Napoleon

STEP 1 Consider the following statements. Which ones reflect things you'd like to have been able to see, hear, or do? Which sound less appealing or perhaps not appealing at all? Rank the statements from 1 through 10, with 1 representing your first preference and 10 your last.

I would like . . .

- to have seen Michelangelo painting the Sistine chapel.
- to have watched Rocky Marciano win the heavyweight boxing championship in 1952.
- to have attended a performance by the famous blues singer, Billie Holiday.
- to have been at Waterloo when Napoleon surrendered.
- to have observed dinosaurs before they became extinct.
- to have seen Anna Pavlova, the Russian ballerina, dance in Tchaikovsky's *Swan Lake* ballet.
- to have walked through the Hanging Gardens of Babylon.
- to have spoken with Confucius, the great Chinese philosopher.
- to have heard the Greek epic poet Homer recite *The Iliad* or *The Odyssey*.
- to have taken a cruise on the Nile River in Queen Cleopatra's barge as the sun was setting.

STEP 2 Compare your ratings with those of a few of your classmates. Briefly explain the reasons for your top one or two choices.

STEP 3 Write two more statements expressing things that you would like to have seen, heard, or done.

▶ **Review of Perfective Infinitive Structures**

EXAMPLES	EXPLANATIONS
Perfective Infinitive **(a)** I'd like **to have seen** the first football game ever played. **(b)** She claimed **to have been** at home all evening. **(c)** I expect **to have finished** my term paper by tomorrow night.	**Forming the Perfective Infinitive** Perfective infinitives have the form *to* + *have* + past participle (*-ed* or irregular verb form).
(d) **To have won** the Boston Marathon was a dream come true for her. **(e)** It is useful **to have reviewed** the chapter before you attend the lecture. **(f)** I would love **to have seen** his face when he opened the present. **(g)** The question **to have been debated** was whether the union should go on strike. **(h)** Research writing is a good course **to have taken.** **(i)** Thanh is too young **to have known better.** **(j)** Those pants were big enough **to have fit** a giant!	**Types of Perfective Infinitive Clauses** Like other infinitives, perfective infinitives occur in a number of clause types in sentences: • subject • postponed subject after introductory *it* • object • adjective • degree complement

EXERCISE 1

In the following passage, Ted Turner, a well-known American businessman, talks with interviewer Studs Terkel about some of the things he would like to have done. Underline the perfective infinitives he uses. The first one has been done as an example.

(1) I would like <u>to have lived</u> a whole bunch of lives. (2) I would like to have gone to West Point or Annapolis and had a military career, I would like to have been a fireman, I would like to have been a state trooper, I would like to have been an explorer, I would like to have been a concert pianist, an Ernest Hemingway, an F. Scott Fitzgerald, a movie star, a big league ballplayer, Joe Namath. (3) I like it all. (4) I would like to have been a fighter pilot, a mountain climber, go to the Olympics and run the marathon, a general on a white horse. (5) A sea captain, back in the days of sailing ships, sailed with Horatio Nelson. (6) I would like to have gone with Captain

Cook to find the Spice Islands, with Columbus, with Sir Francis Drake. (7) I would like to have been a pilot, a privateer, a knight in shining armor, gone on the Crusades. (8) Wouldn't you? (9) I'd like to have gone looking for Dr. Livingston, right? (10) In the heart of darkest Africa. (11) I would like to have discovered the headwaters of the Nile and the Amazon River.

EXERCISE 2

Write five statements about things you would like to have done, using perfective infinitive clauses. Exchange the five statements you wrote with another classmate. Report one or more of your classmate's statements to the rest of the class or a small group, using a *that*-clause with a past perfect verb.

▶ **EXAMPLE:**   Statement: I would like to have heard Jimi Hendrix play the American National Anthem.
Paraphrase: *Olivia wishes that she could have heard Jimi Hendrix play the American National Anthem.*

Note that in the paraphrase, *could* is used as the modal with *wish* as the main clause verb.

EXERCISE 3

Complete the blanks with perfective infinitives. Use the verb in parentheses.

▶ **EXAMPLE:**   She was happy (break) __to have broken__ the record for the one-hundred-meter dash.

1. (a) The elderly gentleman next door considers himself (be) _____ quite a romantic fellow in his younger days. (b) He claims (write) _____ passionate love letters to more than a dozen women. (c) Not all of his letters got the responses he had hoped for, but in his opinion, it truly was better (love) _____ and lost than never (love) _____ at all.

2. David: (a) It was really nice of Hector (give) _____ us his car for our trip to the Grand Canyon. We had a great time.

   Alana: (b) Oh, he was happy (be able to) _____ help you out. (c) I'd really like (go) _____ with you on your trip, but my cousins were visiting that weekend.

3. (a) Jeanne is too smart (believe) _____ the story Russ told her the other day. (b) His story was outlandish enough (convince)_____ her that it was far from the truth.

4. (a) Dear Fran: Accepting that job offer was a wise decision for you (make) _____ . (b) We're glad (have) _____ you as our office mate for the past three years. (c) Good luck! With your talent, we expect you (receive) _____ a big promotion before long.

▶ # Expressing Past Events

Perfective infinitives (*to* + *have* + past participle) express events that are past in relation to a present, past, or future moment of focus.

EXAMPLES	EXPLANATIONS
	Past in Relation to the Present
(a) Jaime is happy **to have finished** his report last night so he can go to the soccer game with us today.	Perfective infinitives signal an event or condition in the past. The event or condition may continue to the present.
(b) Ben considers Phillipe **to have been** his best friend ever since they started college three years ago. (Ben still considers him to be his best friend.)	
	Past in Relation to the Past
(c) Dr. Yamada wanted **to have completed** her research before last August. However her funds for the project ran out.	The event expressed by the infinitive clause may be unfulfilled.
(d) The driver claimed **to have stopped** for the traffic light before the accident occurred.	With verbs that express beliefs or attitudes, such as *claim* or *consider*, the event in the infinitive clause may or may not have actually happened.
	Past in Relation to the Future
(e) Winona expects **to have made** all of her plane reservations by next week.	The event expressed by the infinitive clause may be a future event that takes place before another time in the future.
(f) Winona expects **to make** all of her plane reservations by next week.	We also commonly use infinitives that are not perfective (*to* + verb) to carry the same meaning for future events.
Perfective: Past **(g)** It **was** nice of you **to have done** that.	**Past Tense vs. Present Tense Main Clauses**
	When the main clause is past tense, speakers often use nonperfective infinitives to express the same meanings as perfective ones.
Nonperfective: Past **(h)** It **was** nice of you **to do** that.	
Perfective: Past **(i)** It **is** nice of you **to have done** that. (You did something in the past.)	When the main clause is present tense, use:
	Infinitive *To Express* perfective past meaning nonperfective present or future meaning
Nonperfective: Present, Future **(j)** It **is** nice of you **to do** that. (You are doing something right now or will do something in the future.)	

EXERCISE 4

Complete each blank with a perfective infinitive using the verb in parentheses. Then state which type of meaning each one expresses: past relative to the present, to the past, or to the future.

▶ **EXAMPLE:** I would like (accompany) <u>to have accompanied</u> the Castenada family on their travels across the country.

1. By the end of August, the Castenada family plans (tour) _____ most of the East Coast; they have been traveling in the United States all summer and have only two weeks left.

2. They intended (visit) _____ all of their West Coast relatives before the end of June, but they couldn't because of car trouble.

3. Eight-year-old Ruby Castenada says that she would like (spend) _____ the entire summer at Disneyland.

4. So far, Mr. and Mrs. Castenada consider the highlight of their vacation (be) _____ their camping trip in Michigan.

5. At the beginning of the trip, Tracy, their teenage son, was upset (leave) _____ all his friends for the summer.

6. However, now he admits that he would like (see) _____ even more of the country and hopes to travel again soon.

7. The Castenadas' goal is (visit) _____ all of the continental United States before Tracy goes away to college.

EXERCISE 5

Restate the infinitives in the following quotations as perfective infinitives. If you had to choose one of them for a maxim to live by, which one would you select? Can you think of any other sayings that use perfective infinitives?

▶ **EXAMPLE:** To win one's joy through struggle is better than to yield to melancholy. (Andre Gide, French author)

To have won one's joy through struggle is better than to *have yielded* to melancholy.

1. What a lovely surprise to finally discover how unlonely being alone can be. (Ellen Burstyn, American actress)

2. To endure what is unendurable is true endurance. (Japanese proverb)

3. I would prefer even to fail with honor than to win by cheating. (Sophocles, Greek dramatist)

4. To teach is to learn twice over. (Joseph Joubert, *Pensees*)

5. It is better to be happy for a moment and burned up with beauty than to live a long time and be bored all the while. (Don Marquis, "the lesson of the moth," *Archy and Mehitabel*)

6. Youth is the time to study wisdom; old age is the time to practice it. (Rousseau, *Reveries of a Solitary Walker*)

Progressive and Passive Forms of Perfective Infinitives

EXAMPLES	EXPLANATIONS
(a) I'd like **to have been watching** when Bart received his award for bravery. **(b)** Mr. Park believed the police **to have been guarding** his store when the robbery occurred.	**Progressive Form** *to* + *have* + *been* + verb + *-ing*
(c) Bart would like me **to have been sent** a ticket to the ceremony. **(d)** Mr. Park believed himself **to have been given** false information by the police.	**Passive Form** *to* + *have* + *been* + past participle

EXERCISE 6

Rewrite each of the following clauses as a perfective infinitive clause. The clauses begin with *that, ø-that* (*that* has been deleted), or *when*. Make any word changes that are necessary.

▶ **EXAMPLES:**   *ø-that* clause: Josef wishes he could have discovered the Cape of Good Hope with Diaz.

infinitive clause: *Josef would like to have discovered the Cape of Good Hope with Diaz.*

that-clause: Veronica believes that she was shortchanged.

infinitive clause: *Veronica believes herself to have been shortchanged.*

1. Our English teacher expects that we will finish our oral reports on our favorite celebrities by the end of next week.

2. Henri would prefer that he be the last one to present, but unfortunately for him, he is scheduled to be first.

3. Isela believes she was greatly misinformed by one of her interview subjects.

4. We wish we could have heard more about Shaun's talk with Janet Jackson. (Change *wish* to *would like*)

5. Jocelyn hoped she would be given a chance to interview her favorite author, but the interview didn't work out.

6. Gerard claims that he was sent an autograph from a "major motion picture star," whose identity he is keeping a secret.

7. Sandra reported that Meryl Streep, her favorite actress, had been sitting in front of her at a Carnegie Hall concert.

8. Ty thinks that he has gotten the most interesting interview with a celebrity. (Use *consider* for the main verb.)

9. Berta wishes that she had been eating dinner at the Hollywood restaurant last Friday night because someone told her that her favorite basketball player was there.

10. I will be relieved when I have presented my report since getting up in front of others makes me anxious.

FOCUS **4**

▶ Negative Forms of Perfective Infinitives

EXAMPLES	EXPLANATIONS
	Formal English
(a) The three nations were wise **not to have signed** the agreement until they could discuss it further.	In formal written English, put negative forms (*not, never*, etc.) before the infinitive verbs.
(b) **Not to have been contacted** for a job interview greatly disappointed Daniel.	
(c) During his entire term, Representative Bolski appears **never to have voted** in favor of extra funds for child care.	
	Informal English
(d) **To have not been invited** to the party made her upset.	In less formal English, speakers sometimes put negative forms after *have*.
(e) I seem to **have not brought** the book I meant to give you.	
(f) That woman claims **to have never seen** the money that turned up in her purse.	

EXERCISE 7

Rewrite each of the following sentences so that it contains a negative perfective infinitive clause. Use the pattern for formal written English.

▶ **EXAMPLE:**   It appeared that Dr. Moreau had not been in Marseilles the last weekend in April.

Dr. Moreau appeared <u>not to have been</u> in Marseilles the last weekend in April.

1. In reviewing evidence gathered for the murder trial, Detective Armand believed that the facts had not supported Dr. Moreau's claims of innocence.

2. It was quite strange, Armand mused, that Dr. Moreau had not told his housekeeper he would be away the weekend the murder occurred. (Replace *that* with *for* + noun)

3. Furthermore, the doctor did not seem to remember much about the inn he claimed he had stayed in that weekend. How very odd!

4. Also, the doctor claimed that he had never known the victim, Horace Bix; yet Bix's name was found in his appointment book.

5. All in all, Detective Armand believed that Dr. Moreau had not given the police truthful answers to a number of questions.

Expressing Likes, Preferences, and Dislikes Contrary to Past Fact

	EXAMPLES	EXPLANATIONS
Would + verb *would like*	**(a)** I **would like to have spent** the class period reviewing for the exam. (I would have liked to spend the class period reviewing for the exam.)	Use *would* + verbs with perfective infinitives to express likes, dislikes, and preferences about things that did not happen.
would love	**(b)** My parents **would love to have joined** us for dinner. (My parents would have loved to join us for dinner.)	Alternative forms of these sentences are given in parentheses. The alternative form has a perfective main clause verb and a nonperfective infinitive.
would prefer	**(c)** I **would prefer not to have had** an early morning class. (I would have preferred not to have an early morning class.)	
would hate	**(d)** **Wouldn't you hate to have been** in that crowded room? (Wouldn't you have hated to be in that crowded room?)	
	(e) We **would have liked to have spent** the class period reviewing for the exam.	Native English speakers sometimes use perfective forms for both clauses in speech. Although this pattern would sound fine to many native English speakers, it is not considered standard for written English.

EXERCISE 8

Use the cues below to make sentences expressing a past wish that did not materialize or an unpleasant event that was avoided. Use the standard English pattern of *would like, would love, would prefer,* or *would hate* followed by a perfective infinitive. Make any changes that are necessary, including any needed verb tense changes.

▶ **EXAMPLE:**   be asked to present my report first
   I would like to have been asked to present my report first.

1. take all of my final exams on one day
2. forget the answers to the test questions
3. go to the movies instead of taking the exam
4. be the only one in class without the assignment
5. be given true-false questions for the entire test
6. study geology instead of biochemistry
7. walk into the classroom and find out the teacher was absent
8. be watching music video tapes all afternoon
9. not know that class was canceled
10. present an oral report rather than a written one

EXERCISE 9

Choose any five of the following topics. For each topic, write a statement expressing a past wish. With a classmate, explain the reasons for one or two of your statements.

▶ **EXAMPLE:**   An experience while traveling
   I would prefer to have flown from England to France instead of going by boat across the channel.
   Reason: *The sea was very rough that day and I got seasick.*

1. The way you spent one of your last vacations
2. Your participation in a sports event as an athlete or spectator
3. A course you had to take
4. A paper or report you had to write
5. A meal you had recently
6. An experience you had at a party or other social event
7. (A topic of your choice)

▶ # Expressing Other Emotions and Attitudes with Perfective Infinitives

EXAMPLES	EXPLANATIONS
(a) I **am sorry** to have missed your party.	• *be* + adjective
(b) They **were shocked** to have been treated so rudely.	
(c) **It was generous of you** to have lent us your bicycles.	• *it* + *be* + adjective (+ *of* + noun)
(d) **It is annoying** to have been waiting so long for a ticket.	
(e) **It is a pleasure** to have met you after all these years.	• *it* + *be* + noun phrase
(f) **It was a miracle** to have found the contact lens in the swimming pool.	
(g) **It was fortunate for us** to have discovered the mistake.	• (*it* + *be* + adjective) *for* + noun/objective pronoun
(h) **For them** to have had three plane delays in one day was very unlucky.	
(i) It **must** be exciting to have lived in so many countries!	You may also use modal verbs before *be* with many of the expressions.
(j) It **would** be a disappointment to have missed the parade. I'm glad we made it on time!	

EXERCISE 10

Make sentences with perfective infinitive clauses, using the cues. Use a variety of structures. If you wish, add descriptive words or phrases to expand the sentences.

▶ **EXAMPLES:** Be foolish . . . think that no one would notice
John must be foolish to have thought that no one would notice he had taken the dangerous chemicals.

It was foolish of us to have thought no one would notice we were missing from class.

1. Be a tragedy . . . lose so many homes in the volcanic eruptions

2. Be unwise . . . build a home so close to the volcano

3. Be kind . . . donate your time to volunteer work

4. Show up at the party together . . . be astounding (Start with *for* + noun)

5. Wear jogging shorts . . . was considered improper

EXERCISE 11

Use an expression from Focus 6, Exercise 10, or a similar one to make up a response for each of the situations below. Use a perfective infinitive in your response.

▶ **EXAMPLE:**   You have recently spent three days at the beach house of your parents' friends while they were not there. You are writing them a thank-you note.

It was very generous of you to have let me stay in your beach house during my trip to the coast.

1. You have just remembered that today is the birthday of one of your friends who lives in another city, and you forgot to send her a birthday card. You buy a card and want to write a note to tell her you're sorry.

2. A friend helped you move from one apartment to another. You want to send him a thank-you note.

3. You are having a conversation at a party with someone you have just met. She has been telling you about her trip to see the Summer Olympics.

4. You recently went shopping in a department store. When you tried to purchase something, the salesman kept you waiting for several minutes while he chatted with a friend on the phone. You are writing a letter of complaint to the manager of the store.

5. You are writing a letter to a friend. You want to tell her how fortunate you were recently. You just heard that you were awarded two scholarships to attend school next year.

6. You call up the mother of a friend to thank her for having given a going away party for you before you move to another city.

7. A friend did not show up for a class three sessions in a row. This strikes you as strange because he has never missed a class before. Another friend asks you if you know where he has been, but you don't.

8. Someone you know has recently bought a very expensive new car. The person doesn't have much money, so you think it was an unwise purchase.

▶ # Expressing Uncertainly about Past Events

EXAMPLES	EXPLANATIONS
(a) I **seem to have forgotten** my homework assignment. Oh wait, here it is in my notebook!	After the verbs *seem* and *appear,* perfective infinitives express uncertainty about past events based on present evidence.
(b) This assignment **appears to have been written** rather hastily. **(c)** Hmmm . . . someone **seems to have eaten** all the ice cream.	Sometimes the "uncertainty" is actually a way to avoid directly accusing or criticizing someone.

EXERCISE 12

Make up a sentence with *appear* or *seem* followed by a perfective infinitive for each of the following situations.

1. You go for a job interview. The interviewer asks to see your application form. You realize you must have left it at home. Respond to the question.

2. You are a teacher. One of your students looks as if she is on the verge of falling asleep. Make a comment to her.

3. As you are getting ready to leave the classroom, you discover that you no longer have your notebook, which was with you when you entered the room. Make a comment to the class as they are walking out.

4. You have just finished reading a novel that is the worst one you have ever read. Make a comment to a friend about the author of the book.

5. When the teacher starts going over the homework assignment, you realize that you did the wrong one. The teacher calls on you for an answer. Give an appropriate response.

► # Expressing Obligations, Intentions, and Future Plans

USE

EXAMPLES	EXPLANATIONS
(a) The engineers **were supposed to have checked** all the controls before the shuttle was launched. **(b)** Caroline **was to have spent** the entire summer sculpting, but she ended up working at a bank for a month.	Perfective infinitives may follow phrasal modals *be supposed to* or *be to*. They express past obligations or plans that were not fulfilled.
(c) Do you **plan to have written** your report before Sunday? **(d)** The weatherman **expects** the rains **to have ended** by next weekend.	With verbs such as *plan, intend, hope,* and *expect,* perfective infinitives express a future time before another future time.

EXERCISE 13

Complete the following sentences with information about yourself; use a perfective infinitive clause in each.

► **EXAMPLE:** By tomorrow I intend *to have bought my sister a birthday present*.

1. By next week I plan _____.

2. I intend _____ within the next five years.

3. I was supposed _____ but I didn't because _____.

4. I expect _____ before _____.

5. By _____ I hope _____.

► **Perfective Infinitives with** *Enough* and *Too*

USE

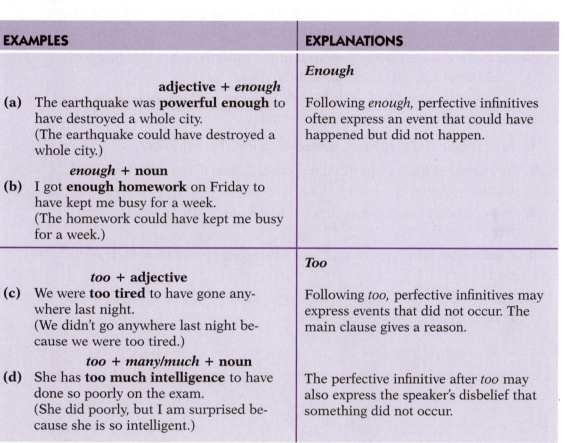

EXAMPLES	EXPLANATIONS
adjective + *enough* **(a)** The earthquake was **powerful enough** to have destroyed a whole city. (The earthquake could have destroyed a whole city.) ***enough* + noun** **(b)** I got **enough homework** on Friday to have kept me busy for a week. (The homework could have kept me busy for a week.)	*Enough* Following *enough*, perfective infinitives often express an event that could have happened but did not happen.
***too* + adjective** **(c)** We were **too tired** to have gone anywhere last night. (We didn't go anywhere last night because we were too tired.) ***too* + many/much + noun** **(d)** She has **too much intelligence** to have done so poorly on the exam. (She did poorly, but I am surprised because she is so intelligent.)	*Too* Following *too*, perfective infinitives may express events that did not occur. The main clause gives a reason. The perfective infinitive after *too* may also express the speaker's disbelief that something did not occur.

EXERCISE 14

Use the phrases below to create sentences about past possibilities using perfective infinitives.

► **EXAMPLE:** poison . . . strong enough

The poison that the child accidentally swallowed was strong enough to have killed her, but fortunately she recovered completely.

1. the noise . . . loud enough
2. they ate enough popcorn . . .
3. fireworks . . . bright enough
4. wind . . . strong enough

5. the weather in Moscow . . . cold enough

6. we heard enough bad news . . .

EXERCISE 15

The following sentences express disbelief about an event or explain why something didn't happen. Combine the ideas in each pair of sentences into one sentence, using a perfective infinitive clause.

▶ **EXAMPLE:** She couldn't have done well in the marathon last fall. She had sustained too many minor injuries.

Combined: *She had sustained too many minor injuries to have done well in the marathon last fall.*

1. My brother couldn't have cheated on a test. He is too honest.

2. You couldn't have stopped taking piano lessons! You have too much talent.

3. Stan couldn't have bought that wild tie himself. He is too conservative.

4. Charmaine didn't stay at that low-level job. She has too much ambition.

5. They couldn't have taken on any more debts. They have too many already.

Use Your English

ACTIVITY 1: LISTENING / WRITING / SPEAKING

Imagine that you have just returned from a two-week vacation. The dates of your vacation were July 14 through the 28th. You will hear four messages that have been left on your telephone answering machine.

STEP 1   Take notes as you listen to each message.

STEP 2   Use your notes to create responses that you could leave on the answering machines of the people who called. Use at least one perfective infinitive form in each response.

STEP 3   Share your favorite responses with a small group of classmates.

ACTIVITY 2: RESEARCH / SPEAKING / WRITING

Interview ten people about regrets—either their greatest regrets or most recent ones. Then write the results of your survey using statements with perfective infinitives. Share the results with your classmates. Here are some examples of paraphrases:

▶ **EXAMPLES:**   Jack's regret: that he stopped dating Shirelle
Paraphrase: Jack is sorry to *have stopped* dating Shirelle.

Risa's regret: that she didn't go to Vienna for her vacation
Paraphrase: Risa is sorry not *to have gone* to Vienna for her vacation.

Blanca's regret: that she never learned Spanish from her mother
Paraphrase: Blanca is sorry never *to have learned* Spanish from her mother.

ACTIVITY 3: SPEAKING/WRITING

Interview one or more classmates about things that they hope or expect to have done or have seen during the next five years. Here are examples of some categories you might consider. Think of others that might be interesting to find out about. (Trips they hope to have made? Classes they expect to have passed? New foods they hope to have tried?)

- Places you hope to have visited
- Hobbies you hope to have engaged in
- Educational degrees you expect to have received
- Possessions you hope to have obtained
- Books you'd like to have read
- Skills you hope to have learned or developed

Present some of your findings in a brief oral report to the class.

ACTIVITY 4: WRITING/SPEAKING

A "tall tale" is a story that contains a great deal of exaggeration for a humorous effect. Imagine that you are at a Tall Tales Convention in which people compete to make up the funniest exaggerations. You have entered the "Enough is Enough Category"; for this competition you must come up with statements like "The sidewalk was hot enough last weekend to have fried an egg on it" or "We made enough food last night to have invited the state of Texas for dinner." Either individually or in teams, make up entries for the competition. Have others vote on the best ones.

ACTIVITY 5: WRITING/LISTENING

Write an imaginary interview or dialogue between you and a famous person who is no longer living. (It could be someone you mentioned in the Opening Task.) In your dialogue use some perfective infinitive phrases. For example, you could ask the person what she or he might like to have done differently if circumstances had been different or if the person had lived at a different time. Or you might have the person comment on what he or she was happy or sorry to have done or how exciting, frustrating, etc. it was to have experienced certain events. Read your dialogue to class members without telling them who the famous person is; see if they can guess the person's identity.

ADJECTIVE COMPLEMENTS IN SUBJECT AND PREDICATE POSITION

UNIT GOALS:

- To use three types of adjective complement structures
- To use adjective complements in subject and predicate position
- To choose among infinitives, gerunds, and *that* clauses

▶**O**PENING **TASK**
Human Beings' Relationship to Animals

STEP 1 As you look over the following list, think about the positive and negative associations each term has.

STEP 2 Jot down your ideas for as many terms as you can with a partner.

Term	Positive	Negative
1. animal research	provides a way to test the safety of drugs and cosmetics	animals dissected, injected, and killed in experiments
2. fur coat		
3. zoo		
4. oil tanker		
5. veal		
6. ivory		
7. pesticide		
8. campground		
9. bullfight		
10. hunting		
11. highway construction		

STEP 3 After your discussion, write down statements about several of the terms, including both positive and negative associations. Here are some sample statements about the first term, animal research:

It is unethical for animals like gorillas and chimpanzees to be used in medical research. That this research tests the safety of drugs and cosmetics is undeniable. But researchers' blindly generalizing the findings from these experiments to human beings does not make sense. In addition, injecting and killing these animals during experiments is inhumane.

▶ **O**verview of Adjective Complements

EXAMPLES	EXPLANATIONS
adjective complement + adjective (a) **Killing these animals** is inhumane.	Adjective complements can appear in subject position in front of linking verbs (such as *appear, be, become, look, remain, seem*) followed by adjectives.
(b) **That the blue whale is becoming extinct** seems sad. (c) **For campers to pollute streams** is irresponsible. (d) **Bulls' being killed** in bullfights appears brutal.	Adjective complements are of three types: • *that*-clause (consisting of *that* + clause) • infinitive (consisting of *for* + noun phrase + *to* + base verb) • gerund (consisting of *'s* + verb + *-ing*)
(e) Joshua appears ready **for the hunting season** to begin. (f) Michelle is eager **for Joshua to shoot a fox.**	The adjectives that precede adjective complements and follow animate subjects generally show positive expectation (e.g., *ready, anxious, happy, eager*, etc.).
(g) Michelle is eager to have a fox coat. (h) **NOT:** Michelle is eager for herself to have a fox coat.	If the main subject and the complement subject are alike, we delete the *for* phrase.

EXERCISE 1

In the following short texts, complete the adjective complements with *that*-clauses, *for/to* infinitives, or gerunds.

▶ **EXAMPLE:** Elizabeth Mann Borghese, who was the daughter of the writer Thomas Mann, taught her dog to take dictation on a special

typewriter. Her dog's __taking dictation__ is amazing.

1. Once a woman was thrown off a yacht and three dolphins rescued her and led her to a marker in the sea. Another time, several fishermen were lost in a dense fog, and four dolphins nudged their boat

   to safety. Dolphins' _____ is well-documented.

2. Mrs. Betsy Marcus' dog Benjy was known to sing "Raindrops Keep

   Fallin' on My Head." For a dog _____ is incredible.

3. At one time, passenger pigeons were very numerous. Now there are none because of massive hunting and the destruction of their natural forest home. That hunters _____ is sad.

4. Jaco, an African gray parrot, could speak German. When his master left the house alone, he said, "God be with you." When his master left with other people, he said, "God be with you all." Jaco's

_____ is fascinating.

5. The dwarf lemur and the mountain pygmy possum were considered extinct. However, in recent years, these animals have reappeared.

For extinct animals _____ is inspiring.

6. Washoe, a female chimpanzee, was taught sign language. She was able to make up words like *drink-fruit* (for watermelon) and *water-bird* (for swan). That Washoe _____ is intriguing.

EXERCISE 2

Imagine that you are an animal instead of a human being. What would make you happy if you were one of the following pets? Write your answers in first person and use one of the adjectives: *anxious, eager, happy,* or *ready.*

▶ **EXAMPLE:**   cat

       *I would be **eager** for my owner to feed me a tuna casserole.*
       *I would be **happy** to lie around in the sun.*

1. horse

2. parrot

3. dog

4. mouse

5. goldfish

6. snake

▶ Adjective Complements in Subject and Predicate Position

EXAMPLES	EXPLANATIONS
(a) I am sorry to say that certain businesses that sell sculptured ivory objects have hired poachers to kill elephants for their tusks. **For poachers to take the tusks from live elephants** is alarming. **That they sell them is** abominable. Worst of all, **elephants' becoming an endangered species because of this** is criminal.	In subject position, adjective complements usually contain a known idea, either previously mentioned or assumed through context.
It **+ linking verb + adjective + adjective complement** **(b)** It is interesting **that medical researchers have made important medical discoveries through animal research.** They need to continue this work. **(c)** It is necessary **for protesters to call for a moratorium on animal testing.** Animals have rights too!	When *that*-clauses and infinitives contain new information, they will more commonly appear in predicate position. We move the *that*-clause or the infinitive to the end of the sentence and add *it* at the beginning.
(d) **NOT:** It is abominable poachers' killing elephants.	Gerunds do not normally occur with *it* constructions.

EXERCISE 3

Fill in the blanks with a variety of appropriate linking verbs and adjectives from the following lists. More than one answer may be correct.

Linking Verbs	Adjectives		
appear	apparent	improper	obvious
be	bad	inappropriate	odd
become	compulsory	irrational	sad
look	depressing	irritating	surprising
remain	disappointing	likely	true
seem	impossible	necessary	unfortunate

► **EXAMPLE:** From all of the evidence, it _____was obvious_____ that the defendant was guilty.

1. Crime is rampant in many parts of the world. That teenagers commit many of these crimes _____.

2. It _____ for children to attend elementary and secondary school in the United States.

3. It was a long, hard winter. Felicia's being shut inside every day _____.

4. It _____ that the president will be reelected if the economy continues to recover.

5. The young man stayed out until 3:00 A.M. For him not to listen to his parents _____.

6. All of the other men had been rehired by the company. John's still being unemployed _____.

7. It _____ for two wrongs to make a right.

8. Everyone knew that President Rabin had been shot. That he had been shot by one of his own people _____.

9. The fashion designer's clothes this season are very extreme. For vinyl to be mixed with fur _____.

10. I have stopped going to the theater on Saturday afternoons. Children's whispering and throwing popcorn in the air _____.

EXERCISE 4

What do you think about the following activities or ideas? Use adjective complements in your answer.

► **EXAMPLES:** (you) saving a little money every month

It's wise (for me) to save because I might need some extra money some day.

OR

My saving money has become essential to my future.

1. (elderly people) skydiving (= jumping from a plane with a parachute on)
2. (you) studying English grammar
3. (your relative) riding a motorcycle without a helmet
4. (cities) banning smoking in all public places
5. (your friend) copying someone else's paper
6. (the government) making alcohol illegal

7. (teachers) creating schools for profit rather than having public schools

8. (a single person) joining a singles club

9. (a poor person) winning the lottery

10. (you) forgetting someone's name

EXERCISE 5

Comment on the following facts found in the *Book of Lists 2* using a *that*-clause in subject position.

▶ **EXAMPLE:** Tigers do not usually hunt humans unless they are old or in-jured. However, a tigress, the Champawat man-eater, killed 438 people in the Himalayas in Nepal between 1903 and 1911.

That so many people were killed in Nepal by a tiger is tragic.

1. Black bears do not usually hurt humans unless they are hungry. When the Alaskan blueberry crop was poor in 1963, black bears at-tacked at least four people, one of whom they killed, because no other food was available.

2. In the central provinces of India, leopards have been known to enter huts and kill humans. One famous leopard, the Panawar man-eater, is reputed to have killed four hundred people.

3. On March 25, 1941, the British ship *Britannia* sank in the Atlantic Ocean. While the twelve survivors sat in a lifeboat, a giant squid reached its arm around the body of one of them and pulled him into the ocean.

4. In South America, people have reported losing fingers, toes, or pieces of flesh while bathing in piranha-infested waters.

5. In 1916, four people were killed as they were swimming along a sixty-mile stretch of the New Jersey coast. The attacker was a great white shark.

EXERCISE 6

Consider your responses during the Opening Task on page 361 and create dialogues with facts about animals, using a *that*-clause and the adjective pro-vided.

▶ **EXAMPLE:** shocking   Q: What's so shocking?

A: ***It is shocking*** *that the oil from the grounded oil tanker killed thousands of innocent animals.*

1. irresponsible   **4.** important

2. encouraging   **5.** outrageous

3. sad   **6.** fortunate

▶ Infinitives, Gerund, and *That* Clauses

EXAMPLES	EXPLANATIONS
(a) Many zoos have instituted stricter laws regarding the care of their animals. **That zoos protect their animals is important.** **(b)** **Zoos' protecting their animals** is important.	Infinitive, gerund, and *that*-clauses have different meanings. *That*-clauses and gerunds refer to actual or fulfilled events. In examples (a) and (b) the adjective complements refer to the fact that zoos actually do already protect their animals.
(c) Many zoos have reported higher numbers of animals dying in captivity. **For zoos to protect their animals** is important.	Infinitives refer to future ideas or potential events. In example (c), zoos potentially can protect their animals (but they don't necessarily do so).

EXERCISE 7

What would be unexpected/odd/surprising/unusual/impossible/strange for the following people to do or to have done? Write a sentence that expresses your idea.

▶ **EXAMPLE:** Eskimos   *Eskimos' living in grass huts would be strange.*

1. dictators
2. busybodies
3. bus drivers
4. procrastinators
5. Napoleon
6. Mahatma Gandhi
7. the ancient Greeks
8. your mother
9. your friend's father
10. our class

EXERCISE 8

Circle the best option and explain your decision.

▶ **EXAMPLE:**   1.   (a) It is heartening that the Beauty Cosmetics Company of London has refused to test its products on animals since its establishment.

(b) It would be heartening for the Beauty Cosmetics Company of London to refuse to test its products on animals.

*(The Beauty Cosmetics Company has actually refused already, so answer **a** with the **that**-clause is correct.)*

1. (a) It is shocking that commercial whalers have almost exterminated the blue whale.

   (b) It would be shocking for commercial whalers to almost exterminate the blue whale.

2. (a) It is sad that dolphins catch diseases from humans at dolphin recreational swim centers.

   (b) It would be sad for dolphins to catch diseases from humans at dolphin recreational swim centers.

3. (a) After an oil spill, it will be important that animals are rescued.

   (b) After an oil spill, it will be important for animals to be rescued.

4. (a) Companies' cutting down the Amazonian rain forests will lead to ecological disaster.

   (b) For companies to cut down the Amazonian rain forests would lead to ecological disaster.

5. (a) For the child to whine seemed annoying to all of the crew.

   (b) The child's whining seemed annoying to all of the crew.

Use Your English

ACTIVITY 1: LISTENING

Listen to the following taped excerpts and circle the appropriate comment that would follow from what you have heard.

▶ **EXAMPLE:** Tonya: *Did you hear the good news?*

Francisco: *No, what?*

Tonya: *Rosa's parents just bought her a car for her birthday.*

(a) That Rosa got a new car for her birthday is amazing.

(b) For Rosa to get a new car will be amazing.

1. (a) It's annoying that such a smart aleck like Tom should have such luck!

   (b) For Harvard to give such an expensive scholarship is annoying.

2. (a) It is essential for human beings to revere animals for their intelligence and strength.

   (b) It is true that many human beings have killed animals in order to obtain food and clothing.

3. (a) That citizens care so much about the needy in Los Angeles is encouraging.

   (b) Citizens' neglecting the needy in Los Angeles will lead to serious consequences.

4. (a) Scientists' working in the Gobi Desert is extraordinary.

   (b) That we now know something about dinosaur parental care is astonishing.

5. (a) It's great that she got a new computer.

   (b) It's great for her to get a new computer.

ACTIVITY 2: RESEARCH/WRITING

Research several animals that are in danger of becoming extinct. Find out how they are dying or being killed. Then, write a short paragraph, giving your feelings and opinions about **one** of these animals. Several suggestions are given below.

California condor	orangutan of Borneo
Arabian oryx	blue whale
spotted owl	giant Panda

ACTIVITY 3: WRITING

What do rosary beads, pistol grips, and dice have in common? They are all made of ivory, sometimes illegally obtained. Hunters cut the tusks from elephants with chainsaws, sometimes while the animals are still alive. Then they sell the tusks to businesspeople who smuggle them out of the country in gas tankers, cargo trucks, or personal luggage. Often political officials collaborate in the crime by issuing false import permits. Great profits are made all around at the elephant's expense.

Imagine that you have bought an ivory figure for $1000 and later learned that the ivory had been illegally obtained. Write a letter of complaint to the company from which you bought the figure. Use statements such as, "I have just learned that the figure I bought from you was made of illegally obtained ivory. Your selling me such an item is outrageous."

ACTIVITY 4: RESEARCH/SPEAKING

Find out how animals have been used in research of one of the following diseases: polio, diphtheria, mumps, hepatitis, diabetes, arthritis, high blood pressure, AIDS, or cancer. As a result of your research, express your opinions in a short oral report on the use of animals in furthering medical progress. Do you feel that it is important or unnecessary?

▶ **EXAMPLE:** *It is important for researchers to use animals in their research . . .*

ACTIVITY 5: SPEAKING/WRITING

Michael W. Fox in his book *Inhuman Society: The American Way of Exploiting Animals* (New York: St. Martin's Press, 1990, p. 46) has expressed his opinion on modern zoos in the following way:

Today's zoos and wildlife safari parks are radically different from the early iron and concrete zoos. It takes money to run a modern zoo, and zoo directors realize that they must compete with a wide variety of leisure-time activities. Concession stands, miniature railroads, and other carnival amusements, as well as dubious circuslike shows with performing chimps or big cats, lure many visitors to some of our large zoos and wildlife parks. What tricks and obedience the animals display are more a reflection of the power of human control than of the animals' natural behavior. Performing apes, elephants, bears, big cats, dolphins, and "killer" whales especially draw the crowds. Man's mastery over the powerful beast and willful control over its wild instincts is a parody of the repression and sublimation of human nature and personal freedom.

STEP 1   In pairs, discuss the preceding paragraph.

- How do modern zoos differ from zoos in the past?
- Do spectators at modern zoos actually have a chance to see an animal's true nature?
- What does the last sentence mean?

STEP 2   Individually, write a short paragraph explaining whether or not you agree with Fox. What statements do you feel are true? What statements do you feel are questionable? (Use at least three adjective complements in your writing.)

NOUN COMPLEMENTS TAKING *THAT* CLAUSES

UNIT GOALS:

- To use noun complements to explain abstract nouns
- To distinguish *that* clause noun complements from restrictive relative clauses
- To use *that*-clause noun complements in subject position to signal known or implied information
- To use *the fact* + *that* noun complements appropriately
- To use *that* clause noun complements after transitive adjectives and phrasal verbs

▶ OPENING TASK

Explaining Natural Phenomena

How good are you at explaining natural phenomena? Would you be able to explain why the North American and South American eastern coastlines and the Eurasian and African western coastlines appear to be mirror images of each other?

One account for this phenomenon is the theory that all of these continents once formed a single continent and subsequently moved apart.

STEP 1 Discuss some of the following questions with your classmates. Try to write down the facts that could explain these intriguing natural events.

1. What explains the observation that in some parts of the world leaves change color and fall from the trees each year?

2. What explains the observation that shooting stars speed across the sky?

3. What explains the fact that there are oases in desert environments?

4. What accounts for the fact that some rainbows are partial and some are full?

5. What could illustrate the idea that physical activity is difficult at high altitudes?

6. What could illustrate the law that heat flows from a warm place to a cooler place?

7. What fact could explain why the sun and moon appear larger near the horizon?

8. What fact could account for a person's reflection appearing upside down in a spoon?

STEP 2 Now add a few questions of your own about other intriguing natural events that you are curious about. Once you have written your questions, see if your classmates know the facts that explain them.

Overview of Noun Complements

EXAMPLES	EXPLANATIONS
(a) The theory **that water expands when it is frozen** is testable. (b) The requirement **for workers to wear safety glasses** is important.	Noun complements are of two types: *that*-clauses and infinitives. • The *that* clause is a way of explaining the noun. • The *for-to* infinitive also explains the noun. • Both types of complements follow abstract nouns. Many abstract nouns have verb counterparts (*requirement/require, advice/advise, reminder/remind,* etc.).
Abstract Nouns (+ *That* Clause): *answer · · · · news · · · · · request* *appeal · · · · notion · · · · statement* *axiom · · · · possibility · · suggestion* *fact · · · · · proposal · · · theory* *hypothesis · reminder · · thesis* *idea · · · · · reply*	With some abstract nouns, we use a *that*-clause to form noun complements.
Abstract Nouns (+ Infinitives): *advice · · · · · permission · · request* *appeal · · · · · plan · · · · · · requirement* *command · · · preparation · suggestion* *instruction · · proposal · · · tendency* *motivation · · recommendation* *order · · · · · reminder*	Another group of abstract nouns takes infinitives.
(c) Most people understand the recommendation **that citizens should pay higher taxes.** (d) Most people understand the recommendation **for citizens to pay higher taxes.**	Some nouns, such as *request, recommendation, and suggest* may take either a *that*-clause or an infinitive as a complement.
(e) The fact **that students must pay higher tuition** disappoints us. (f) We read about the need **for more volunteers to help the poor.**	Noun complements may appear with nouns in subject or object position.

EXERCISE 1

Underline each noun complement. Circle the abstract noun that precedes it.

▶ **EXAMPLE:** Early scientists believe (the notion) that matter could be divided into four basic elements: earth, water, air, and fire.

1. The tendency for liquids to turn into gases is well-known.
2. Moisture in the air provides the catalyst for industrial fumes to react and form acid rain.
3. Galileo proposed the hypothesis that all falling bodies drop at the same constant speed.
4. The possibility for a sailor to get lost at sea is low if he or she has a compass.
5. The idea that people can survive without light is nonsense.
6. The fact that overhead cables sag on a hot day proves that solids expand when heated.

EXERCISE 2

Summarize the information from the text by completing the statements that follow.

SOLAR RAYS AND OUR SKIN

The increase of hydrofluorocarbons in the atmosphere is dangerously depleting the earth's ozone layer. The effect of this is that people are having greater exposure to ultraviolet light rays. Can these solar rays increase the chances of skin cancer? Yes, in fact, they increase the cases of malignant melanoma—the deadliest type.

According to The American Cancer Society, hundreds of thousands of new cases of skin cancer will be diagnosed in the United States each year. About five percent of these will be malignant melanoma. To prevent more cases, many doctors say that people should stay out of the sun altogether. This is especially true for redheads and blondes with freckled skin. At the very least, a person should cover up and wear a sunscreen with a high sun-protection factor (15, 25, or 30) during the periods of the day when ultraviolet rays are strongest.

A good example of an anti-skin-cancer campaign comes from Australia. Life-guards in the state of Victoria wear T-shirts with the slogan "SLIP! SLOP! SLAP!" which means slip on a shirt, slop on some sunscreen, and slap on a hat. Although these hints may not please all sunbathers on beaches around the world, they might very well save their lives.

▶ **EXAMPLE:** The news that <u>hydrofluorocarbons are depleting the earth's ozone layer</u> is alarming.

1. The fact that _____ indicates why there has been an increase in cases of malignant melanoma.

2. The fact that _____ explains why blondes and redheads burn easily.

3. The fact that _____ is evidence that ultraviolet rays can cause skin cancer.

4. The doctors' recommendation for _____ is not very popular.

5. The amusing reminder for _____ has changed the sunbathing habits of people in Australia.

EXERCISE 3

Reread the questions in the Opening Task on page 373 and answer them, using a *that* clause in object position.

▶ **EXAMPLE:** What explains the observation that "shooting stars" speed across the sky?

The observation that "shooting stars" speed across the sky can be explained by meteorites' burning up as they hit the earth's atmosphere.

That Clause Noun Complements versus Restrictive Relative Clauses

EXAMPLES	EXPLANATIONS
(a) The story **that she opened a restaurant** is untrue. (b) The requirement **that students do their homework** is necessary.	A *that*-clause noun complement defines an idea. In (a), *opening a restaurant* is "the story." The sentence still makes sense even if *the story* is deleted. In this sentence, *which* cannot replace *that*. Likewise in (b), the main idea of the sentence is kept even if *the requirement* is omitted.
(c) The story **that/which she told** was untrue. (d) The requirement **that/which students must follow** is outdated.	A restrictive relative clause limits an idea. *The story* in (c) relates to a particular story, the one that she told. The sentence will not make sense if *the story* is deleted. In this sentence, *which* can replace *that*. The same is true in (d), where the sentence will not make sense if *the requirement* is deleted.

EXERCISE 4

Which sentence in each of the following pairs contains a noun complement? Circle your choice.

▶ **EXAMPLE:** (a) The idea that they didn't question the witnesses was shocking.
     (b) The idea that he had was exciting.

1. (a) Many people dispute the fact that human beings evolved from apes.
   (b) Many people accept the fact that he just mentioned.

2. (a) The suggestion that she included in the letter will never be followed.
   (b) The suggestion that a person should warm up before jogging is important.

3. (a) The reply that she did not need help came as a surprise.
   (b) The reply that contained important information was received too late.

4. (a) I believe the theory that opposites attract.
   (b) I believe the theory that my uncle proposed.

5. (a) The news that was relayed on Thursday was disappointing.
   (b) The news that the war had started depressed everyone.

▶ *That* **Clause Noun Complements in Subject Position**

EXAMPLES	EXPLANATIONS
(a) Harry had to write many papers in college. He never learned how to type. **The idea that Harry graduated from college without knowing how to type** astonishes me.	*That* clause noun complements in subject position contain known or implied information. The predicates comment upon the facts or ideas contained in *that* clauses following *the fact/idea/news,* etc.).
(b) When Teresa was diagnosed with cancer, everyone thought that she would not survive. Then, after several months of chemotherapy, the doctor said he could see no trace of the disease. **The fact that she was cured** is a miracle.	

EXERCISE 5

The following paragraphs describe amazing facts about famous people. Make observations about each set of facts using a *that*-clause following the *fact/idea/news,* etc.

▶ **EXAMPLE:** When Beethoven was twenty-eight years old, he became deaf. In spite of this, he was still able to compose music.

The fact that Beethoven composed music while he was deaf is amazing.

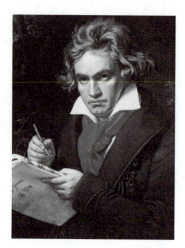

1. Marie Antoinette and Louis XVI ate very well, while their Parisian subjects could not afford bread. When hearing of this, the unsympathetic queen is reported to have said, "Why, then, let them eat cake."

2. United States President Richard Nixon resigned from office in 1974 after a very serious governmental scandal. His Republican associates who were interested in having him reelected had installed wiretaps at the headquarters of the Democratic National Committee at the Watergate Hotel. Rather than being honest, Nixon tried to cover up the scandal and this led to his downfall.

3. In 1919, Rudolph Valentino, a famous American movie star, married Jean Acker. In his silent films, he played the part of the great lover. But, on the wedding day, Acker ran away and Valentino never consummated his marriage with her.

4. For years, athletes did the high jump by jumping sideways or straddling over the bar. Then, Dick Fosbury discovered that he could break world records by going over head first, flat on his back. The technique is now called the Fosbury Flop.

5. The Japanese had long revered their emperor as divine. However, Emperor Hirohito destroyed this image by announcing to his people in 1946 that it was a false conception that he was descended from God. In fact, even at the early age of fourteen, Hirohito had doubted his own divinity.

▶ *The Fact That . . .*

EXAMPLES	EXPLANATIONS
(a) **Less formal:** The fact that she refused the money showed her sense of pride. **(b)** **Formal:** That she refused the money showed her sense of pride. **(c)** **Less formal:** People generally acknowledge the fact that Japan must find alternate ways to use its space. **(d)** **Formal:** People generally acknowledge that Japan must find alternate ways to use its space.	*The fact* + *that* clause noun complements in (a) and (c) are similar in meaning to the *that* clauses in (b) and (d); however, we generally consider them less formal.
(e) **Wordy:** He believed the fact that his daughter had been kidnapped, and he understood the fact that he would need to pay a ransom. **(f)** **Concise:** He believed that his daughter had been kidnapped, and he understood that he would need to pay a ransom.	In writing, overuse of *that* clauses in object position with *the fact* can lead to wordiness. In most cases, it is better to use the simple *that* clause.
(g) The detectives concealed **the fact that** they had searched the room. **(h)** The soldiers accepted **the fact that** they had been defeated. **(i)** The police officers disregarded **the fact that** they needed a search warrant. **(j)** NOT: The police officers disregarded that they needed a search warrant.	Certain verbs (such as *accept, conceal, discuss, dispute, disregard, hide, overlook, support*) require the use of *the fact that* clauses in object position, however.

EXERCISE 6

The following passage contains too many *the fact that* clauses. Underline instances of *the fact* in the text. Then, cross out those that do not seem necessary or are incorrect.

(1) Citizens may believe ~~the fact~~ that they are safe from hazardous wastes, but they are misled. (2) Hundreds of chemical companies say the fact that they are disposing of toxic wastes, yet they conceal the fact that they are illegally dumping them or improperly disposing of them. (3) The tragic result is the fact that dangerous wastes are seeping into the water supply. (4) Although many man-

ufacturers do not want to accept the fact that they need to find alternate means of disposal, environmental agencies are forcing them to do so. (5) Unfortunately, it has been too late in some cases. (6) The fact that residents who live near toxic wastes sites often have greater chronic respiratory and neurological problems than people who do not supports the fact that toxic waste is a major health issue. (7) Chemical companies can no longer overlook the fact that something must be done. (8) Experts claim the fact that landfills having double liners is one solution. (9) Companies also need to accept the fact that recycling and substituting hazardous chemicals for safer ones in their products will greatly improve the situation for their communities.

FOCUS **5**

▶ *That*-Clause Noun Complements Following Transitive Adjectives and Phrasal Verbs

EXAMPLES	EXPLANATION
(a) He is tired of **the fact that she refuses to see him.** **(b)** NOT: He is tired of that she refuses to see him. **(c)** He played down **the news that his team won.** **(d)** NOT: He played down that his team won.	When *that*-clause noun complements follow transitive adjectives (adjective taking a preposition + a noun phrase) or phrasal verbs, they must be *the fact/news/idea/theory*, etc. *that*-clauses rather than simple *that*-clauses.

Examples of Transitive Adjectives	Examples of Phrasal Verbs
disappointed in *worried about* *proud of* *sick of* *tired of*	*play down* *long for* *give in* *face up to* *put up with*

EXERCISE 7

Imagine that a very wealthy entrepreneur has just lost his fortune. Comment upon the circumstances of his condition using the words below and the fact/idea/news, etc. that clauses.

▶ **EXAMPLES:** businessman (face up to)

The businessman had to face up to the fact that he had lost his millions.

1. his mother (worried about)
2. negligence (account for)
3. his creditors (wary of)
4. his employees (indignant at)
5. his wife (put up with)
6. the lawyers (proud of)

EXERCISE 8

Suppose you saw people doing the following strange actions. What facts would you bring up in order to help clear up their confusion? Write a sentence about what you would say.

▶ **EXAMPLES:** reading a book upside down

I would bring up the fact that it is easier to read a book while sitting up.

1. washing the dishes with laundry detergent
2. making lasagna without cheese
3. playing soccer with a baseball
4. taking pictures without film in the camera
5. watching a TV with no sound
6. spelling the word *fish* with *ph* before *i* instead of *f.*

EXERCISE 9

The following sentences review the structures learned in this unit. Correct those that contain errors or are too wordy according to formal writing rules. Write **OK** next to those that are correct.

▶ **EXAMPLES:** The teacher overlooked the fact that Hung had not done his homework. *OK*

The fact that she made a confession ^{was} untrue.

1. Tom believes the fact that light travels faster than sound.
2. The request for her to stop smoking was ignored.
3. The fact that the automobile increased the distance a person could travel made it possible for a person to live and work in different places.
4. She is tired of that she always has to wash the dishes.
5. We are concerned about that there will be no more food.
6. I am grateful for the fact that the doctor assisted me in my decision.
7. Did the glasses help to conceal the fact that he had a scar on his left eyelid?
8. The fact that Mary finished her homework.
9. The fact that twenty million Russians died during World War II is tragic.
10. The request that we ignore the crime was considered unacceptable.

11. Do you agree the statement that blondes have more fun?

12. That Jerome passed the bar examination made it possible for him to practice law.

EXERCISE 10

What will the world be like in the third millennium? In a book called *Megatrends* 2000 (New York: Morrow, 1990) John Naisbett and Patricia Aburdene describe what they believe will transform the world, or, in some cases, American culture. Here are some of their predictions:

1. The English language will become the world's first truly universal language.

2. Nations, especially the "superpower" countries, will regard war as an obsolete way of solving problems.

3. Even as peoples of the world communicate more closely, individual cultures will increasingly find their unique qualities important and seek to preserve racial, linguistic, national, and religious traditions.

4. The arts will replace sports as American society's dominant leisure activity; Americans will consider alternatives to attending sports events such as football and baseball.

5. The trend of the future in the global economy is "downsizing": producing and using smaller, lighter, and more sophisticated products (for example, smaller computers, lighter building materials, electronic impulses used for financial transactions instead of paper).

6. In the first decade of the third millennium, we will think it quaint that women in the late twentieth century were excluded from the top levels of business and politics.

7. The world's nations will increasingly cooperate to address global environmental problems.

Which of these hypotheses do you consider almost a certainty by the end of the twenty-first century? Which do you think probable? Which do you find unlikely developments? Fill in the following blanks with your opinions.

▶ **EXAMPLES:** I agree with the idea that ___the arts will become popular, but I do not___ ___believe that Americans will lose their love of football.___

The prediction that ___English will be the world's universal language is___ ___already true___.

1. I am skeptical of the notion that _____.

2. The tendency for _____.

3. I believe the statement that _____.

4. The suggestion that _____.

5. I doubt the possibility that _____.

Use Your English

ACTIVITY 1: LISTENING/ SPEAKING

STEP 1 Listen to the interview between a university admissions officer and several interested high school seniors. Take note of any interesting facts you hear.

STEP 2 Describe the interesting facts you learned to a classmate. Use as many noun complements as you can.

▶ **EXAMPLE:** *The fact that the admissions officer mainly looks at GPA and college entrance examination scores surprises me.*

ACTIVITY 2: SPEAKING

Discuss the specific reasons behind some of the following environmental problems: pollution of cities, extinction of animals, toxic waste, etc.

▶ **EXAMPLE:** *The fact that people have continued to drive gasoline engines has created the pollution problem in cities.*

ACTIVITY 3: READING/WRITING

In the Opening Task on page 373, you discussed certain natural facts. Investigate one or more issues mentioned there (meteorites, rainbows, oases, lightning, eclipses, etc.) or one of your own and write a short report explaining what facts give them the unusual properties that they have. Use at least three noun complements in your report.

▶ **EXAMPLE:** *Some people say that lightning never strikes the same place twice. However, the fact that we cannot scientifically predict when or where lightning will strike makes it difficult to refute this idea . . .*

ACTIVITY 4: LISTENING/SPEAKING

Watch a mystery or detective program on TV or at the movies with your class-mates. Discuss why the central characters were not able to solve the mystery or crime sooner than they did. What facts were concealed, disregarded, or over-looked? What facts finally led to the solution of the mystery?

▶ **EXAMPLE:** *The mother concealed the fact that Tony had a twin brother. The fact that Tony had a twin brother made the police finally realize that it was Tony's twin, Jimmy, who was guilty.*

ACTIVITY 5: READING/WRITING

Read several editorials or opinion essays. Then write your own view of the ideas in the essays by using noun complements.

▶ **EXAMPLE:** *The idea that people should not be allowed to own weapons makes sense.*

SUBJUNCTIVE VERBS IN *THAT* CLAUSES

UNIT GOALS:

- To use subjunctive verbs in *that* clause complements with verbs of advice and urging
- To use subjunctive verbs in noun complements that refer to nouns of advice or urging
- To use subjunctive verbs in adjective complements

▶ OPENING TASK
Solving Problems

It is not uncommon for two different people or groups of people to disagree about the rightness of an issue or the solution to a problem. Often another person who does not favor either side will be called in to serve as an arbitrator. For this task, one or more classmates should role-play each side of one or more of the following issues. One other person, as the arbitrator, should listen, ask questions, and give recommendations to the two parties (for example, *I suggest that* _____; *I recommend that* _____; *I propose that* _____).

Case #1

A young woman would like to attend an all-male college. The president of the college wants to maintain the one-hundred-year tradition of an all-male campus.

Case #2

A girl was in a serious car accident one year ago. She has been in a coma ever since and is not expected to recover. The doctors want to keep her alive. The girl's mother sees that there is no hope for her recovery and would like to remove her from the life-support system.

Case #3

A father keeps his children at home rather than sending them to school because he feels children are being taught ideas against his religion. The school board feels it is unlawful to prevent children from getting a well-rounded education.

Case #4

A supervisor fires a worker because the supervisor believes he is often late, undependable, and disrespectful. The worker denies these charges and claims that he is overworked and called names by his supervisor.

▶ **Subjunctive Verbs** in *That* **Clauses**

EXAMPLES	EXPLANATIONS
(a) The arbitrator recommends that Susan not **be** fired. **(b)** It was stipulated that he **abandon** the plans.	*That* clause complements of verbs of advice and urging must contain a present subjunctive verb.
(c) Her father demanded that they **be** back by 12:00. **(d)** The committee stipulated that Mary **follow** all of the instructions.	The subjunctive verb is the base form of the verb: *be, go, take,* etc. We use the base form for all singular and plural subjects.
(e) **Formal:** The president insisted that the meeting **begin** on time. **(f)** **Informal:** Jody suggested that we **should eat** at 6:00.	For a similar yet less formal effect, use *should* + base form instead of the subjunctive.

Verbs of advice and urging that require subjunctive verbs in *that*-clauses:

advise	*insist*	*prefer*	*stipulate*
beg	*move*	*propose*	*suggest*
command	*order*	*recommend*	
demand	*pledge*	*request*	
determine	*pray*	*require*	

EXERCISE 1

During the Opening Task on pages 386 and 387, what were some of the recommendations that the arbitrator made to the conflicting parties?

▶ **EXAMPLE:** *He suggested that the president reconsider the all-male policy.*

EXERCISE 2

Use the following base sentence to make comments about each of the situations in items 1 through 6. Fill in the first blank with the correct form of the verb in parentheses and the second blank with a subjunctive verb or *should* + base form, whichever is more appropriate.

Base sentence: She (or he) _____ that he (or she) _____.

▶ **EXAMPLE:**   A boss to her employee (recommend)

  She _recommends_ that he _call her tomorrow_.

   1. A friend who wants to give another friend some information (insist)
   2. An actor to a director who may offer him a part in a play (suggest)
   3. A doctor to a patient who might have a deadly disease (require)
   4. A neighbor to another neighbor who is too busy to talk (propose)
   5. A father to an unsuitable companion for his daughter (forbid)
   6. A salesperson to a customer (advise)

FOCUS **2**

▶ Subjunctive Verbs in Noun Complements

EXAMPLES	EXPLANATION
(a) Suggest: **The suggestion that he be fired** was met with resistance. **(b)** Request: She didn't listen to **his request that she take a sweater.** **(c)** Advise: **His advice that she be set free** was unwise.	Nouns that come from verbs of advice and urging may also take a *that* clause with a subjunctive verb. Some of these nouns are *advice, command, decision, demand, order, pronouncement, recommendation, request,* and *suggestion.*

EXERCISE 3

Imagine that you live in an apartment complex surrounded by some very disagreeable neighbors in apartments 4A through 4F. Answer the following questions, using the prompts provided and a subjunctive complement.

▶ **EXAMPLE:**   What did the man in 4A do when you told him his music was too loud?

  ignore/suggestion

  He ignored my suggestion that he turn down the stereo.

1. What did the person in 4B do when you asked her to return your watering can?

   not heed/proposal

2. What did the man in 4C do when you wanted him to stop being a Peeping Tom?

   laugh at/demand

3. What did the woman in 4D do when you told her to stop stomping around?

   not listen to/demand

4. What did the man in 4E do when you asked him not to come home drunk?

   refuse to pay attention to/request

5. What did the couple in 4F do when you advised them to give their dog away?

   ignore/advice

EXERCISE 4

Imagine that you have a friend Yang, whose family has given him a great deal of advice about how to succeed on his new job as a computer programmer. Which advice of Yang's family do you think was useful and which wasn't? Write a sentence that expresses your opinion of each family member's suggestion.

▶ **EXAMPLE:**   Uncle/flirt with the secretaries
   His uncle's advice that he flirt with the secretaries was not appropriate.

Note: Try to use as many advice or urging nouns as you can.

Family Member	Advice
Uncle	flirt with the secretaries
Grandfather	be accurate in your math
Mother	be friendly
Sister	bring your boss coffee every day
Brother	be in good physical condition
Aunt	work overtime without pay
Father	act confident

Subjunctive Verbs in Adjective Complements

EXAMPLES	EXPLANATION
(a) **That he type** is essential.	Adjective complements can sometimes take subjunctive verbs. This is true when advice adjectives like *advisable, desirable, essential, imperative, important, mandatory, necessary, requisite, urgent,* and *vital* are in the main clause.
(b) It is essential **that he type.**	
(c) **That she be punctual** is important.	
(d) It is important **that she be punctual.**	

EXERCISE 5

STEP 1 Using the information from the following job advertisements, fill in the following statements with *that*-clauses containing subjunctive verbs.

236 Employment	**236 Employment**	**236 Employment**
Accountant ★ Accounting firm seeks individual w/ min 2 yr exp. Good communication skills & ability to assist clients. Biling Chinese required. Previous exp in CPA firm a plus. Call Mr. Tang 213-627-1409	**Customer Service** 30 Jobs Temp to Perm **WANTED!** People with good Customer Service skills that can work 3:30pm to12am 5pm-9pm. If you can, we need you ASAP Call! 458-4847-6666	**File Clerk** Min. 1 yr exp in law file rm. Knowledge of ofc equipment. Ability to work without supervision. Good command of English for switchboard relief. Mrs. Jacobsen 310-395-6662
Accountant Executive Local firm has a fabulous opportunity for a tax accountant. Two + years tax or accounting experience, a strong client service mentality, and a team oriented approach required. Position can be full time. Send in resume 555 East King. Big City Pa 34543	**Drivers-Shuttle** ★ AIRWAY Shuttle needs outstanding drivers for day and eve shifts. Must be clean-cut, highly ethical, energetic. Great benefits and friendly environment. AIRWAY 818-775-8156	**Grocery** Fox's market has immediate! openings for part-time or full-time meat cutters. Vacation, Life insurance, Medical insurance, Profit sharing. Call 333-4444
Chemist ★ Stable, fast-growing company seeks chemist for formulation of industrial products. Must have BS degree chemistry & min. 5 yrs. exp. Nonsmoker preferred. Excellent benefits. Redex Co. 714-773-2221	**Education:** Elementary Principal Twelve month postion available on or before January 1, 2001. Elementary teaching experience and elementary certification required. Knowledge certification required.	**Manager** ★ 10 new Asst. Managers for marketing & sales needed. No exp. necessary. We will train. Must be 18 & older. Must have car. Work in a wild & crazy office. Super's 818-774-8234
Customer Service lot of work full-time. Fax resume to 234-345-4567		**Nurse** ★ Opportunity for career-minded RN. Participate in clinical trials & oversee needs for patients on daily basis. Need good track record of exp. be able to learn fast, self-starter. If interested, call Westside Hospital 213-454-6210

▶ **EXAMPLE:** It is important <u>that the accounting applicant be bilingual in Chinese and English</u>. (accountant)

1. _____ is essential. (chemist)

2. It is mandatory _____. (shuttle driver)

3. _____ is desirable. (file clerk)

4. It is imperative _____. (manager)

5. It is necessary _____. (nurse)

STEP 2 Create five more of your own sentences with information from the ads.

Use Your English

ACTIVITY 1: LISTENING/ WRITING

Listen to the recording of a radio broadcaster who gives people advice about relationships.

STEP 1 Jot down notes about each of the problems and the advice given.

	Problem	Advice
a. Female Caller:		
b. Male Caller:		

STEP 2 Now write a short paragraph summarizing your opinion of the broadcaster's advice to these two callers. Use at least two subjunctive complements in your writing.

ACTIVITY 2: READING/WRITING

The owner of a factory has been losing a great deal of money, and he realizes that he must let five of his employees go. You and a partner, the company's personnel manager and assistant personnel manager, must review the performance of the ten most problematic employees.

STEP 1 Read each of the problems of the employees and jot down exactly what the employee did that was inappropriate.

STEP 2 Discuss which employees have the most serious problems.

STEP 3 Make checkmarks in the right columns indicating which five employees you need to fire and which five you wish to retain.

STEP 4 Write a short report to the owner of the factory, explaining your decision.

▶ **EXAMPLE:** *Dear Mr. Johnson,*
Related to your last request, I have determined which five employees should be dismissed. I suggest that Dawn M. be fired because she has missed thirty days of work during the last three months . . .

Name	Problems	Examples	Fire	Retain
Dawn M.	absenteeism	missed 30 days of work		
Homer O.	lack of ambition			
Gunnar F.	criminal background			
Sang S.	incompetence			
Fern M.	laziness			
Sherry B.	alcohol problem			
Maggie W.	clumsiness			
Ly P.	dishonesty			
Mina A.	disagreeableness			
Ann K.	loose morals			

ACTIVITY 3: READING/WRITING

Read at least five advice letters and responses in the newspaper from the columns of "Ann Landers," "Dear Abby," and "Miss Manners." Summarize the problems and the advice given to persons requesting the advice.

▶ **EXAMPLE:** *A man had attempted many times to quit smoking. Counseling, nicotine chewing gum, and "cold turkey" were all ineffective. Abby suggested that he try acupuncture.*

ACTIVITY 4: SPEAKING/WRITING

Have you or any of your classmates ever paid for something that was defective or did not work (for example, a piece of clothing, a gadget, a machine)? Or have you ever paid for a service you discovered later had not been performed (for example, had your car fixed, your computer repaired, your watch cleaned)? How did or would you request the salesperson or service provider to correct these mistakes? Summarize your own and your classmate's responses.

▶ **EXAMPLE:** *Jocelyn suggested that the saleswoman replace the sweater because of the unraveling yarn.*

ACTIVITY 5: READING/WRITING

Select a letter to the editor in a newspaper or an editorial that discusses a political, environmental, or civic problem.

STEP 1 Summarize the issue.

STEP 2 State the writer's position.

STEP 3 List any solutions/suggestions made by the writer. Use at least two subjunctive complements in your list.

ACTIVITY 6: READING/SPEAKING

Over a thousand years ago, Anglo-Saxon and Scandinavian wizards and magicians used the power of runes to divine their future. Runes are alphabetic characters used much like tarot cards or I-Ching ideograms to obtain divine guidance on life's questions. You will have a chance to test the power of runes as a guide in the following activity.

STEP 1   Form groups of three or four students. Think of a question you would like answered about some area of your life (such as work, relationships, travel, or money).

▶ **EXAMPLE:** *How will I get home for the holidays?*

STEP 2   Point to one of the runes on the chart on page 399.

▶ **EXAMPLE:** *YR*

STEP 3   Choose a number between 10 and 30 and move your finger clockwise the number of spaces you selected.

▶ **EXAMPLE:** *13*

STEP 4   The rune you land on is your oracle. Read the text about this rune.

▶ **EXAMPLE:** *Hagal*

STEP 5   Share your question with your classmates and paraphrase your rune's "advice."

▶ **EXAMPLE:** *It suggested that I be on my guard because my prospects may change unexpectedly and it urged that I be cautious and patient.*

RUNES

THE SELF: This rune symbolizes a human being. It counsels you to exhibit your generosity, friendship, and altruism. It represents your positive character traits, those which you must draw upon to improve yourself.

- Advice: You possess genuine power over events and you will find the solution to your problem within yourself. Only within yourself.

PARTNERSHIP: This rune signifies collective effort. It speaks of exchanges in an atmosphere of generosity and peace. In your job, teamwork will pay off. In love, it's an omen for a solid relationship, a meeting of minds and hearts.

- Advice: Be warned against hesitation or selfishness. It's by thinking of others, by offering a gift, or simply by giving pleasure that you will be fulfilled.

GROWTH: This is the symbol of achievement, the completion of a project. It also signifies fertility, birth, completion, and renewal. An end or a beginning.

- Advice: You are on the brink of a new departure. Have faith.

CONSTRAINT: The rune of the master of us all: time. Now is the moment to free yourself of material things and cultivate the life of the mind. Be patient, careful, and resolute. Thought is preferable to action.

- Advice: The mind rules. Don't be grasping in your pursuit of success. Don't rush things. Wisdom alone will lead you to accomplishment.

FLOW: This is the quintessential female rune. It augurs well for everything that touches on artistic creativity, summoning up your re-

serves of intuition and imagination. Talents that are hidden will come to the fore. Work with them!

- Advice: Don't give in to doubt. Let your deepest desires express themselves. Don't question your abilities.

WARRIOR: This is an arrow shot into the air. In your work life, this means you should get a project rolling and have both a competitive spirit and a will to win. In love, it suggests passion, sex, and fertility.

- Advice: Act firmly and positively. Rely only on yourself, your energy, and your desires. It's simple: Motivate yourself.

DISRUPTION: This rune is like a disruptive hailstorm. It represents the random in life—its problems and everyday frustrations.

- Advice: Be on your guard: Your prospects may change unexpectedly. Only caution and patience will lead you to success because the final decision is out of your hands.

THE UNKNOWABLE: This mysterious oracle reserves the right to remain silent and to withhold all advice.

SIGNALS: This rune deals with knowledge and learning. It is telling you that some sort of test awaits, one in which you may need the help of someone who is an expert.

- Advice: Study the situation thoughtfully. Express your wishes but don't decide anything off the top of your head.

FERTILITY: This especially concerns the family. It predicts the birth of a child, a marriage, or the improvement of life in the home. In matters of health, it foresees a healing process.

- Advice: Tenderness and care will bring about growth. You're only just at the beginning, but soon the results will be visible.

INITIATION: This is an enigmatic sign that speaks of hidden happenings. It stresses the importance of mystery, the revelation of a secret, and the possibility of finding something or someone. It's the rune of second chances.

- Advice: Follow your intuition. The solution to the problem lies not in what you can see but in what you can feel.

SEPARATION: The rune suggests a change concerning material goods, cultural heritage, legacies, or money in general. Professionally, efforts must be made to stabilize a certain situation.

- Advice: Expect some difficulties or delays. Good things come to those who wait. Avoid flighty behavior, doing too many things at once, or spending too much.

JOURNEY: This signifies a journey or a major move. It can indicate the arrival of good news or an important change. Professionally, your activities are successful—plans may change and any negotiations will end favorably for you.

- Advice: Be prepared to change course, to travel, to be more open-minded.

PROTECTION: A very positive rune. It speaks of being protected by an important person, whether at work or in love. You have a lot of self-confidence because this is a splendid time for you.

- Advice: Positive change is in the offing. Control your emotions and be ready to meet all challenges.

OPENING: An optimistic sign, a good omen of beginnings (or renewals). If you are ill, this rune signifies a healing or cure. In affairs of the heart, it indicates the start of an intimate relationship.

- Advice: The time is for action, not surrender. In love, it promises good times.

STRENGTH: Growth and rewarding change, especially in your professional life. You should act energetically, for new responsibilities are yours for the taking. Your abilities will be put to the test.

- Advice: Act with determination and do your best. Your work conditions may noticeably improve.

BREAKTHROUGH: Another positive rune that signifies prosperity and improvement. It represents the light after darkness, and triumph over adversity.

- Advice: Take full advantage of opportunities when they arise. Remain serene and upbeat.

GATEWAY: You will soon receive good news that may change your life. But you will have to make a decision that will require a lot of thought.

- Advice: Learn to listen to the opinions of others. Seek out help and wait for the right moment to act. If you don't have enough self-confidence, hold off.

DEFENSE: This rune involves danger that can, and should, be overcome. In fact, the goal you wish to attain is within reach, but you have to become more flexible and change your way of seeing things.

- Advice: This is just a warning. You can improve the situation by questioning the way you think and changing the way you act.

SIGEL

WHOLENESS: This represents luck, victory, and the fulfillment of your hopes. In all areas of your life (work, love, health, etc.), energy is on the upswing.

- Advice: Take advantage of it.

POSSESSIONS: This is very positive, an omen of increased wealth. New financial opportunities are the order of the day. It's also a symbol of victory, struggle, and an obstacle overcome.
FEOH

- Advice: Consolidate your gains and persevere along your path. Material reward will soon follow.

JARA

HARVEST: This rune symbolizes what has been sown and will soon be reaped. Thus, it speaks of work, perseverance, and patience. The earth has a natural cycle: planting and harvesting.

- Advice: You are on the right path, the one that leads you to a reward. Don't stop halfway. But don't forget, things take time.

IS

STANDSTILL: This involves obstacles, a cooling in your relations with others. At work, it can mean a loss of motivation. Passivity may get the better of you. In love, a relationship may lose passion and ardor.

- Advice: For the moment, put your plans on hold. Before you act, wait for the situation to improve on its own.

EH

MOVEMENT: This motion can involve a change of job, a business trip, a long journey, or a new home. This rune is a source of progress, demanding that you keep an open mind.

- Advice: Be prepared to take control and get ready to adapt. Your horizons are broadening. Get rid of your hang-ups and throw yourself into an adventure.

WYN

JOY: You'll get pleasure from your work. Your artistic talents or manual skills will be unleashed. Joy will be found in your love life, through emotional and physical fulfillment. A change is coming, if your enthusiasm doesn't flag.

- Advice: Use your creative gifts and your intuition to achieve your goals. Everything depends on how much fun you get out of accomplishing things.

GYFU
BEORC
MAN
NYD
WYN
LAGU
EH
TIR
IS
HAGAL
JARA
WYRD
FEOH
OS
SIGEL
ING
YR
PEORTH
THORN
ODAL
DAEG
RAD
UR
EOLH
KEN

Thorsons, an imprint of Harper Collins Publishers. Limited Extracts and material from *The Runic Workbook* by Tony Willis.
Layout reprinted with permission from *Elle* Magazine © 1991 ELLE Publishing L. P.

EMPHATIC STRUCTURES

Emphatic *Do, No* versus *Not*

UNIT GOALS:

- To use emphatic *do* to add emphasis to a sentence
- To choose *no* versus *not* to emphasize a negative statement

▶ **OPENING TASK**

Looking at Consumer Needs

Advertising agencies spend a lot of time and money finding out what consumers like and dislike. VALS (Values and Lifestyles) typology* is a system for describing different types of consumers. Imagine that you work for an advertising agency and that you are trying to identify the likes and dislikes of potential consumers. Use the VALS typology to help you make your decision.

*VALS typology was developed by SRI, an important research service.

STEP 1 Read the VALS (for Values and Lifestyles) descriptions. List items or services that you think the nine groups of consumers would and would not want to purchase.

STEP 2 Conduct a mock advertising agency meeting where you convince members of your team of the needs of each type of consumer.

> ▶ **EXAMPLE:** *Survivors really do need medical care!*
>
> *Survivors will have no money for luxuries.*
>
> *Survivors won't buy any expensive fur coats, but they **will** buy practical warm woolen ones!*

VALS Typology Consumer Types	Consumer Items or Services that Would and Would Not Appeal to Group
1. Survivors: Old, intensely poor, fearful, depressed, despairing. This group represents about 4 percent of the adult population.	NEED: good medical care DON'T NEED: luxuries (expensive fur coats, etc.)
2. Sustainers: Living on the edge of poverty, often unemployed, angry, resentful, sentimental, family-oriented, intensely patriotic, deeply stable. This group represents about 7 percent of the adult population.	
3. Belongers: Mostly female, traditional, conventional, contented, sentimental, family-oriented, intensely patriotic, deeply stable. This group is the largest in the typology, accounting for about 38 percent of the adult population.	
4. Emulators: Youthful, ambitious, status conscious, clerical or skilled blue collar, want to appear successful, to make it big. A relatively small group, accounting for about 10 percent of the adult population.	
5. Achievers: Middle-aged, more heavily male, most affluent group, leaders, materialistic, self-assured, successful. "Mover and shakers," these people make up over 20 percent of the adult population.	
6. I-Am-Me's: Young, often students, narcissistic, fiercely independent, individualistic, impulsive, dramatic. Next to the smallest group in the typology, accounting for only 3 percent of the adult population.	
7. Experientials: Youthful, artistic, seeking direct experience and inner growth. This group accounts for 5 percent of the adult population.	
8. Societally Conscious: Affluent (second only to Achievers), most highly educated of all VALS types, mature, successful, concerned with social issues, leaders. Account for about 11 percent of the adult population.	
9. Integrateds: Combine the power of the Achievers with the sensitivity of the Societally Conscious, mature, tolerant, understanding. Represent only about 2 percent of the adult population.	

Source: J. Niefeld. *The Making of an Advertising Campaign.* Englewood Cliffs, N.J.: Prentice Hall, 1989.

▶ **Emphatic *Do***

EXAMPLES	EXPLANATIONS
(a) I ***will*** write you a letter as soon as I arrive. **(b)** He ***is*** going to Mexico during the winter break. **(c)** Sally ***has*** finished her homework. **(d)** Todd ***is*** a world-class swimmer.	We can add emphasis to a sentence by stressing the auxiliary or the *be* verb.
(e) I ***do*** believe in miracles. **(f)** Professor Dean ***did*** get her conference paper accepted.	In sentences where there is no auxiliary or *be* verb, we can add *do* and stress it for emphasis.
(g) Juan ***really does*** know the answer to the question. **(h)** They ***certainly did*** see us at the exposition.	We often add extra emphasis with an emphatic adverb like *really* or *certainly* and a strongly stressed *do*.

EXERCISE 1

Read the following script for a radio commercial aloud. Then go over it again silently and underline examples of emphatic *do*.

It is no secret that many famous people, including Napoleon, Catherine the Great, Pope Julius II, and even the Queen of England loved silk clothes. In the thirteenth century Marco Polo traveled the "Silk Road" and brought silk to Venice. You can be sure that Italian royalty did value this precious fabric. Some of the designs embroidered into their clothing were copies of frescoes designed by Leonardo da Vinci.

Today, there are no world-class dress designers who have not used Italian fabrics made of Chinese silk yarn. Oscar de la Renta has said, "What diamonds do for the hand, silk does for the body." Silk does have a luxurious and romantic quality. Silk dresses and suits do add beauty and style to any wardrobe.

You do want to be considered as successful as those who know what quality is, don't you? No one who is anyone should be without this unique fabric. Do buy a silk outfit today!

Some Ways to Use Emphatic *Do*

EXAMPLES	EXPLANATIONS
(a) A: You have a good thesis. B: Really? A: Yes, you really **do** have a good thesis.	Emphatic *do* can: • add emphasis to a whole sentence.
(b) **Do** come in! **(c)** **Do** give him my best regards!	• add emphasis to an imperative. This use of emphatic *do* softens a command and shows polite encouragement.
(d) A: You didn't lock the back door. B: You're wrong. I **did** lock it.	• contradict a negative statement. This use of emphatic *do* is very common in arguments. In such situations, the *do* verb generally refers back to a previous statement.
(e) A: Bob didn't cheat on the test. B: Then, what **did** happen? OR Who **did** cheat? OR What **did** he cheat on?	• be used to ask a clarification question about a previously mentioned negative statement.
(f) It was no surprise to me. He seldom **did** complete his homework. **(g)** To make a long story short, she always **does** get her own way.	• add emphasis to a verb used in connection with an adverb of frequency such as *never, rarely, seldom, often,* or *always.*
(h) I'm relieved that he **does** have his credit card (because I thought he might have forgotten it).	• emphasize a positive result regarding something that had been unknown or in doubt.
(i) Even though I do not usually enjoy fiction, I **did** enjoy John King's latest novel.	• indicate strong concession bordering on contrast.

EXERCISE 2

Circulate around the room and give at least ten compliments to other students using the auxiliary, *be*, or emphatic *do* verbs.

▶ **EXAMPLES:** *You **have** done your hair very nicely.*
*You certainly **are** wearing a beautiful necklace.*
*That certainly **is** a nice shirt.*
*I really **do** like your loafers.*

EXERCISE 3

Use *do* structures to make the following invitations, requests, or suggestions.

▶ **EXAMPLE:** suggestion to sit down
Do sit down.

1. invitation to put a friend's bags in your room
2. request to come early to the party
3. suggestion to tell the children to quiet down
4. invitation to have some more punch
5. request to put the money in a safe place
6. suggestion to turn off the lights when you leave the conference room
7. invitation to have a bite to eat
8. request to let relatives know you'll be late for your visit

EXERCISE 4

Bruce and Gary are brothers, but they often have arguments. Read the following argument and cross through all the places where you think it is possible to use emphatic *do*. Rewrite those sentences with an appropriate form of the *do* verb. The first one has been done for you.

Bruce: Did you take my flashlight? I can't find it anywhere.

Gary: Well, I haven't got it. I always return the stuff I borrow.

Bruce: No, you don't.

Gary: That's not true! ~~I return the things I borrow~~! *I do return the things I borrow!* It's probably on your desk. I bet you didn't look for it there.

Bruce: No, I looked on my desk, and it's not there.

Gary: Well, don't blame me. You can't find it because you never clean your room.

Bruce: I clean my room!

Gary: Oh, no you don't!

Bruce: I certainly clean it up! I cleaned it up last night as a matter of fact.

Gary: You didn't.

Bruce: I really cleaned it up last night. Hey, there's my flashlight under your bed.

Gary: Well, I didn't put it here.

Bruce: I bet you put it there. Anyhow, that proves it: You take my stuff and you don't return it.

Gary: I told you before: I return everything I borrow. You just don't look after your things properly.

Bruce: I look after my things. Anyway, from now on, I'm going to lock my door and keep you out.

Gary: You can't. That door doesn't have a key.

Bruce: That's where you're wrong. It has a key and I'm going to lock you out!

Gary: Oh, be quiet!

Bruce: Do you know something? You make me sick. You really make me sick.

Gary: You make me sick too!

Get together with another student and take the parts of Gary and Bruce. Read the dialogue, paying particular attention to the stress patterns of emphatic *do*. If possible, record yourselves and listen to how emphatic you sound.

▶ **N**ot versus **N**o

EXAMPLES	EXPLANATIONS
(a) They do not have any suggestions for the project. They have **no** suggestions for the project. **(b)** Norwegian tourists did not come to Miami this year. **No** Norwegian tourists came to Miami this year.	To emphasize a negative statement, we can use *no* + noun in place of *not/-n't* + verb.
(c) I have **no** fear of flying. **(d)** She is taking the bus because she has **no** car today. **(e)** He has **no** chairs in his apartment.	We use *no* with noncount nouns, singular count nouns, and plural count nouns.
(f) They are indebted to **no one**. **(g)** I saw **nobody** by the river. **(h)** He managed **nothing** well. **(i)** That business decision led him **nowhere**.	We can combine *no* with other words to make compounds. *no + one = no one* *no + body = nobody* *no + thing = nothing* *no + where = nowhere*
(j) Mike does**n't** have **any** money. **(k)** We have**n't** seen **any** pelicans all day. **(l)** **NOT:** She won't earn no money.	In standard English, a negative sentence (with *not* after the first auxiliary verb or *be*) with a second negative component uses *not . . . any*.

EXERCISE 5

STEP 1 Match the first part of the sentence in column A with something from column B that makes sense and is grammatical. The first one has been done for you.

Lily went to a party last night.

A

1. She had hoped to make some new friends, but she didn't meet

2. She had to drive home, so she didn't drink

3. She was very hungry, but when she arrived there wasn't

4. She talked to a few people, but she didn't have

5. Some people were dancing, but Lily didn't have

6. She wanted to sit down, but there weren't

7. Finally, she said to herself: "This party isn't

8. So she went home early and decided not to go to

B

a. any food left.

b. anyone to dance with.

c. any more parties.

d. anyone interesting.

e. any fun!"

f. any alcohol.

g. anything to say to them

h. any chairs.

STEP 2 Rewrite each sentence of Step 1 using *no* or an appropriate *no* + compound. Change the verbs as necessary. The first one has been done for you.

1. *She had hoped to make some new friends, but she met nobody interesting.*

EXERCISE 6

Edit the following speech for errors with negative constructions. When you are finished, read it aloud to a partner and see if there are any more changes you want to make. The first sentence has been edited as an example.

(1) The year 2025 ~~no is~~ *is not* as far away as it might seem. (2) Today we don't have no direction. (3) If we don't get any direction, our dream for our nation is sure to explode. (4) No children will have the things we had. (5) There isn't nobody who cannot benefit from the few principles I will share with you today. (6) Please listen carefully. (7) If you don't listen to anything I say, the consequences will be fatal.

(8) First, it isn't good for nobody to feel that they deserve everything when they don't put any sweat and struggle in getting it. (9) Even more, this nation can't tell nobody nowhere that it is entitled to world leadership just because

they had it in the past. (10) You can never take nothing for granted in this country. (11) I hope you will work hard to achieve.

(12) Next, I believe that no people should set goals and then do anything not to achieve them. (13) If you set a goal, work hard and humbly to accomplish it. (14) Even if you don't get no credit, it is important to keep trying because you and your maker know what you accomplished.

(15) Another important piece of advice is not to work just for money. (16) Money alone can't strengthen nobody's family nor help nobody sleep at night. (17) Don't let nobody tell you that wealth or fame is the same as character. (18) It is not O.K. to use drugs even if everyone is doing it. (19) It is not O.K. to cheat or lie even if every public official does.

(20) Finally, no person should be afraid of taking no risks. (21) No anybody should be afraid of failing. (22) It shouldn't matter to nobody anywhere how many times you fall down. (23) What matters is how many times you get up.

(24) Let's not spend no more time talking. We are all responsible for building a decent nation to live in! Let's not let no more minutes pass.

FOCUS **4**

USE

When to Use *No* for Emphasis

EXAMPLES	EXPLANATIONS
(a) I didn't have any friends when I was a child. **(b)** I had **no** friends when I was a child.	Statements using *no* as the negative word instead of *not* emphasize what is missing or lacking. In speaking, we often stress the word *no* for extra emphasis.
(c) NEUTRAL: I didn't meet anybody interesting at the party. **(d)** EMPHATIC: I met **nobody** interesting at the party. **(e)** NEUTRAL: I didn't learn anything new at the conference. **(f)** EMPHATIC: I learned **nothing** new at the conference.	*No* + compound also emphasizes what is missing or lacking. Sentence (c) sounds neutral, a statement of fact. Sentence (d) sounds more emotional, emphasizing the lack of interesting people.

EXERCISE 7

Lily is describing the party (in Exercise 5) to her best friend and is telling her what a miserable time she had. Imagine you are Lily and try describing the party from her point of view, emphasizing all the negative aspects of the evening. If possible, record yourself and listen to see how emphatic you sound.

EXERCISE 8

Emphatic language is very common in public speeches. Read aloud the extracts from speeches below and notice the different ways each speaker uses language to emphasize his message. Underline any examples that you can find of the emphatic language discussed in this unit. Do you notice any other techniques the speakers use to get their points across?

1. Jesse Jackson: Speech to the Democratic National Convention, July 20, 1988

When I was born late one afternoon, October 8, in Greenville, South Carolina, no writers asked my mother her name. Nobody chose to write down our address. My mama was not supposed to make it. You see, I was born to a teenage mother who was born to a teenage mother. I understand. I know abandonment and people being mean to you, and saying you're nothing and nobody, and can never be anything. I understand . . . I understand when nobody knows your name. I understand when you have no name . . . I really do understand.

2. Donald Kagan: Address to the Class of 1994 of Yale College, September 1, 1990

We now have the mechanisms that do permit the storage of data in staggering amounts and their retrieval upon demand. And one of the by-products is the approaching end of the age of specialization. The doom of the specialist draws closer every time someone punches the keys on a word processor. Of course, we will still need doctors, lawyers, plumbers, and electricians. But will there still be a brisk market for all the specialties we have fostered in the economic and social fields? I doubt it. The future will belong to those who know how to handle the combinations of information that come out of the computer, what we used to call the "generalist." The day of the generalist is just over the horizon and we had better be ready for it.

Use Your English

ACTIVITY 1: LISTENING/ WRITING/SPEAKING

STEP 1 Listen to the lecture on how to create a good advertisement. Take notes and pay special attention to the suggestions given.

STEP 2 Summarize the speaker's advice in a short paragraph.

▶ **EXAMPLE:** *A good ad should have three main ingredients. The ad should include information about the product and its unique advantage. . . .*

STEP 3 Now revise your paragraph so that it sounds more emphatic. Use some of the techniques you have learned in this chapter.

STEP 4 Now read your paragraph aloud to a classmate, stressing words appropriately.

ACTIVITY 2: WRITING/ SPEAKING/LISTENING

STEP 1 Organize a political campaign in class. Divide into groups. Each group represents a new political party. With your group, create a name and draw up a list of all the things you stand for and all the things you will do if you are elected.

STEP 2 Make a poster representing your beliefs and prepare a short speech to persuade people to vote for you. Each member of your group should be prepared to speak on a different aspect of your party's platform.

STEP 3 Give your speeches to the rest of the class and decide who has the most persuasive approach. If possible, record your speech and afterward listen to what you said, taking note of any emphatic structures you used and how you said them.

ACTIVITY 3: SPEAKING/WRITING

STEP 1 Get together with another student. Think of a relationship or a situation in which people often have disagreements (for example, parent/child; brother/sister, boyfriend/girlfriend, spouse/spouse, roommate/roommate, and so on). Choose one such relationship and brainstorm all the possible issues these people might argue about.

STEP 2 Choose one issue and take the role of one of the people in the situation (your partner takes the role of the other). Create the argument these two people might have on this issue. Write your dialogue and prepare to perform it in front of the class. Before you perform, check to see how emphatically you state your point of view.

STEP 3 Perform your dialogue for the class.

ACTIVITY 4: RESEARCH/WRITING/SPEAKING

STEP 1 Think of someone famous whom you truly admire because of his or her ideas. This person could be an important figure in any field, such as:

Communications	Peter Jennings, Connie Chung, Larry King
Politics	Geraldine Ferraro, Keizo Obuchi, Nelson Mandela
Business	Bill Gates, Stephen Covey, Rupert Murdoch
Entertainment	Stephen Spielberg, Celine Dion, Oliver Stone

STEP 2 Go to the library and do some research about the person you have selected by using encyclopedias, *The Reader's Guide*, biographical references, speech references, etc.

STEP 3 Write a short essay describing what traits, activities, or ideas of this person impress you the most.

STEP 4 Give a speech to your classmates convincing them of the admirable traits, activities, and ideas of this person. Use as many emphatic structures from this unit as you can.

▶ **EXAMPLES:** *Even though some people think Barbara Walters is an egotistical newsreporter, she does deliver informative news.*

Steves Covey's simple behavioral principles really do apply as much to the workplace as to the home.

There is no Hollywood producer as political as Oliver Stone.

FRONTING STRUCTURES FOR EMPHASIS AND FOCUS

UNIT GOALS:

- To know what kinds of structures can be moved to the front of sentences for emphasis
- To know when to change the subject/verb order for fronted structures
- To use fronted negative forms for emphasis
- To use fronted structures to point out contrasts and focus on unexpected information

 O PENING TASK

Film Scenarios

When someone mentions the film industry, we usually think first of actors and directors. When film awards are handed out, however, we are reminded that behind all good movies stand creative scriptwriters.

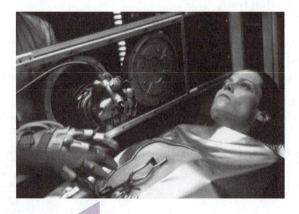

STEP 1 Form groups with members of your class. Each group will be a team of scriptwriters. Imagine that you are being considered for a film company contract based on your imaginative ideas.

STEP 2 For the scenario or scenarios below that your group chooses or is assigned, think of a completion for the last line of dialogue or description.

STEP 3 When the groups have finished, take turns reading the scenarios along with the completions. As a class, you may want to vote on the ones you think are the most creative.

FILM 1: SCIENCE FICTION

SCENARIO: For weeks the townspeople of Spooner, a small lake resort town, have observed signs that something horrible has invaded their community. Trees, shrubs, and even the flowers have begun to die. Dogs howl at night and cats are afraid to go out. One summer Saturday night, many of the townsfolk are, as usual, celebrating the end of the week at the local dance hall, when they become aware of an eerie green glow outside. They rush out to see what it is. Moving slowly toward them across a field is . . .

FILM 2: HORROR STORY

SCENARIO: Ten people have agreed to spend a week in a large and very old mansion on the edge of town. Strange events have occurred in this house over the past few years, and the people assembled this evening want to find out if there is truth to rumors that the house has been cursed. They are all seated at the dining room table, with their leader, Madame Montague, at the head.

Madame Montague: My friends, you all know why we are here. Before we spend another hour in this house, there is one thing that I must demand of all of you. Under no circumstances should . . .

FILM 3: ROMANCE

SCENARIO: Max and Ramona are a young couple in their twenties who have been dating for a year. Max is passionately in love with Ramona and wants to marry her, but he's not sure if she's as much in love with him as he is with her. Max is trying to find out how Ramona feels about him.

Max: Ramona, you know how much I love you. (Long pause. No response from Ramona.) Tell me honestly, what do you think of me?

Ramona: Max, never have . . .

FILM 4: MYSTERY

SCENARIO: Detective Hendershot has been called to the scene of a crime—a murder, to be exact. He is now in the master bedroom, where the unfortunate victim was discovered. Hendershot opens and searches the dresser drawers one by one, hoping to find the murder weapon or some other clue to the crime. He opens the last drawer, the bottom one, and sifts through its contents. There, buried under a pile of silk scarves, is . . .

FILM 5: ADVENTURE STORY

SCENARIO: After three days of wandering aimlessly in the heart of the Brazilian rain forest, a group of scientists have to admit that they are hopelessly lost. The head of the expedition, Professor Winbigler feels it is time to warn the others of a great danger to them that she has encountered while separated from the group.

Professor Winbigler: My fellow scientists, I didn't want to tell you this, but now that I fear we may not get out of here for a while, I believe you should be alerted. Far more threatening to our survival than the poisonous snakes and spiders are . . .

► Fronted Structures

EXAMPLES		EXPLANATIONS
(a) **Not Fronted** The townspeople went outside **because they were curious.**	**(b)** **Fronted Because they were curious,** the townspeople went outside.	In English, you can place special emphasis on some ideas by moving words or phrases from their usual place in a sentence to the front of the sentence. This process is called "fronting," and the resulting structures are known as "fronted structures."
(c) I would **not** leave this town **for anything.**	**(d)** **Not for anything** would I leave this town.	
(e) **The storm was** so terrible that many people lost their homes.	**(f)** So terrible **was the storm** that many people lost their homes.	**Subject-Verb and Subject-Auxiliary Order** When you front some structures, the word order in the rest of the sentence changes. The order of the subject and verb or the subject and the auxiliary is reversed (inverted). The verb or the auxiliary comes before the subject instead of after it. These structures will be shown in Focus 3 and Focus 4.

EXERCISE 1

In the dialogue below, a group of friends who have just been backpacking in the mountains are telling some other friends about their trip. Each numbered sentence contains a fronted structure. For these sentences, underline the subject and circle the main verb and any auxiliaries. If the subject and the verb (or the subject and an auxiliary) have been inverted, write "I" at the end of each sentence.

▶ **EXAMPLE:**   Not once ⟨did⟩ we ⟨see⟩ a wild animal. **I**

Karen: Well, to begin with, we had to hike straight uphill for six miles. I couldn't believe how steep it was! (1) Never have I been so tired in my whole life!

Toshi: Really! Listen, next time all the food will be freeze-dried. (2) Not for anything would I carry a twenty-pound pack uphill again!

Phan: (3) At dusk we finally got up to our campsite; it was gorgeous! We were on the shores of a pristine mountain lake, surrounded by pine trees. (4) Nowhere could we see another person.

Kent: (5) However, no sooner had we dropped all our stuff on the ground than the storm clouds rolled in. (6) In a big hurry we unpacked everything we had.

Mario: (7) Yeah, and not until then did I discover that I hadn't packed my rain poncho.

Karen: (8) Neither had the rest of us.

Toshi: We tried to pitch the tents as fast as we could but it wasn't fast enough. (9) With every stake we pounded in, it seemed to rain harder. (10) Not only did we get soaked, but some of our food got wet too.

Phan: But fortunately the storm ended almost as quickly as it had started. (11) And on the other side of the lake the most beautiful rainbow appeared.

Mario: All in all, even though it was a hard climb getting there, it was worth it. (12) You know, seldom do you realize how peaceful life can be until you get away from civilization!

▶ Inversion of Subjects and Auxiliaries and Verbs with Fronted Structures

Fronted Structures that Do Not Require Inversion

ADVERBIAL NOT FRONTED		FRONTED ADVERBIAL		TYPE OF ADVERBIAL
(a)	She works on her novel **during the evenings.**	(b)	**During the evenings** she works on her novel.	Time
(c)	Detective Wagner sorted the evidence **with great care.**	(d)	**With great care,** Detective Wagner sorted the evidence.	Manner
(e)	Something strange must be happening **if the dogs are howling.**	(f)	**If the dogs are howling,** something strange must be happening.	Condition
(g)	Max showered Ramona with gifts **in order to win her heart.**	(h)	**In order to win her heart,** Max showered Ramona with gifts.	Purpose
(i)	The townspeople left **because they were afraid.**	(j)	**Because they were afraid,** the townspeople left.	Reason
(k)	The group would meet in the living room of the old mansion **every night.**	(l)	**Every night** the group would meet in the living room of the old mansion.	Frequency (after verbs)

Fronted Structures that Require Inversion

NOT FRONTED	FRONTED WITH INVERSION	STRUCTURE
(m) The townspeople *were* **so afraid** that they hardly ventured out of their neighborhoods.	**(n)** **So afraid** *were* the townspeople that they hardly ventured out of their neighborhoods.	Adverbials of extent or degree (*so* + adjective/adverb + *that*)
(o) A small boy *was* **in the library.**	**(p)** **In the library** *was* a small boy.	Adverbials of position when the main verb is *be*
(q) We *have* **never** *seen* such generosity.	**(r)** **Never** *have we seen* such generosity.	Negative adverbials of frequency that come before the main verb (*never, rarely, seldom*)
(s) Max *would* **not** leave Ramona **for anything.**	**(t)** **Not for anything** *would* Max *leave* Ramona.	Other negated structures
(u) A beam of light *was* **moving toward them.**	**(v)** **Moving toward them** *was* a beam of light.	Present participles + modifiers
(w) A note *was* **stuck in a branch of the willow tree.**	**(x)** **Stuck in a branch of the willow tree** *was* a note.	Past participles + modifiers
(y) The cinematography of this movie *is* **more interesting than** the plot.	**(z)** **More interesting than** the plot of this movie is the cinematography.*	Comparative structures
(aa) (Paraphrase: The soldiers *did not know* that the enemy was just over the hill.)	**(bb)** **Little** *did* the soldiers *know* that the enemy was just over the hill.	Implied negation Because the negation is implied rather than explicit, there is no non-fronted form with *little*.

*Note in (z) that the phrase *of this movie* has also been moved to the front to give the reader more information at the beginning of the sentence

Optional Inversion with Fronted Structures

ADVERBIAL NOT FRONTED	FRONTED ADVERBIAL	TYPE OF ADVERBIAL
(cc) A leopard appeared **from the western hills.**	**(dd) From the western hills** a leopard *appeared.* (No inversion) **(ee) From the western hills** *appeared* a leopard. (Optional inversion)	Direction
(ff) An old woman sits **on the park bench.**	**(gg) On the park bench** an old woman *sits.* (No inversion) **(hh) On the park bench** *sits* an old woman. (Optional inversion)	Position, when the main verb is not *be.*

EXERCISE 2

Use the cues in parentheses to add adverbial phrases or clauses to the end of each sentence. Then to emphasize the description you added, move it to the front of a new sentence. You will need to write two sentences for part a. and two for part b. If you wish, you can add other descriptive words or phrases. Be creative; try to use new vocabulary!

▶ **EXAMPLES:** The odd creatures were standing in front of them. (a. manner)

1. *The odd creatures were standing in front of them with hungry looks on their angular faces.*
2. Fronted: *With hungry looks on their angular faces, the odd creatures were standing boldly in front of them.*

The scientists heard a piercing shriek. (b. time)

1. *The scientists heard a piercing shriek shortly before dawn.*
2. Fronted: *Shortly before dawn, the scientists heard a piercing shriek.*

1. The townspeople were absolutely terrified. (a. time b. frequency)
2. Detective Hendershot will find the murderer. (a. condition b. manner)
3. The group explored the nooks and crannies of the old house. (a. time b. purpose)

4. The scientists wandered. (a. direction b. purpose)

5. Professor Winbigler faithfully writes in her journal. (a. position b. condition)

EXERCISE 3

Use an appropriate word or phrase from the list below to complete the blanks with fronted structures.

little did I know	peeking out from under
not for anything	a snowdrift
never	stuffed into the toe
sitting at the bottom of the hill	so embarrassed
coming toward me from the right	worse than the beginning of
	my excursion

I'm not sure if I ever want to go skiing again. (1) _____ have I felt so frustrated trying to have fun! First, I had trouble just getting on the boots and skis I had rented. One of the boots wouldn't fit; then I discovered that (2) _____ was an old sock. I was so nervous that I hadn't realized what it was. Next I discovered that getting to the top of the hill on the chair lift was no small feat. (3) _____ that one could fall numerous times before even getting started. Once I made it to the top, I couldn't believe how small everything looked down below. (4) _____ was a tiny building that I recognized as the chalet. My first thought was: (5) _____ am I going to go down this slope. As it turned out, my first thought was probably better than my second, which was to give it a try. (6) _____ was the end of it. As I raced uncontrollably down the slope terrified, I suddenly saw that (7) _____ was another skier. We collided just seconds later. (8) _____, I muttered an apology. That was it for me for the day. (9) _____ did I feel that I spent the rest of the afternoon finding out how to enroll in a beginning ski class.

▶ **P**atterns of Inversion with Fronted Structures

EXAMPLES		EXPLANATIONS
Not Fronted	**Fronted**	**Pattern 1: Simple Verbs**
(a) I never **said** such a thing!	**(b)** Never **did I say** such a thing!	When you front a structure requiring inversion and the sentence has only a simple verb, add *do* except when the main verb is a form of *be*.
(c) **She walked** so slowly that it took her an hour to get to school.	**(d)** So slowly **did she walk** that it took her an hour to get to school.	
(e) **Max could** never have left Ramona.	**(f)** Never **could Max** have left Ramona.	**Pattern 2: Complex Verbs**
(g) **They would** not stay in that house for anything.	**(h)** Not for anything **would they** stay in that house.	Complex verbs have a main verb and one or more auxiliaries. In sentences with complex verbs, invert the first auxiliary and the subject.
(i) **The director is** seldom here on time.	**(j)** Seldom **is the director** here on time.	**Pattern 3: *Be* Verbs**
(k) **The speaker was** so boring that many in the audience fell asleep.	**(l)** So boring **was the speaker** that many in the audience fell asleep.	When the verb is *be* with no auxiliaries, invert the subject and *be*.
		Pattern 4: ***Be* + Auxiliary Verbs**
(m) **There has** never been so much excitement in this town.	**(n)** Never in this town **has there** been so much excitement.	In sentences with fronted adverbials, invert the first auxiliary and the subject.
(o) **The dust has been** more annoying than the noise during the remodeling of the library.	**(p)** More annoying than the noise **has been the dust** during the remodeling of the library.	In sentences with fronted comparatives, put both the auxiliary and *be* before the subject.

EXERCISE 4

After each of the following phrases, add a main clause that expresses your opinions or provides information. If the fronted part is a position adverbial, use a *be* verb to follow it.

▶ **EXAMPLES:**   Near the school
Near the school is a small coffee shop.

So puzzling . . . that
So puzzling was the homework assignment that most of us didn't finish it.

1. Seldom during the past few years
2. More fascinating than my English class
3. Rarely during my lifetime
4. In my bedroom
5. More important to me than anything
6. Seldom in the history of the world
7. More of a world problem than air pollution
8. So interesting . . . that
9. Stored in the recesses of my brain, never to be forgotten,
10. Waiting for me in the future
11. In the front of my English textbook
12. Better than ice cream for dessert
13. Loved and respected by many admirers
14. So terrible . . . that

EXERCISE 5

Make up a sentence in response to each of the following. Use a fronted structure for emphasis.

▶ **EXAMPLE:**   Describe what is in some area of your classroom.
In the back of our classroom are posters of many countries of the world and a large map of the world.

1. State how exciting something is to you by comparing it in degree to something else. (Start with "More exciting . . .")
2. Tell how infrequently you have done something.
3. Describe how angry you were in a certain circumstance. (Start with "So angry . . .")
4. Describe how happy you were in another circumstance.

▶ Fronted Negative Forms: Adverbials

For all of these fronted negative adverbials below, you must invert the subject and auxiliary or the subject and the simple verb.

Adverbs and Adverb Phrases

WORD/PHRASE	NOT FRONTED	FRONTED
never	**(a)** I have **never** laughed so hard!	**(b)** **Never** have I laughed so hard!
not once	**(c)** I have **not** missed my Portuguese class once this semester.	**(d)** **Not once** have I missed my Portuguese class this semester.
not for + (noun)	**(e)** I would **not** commute four hours a day **for all the money in the world!**	**(f)** **Not for all the money in the world** would I commute four hours a day!
not until + (noun)	**(g)** She did **not** realize the ring was missing **until the morning.**	**(h)** **Not until the morning** did she realize the ring was missing.
not since + (noun)	**(i)** We have **not** had so much rain **since April.**	**(j)** **Not since April** have we had so much rain.
under no circumstances	**(k)** You will **not** be allowed to leave **under any circumstances.**	**(l)** **Under no circumstances** will you be allowed to leave. (*not any → no*)
in no case	**(m)** We can **not** make an exception **in any case.**	**(n)** **In no case** can we make an exception.
in no way	**(o)** This will **not** affect your grade **in any way.**	**(p)** **In no way** will this affect your grade.
no way (informal)	**(q)** I am **not** going to miss that concert **for any reason!**	**(r)** **No way** am I going to miss that concert.
nowhere	**(s)** I have **not** been **anywhere** that is as peaceful as this place.	**(t)** **Nowhere** have I been that is as peaceful as this place.

Adverb Time Clauses

CLAUSE	NOT FRONTED	FRONTED
not until + clause	**(u)** I will **not** believe it **until I see it!**	**(v)** **Not until I see it** will I believe it!
not since + clause	**(w)** I have **not** had so much spare time **since I started high school.**	**(x)** **Not since I started high school** have I had so much spare time.

EXERCISE 6

Add the negative fronted structure in parentheses to the following sentences for emphasis. Make any other changes that are necessary.

▶ **EXAMPLE:** I hadn't ever been so upset. (never)
Never had I been so upset.

1. We can't let you retake the examination. (under no circumstances)
2. I haven't missed a class. (not once)
3. Homer won't miss graduation. (not for anything)
4. This didn't change my attitude about you. (in no way)
5. I won't tell you my secret. (not until + a time phrase)
6. She hasn't allowed any misbehavior. (in no case)
7. You may not have access to the files. (under no conditions)
8. I wouldn't trade places with him. (not for a million dollars)

EXERCISE 7

Complete the following with a statement based on your experience or opinions.

1. Not since I was a child . . .
2. Not until I am old and grey . . .
3. Not until years from now . . .
4. Not since I started . . .
5. Nowhere . . .
6. Not for anything . . .

▶ Fronted Negative Forms: Objects and Conjunctions

As with the negative adverbials in Focus 4, these fronted structures require subject-auxiliary or subject-verb inversion.

Noun Phrase Objects

PHRASE	NOT FRONTED	FRONTED
not + singular noun*	**(a)** The sky was brilliant; he could **not see one cloud** in any direction.	**(b)** The sky was brilliant; **not one cloud** could he see in any direction.
	(c) We will **not** spend **another penny** on your education unless your grades improve.	**(d)** **Not another penny** will we spend on your education unless your grades improve.

*A plural form is possible with *no* (*no clouds could he see*), but the emphasis would not be as strong as with the singular form.

Conjunctions

WORD/ PHRASE	NOT FRONTED	FRONTED
neither, nor	**(e)** I have no idea why the mail didn't come.	
	(f) My mother **doesn't either.**	**(g)** **Neither** does my mother.
	(h) My sister **doesn't either.**	**(i)** **Nor** does my sister.
	(j) **No one** else does **either.**	**(k)** **Neither** does anyone else.
not only (. . . *but also*)	**(l)** Frozen yogurt does **not only** taste good, but it's also good for you.	**(m)** **Not only** does frozen yogurt taste good, but it's also good for you.
no sooner (. . . *than*)	**(n)** The exam had **no sooner** started than we had a fire drill.	**(o)** **No sooner** had the exam started than we had a fire drill.

EXERCISE 8

After each of the following statements, add a sentence using the fronted negative in parentheses.

▶ **EXAMPLE:** The German swimmers did not win any medals at the Olympics. (Nor)
Nor did any swimmers from France or the United States.

1. I tried to do the homework but I couldn't understand the assignment. (neither)
2. I've been working on this math assignment almost the entire night. (not one more minute)
3. The main star of the film could not get along with the director. (nor)
4. I just love to visit large cities. (not only)
5. Look how skinny that model is! (not one ounce of fat)
6. We do not want to buy products from companies who use dishonest advertising. (not another dollar)
7. Leon was sorry he had decided to go sailing. (no sooner)
8. Our art history professor will not accept late papers. (neither)
9. Learning Greek could help you in several ways. (not only)
10. It has been reported that the terrorists will not release their hostages. (nor)

► **Fronted Structures: Emphasizing, Contrasting, and Focusing on Unexpected Information**

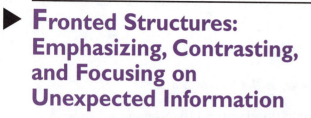

EXAMPLES	EXPLANATIONS
Emphasis (a) **In the evenings** she writes. It is a time when the house is quiet and peaceful and she can concentrate.	**Adverb Phrases** Reasons for fronting: • to emphasize information • to point out contrasts
Contrast (b) **In the evenings** she writes. **The mornings** are devoted to gardening and **the afternoons** to her job at a publishing company.	For adverbials of time, place, or frequency, the context determines whether contrast or some other kind of emphasis is intended.
Emphasis (c) **On the first floor of the store** are men's clothes. This floor also has luggage.	The fronting of contrast phrases emphasizes parallel structures. Parallelism of this kind is a stylistic device used to stress ideas and create rhythm.
Contrast (d) **On the first floor of the store** are men's clothes. **On the second floor** are women's clothes and linens.	
(e) Who could be at Sara's door at this late hour? Sara squinted through the peephole to see who the mystery caller was. **Participle** **Focus on Subject** **Staring back at her** was her long-lost brother. **Comparative** (f) **More important to me than anything else** **Focus on Subject** is my family.	**Participle Phrases and Comparatives** Reason for fronting: • to emphasize a subject that contains new or unexpected information by moving it to the end of the sentence.

EXAMPLES	EXPLANATIONS
(g) **Never** have I seen such a display of bravery! **(h)** **Not until the last votes were counted** would the senator admit defeat. **(i)** **Under no circumstances** may you enter this building after midnight. **(j)** **Not a single promise** did he make that wasn't eventually broken.	**Negative Structures** Reasons for fronting:* • to emphasize unusual or unexpected actions or events • to stress particular aspects of events or actions • to create strong commands that prohibit actions • to emphasize the "negativeness" of things, events, or actions

*These uses often overlap; a fronted negative may emphasize in several different ways.

EXERCISE 9

State what you think is the main reason for fronting each of the underlined structures. Do you think it is primarily for (1) emphasis of the fronted structure, (2) contrast of the structure, or (3) focus on a delayed subject that contains new or unexpected information?

1. <u>Only when Marta drives</u> does she get nervous. At other times she's quite calm.

2. The phone rang. Howard was sure it was his best friend Miguel calling. Picking up the phone, he shouted, "Yo!" <u>Responding to his greeting</u> was his biology professor.

3. <u>Not since I was in elementary school</u> have I been to the circus. Believe me, that was a long time ago!

4. Welcome to the Little River Inn. We hope you will enjoy your stay here. <u>To your right</u> is a cooler with ice and the soft-drink machines. <u>To your left and around the corner</u> is the swimming pool and jacuzzi.

5. <u>To start this lawnmower,</u> you need to pull the cord very hard and quickly. To keep it going, you should set the lever in the middle.

6. Minh heard a noise coming from underneath his parked car. Getting down on his knees, he looked under the front of it. <u>There, crouched on the right front tire</u> was a tiny kitten.

7. <u>Not until I hear from you</u> will I leave. I promise I'll stay here until then.

8. <u>During the long winters</u> Bonnie does a lot of reading. She loves to lounge by the fire with a good book.

9. The crowd was waiting excitedly to see who would win this year's Boston marathon. <u>A few minutes later, across the finish line</u> came a runner from Kenya.

10. <u>Had I known the movie was so long,</u> I doubt I would have gone to see it. I had no idea that it would last for five hours!

EXERCISE 10

In each of the students' responses to the teacher's questions below, there is something wrong either with the **form** of the statement or the **use** in context. Identify the problem. Correct errors in form and explain problems with usage.

1. **Teacher:** Meeyung, is it true that you got to see the fireworks during the Statue of Liberty's anniversary celebration?

   Meeyung: Oh yes! Never I have seen such a beautiful display of fireworks!

2. **Teacher:** Alex, the bell rang five minutes ago. Please turn in your exam.

   Alex: Hey, no way am I turning this in.

3. **Teacher:** Wilai, I don't seem to have your homework. Did you turn it in to me?

   Wilai: No, I'm sorry, never have I turned it in.

4. **Teacher:** Javier, did you find that chapter explaining verb tenses helpful?

   Javier: Yes, not only it helped me with present perfect but it also explained conditionals well.

5. **Teacher:** Patrice, I'm really sorry to hear you've been so ill. I hope you're better now.

   Patrice: Thank you. I *was* really sick all month. No sooner I got rid of the flu when I got pneumonia.

6. **Teacher:** Kazuhiko, I could help you after class if you can stay for a while.

   Kazuhiko: I'm sorry. Not for an hour could I stay because I have another class at 4:30.

Use Your English

ACTIVITY 1: LISTENING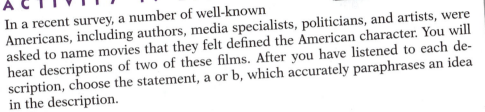

In a recent survey, a number of well-known Americans, including authors, media specialists, politicians, and artists, were asked to name movies that they felt defined the American character. You will hear descriptions of two of these films. After you have listened to each description, choose the statement, a or b, which accurately paraphrases an idea in the description.

Pollyanna
a. Americans have never hated or envied the rich.
b. Americans have never hated the rich, just envied them.

Mr. Smith Goes to Washington
a. Political corruption in Washington continues until an innocent man from a small town arrives.
b. Political corruption in Washington stops before an innocent man from a small town arrives.

ACTIVITY 2: WRITING/SPEAKING

Make a list of some things you believe you would **never** do under any circumstances. For emphasis, start your statements with a negative word or phrase. Then share your list with one or more classmates to see if they also would never do the things on your list, and have them discuss their lists with you. Finally, write a summary of your discussion, pointing out your similarities and differences on this topic.

▶ **EXAMPLES:** *Under no circumstances would I take an advanced course in physics.*

No way would I ever eat squid. (informal usage)

ACTIVITY 3: WRITING/SPEAKING

Advertisements and commercials often use strong claims to sell products. Imagine that you are a copywriter for an ad agency. Team up with another classmate. With your partner, choose a product (one that already exists or make one up) to sell; write an advertisement for either print media (magazine, newspaper), radio, or television. In your ad, use at least two fronted structures to emphasize something about your product. Present your ad/commercial to the class, and give them a chance to discuss your claims.

ACTIVITY 4: WRITING

Write a paragraph in which you describe one of the following:

- the contents of a room as someone might see the room upon entering it.
- a machine or appliance with a number of parts.

Use some fronted adverbials of position for contrast or emphasis in your description.

▶ **EXAMPLES:** *As you come into the living room, there is a large chintz sofa. In front of the sofa is a maple coffee table. To the left of it is an end table that matches the coffee table, and to the right stands a bookcase. On top of the bookcase sits my favorite vase. It's a deep turquoise blue.*

The parts of my computer include the monitor, the printer, the computer itself, and the control panel. On the control panel are four switches. To the far left is the switch for the computer. Next to it is the switch for the monitor. To the right of the monitor switch is the one for the printer.

ACTIVITY 5: SPEAKING

With a partner or in a small group, describe an event that affected you strongly; for example, a time when you were especially happy, excited, angry, frightened, surprised, etc. Use a fronted structure, such as a comparative, to emphasize the way you felt.

ACTIVITY 6: WRITING

Write a review or synopsis of a book, television show, or movie that you especially liked or disliked. Use some fronted structures for emphasis, contrast, or focus.

FOCUSING AND EMPHASIZING STRUCTURES

It-Clefts and Wh-Clefts

UNIT GOALS:
- To use *it*-cleft sentences to put special emphasis on information
- To know what parts of a sentence can be used for focus in *it*-clefts
- To know how to use other kinds of cleft sentences for questions and statements
- To use *wh*-clefts to put focus on information at the end of sentences

▶ **O P E N I N G   T A S K**
How Does Birth Order Influence Personality?

You may have at times judged someone's behavior according to their position in a family as the oldest, youngest, middle, or only child. For example, you might have considered a friend's "take charge" attitude as characteristic of an oldest child or a brother's or sister's "spoiled" behavior the result of being the youngest. If you are an only child, you may have heard the generalization that only children are very confident.

STEP 1 Read the following observations about personality traits associated with particular birth orders that were made by two clinical psychologists.

Personality Traits Associated with Birth Orders

(a) tends to be self-critical and perfectionist

(b) is often the most secretive

(c) is usually very comfortable with older people

(d) tends to be skilled at defending himself or herself

(e) may sometimes try to be all things to all people

(f) as a child, may find others of the same age immature

(g) often feels most obligated to follow the family rules and routines

(h) may be confused about self-image as a result of being simultaneously welcomed, adored, bossed around, and disliked by siblings

(i) tends to be the most conservative

(j) is typically self-sufficient

(k) often subject to self-doubt due to not being taken seriously by family members

(l) may often feel like a "fifth wheel" (a feeling of not belonging or being an "extra")

From: Bradford Wilson and George Edington, *First Child, Second Child* . . . . New York: McGraw-Hill, 1981.

STEP 2 Based on your knowledge of your family members personalities (including yours) and the personalities of friends whose birth order you know, guess which order each trait characterizes: the only child, the oldest child, the middle child, or the youngest child. Here are answers to (a) and (b):

(a) *It's the oldest child who's often the most self-critical and perfectionist.*
(b) *It's the middle child who tends to be secretive.*

STEP 3 After you have guessed a birth order for each trait, briefly discuss your choices in small groups.

STEP 4 As a class, share results of your group discussions: Which ones did you most often agree about? Which resulted in the most differing guesses?

STEP 5 Check the answers to this task on page A-16. Comment on ones that surprised you the most.

▶ **EXAMPLE:** *What surprised me the most is that the middle child is often secretive. My brother's girlfriend is a middle child and she tells everyone about everything!*

► Structure of *It*-Cleft Sentences

EXAMPLES		EXPLANATION
(a) **No Special Emphasis:** My brother is conservative, not me. **(b)** **Emphasis: It is my brother** who is conservative, not me!		*It*-cleft sentences put special emphasis on one part of a sentence. The part that is emphasized is introduced by it and a form of *be*.
	Focus Element	**Clause**	"Cleft" means to divide. The cleft sentence divides a sentence into two parts: (1) a focus element and (2) a clause beginning with *that, who, when, or where*.
(c)	It is the youngest child	who is often both a rebel a charmer.	
	Sing. Plural		The verb is singular even when the focus element is plural.
(d)	It **is** oldest children and only children	who tend to be the most assertive.	
	Future		
(e)	It **will be** on a Saturday	that we leave, not a Sunday.	The *be* verb is usually present tense. However, we also use other tenses.
	Past		
(f)	It **used to be** my mother	who did all the cooking, but now we all help.	
(g)	It **must** be red wine	that stained this carpet.	We can use modal verbs in cleft sentences to express degrees of probability.
(h)	It **can't** be the youngest child	who is the most conservative.	

EXERCISE 1
Complete each blank below with a word or phrase that fits the context.

1. It couldn't be _____ who are confused about self-image because they don't have any siblings.

2. I think it must be _____ who often has the self-image problem because the older ones might have mixed feelings about the baby of the family.

3. It might be _____ who is generally self-sufficient because as a child he or she might have had to do a lot of things alone.

4. Psychologists Wilson and Edington claim that, of all birth order positions, _____ the middle child who is apt to be the most popular among other people.

5. The two psychologists say it is _____ who may be fearless and have a strong sense of exploration because that child often feels protected by older siblings.

6. They have also observed that _____ who tend to have difficulty dealing with interruptions from others because they did not have brothers or sisters who interrupted them.

▶ Focus Elements in Cleft Sentences

We can focus on various parts of a sentence in the focus element of cleft sentences.

CLEFT SENTENCE	FOCUS	ORIGINAL SENTENCE
(a) It is **the President** who appoints the cabinet.	Subject	The President appoints the cabinet.
(b) It is **the cabinet** that the President appoints.	Direct object	
(c) It is **the Speaker of the House** with whom the President often disagrees. (formal)	Object of preposition	The President often disagrees with the Speaker of the House.
(d) It is **the Speaker of the House** that the President often disagrees with. (less formal)		
(e) It was **an awful shade of yellow** that they painted the Oval Office.	Complement (noun)	They painted the Oval Office an awful shade of yellow.
(f) It was **greenish yellow** that they painted it.	Complement (adjective)	They painted it greenish yellow.
(g) It was **due to illness** that the Vice-President resigned.	Prepositional phrase	The Vice-President resigned due to illness.
(h) It was **after World War II ended** that the baby boom began in the United States.	Dependent clause	The baby boom began in the United States after World War II ended.
(i) It was **to ensure the right of women to vote** that the Twelfth Amendment to the Constitution was passed.	Infinitive or Infinitive clause	The Twelfth Amendment to the Constitution was passed to ensure the right of women to vote.

EXERCISE 2

Restate the following sentences about the United States civil rights movement of the 1960s to emphasize the information indicated in parentheses. Change any other wording as necessary.

▶ **EXAMPLE:** Black students staged the first sit-in at a lunch counter in Greensboro, North Carolina, in 1960. (Emphasize the date)

It was in 1960 that black students staged the first sit-in at a lunch counter in Greensboro, North Carolina.

1. White and black civil rights workers sat together in "white only" sections of restaurants and other public places to protest segregation. (Emphasize the purpose.)

2. In 1962, President Kennedy sent United States marshalls to protect James H. Meredith, the first black student at the University of Mississippi. (Emphasize the place.)

3. The civil rights movement reached a climax in 1963 with the march on Washington. (Emphasize the event.)

4. Martin Luther King, Jr., delivered his famous "I Have a Dream" speech during the march on Washington. (Emphasize the speech.)

5. Three young civil rights workers were tragically murdered in Mississippi on June 22, 1964. (Emphasize the date.)

6. Martin Luther King, Jr., led civil rights marches in Selma, Alabama, and Montgomery, Mississippi, in 1965. (Emphasize the places.)

7. King was assassinated by James Earl Ray in Memphis, Tennessee, in 1968. (Emphasize the assassin.)

8. We now celebrate the achievements of this great civil rights leader in January. (Emphasize the month.)

EXERCISE 3

Imagine that each of the situations below is true. Provide an explanation, either serious or humorous, emphasizing the reason.

▶ **EXAMPLE:** You were late to class yesterday.

It was because the bus didn't come that I was late to class.

1. You didn't have an assignment done that was due.

2. You missed a medical appointment.

3. You forgot a relative's birthday. (You choose the relative.)

4. You didn't eat anything for two days.

5. You stumbled and fell crossing the street.

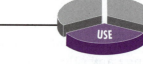

▶ *It*-Clefts in Spoken and Written Communication

EXAMPLES	EXPLANATIONS
(a) **It is the middle child** who is most secretive. (The middle child is distinguished from the eldest and youngest children.)	**Distinguish Member of a Group** *It*-cleft sentences can distinguish one member of a group as having certain qualities.
(b) **It is only love** that can bring world peace. (Love is the only thing that can bring world peace.) **(c)** **It is only my best friend** who can cheer me up when I'm down. (My best friend is the only person who can cheer me up.)	In some cases the "group" may include all other things or people. We use *only* before the focus element to convey this meaning.
(d) A: I think the youngest child is the one who tends to be secretive. B: I don't agree. **It's the middle child,** I think, who is most secretive. **(e)** What color paint is this? **It was blue** that I ordered, not green!	**Express Contrast** We sometimes use cleft sentences to point out a contrast or to note something that is commonly believed but not true. In spoken English, the contrasting word or phrase receives extra stress. In (e), *blue* is stressed because it contrasts with *green*.
(f) **It was out of concern** that we called our neighbor to see if she was all right. **(g)** **It was for a general education requirement** that I took art history.	**Emphasize Purpose or Cause** *It*-clefts can also emphasize the purpose or cause of something. These often include prepositional phrases beginning with *out of* or *for*.

EXERCISE 4

Which person in your family or circle of friends best matches the following descriptions? In your response, use a cleft sentence beginning with *it is* (or *it's*). Also, try to paraphrase (put in your own words) the description.

▶ **EXAMPLE:** would be most likely to complain about young people's behavior

It's my grandmother who would be most likely to complain about the way young people act.

1. tends to watch the most TV

2. has the best sense of humor

3. would be most likely to park a car and forget where it was

4. has the most trouble getting up in the morning

5. is the most artistic

6. would be most likely to stop and help if he or she saw someone in trouble

7. most often tries to get out of doing housework

8. most enjoys gossiping

EXERCISE 5

Complete each blank by choosing a word from the list below for a focus element and creating a cleft sentence. The first has been done as an example.

anger   music
curiosity   pride
faith   a sense of humor

1. ___It was anger___ that made God banish Adam and Eve from the Garden of Eden, according to the Judeo-Christian Bible.

2. _____ that often keeps us from admitting our mistakes.

3. _____ that caused Pandora's downfall in the Greek myth; she had to find out what was in the box.

4. _____ that has been called the language of the soul.

5. _____ that keeps most of us from taking ourselves too seriously and helps us to deal with the ups and downs of life.

6. _____ that has helped many people withstand religious persecution.

Exercise 6

Imagine you have been asked to edit a reference book for errors. Unfortunately, much of the book turns out to be a collection of misinformation. As you read each "fact" below, identify the incorrect part. Write a sentence indicating what needs to be corrected, using a cleft sentence to highlight that element.

▶ **EXAMPLE:** Mark Twain wrote the classic novel *Huckleberry Flan* in 1884.

Correction: *It is **Huckleberry Finn** that Mark Twain wrote.*

1. The United States Congress first began meeting in Washington State in 1800.

2. New York City has two baseball teams: the Mets and the New York Blue Jays.

3. One of the most famous tragedies of all times, *Romeo and Juliet* was written by Moliere in 1595.

4. Christopher Columbus sailed to India in 1492.

5. United States astronauts first landed on Mars in 1969.

6. In 1260 Kublai Khan founded the Yuan dynasty in Japan.

7. Leonardo da Vinci painted the famous *Moaning Lisa* around 1500.

8. The brain, the spinal cord, and the nerves are parts of the body's digestive system.

9. Nefertiti ruled India along with her husband King Akhenaton during the 14th century B.C.

EXERCISE 7

STEP 1 Make lists of your four favorite foods, your four favorite movies (or TV programs), and your four favorite school subjects.

STEP 2 To indicate which item ranks highest in each of the three lists, fill in the blanks of the sentences below. Share one of your responses with classmates.

1. I love to eat _____ , _____ , and _____.
But it is _____ that I would choose if I had to eat only one food for a week.

2. I could watch _____ , _____ , and _____
quite a few times, but it is _____ that _____ .

3. I enjoy _____ , I like to study _____ , and I
also like _____. However, if _____ , it is
_____ that I would choose.

STEP 3 Make up another list of four favorite things of some other category (e.g., books, sports). Then write a sentence using the pattern in step 2.

FOCUS **4**

▶ *It*-Clefts: **Emphasizing Time, Place, and Characters**

EXAMPLES	EXPLANATION
(a) It was **in the early spring** that Sylvia finally felt well enough to make the trip to Budapest. **(b)** It was **on a cold day in February, 1860,** that Abraham Lincoln delivered his eloquent Cooper Union speech against slavery. **(c)** It was **in Barbizon** that Rousseau founded the modern school of French landscape painting. **(d)** It was **Shakespeare** who inspired Beethoven's creation of his String Quartet opus 18, number 1.	In narratives such as stories or historical accounts, we may use cleft sentences to emphasize the time, place, characters (or real people) in the narrative.

EXERCISE 8

Choose one feature to highlight in the following historical facts and write an introductory sentence for a historical narrative about each.

▶ **EXAMPLES:** *It was **Cheops** who started building the pyramids in Egypt around* 2700 B.C. (Emphasizes person)

*It was **around 2700 B.C.** that Cheops began building the pyramids in Egypt.* (Emphasizes date)

Person	Date	Place	Event
Cheops (king)	around 2700 B.C.	Egypt	started building the Pyramids
Machiavelli (statesman)	1513	Florence, Italy	accused of conspiracy
John James Audubon (artist)	April 26, 1785	Cayes, Santo Domingo	born
Emily Dickinson (poet) (poet)	1862	Amherst, Massachusetts	began correspondence with Thomas Wentworth Higgins
Joaquium Machado de Assis (writer)	1869	Rio de Janeiro, Brazil	married Portuguese aristocrat, Carolina de Novaes
Jean Sibelius (composer)	1892	Helsinki, Finland	wrote the symphonic poem "Kullervo"
Aung San Suu Kyi	1991	Mynamar	received word that she had won the Nobel Prize

FOCUS **5**

▶ **O**ther Forms of Cleft Sentences

EXAMPLES	EXPLANATIONS
(a) **Who was it** that gave you that information? **(b)** **Why was it** (that) they decided to move? **(c)** **When was it** (that) you left Shanghai?	**Wh-Cleft Questions** In *Wh*-questions, *it* and *be* are inverted, changing the order to *be + it* after the question word (question word + *be + it*). In examples (b) and (c), *that* is in parentheses because it is optional.
(d) **Was it out of pity** (that) he let the old man move into his house? **(e)** **Is it Spanish 3** (that) you're taking this quarter?	**Yes-No Cleft Questions** We must also invert *it* and *be* in yes-no questions.
(f) **What a nice essay it was** (that) you wrote about your father!	**What a + Noun Phrase** This type of cleft sentence (*What a* + noun phrase + *it + be*) expresses wonder, delight, admiration, or surprise.
(g) I told you before (that) **it was Marsha who called you, not Marianne.** **(h)** The President announced (that) **it was because he was ill that he would not be seeking re-election.**	**That Clauses** As you have seen in some exercises in this unit, focus elements may be that clauses in reported speech.

EXERCISE 9
Make up a cleft sentence for each situation that follows to emphasize some piece of information.

▶ **EXAMPLE:** You told a friend that *Braveheart* was going to be on TV on Monday night. He thought you said Tuesday and missed seeing it. Tell him what you said.

I told you it was on Monday night that it was going to be on, not Tuesday!

1. You're not sure why a customer service representative at a bank wanted to know your place of birth for a checking account application you were filling out. Ask him.

2. You want to compliment a classmate on a great speech that she gave in class the day before.

3. You've been listening to a history lecture about China and missed hearing the date when the Chinese revolution ended the Manchu dynasty. Politely ask your instructor to tell you the date again.

4. You and your family are watching the news. The newscaster has just announced the cause of a major plane crash to have been an engine failure. A member of your family was distracted and didn't hear this information. Tell him or her what the newscaster said.

5. You have been trying to call a close friend for three hours, but the line has been busy. You wonder who she could be on the line with. When you finally get through, you ask her.

► *Wh*-Clefts

EXAMPLES	EXPLANATIONS
(a) What the world needs **is peace and justice.** **(b)** What we want **is a woman in the White House.**	Unlike *it*-clefts, *wh*-clefts put focus on information at the end of the sentence.
Assumption **Be** **Focus** **(c)** **Where** he goes **is** a mystery to me. **(d)** **What** Barbara Tomas offers **is** honesty and compassion. **(e)** What she is **is** a brilliant politician.	The assumption (what we already know or understand) is introduced by a *wh*-word. The focus adds new information. A form of *be* links the two parts of the sentence. When the sentence has two *be* verbs, the second *be* links the two parts. In spoken English, the first *be* verb would be stressed and followed by a pause. (What she *is* is . . .)

EXERCISE 10

Match the phrases in column A with the appropriate word or phrase from column B. Connect them with an appropriate form of *be* and write complete sentences. The first has been done as an example.

▶ **EXAMPLE:** 1. *What a lepidopterist specializes in **is** the study of moths and butterflies.*

A
1. What a lepidopterist specializes in
2. What Florida produces
3. What Alexander Graham Bell invented
4. What Martin Luther King, Jr., believed in
5. Where the United States President lives
6. Where the capital of South Korea is
7. What "mph" means
8. Where the Pyramids are located
9. What Brazilians speak
10. What most Americans eat at Thanksgiving
11. What Jimmy Carter was

B
turkey
Seoul
Portuguese
the study of moths and butterflies
in Egypt
the 39th President
racial equality
in the White House
citrus fruit
the telephone
miles per hour

▶ ## Using *Wh*-Clefts for Emphasis

EXAMPLES	EXPLANATION
(a) A: How much money does the director earn? B: **What she earns** is none of your business!	*Wh*-clefts are more common in spoken English than in written English. The *Wh*-phrase often refers to a statement or idea that has been previously expressed.
(b) A: Mozart wrote plays. B: Actually, **what Mozart wrote** was music. Perhaps you mean Moliere.	

EXERCISE 11

Rewrite the underlined words using a *Wh*-cleft. Then act out the conversations with a partner, using appropriate emphasis. The first has been done as an example, with the emphasis in italics.

1. Matt: Henry drives a Porsche.
   David: Are you kidding? <u>He drives a Ford.</u>
   Matt: Really? He told me it was a Porsche.

   EXAMPLE: *Wh*-cleft: *What he drives is a **Ford**.*

2. Frank: Margo tells me you're a painter.
   Duane: That's right.
   Frank: Do you sell many of your paintings?
   Duane: Well, actually, <u>I paint houses.</u>

3. Nick: I'm tired. I think I'm going to take a nap.
   Lisa: Nick, <u>you need some exercise.</u> That will make you feel much better than a nap, I think.

4. Teacher: Do you have any suggestions about how we can improve this class?
   Fusako: <u>We'd like less homework.</u>
   Ricardo: <u>And we'd prefer a test every week.</u>
   Soraya: <u>And I need more grammar to pass my writing exam.</u>
   Bernadine: <u>And I'd like a different textbook.</u> This one isn't very challenging.

5. Howard: Do you know Barry? He writes novels.
   Tessa: I don't think that's true. <u>He writes instruction manuals for computer programs.</u>

6. Lia: What are you getting Carol and Bart for their wedding?
   Shelley: <u>They'd really like a microwave,</u> but I can't afford it, so I'm getting them a coffee grinder.

Use Your English

ACTIVITY 1: LISTENING/SPEAKING

Divide the class into two or three teams for a quiz show competition. On the tape you will hear questions followed by a choice of three answers. After each question and possible answers, the teacher will stop the tape. Teams will take turns giving answers, which must be in the form of a cleft sentence. For each correct answer, a team will receive two points. Both the answer and the form must be correct to be awarded the points.

▶ **EXAMPLES:** Who was president before Bill Clinton?
(a) Jimmy Carter   (b) George Bush   (c) Ronald Reagan

Correct answer: *It was George Bush who was president before Clinton.*

What does a baseball player get when he or she hits a ball out of the park?
(a) an out   (b) a triple   (c) a home run

Correct answer: *What the player gets is a home run.*

ACTIVITY 2: WRITING/SPEAKING

Make up five descriptions that could be used for members of your class. Write your descriptions as verb phrases, similar to Exercise 1. (Be careful not to write any descriptions that would offend anyone or hurt someone's feelings!) Write down who you think best fits the description. Take turns reading your descriptions and have classmates say who they think matches each, using a cleft sentence. Then tell them whether you agree or disagree. Here are a few examples to get you started:

▶ **EXAMPLE:** A: *Tells the funniest stories*
B: *I think it's Josef who does that.*
A: *I agree.*

ACTIVITY 3: WRITING

People who are against the government's controlling the sales of guns often say "It's not guns that kill; it's people who kill." Do you agree with this logic? Write a paragraph or essay giving your opinion about this statement.

ACTIVITY 4: WRITING

Consider some films you have seen or books, poetry, or short stories that you have read. For each, what was one of the main things you admired or that you felt made it good? Write your responses in a list. Then elaborate one of them by writing a paragraph about it. Here are a few examples of the types of comments that might be made:

▶ **EXAMPLE:** *It is the beautiful cinematography and interesting story that make* Out of Africa *such an enjoyable movie.*

ACTIVITY 5: WRITING OR SPEAKING

Write a narrative paragraph describing the place, time, and other significant information about one of the following:

- The circumstances of your birth or someone else's you know
- A historical event
- A current event

To begin your narrative, choose one of the features to highlight in a cleft construction as was shown in Focus 4 on page 441. If time permits, read your paragraph to classmates in small groups.

ACTIVITY 6: WRITING

Which of the personality traits listed in the Opening Task seem to fit you or members of your family? Write a paragraph describing who it is that they fit.

Appendices

Appendix 1A   Present Time Frame

Form	Example	Use	Meaning
SIMPLE PRESENT base form of verb or base form of verb + *-s*	Many plants **require** a lot of sun to thrive.	timeless truths	now
	Luis **works** every day except Sunday.	habitual actions	
	We **think** you should come with us.	mental perceptions and emotions	
	Veronica **owns** the house she lives in.	possession	
PRESENT PROGRESSIVE *am/is/are* + present participle (verb + *-ing*)	They **are** just **finishing** the race.	actions in progress	in progress now
	She **is picking** straw-berries this morning.	duration	
	Someone **is pound-ing** nails next door.	repetition	
	My friend **is living** in Nova Scotia for six months.	temporary activities	
	I **am changing** the oil in my car right now.	uncompleted actions	
PRESENT PERFECT *have/has* + past participle (verb + *-ed* or irregular form)	She **has attended** the university for four years; she will graduate in June.	situations that began in the past, continue to the present	in the past but related to now in some way
	I **have read** that book too. Did you like it?	actions completed in the past but related to the present	
	The movie **has** just **ended.**	actions recently completed	

Form	Example	Use	Meaning
PRESENT PERFECT PROGRESSIVE *have/has* + present participle (verb + *-ing*)	I **have been dialing** the airline's number for hours it seems. I can't believe it's still busy.	repeated or continuous actions that are incomplete	up until and including now
	This weekend Michelle **has been participating** in a job fair which ends on Sunday afternoon.		

Appendix 1B Past Time Frame

Form	Example	Use	Meaning
SIMPLE PRESENT	So yesterday he **tells** me he just thought of another way to get rich quick.	past event in informal narrative	at a certain time in the past
SIMPLE PAST verb + *-ed* or irregular past form	We **planted** the vegetable garden last weekend.	events that took place at a definite time in the past	at a certain time in the past
	Pei-Mi **taught** for five years in Costa Rica.	events that lasted for a time in the past	
	I **studied** English every year when I was in high school.	habitual or repeated actions in the past	
	We **thought** we were heading in the wrong direction.	past mental perceptions and emotions	
	Jose **had** a piano when he lived in New York.	past possessions	
PAST PROGRESSIVE *was/were* + present participle (verb + *-ing*)	When I talked with him last night, Sam **was getting** ready for a trip.	events in progress at a specific time in the past	in progress at a time in the past

Form	Example	Use	Meaning
PAST PERFECT *had* + participle (verb + *-ed* or irregular form)	My parents **had lived** in Hungary before they moved to France.	actions or states that took place before another time in the past	before a certain time in the past
PAST PERFECT PROGRESSIVE *had* + *been* + present participle (verb + *-ing*)	We **had been hurrying** to get to the top of the mountain when the rain started.	incomplete events taking place before other past events	up until a certain time in the past
	I **had been working** on the last math problem when the teacher instructed us to turn in our exams.	incomplete events interrupted by other past events	

Appendix 1C   Future Time Frame

Form	Example	Use	Meaning
SIMPLE PRESENT	Takiko **graduates** next week.	definite future plans or schedules	already planned or expected in the future
	When Guangping **completes** her graduate program, she will look for a research job in Taiwan.	events with future time adverbials (*before, after, when*) in dependent clauses	
PRESENT PROGRESSIVE	I **am finishing** my paper tomorrow night.	future intentions	already planned or expected in the future
	Amit **is taking** biochemistry for two quarters next year.	scheduled events that last for a period of time	

Form	Example	Use	Meaning
BE GOING TO FUTURE *am/is/are going to* + base verb	The train **is going to arrive** any minute.	probable and immediate future events	at a certain time in the future
	I **am going to succeed** no matter what it takes!	strong intentions	
	Tomorrow you**'re going to be glad** that you are already packed for your trip.	predictions about future situations	
	We **are going to have** a barbecue on Sunday night.	future plans	
SIMPLE FUTURE *will* + base verb	It **will** probably **snow** tomorrow.	probable future events	
	I **will give** you a hand with that package; it looks heavy.	willingness/promises	
	Tomorrow **will be** a better day.	predictions about future situtations	
FUTURE PROGRESSIVE *will* + *be* + present participle (verb + *-ing*)	I **will be interviewing** for the bank job in the morning.	events that will be in progress at a time in the future	in progress at a certain time in the future
	Mohammed **will be studying** law for the next three years.	future events that will last for a period of time	
FUTURE PERFECT *will* + *have* + past participle (verb + *-ed* or irregular verb)	He **will have finished** his degree before his sister starts hers in 2001.	before a certain time in the future	future events happening before other future events
FUTURE PERFECT PROGRESSIVE *will* + *have* + *been* + present participle (verb + *-ing*)	By the year 2000, my family **will have been living** in the U.S. for ten years.	up until a certain time in the future	continuous and/or repeated actions continuing into the future

All passive verbs are formed with *be* + or *get* + past participle.

SIMPLE PRESENT *am/is/are* (or *get*) + past participle	That movie **is reviewed** in today's newspaper. The garbage **gets picked up** once a week.
PRESENT PROGRESSIVE *am/is/are* + *being* (or *getting*) + past participle	The possibility of life on Mars is being **explored.** We **are getting asked** to do too much!
SIMPLE PAST *was/were* (or *got*) + past participle	The butterflies **were observed** for five days. Many homes **got destroyed** during the fire.
PAST PROGRESSIVE *was/were* + *being* (or *getting*) + past participle	The Olympics **were being broadcast** worldwide. She **was getting beaten** in the final trials.
PRESENT PERFECT *has/have* + *been* (or *gotten*) + past participle	The information **has been sent.** Did you hear he**'s gotten fired** from his job?
PRESENT PERFECT PROGRESSIVE *has* + *been* + *being* (or *getting*) + past participle	This store **has been being remodeled** for six months now! I wonder if they'll ever finish. It looks as though the tires on my car **have been getting worn** by these bad road conditions.
PAST PERFECT *had* + *been* (or *gotten*) + past participle	The National Anthem **had** already **been sung** when we entered the baseball stadium. He was disappointed to learn that the project **had**n't **gotten completed** in his absence.
FUTURE *will* + *be* (or *get*) + past participle *be going to* + past participle	The horse races **will be finished** in an hour. The rest of the corn **will get harvested** this week. The election results **are going to be announced** in a few minutes.

FUTURE PERFECT *will* + *have* + *been* (or *gotten*) + past participle	I bet most of the food **will have been eaten** by the time we get to the party. The unsold magazines **will have gotten sent** back to the publishers by now.
FUTURE PERFECT PROGRESSIVE *will* + *have* + *been* + *being* (or *getting*) + past participle	Our laundry **will have been getting dried** for over an hour by the time we come back. I'm sure it will be ready to take out then. NOTE: The *be* form of this passive tense is quite rare. Even the *get* form is not very common.
PRESENT MODAL VERBS modal (*can, may, should,* etc.) + *be* (or *get*) + past participle	A different chemical **could be substituted** in this experiment. Don't stay outside too long. You **may get burned** by the blazing afternoon sun.
PAST MODAL VERBS modal (*can, may, should,* etc.) + *have* + *been* (or *gotten*) + past participle	All of our rock specimens **should have been identified** since the lab report is due. The file **might have gotten erased** through a computer error.

APPENDIX 3   Sentence Connectors

Meaning	Connectors

Addition
    Simple addition
    Emphatic addition
    Intensifying addition
	also, in addition, furthermore, moreover,
	what is more (what's more), as well, besides
	in fact, as a matter of fact, actually

Alternative	*on the other hand, alternatively*
Exemplifying	*for example, for instance, especially, in particular, to illustrate, as an example*
Identifying	*namely, specifically*
Clarifying	*that is, in other words, I mean*

Meaning	Connectors
Similarity	*similarly, likewise, in the same way*
Contrast	*however, in contrast, on the other hand, in fact*
Concession	*even so, however, nevertheless, nonetheless, despite (+ noun phrase), in spite of (+ noun phrase), on the other hand*
Effects/Results	*accordingly, as a result, as a result of (+ noun phrase), because of (+ noun phrase), due to (+ noun phrase), consequently, therefore, thus, hence*
Purpose	*in order to (+ verb), with this in mind, for this purpose*

APPENDIX 4   Gerunds and Infinitives

Appendix 4A   Overview of Gerunds and Infinitives

Examples	Explanations
	Infinitives (*to* + verb) or gerunds (verb + *ing*) can have various functions in a sentence:
(a) **To know many languages** would thrill me. (b) **Speaking English** is fun.	• subject
(c) His dream was **to sail around the world.** (d) Her hobby is **weaving baskets.**	• subject complement
(e) Paco hopes **to see the play.** (f) Carol remembered **mailing the package.**	• object
(g) By **studying hard,** you can enter a good school. (h) Thank you for **helping me.**	• object of preposition (gerunds)
(i) I don't understand the need **to take a ten-minute break.** (j) The instruction **to wear safety goggles** has saved many people's eyes.	• noun complement (infinitives)
(k) I am sorry **to inform you of the delay.** (l) They were pleased **to meet you.**	• adjective complement (infinitives following adjectives)

Appendix 4B   Verbs Followed by Infinitives and Gerunds

to + verb

EXAMPLE: Julia hates to be late.

List A

As mentioned in Unit 18, Focus 4, some of the verbs in List A may also take gerunds if an actual, vivid or fulfilled action is intended. (Example: Julia hates being late.)

Verbs of Emotion

care	loathe
desire	love
hate	regret
like	yearn

Verbs of Choice or Intention

agree	plan
choose	prefer
decide	prepare
deserve	propose
expect	refuse
hope	want
intend	wish
need	

Verbs of Initiation, Completion, and Incompletion

begin	manage
cease	neglect
commence	start
fail	try
get	undertake
hesitate	

Verbs of Request and Their Responses

demand	swear
offer	threaten
promise	vow

Verbs of Mental Activity

forget	learn
know how	remember

Intransitive Verbs

appear	seem
happen	tend

Other Verbs

afford (can't afford)	continue
arrange	pretend
claim	wait

List B

object + *to* + verb

EXAMPLE: She reminded us to be quiet.

Verbs of Communication

advise	permit
ask*	persuade
beg*	promise*
challenge	remind
command	require
convince	tell
forbid	warn
invite	urge
order	

Verbs of Instruction

encourage	teach
help	train
instruct	

Other Verbs

expect*	prepare*
trust	want*

Verbs of Causation

allow	get
cause	hire
force	

* Can follow pattern A also.

List C

verb + *-ing*

EXAMPLE: Trinh enjoys playing tennis.

Note that when the subject of the gerund is stated, it is in possessive form.

We enjoyed his telling us about his adventures.

Verbs of Initiation, Completion and Incompletion

avoid	give up
begin	postpone
cease	quit
complete	risk
delay	start
finish	stop
get through	try

Verbs of Communication

admit	mention
advise	recommend
deny	suggest
discuss	urge
encourage	

List C (continued)

Verbs of Ongoing Activity

continue	keep
can't help	keep on
practice	

Verbs of Mental Activity

anticipate	recall
consider	remember
forget	see (can't see)
imagine	understand

Verbs of Emotion

appreciate	like	miss	resent
dislike	love	prefer	resist
enjoy	mind (don't mind)	regret	tolerate
hate		can't stand	

APPENDIX 5   Preposition Clusters

in + noun + *of*	*on* + noun + *of*	*in* + *the* + noun + *of*	*on* + *the* + noun + *of*
in case of	on account of	in the course of	on the advice of
in charge of	on behalf of	in the event of	on the basis of
in place of	on top of	in the habit of	on the part of
in lieu of	on grounds of	in the name of	on the strength of
in favor of		in the process of	on the face of

Other Combinations

in by means of	in return for	at odds with	with the exception of
with respect to	in addition to	for the sake of	

Appendix 6A   General Types of Relative Clauses

Example:	Noun Phrase in Main Clause	Relative Pronoun in Relative Clause
(a) <u>The contract</u> **that** was signed yesterday is now valid. (S S)	Subject	Subject
(b) <u>The contract</u> **that** he signed yesterday is now valid. (S O)	Subject	Object
(c) I have not read <u>the contract</u> **that** was signed yesterday. (O S)	Object	Subject
(d) I have not read <u>the contract</u> **that** he signed yesterday. (O O)	Object	Object

Appendix 4B   Relative Clauses Modifying Subjects

Example:	Types of Noun in Main Clause	Relative Pronouns	Function of Relative Pronoun
(a) A person **who/that** sells houses is a realtor.	person	who/that	subject
(b) The secretary **whom/that** she hired is very experienced.		whom/that	object of verb
(c) The employees **to whom** she denied a pay raise have gone on strike.		whom	object of preposition
(d) Clerks **whose** paychecks were withheld must go to the payroll office.		whose (relative determiner)	possessive determiner
(e) The mansions **that/which** were sold last week were expensive.	thing or animal	that/which	subject
(f) The computer **that/which** they purchased operated very efficiently.		that/which	object of verb
(g) The division **whose** sales reach the million-dollar point will win a bonus.		whose (relative determiner)	possessive determiner

Appendix 6C   Patterns of Relative Adverbial Clauses

Relative Adverbs with Head Nouns

Head Noun	Relative Adverb	Clause
a place	where	you can relax
a time	when	I can call you
a reason	why	you should attend

Relative Adverbs without Head Nouns

Relative Adverb	Clause
where	he lives
when	the term starts
why	I called
how	she knows

Head Nouns without Relative Adverbs

Head Noun	Clause
the place	we moved to
the time	I start school
the reason	they left
the way	you do this

Appendix 7A   Verb Complements

that	*for-to*	*'s gerund*	*Type*
			SUBJECT basic order
(a) That Tom spent the whole day shopping surprised us.	**(b) For** Tom **to** spend the whole day shopping would surprise us.	**(c)** Tom**'s spending** the whole day shopping surprised us.	
(d) It surprised us **that** Tom spent the whole day shopping.	**(e)** It would surprise us **for** Tom **to** spend the whole day shopping.	**(f)** It surprised us— Tom**'s spending** the whole day shopping. (When this structure occurs, there is a pause between the main clause and the complement.)	complement after *it* + verb
		OBJECT	
(g) We hope **that** the the children take the bus.	**(h)** We hope **for** the children **to** take the bus.	**(i)** not applicable	indicative form
(j) Ms. Sanchez suggests **that** he wait in the lobby.	**(k)** not applicable	**(l)** not applicable	subjunctive form

Appendix 7B   Adjective Complements

that	*for-to*	*'s gerund*	*Type*
			SUBJECT basic order
(a) That Lisa went to the meeting was important.	**(b) For** Lisa **to** go to the meeting was important.	**(c)** Lisa**'s going to** the meeting was important.	
(d) It was important **that** Lisa went to the meeting.	**(e)** It was important **for** Lisa **to** go to the meeting.	**(f)** It was important— Lisa**'s going** to the meeting. (When this structure occurs there is a pause between the main clause and the complement.)	complement after *it* + verb

that	*for-to*	*'s gerund*	*Type*
(g) Mr. Walker is happy **that she works** at the company.	**(h)** Mr. Walker is happy **for** her **to** work at the company. (This structure only occurs with a subset of adjectives like *ready, anxious, happy, eager,* etc.)	**(i)** not applicable	PREDICATE indicative form
(j) Chong demands **that she be** on time.	**(k)** not applicable	**(l)** not applicable	subjunctive form

Base Form	Simple Past	Past Participle	Base Form	Simple Past	Past Participle
arise	arose	arisen	leave	left	left
awake	awoke	awoken	let	let	let
bet	bet	bet	lie	lay	lain
beat	beat	beaten	lose	lost	lost
become	became	become	make	made	made
begin	began	begun	mean	meant	meant
bite	bit	bitten	meet	met	met
bleed	bled	bled	pay	paid	paid
blow	blew	blown	put	put	put
break	broke	broken	read	read	read
bring	brought	brought	ride	rode	ridden
build	built	built	ring	rang	rung
buy	bought	bought	rise	rose	risen
catch	caught	caught	run	ran	run
choose	chose	chosen	say	said	said
come	came	come	see	saw	seen
cost	cost	cost	sell	sold	sold
cut	cut	cut	send	sent	sent
do	did	done	set	set	set
draw	drew	drawn	shake	shook	shaken
dream	dreamt/dreamed	dreamt/dreamed	shine	shone/shined	shone/shined
drink	drank	drunk	shut	shut	shut
drive	drove	driven	sing	sang	sung
eat	ate	eaten	sink	sank	sunk
fall	fell	fallen	sit	sat	sat
feel	felt	felt	sleep	slept	slept
fight	fought	fought	speak	spoke	spoken
find	found	found	spend	spent	spent
fly	flew	flown	stand	stood	stood
forget	forgot	forgotten	steal	stole	stolen
forgive	forgave	forgiven	strike	struck	struck
freeze	froze	frozen	swing	swung	swung
get	got	gotten	swim	swam	swum
give	gave	given	take	took	taken
go	went	gone	teach	taught	taught
grow	grew	grown	tear	tore	torn
hang	hung	hung	tell	told	told
hear	heard	heard	think	thought	thought
hide	hid	hidden	throw	threw	thrown
hit	hit	hit	understand	understood	understood
hold	held	held	wake	woke	woken
hurt	hurt	hurt	wear	wore	worn
keep	kept	kept	win	won	won
know	knew	known	wind	wound	wound
lay	laid	laid	write	wrote	written
lead	led	led			

Answer Key (for puzzles and problems only)

Answer to Internet Frequently Asked Questions in Exercise 1 (page 15)

1. It *is* acceptable to send coconuts through the mail without wrapping them.
   True
2. A mime *had* a heart attack during his performance. People *thought* it was part of his act. He *died*.
   False
3. A penny falling from the top of the Empire State Building *will embed* itself in the pavement.
   False
4. Fast-food shakes that aren't marked "dairy" *have* no milk in them.
   True
5. Albert Einstein did poorly in school.
   False
6. Green M & M candies *are* an aphrodisiac.
   False
7. Contact lenses *will stick* to your eyeballs if you weld something while wearing them.
   False
8. If mold grows on a Twinkie, the Twinkie *digests* it.
   False

Answers of Opening Task (page 433)

a) oldest, b) middle, c) only, d) youngest, e) middle, f) only, g) oldest, h) youngest, i) oldest, j) only, k) youngest, l) middle

Exercises (second parts)

List of Words for Short-Term Memory Experiment (page 57)

book, hand, street, tree, sand, rose, box, face, pencil, nail, pan, dog, door, school, shoe, cloud, watch, lamp, stair, glue, bottle, card, movie, match, hammer, dance, hill, basket, house, river

Definition of the Serial Position Effect (page 57)

If a person is asked to recall a list of words in any order immediately after the list is presented, recall of words at the beginning and end of the list is usually best; words in the middle of a list are not retained as well. This observation is based on a model of learning that assumes the first words are remembered well because they are rehearsed and because short term memory at that point is relatively empty. The last words are remembered well because they are still in the short-term memory if the person tries to recall immediately.

Opening Task (page 126)

Student B

Guess the Correct Answer:

1. (a) seahorse, (b) boa constrictor, (c) Canadian goose
2. (a) *War and Peace* by Leo Tolstoy, (b) *The Great Gatsby* by F. Scott Fitzgerald, (c) *Pride and Prejudice* by Jane Austen
3. (a) Thomas Edison, (b) Richard Nixon, (c) Henry Thoreau
4. (a) mucker, (b) hooker inspector, (c) belly builder

Create a Definition: (* indicates the correct answer)

5. a fly
   It is actually classified as a beetle.
   (a) dragonfly, (b) flycatcher, *(c) firefly
6. a person
   He or she pretends to be someone else.
   (a) cornball, *(b) imposter, (c) daytripper
7. a jar
   Ancient Greeks and Romans used it to carry wine.
   *(a) amphora, (b) amulet, (c) aspartame

8. a piece of clothing
   It is composed of loose trousers gathered about the ankles.
   (a) bodice, (b) causerie, *(c) bloomers

UNIT 8

Opening Task (page 140)

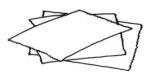

Paper
About A.D. 105

Magnetic Compas
1100s

Television
1920s

Safety Elevator
1853

Typewriter
1867

Laser
1960

Telephone
1876

Gasoline Automobile
1885

Airplane
1903

Credits

Text Credits

Text in Exercise 1 on p. 3 adapted from *The Hunger of Memory* by Richard Rodriguez. Reprinted by permission of David R. Godine, Publisher, Inc. Copyright © 1982 by Richard Rodriguez.

Text in Exercise 3 on p. 5 and Exercise 5 on p. 9 adapted from Studs Terkel, *The Great Divide*, © 1988 by Studs Terkel. Reprinted with permission of Pantheon Books, a division of Random House, Inc.

Text in Exercise 1 on p. 15 from "The Internet's Believe It or Not." Reprinted with permission by Terry Chan.

Text in Exercise 3 on p. 17 from Annie Dillard, *Pilgrim at Tinker Creek*, Copyright © 1974 by Annie Dillard. Reprinted by permission of Harper-Collins Publishers, Inc.

Text in Exercise 4 on p. 17 from "Get a Cyberlife," by Peggy Orenstein, which originally appeared in the May/June 1991 issue of *Mother Jones Magazine*, © 1991, Foundation for National Progress.

Text in Exercise 7 on p. 21 from James Thurber, *Thurber's Dogs, A Collection of the Master's Dogs; Written and Drawn, Real and Imaginary, Living and Long Ago.* Copyright © 1955 by James Thurber. Copyright renewed 1983 by Rosemary A. Thurber. Reprinted by arrangement with Rosemary Thurber and the Barbara Hogenson Agency.

Text in Exercise 8 on p. 22 from J. Michael Kennedy, "It's the Hottest Little Ol' Race in Texas," *Los Angeles Times*, September 2, 1991.

Text in Exercise 15 on p. 29 from Edith Hamilton, *Mythology*. Copyright 1942 by Edith Hamilton. Reprinted with permission by Magad F. Riad Cloriad and Associates.

Text in Exercise 1 on p. 39, and Exercise 9 on p. 50, adapted from *The Gallup Poll Monthly*, February 1991, with permission of The Gallup Organization, Inc.

Text in Exercise 11 on p. 70 adapted from *The Guinness Book of World Records*. Reprinted with permission by Guiness World Records Limited.

Text in Focus 7 on p. 71 from "Busy and Smart Too," *Los Angeles Times*, August 18, 1996.

Text in Exercise 12 on p. 72 adapted from "Decoding of Microbe's Genes Sheds Light on Odd Forms of Life." Reprinted with permission by the Associated Press.

Text in Focus 6 on p. 84 adapted from P. Master, "Teaching the English Article System, Part II: Generic versus Specific," in *English Teaching Forum*. July 1988.

Text in Exercise 18 on p. 96 adapted from S. Hall, *Invisible Frontiers*. New York: The Atlantic Monthly Press, 1987. Reprinted with permission.

Text in Exercise 19 on p. 97 adapted from F. Bloom "Introduction: Science Technology, and the National Agenda: in a report by the Committee on Science, Engineering, and Public Policy of the National Academy of Sciences, National Academy of Engineering, institute of Medicine entitled *Frontiers in Science and Technology: A Selected Outlook*. Reprinted with permission by the National Academy of Sciencies.

Situations 1 through 3 on p. 101 and Exercise 1 on p. 103 adapted from Deborah Tannen, *You Just Don't Understand: Women and Men In Conversation*.

Text in Exercise 2 on p. 104 from Lewis Thomas, *The Medusa and the Snail*. New York: Bantam Books, 1979, p. 167.

Text in Exercise 4 on p. 106, adapted from C. Wade and C. Tavris, *Psychology*. New York: Harper and Row, 1987.

Text in Activity 4 on p. 138 from *Hutchinson Pocket Encyclopedia*. London: Helicon, 1987. Reprinted with permission by Deirdre Luzwick.

Illustration on p. 155 from *Endangered Species: Portraits of a Dying Millennium*. Copyright © 1992 by Deirdre Luzwick. Reprinted by permission of HarperCollins Publishers, Inc

Text in Exercise 3 on p. 160: Reprinted with the permission of Macmillan General Reference, a wholly owned subsidiary of IDG Books Worldwide, Inc., from ARTHUR FROMMER'S NEW WORLD TRAVEL, by Arthur Frommer, Copyright © 1988 by Frommer Books, a division of Macmillan Publishing.

Text in Opening Task on p. 199 adapted from Maria Leach, *The Beginning: Creation Myths around the World*. New York: HarperCollins Publishers, 1956.

Text in Focus 4 on p. 233 and Exercise 6 on p. 234 from *A Brief History of Time: From the Big Bang to Black Holes*. by Stephen Hawking. Copyright © 1990 Stephen Hawking. Reprinted by permission of Bantam Books.

Text in Exercise 12 on pp. 262–263 from Isaac Asimov, *Earth: Our Crowded Spaceship*, Greenwich, Connecticut: Fawcett, 1974.

Text in Exercise 6 on p. 309 from U.S. Immigration and Naturalization Service.

Photo Credits

Page 1, photo by CORBIS/Bob Kristi; photo by CORBIS/Joseph Sohm, ChromoSohm Inc. Page 12, photo by THE STOCK MARKET/Tom Stewart/© 98. Page 13, photo by CORBIS/Tom Nebbia. Page 19, photo by Jonathan Stark for Heinle & Heinle. Page 22, photo by CORBIS/Kelly-Mooney Photography. Page 25, THE FAR SIDE © 1985 FARWORKS, INC. Used by Permission. All rights reserved. Page 29, Reprinted by permission of U.F.S. Inc. Page 36, photo (left) by THE STOCK MARKET/ © Rich Meyer; photo (right) by THE STOCK MARKET/ © 90 Tom Tracy. Page 39, photo by CORBIS/Laura Dwight. Page 51, photo by CORBIS/Grant. Page 56, photo by Jonathan Stark for Heinle & Heinle. Page 76, photo by CORBIS/Paul A. Souders. Page 81, photo by Jonathan Stark for Heinle & Heinle. Page 85, photo by Jonathan Stark for Heinle & Heinle. Page 100, photo by THE STOCK MARKET/ © 1995 Rob Lewine. Page 104, photo by Jonathan Stark for Heinle & Heinle. Page 114, photo by Jonathan Stark for Heinle & Heinle. Page 117, photo by Jonathan Stark for Heinle & Heinle. Page 149, photo (top right) by CORBIS/Steven Chenn; photo (middle left) by THE STOCK MARKET/David Stocklein © 1987; photo (middle right) by THE STOCK MARKET/ © Roy Morsch; photo (bottom left) by THE STOCK MARKET/Copyright, George W. Disario 1993; photo (bottom right) by THE STOCK MARKET/ © 94 David Stoecklein. Page 156, photo by CORBIS/Ric Ergenbright. Page 180, photo by Jonathan Stark for Heinle & Heinle. Page 187, photo by CORBIS/Bob Krist. Page 198, photo by CORBIS/Paul Thompson. Page 243, photo by Jonathan Stark for Heinle & Heinle. Page 244, photo (left) by Jonathan Stark for Heinle & Heinle; photo (right) by Jonathan Stark for Heinle & Heinle. Page 264, photo (left) by CORBIS/Jonathan Blair; photo (middle) by CORBIS/Kevin R. Morris, photo (right) by CORBIS/Charles O'Rear. Page 278, photo by CORBIS/WildCountry. Page 285, photo by CORBIS/Bettmann. Page 298, photo (left) by Jonathan Stark for Heinle & Heinle; photo (right) by CORBIS/Peter Turnley. Page 301, photo by Jonathan Stark for Heinle & Heinle. Page 335, photo by CORBIS. Page 340, photo by CORBIS/Archivo Iconografico, S.A. Page 360, photo (left) by CORBIS/Vince Streano; photo (right) by CORBIS/ © Archivo Iconographico, S.A. Page 386, photo by CORBIS/Laura Dwight. Page 400, photo (left) by CORBIS/Jennie Woodcock; photo (right) by CORBIS. Page 405, photo by Jonathan Stark for Heinle & Heinle. Page 409, photo by CORBIS/AFP. Page 412, photos by Photofest. Page 415, photo by CORBIS/Brain Vikander. Page 432, photo (left) by CORBIS/Laura Dwight; photo (right) by CORBIS/Paul A. Souders.

Index

results
  sentence connectors to express, 200
  subordinating conjunctions expressing, 201
  unreal conditions expressed using modal
    perfect verbs, 237–239
rhetorical questions using discourse organizers,
  246, 257, 258–261

seasons, Ø used with, 84
seem, 353
seldom, 417
semicolons, sentence connectors using, 222
sentence connectors, 198–225
  added ideas using, 200
  addition connectors as, 203–206
  alternative connectors as, 207–208
  clarification using, 200, 210
  commas used with, 222
  concession connectors as, 216
  contrast expressed using, 200, 215
  coordinating conjunctions as, 201
  dependent clauses and, 201
  effect/result expressed using, 219
  emphatic addition using, 203–204
  emphatic vs. intensifying addition using, 204
  examples using, 200, 209
  identifying connectors as, 209
  independent clauses joined by, 201
  intensifying addition using, 204
  punctuation for, 222
  purpose expressed using, 220
  results expressed using, 200
  semicolons used with, 222
  similarity connectors as, 200, 212–214
  simple addition using, 203
  subordinating conjunctions as, 201
  time sequences using, 200
sequence of topics expressed using discourse
  organizers, 246, 248–251
shall have in modal perfect verbs, 240, 241
should have
  modal perfect verb use of, 229, 233, 241
should
  passive verb tenses using, 61
  subjunctive verbs in *that* clauses and, 388
signaling topic shifts using discourse organizers,
  246, 257
similarity expressed using sentence connectors,
  200, 212–214
similarly, 200, 212, 222
simple aspect, 2
simple form of gerund, 320–323
simple form of infinitive, 320–323
simple future tense (*See also* future tense), 2,
  14–15, 31
simple past tense (*See also* past tense), 2, 14–15,
  28
simple present tense (*See also* present tense), 2,
  14–15, 26, 28, 31
simple tense, 14–15

since
  reduced adverb clause using, 286, 288
  subordinating conjunction use of, 201
singular nouns, as reference word, 102
singular/plural agreement with subject/verb
  agreement, 38
so that, subordinating conjunction use of, 201
so
  coordinating conjunction use of, 201
  subordinating conjunction use of, 200
so + adjective/adverb + that, 417
some, relative adverbs modifying nouns using,
  174–177
source of information, preposition clusters to
  identify, 310–311
space, as reference word, 110
specifically, 209
start, 324
stative verbs, passive, 62–63, 64–66
stopped, 324
subject clauses, perfective infinitives used in,
  342–343
subject
  adjective complements used in, 362–366
  gerunds as, 318
  infinitives as, 318
  inversion (reversal) of subject–verb order in
    fronting structures, 414–421
  noun complements used as, 374, 378–379
  passive verbs used in, 71–73
  relative clauses to modify, 126–138
  restrictive relative clause and, 129
  subject complements, gerunds and infinitives
    as, 318
subject/verb agreement, 36–55
  -*s* and present-tense verbs, 38
  abstract nouns and, 44–46
  adjective-derived nouns and, 44–46
  arithmetical operations and, 47
  clauses subject and, 47
  collective nouns and, 44–46, 49
  compound prepositions and, 40
  correlative conjunctions and, 42–43
  either...or and, 52–53
  exceptions to rules regarding, 52–53
  fractions and, 49–51
  gerund clauses and, 47
  head noun identification for, 40–41
  infinitive clauses and, 47
  mass nouns and, 44–46
  modifying phrases and, 38
  neither...nor and, 52–53
  noncount nouns and, 44–46, 49
  not noun phrases and, 40
  noun clauses and, 49
  noun phrases and, 38
  pair and, 47
  percentages and, 49–51
  prepositional phrases and, 40, 52
  pronoun phrases and, 38